D1130665

In the Cool

of the

Evening

The Distilled Wisdom of:
Dr. Vernon S. Broyles, Jr.

First printing 1992
Second printing 1999
Third printing 2006

Big Canoe Chapel
10455 Big Canoe
Big Canoe, GA 30143

Dedication

This book is dedicated to the memory of Dr. Vernon S. Broyles, Jr., author of this work and a primary founder of Big Canoe Chapel. Dr. Broyles served as Chaplain here from 1977 until his death on February 13, 1992.

This collection of daily devotional readings was compiled and edited by the staff of Big Canoe Chapel to commemorate the fifteenth anniversary of the Chapel's first services on December 24, 1977.

Acknowledgments

We are gratefully indebted to North Avenue Presbyterian Church for loaning their collection of columns written by Dr. Broyles from 1960-65.

No one person spent more time on this project than did Kathleen Ingram, the Chapel's office manager. She not only gave countless hours of overtime needed to meet the printer's deadline, but she did so with a cheerful disposition and a willing heart. Without Kathleen this project would have been almost impossible.

Charlene Terrell served as an editor and selected the verses of scripture or appropriate quotes that appear at the beginning of each devotional. She wrote the text for the jacket cover and helped edit the second edition.

We are most grateful to Mrs. (Eloise) Vernon S. Broyles, Jr. for allowing us to use the cover photograph of Dr. Broyles. This photograph is a copy of a portrait painted by the acclaimed portraitist Minnette Bickel. The portrait was a gift to Big Canoe Chapel from Dr. and Mrs. C.L. Chandler, Jr.

We are indebted to Walter Elcock, treasurer at the time of the first printing and to current treasurer Tom Patton and to the Chapel Board of Trustees for their overwhelming support.

Dr. D. Wayne Smith, president of The Friendship Force and our assistant chaplain, took time from his busy schedule to write the introduction to this collection.

A special thanks goes to all these who helped with the final proofreading of the manuscript: Elly Baker, Bob Battle, Jack Bergman, Sue Bergman, Louise Chumley, Lucretia Davenport, Pat Hillman, Patty Libby, Betty Miller, Fred Miller, Dave Terrell, Dick Warmels and Connie Warmels.

Elly Baker, Jack and Sue Bergman, Dave Terrell and Betty and Heath Laughlin also proofread the second edition manuscript.

FOREWORD

"In the Cool of the Evening" was first compiled in 1992 as a memoriam to Dr. Vernon S. Broyles following his death in February of that year. Copies sold out quickly and a second printing followed several years later. Though written decades earlier, the devotionals contained in this volume remain as fresh, true, inspirational and useful as the day they were written. Dr. Vernon S. Broyles' words have indeed withstood the test of time.

Countless people of all ages have been blessed and sustained by these devotionals. Because of this, a generous anonymous donor has made possible a third printing. Dr. Broyles would be very pleased to know that his words of wisdom continue to be a source of inspiration to those who seek a walk with God...*In the Cool of the Evening.*

Introduction

Will Rogers said that he never met a man he didn't like. Vernon S. Broyles, Jr. went far beyond the American humorist of the Great Depression era. Vernon Broyles never met a man, woman, adolescent, child, dog, cat or even a monkey that he didn't like!

This amazing and humble servant of God befriended people of all estates: the poor in need and the rich in need. The smallest child with an inquisitive mind, as well as those to whom the world looked in awe for their achievements, were "just folks" to Vernon Broyles. He loved them all and the sincerity of his love made them know it.

Vernon Broyles didn't just like people. He believed in them. He made them feel as if they could hang the moon. This was no "put-on act" with the gentle man who moved to Atlanta from Canton, Mississippi to become the pastor of the staid old North Avenue Presbyterian Church in the 1940s. Because he believed in people, they started believing in themselves. Because he honestly loved them, they were able to love others around them..."where you live, work and play," as he so often said.

But make no mistake about it, Vernon Broyles was no stranger to the reality of sin. He recognized that an evil power is at work in the world, attempting to cause people to self-destruct. Countless numbers of people who were on such a self-destructive course sought him out for his counsel. After those sessions most went away with no specific advice from this caring and concerned counselor, but left better equipped to fight the Enemy and to untangle the knots of the cords which were binding them. They went away knowing that a man of God loved them and believed in them in just the way the Bible told them that God loved them and believed in them. It wasn't so much what they had heard that helped them to face and fight their problems. Most of the time the strongest counsel the "good doctor" would give was this: "Read your Bible. Read it every day and it won't be long until you meet the Author of the Book Himself."

This collection of the writings of Vernon S. Broyles, Jr. has been lovingly compiled and edited into a daily devotional format. These writings appeared in the Atlanta Constitution in the early 1960s. In those days, which are so vastly different from today, thoughtful people would read the wisdom of Vernon Broyles daily and it would help them live the abundant life of which Jesus spoke in the Gospel of John.

"In the Cool of the Evening" has will be a fitting tribute to the memory of Vernon Seba Broyles, Jr. if those whom he loved and believed in will make it a habit each day to read and meditate on one of his writings. If read along with a passage from the Bible and concluded with a time of personal prayer, I predict that we will find our lives continuing to be blessed by this man who was such a great gift of God to all of us on whom his shadow fell.

For those of you who never knew Dr. Broyles, you can know him now by reading this second printing of his inspiring words recorded in "In the Cool of the Evening".

Wayne Smith

JANUARY

JANUARY 1: NO MAN or company of men, no power on earth or heaven can touch that soul which is abiding in Christ without first passing through His encircling presence and receiving the seal of His permission. If God be for us, it matters not who may be against us; nothing can disturb or harm us, except He shall see it is best for us.

Hannah Whitall Smith

UNENDING TRUTHS FOR THE NEW YEAR

As we enter a New Year, we cannot help hoping it will be a good year. We cast about for some solid basis that we can depend on to make it a good year. We want some foundation to build on that will not change. Here are some things that will not change regardless of what happens and in which we can find security for our living.

1. The love of God revealed in Jesus Christ will be the same. Christ is the same yesterday, today and forever. In all your ways, He will be seeking you to give you His divine gifts of forgiveness and strength and hope.

2. The moral law of God will not change. The 10 Commandments and the Sermon of the Mount reveal what duty God requires of man. There is no so-called advance of man in any branches of learning that allows him to escape the requirements of the moral law. If your year is to be better, doing the will of God is not just a religious demand; it is an absolute necessity.

3. The affections of the family circle will remain the basis for all real human happiness. The home is first in importance to every individual. No amount of worldly success will mean much if the affections of the family circle are marred by discord.

4. The necessity to worship God will not change. There is a miracle present when men, women, and children gather to worship God. God made us so that we are incomplete without regular worship.

It is in worship that God gives His love and reveals His will. It is in worship that the family circle is kept secure. No excuse that you can give is good enough to keep your soul from dying within you if you fail to worship God through your own choice.

If you and I will open our hearts to God's love and seek to do His will in our daily lives, if we will do what we can to keep family ties strong, and will all bow in reverent worship, it will be a good year. In the midst of all the changes that force themselves upon us, these things abide as the foundation of a good life.

JANUARY 2   LORD...tell me clearly what to do, which way to turn.

Psalm 5:8 (LB)

THERE ARE TWO WAYS TO REACT TO THE BEGINNING OF A NEW YEAR

It used to be that almost every family would sit down together, from the smallest to the oldest member, and write out resolutions for the new year. They actually believed they could improve some things. All of us at times feel that we are caught in the trap of life. We peer over the rim of a new year and only see the shadows. Life to us seems just a cycle of the same old things.

But life is not intended to be this way. God so made us that around our lives there should always be the radiance of newness. There are really only two basic ways to react to the coming year. You can run from the new year or you can try to find the answer for it.

1. Too many of us run from life. The books we buy are primarily "escape reading." Some people try to drink their way into escape. Approximately 15 to 20 million pills are taken every night in the United States to insure sleep. We don't like to lie awake at night and think about life. We want relief. At the same time, the faster we run from life, the more afraid we get.

2. We can face life. We can find the answer to the longing within us for newness.

Christ stands on the threshold of the new year. He says simply, "Behold, I make all things new." He is speaking to every person alive. If you are afraid of life or are running from life, He invites you listen to Him since He would make life new for you. He speaks to you whether you are rich or poor, sick or well, happy or sad. Whatever circumstance is yours, He can touch it so that it is never quite the same again. He can make it new! The Gospel of Jesus Christ is not a gospel of good health or good cheer. It is a gospel of good news to those who have need. If life has lost its luster, Jesus Christ invites you to come.

Whatever it brings, you can have total assurance that a provident and loving God is completely in control of all things. You can have the assurance that "all things (even if they appear to be things you fear) will work for good to those who love God."

If you have not yet entrusted your life to Jesus Christ, don't venture further into a new year without Him. If you do, this year will be just like all other years but if you entrust your life to Him, this year will be the year when life became new and took on the meaning it was intended to have.

JANUARY 3   FOR do I now persuade men, or God? or do I seek to please men? for if I yet pleased men, I should not be the servant of Christ.

Galatians 1:10 (KJ)

THE FOUNDATION MUST BE KEPT SECURE

In past Christmas holidays, there was some barring of Christmas trees in certain schools. They were barred because they represented religion. This is a long way from the way of life brought to these shores by the founders of this country. The attacks upon the Christian faith grow in our land. If they continue and if they are upheld by our courts, then the American way of life as we have known it will pass away.

Upon what then will morality and truth and justice rest? Nothing is left but the current whims of men and who is there to say one man's whim is better than another's? If the final reference for character is not the will of God revealed in the Judeo-Christian Bible, then where is it?

The weakening of our religious foundations is already reaping a deadly harvest. The evidence is everywhere. Years ago Mr. Hoover said in a speech to the American Legion: "There must be a moral awakening in every home of our country. Disrespect for law and order is a tragic moral illness. Our city streets are jungles of terror.

"Every strong nation in history has lived by an ideal and has died when its ideals were dissipated. We can be destroyed only by our own gullibility. It is what a nation has in its heart, rather than what it has in its hand, that makes it strong. The nation that honors God is protected and strengthened by Him. We are a God-loving people. This is our greatest strength. Let our national motto always be: 'In God We Trust.'"

Morality without God loses its meaning. Character building without God becomes play-acting. Education without God loses its direction and its purpose. Justice without God loses its foundations. Welfare without God loses its heart. Work without God loses it significance. Pleasure without God becomes license. A person without God loses his soul. A nation without God loses its life.

It is a serious thing when a people seek to separate any part of their private or common life from the open honoring of the worship of God. In Him we live and move and have our being. The place God holds at the center of the life of every institution of men is an urgent concern for everyone who cares.

JANUARY 4
WATCH out that no bitterness takes root among you, for as it springs up, it causes deep trouble.

Hebrews 12:15 (LB)

THE CROSS HAS POWER TO END HATREDS

There is danger that we are going to be engulfed by hatred and enmity unless we find an answer to it. The fire is spreading rapidly in individuals and in groups here at home and all over our world. It destroys marriages, it divides neighborhoods, it inflames groups of different nationalities and races.

What is the answer? Education can do certain things but it is naive indeed to believe it can lessen the hatred in a human heart. Others offer economic answers. Abolish poverty, divide the wealth and men will live together in peace.

We will all do well to consider afresh the Christian answer. Paul makes the answer clear. He was an authority on hatred, having exhibited enmity toward all not of his clan and race and nation. Education and economic security and privilege had only fed the fires of his hatred.

Then one day he met and accepted Jesus Christ in a personal encounter. He found himself reconciled to God by the cross of Christ. He discovered that the fires of his hatreds were put out and that the walls that divided him from others were destroyed. He found that in Christ, enmity was destroyed and that God made a new man of him. He found that God made of believers a fellowship of those bonded together by love. In this fellowship the barriers that divided men and women, rich and poor, educated and ignorant, Jew and Gentile, were abolished.

In spite of all its failures and in spite of all the criticism hurled at it, the church today is the one hope against the enmities of our day. The church as you and I know it fails often enough to deserve

5

criticism. However, more perfectly than anywhere else on earth, it does show forth the power of God in Christ to destroy the barriers that divide men.

Here men and women find harmony in marriage. The rich and the poor, the ignorant and the educated and men of different races, do live and work together in peace and with mutual love and respect.

JANUARY 5   AND yet shew I unto you a more excellent way.

I Corinthians 12:31 (KJ)

THE BIGNESS THAT PLAGUES MANKIND

The darker the night, the more grateful we are for the light. As the events of our day grow more alarming, we can be ever more grateful for the Christian gospel. We may be on the threshold of a revival of faith. The power structures threaten the very existence of the individual. These power structures have many names: big business, big labor, automation, organized welfare (public and private) and social conformity. They have one thing in common: the enslavement of individuals for what is often presented as the good of the whole. This too often degenerates into the "good" of the manipulators of the power structure.

This has always been true. Christ lived in the midst of power structures of government and society far stronger and harsher than ours. He planted the seed of the Gospel, and the seed grew until the rigid structures were cracked and broken.

Christ gave to individuals a new confidence in themselves, so great a confidence that no tyranny could hold them and no misfortune discourage them. The slave and the outcast became convinced that they were loved by God, adopted as the children of God, under the special care of God. The man of influence and power came to see himself as the servant of God. In the church, the fellowship of believers, the barriers that divided men were dissolved by the love of God revealed in Christ.

6

In Christ men saw afresh that God is concerned with each individual, his conduct, his successes, his failures, his sicknesses, his sorrows, his hopes, his discouragements. In Christ, God revealed His concern for all people in all the world. His determination is that all man's history shall serve His final purpose of man's salvation.

Man began to live again with hope for himself and for his world. There began that long line of individuals living as citizens of Heaven in God's world. From these has come our richest heritage of human dignity, political freedom and moral integrity.

The solution of our problems does not finally lie in human power structures. The solution begins at the heart of an individual where God enters by faith to change a person from a slave of circumstance to a child of God.

JANUARY 6   **GOD'S goodness hath been great to thee. Let neither day nor night unhallowed pass, but remember what the Lord hath done.**

Shakespeare

LIFE IS UNCERTAIN, BUT GOD IS NOT

Can you face your day in the confidence that you will be able to successfully meet its demands? It is not easy. Many carry heavy burdens that seem to get no lighter. Many face threats to their security and happiness. Others are just confused by the many demands made on them.

Some are entangled in the results of yesterday's misdeeds and see no hope for the present. Some get so concerned over the multitude of bad things that are happening until they see no hope for the future. So many of us face each day carrying in our minds the mistakes of the past, the burdens of the present and the fears of tomorrow. It is a wonder more people don't break down than do.

It does not help much to be told to cheer up. We get tired of lifting ourselves up by our own bootstraps. We feel like the man who was told: "Cheer up, things could be worse." He cheered up and, sure enough, they got worse.

If you are having trouble finding strength for the day, God stands ready to give you help in your need. We are not made to meet our days in our own strength.

God offers you forgiveness for your misdeeds. You carry no sin He will not forgive. In the cross and resurrection He bears our sins in His own body. If you will let Him have your misdeeds in penitence, He will take from them their power to destroy your present and your future. You can trust God with your past.

God offers you strength for the day. The promise of Christ: "Lo, I am with you" is God's assurance that He lives in you and is by your side. The Bible is full of the promises of God for those who are willing to trust Him. If you will let Him into your heart, you will find these promises to be true. At the end of the day you will find that often, to your surprise, there has been wisdom you yourself did not possess and victories you never thought you could win.

We cannot control our future. Unexpected things happen to disrupt our plans. The things of this world on which we seek to build security are taken from us. Circumstances and people over which we have no control often determine what happens to us. God promises us that if we will love and trust Him, He will make all those things work for good.

**JANUARY 7   TEACH us to number our days aright, that
we may gain a heart of wisdom.**

Psalm 90:12 (NIV)

THE AGED NEED MORE THAN RECREATION

A White House conference on aging was held some years ago. Dr. Abraham J. Heschel of the Jewish Theological Seminary made a talk that can be read with profit by all. The following is taken from this talk and I hope it will be helpful.

"What we owe to the old is reverence, but all they ask for is consideration, attention, not to be discarded and forgotten. What they deserve is preference but we do not even grant them equality. One father finds it possible to sustain a dozen children, yet a dozen children find it impossible to sustain one father.

"The typical attitude to old age is characterized by fear, confusion, absurdity, self-deception and dishonesty. Old age is something we are all anxious to attain. However, once attained, we consider it a defeat, a form of capital punishment. Enabling us to reach old age, medical science may think it gave us a blessing; however, we continue to act as if it were a disease.

"How to save the old from despondency, despair? How to lend beauty to being old? While we do not officially define old age as a second childhood, some of the programs we devise are highly effective in helping the aged to become children. The preoccupation with games and hobbies, the over-emphasis upon recreation, while certainly conducive to eliminating boredom temporarily, hardly contribute to inner strength. The effect is rather a pickled existence preserved in brine with spices.

"For thousands of years human existence was not simply confined to the satisfaction of trivial needs. Through prayer and ritual man was able to remain open to the wonder and mystery of existence, to lend a tinge of glory to daily deeds. Modern man has discarded ritual, failed to learn the art of prayer, but found a substitute for both in occupational routine. He severed relations to God, to the cosmos, or even to his people but became engrossed in the search for success. Upon his retirement from business or labor, games and hobbies, the country club or golf take the place of church, synagogue, ritual and prayer.

"The sense of significant being is a thing of the spirit. Stunts, buffers, games, hobbies, slogans, are all evasions. What is necessary is an approach, a getting close to the sources of the spirit.

"The goal is not to keep the old man busy but to remind him that every moment is an opportunity for greatness. Inner purification is at least as important as hobbies and recreation. The elimination of resentments, of bitterness, of jealousies, of wranglings, is certainly a goal for which one must strive.

"Old men need a vision, not only recreation. Old men need a dream, not only a memory. It takes three things to attain a sense of significant being: God, a soul, a moment. And the three are always there. Just to be is a blessing. Just to live is holy."

JANUARY 8   OH, for a thousand tongues to sing my great Redeemer's praise.

Charles Wesley, Hymn

CHRIST'S CHURCH: A SOCIETY OF SINNERS

Jesus Christ was crucified by the people of His day because He made certain decisions. These decisions will lead to rejection and loss in our day. Selfish and evil men will not tolerate people who "deny themselves and take up their cross daily and follow Christ." Yet in our strange world, men are changed and evil overcome only through those who follow Christ in bearing man's sin and evil in their own bodies and minds. Only in the fellowship of suffering is the power of the resurrection possible.

Christ chose to do the will of God as shown to Him at any cost. A second decision made the cross more certain. He decided to build His Kingdom out of sinners. He founded the only society on earth whose one qualification is that you shall be unworthy to join. His choice of close friends offended the good people of His day. Peter is typical of the unpromising groups he gathered. Matthew was an outsider to all decent people. The religious people could not tolerate Jesus' mingling socially with people they considered of low reputation.

Jesus chose His church from those who were sinners and knew it. He chose a prostitute instead of Simon the Pharisee; the beggar Lazarus instead of Dives; Zacchaeus instead of the religious leaders

10

of Jericho; the Prodigal instead of the correct son who stayed home; the poor over the rich; the sick and crippled over the well and healthy; the Good Samaritan over the priest and Levite. He came to seek and to save the lost. The people of privilege resented it and finally could abide Him no longer. They crucified Him.

Today, the church stands in grave danger because of its respectability. All too much we who are Christian seek to evade the places where men suffer the results of their own sin and the sins of others. Instead of seeking in Christian love those outside accepted moral excellence, we too often relieve our consciences by critical attack.

Few "established" churches are marked by contact with the poor, the downtrodden, the outcast, the man or woman caught in private and public conduct which people believe to be wrong.

Those who would seriously follow Jesus into the highways and hedges will learn what it means to bear a cross.

Since the church of Christ is a society of sinners, it may be that the chief qualification of most of us who are Christian is our pride, which has kept us from following Him.

JANUARY 9   SO if the Son sets you free, you will indeed be free...

John 8:36 (LB)

THERE'S A SURE WAY TO KNOW FREEDOM

Freedom involves man's relationship to God and nowhere else does freedom have any real roots. This should not seem strange. God created us. God loves us. God guides and governs us. We have an eternal destiny. The real reason this does not make much sense today is so few of us believe it.

Everybody is talking about freedom. Yet freedom is being lost while we talk.

1. Freedom is being threatened by our national urge to be alike. We laugh about the similarity between us, but we are losing freedom in our fear of being different from each other. Like a bunch of scared steers, we crowd together. We are wearing the same cloths, doing the same things, listening to the same programs, ashamed or afraid to get out-of-step. It is costing us some of our freedom.

2. Freedom is threatened by government. Government always threatens freedom. We may lose our freedom by seeking to hide under government in order to be secure. Sooner or later, we must make up our minds whether we will be secure or whether we will be free. We cannot have it both ways.

3. Money never made a man free. Standards of living never made anybody free. It makes slaves of people but makes no man free.

4. Education never made any man free. We have all read long articles about education being the foundation of freedom. Free men create education, but education does not create free men.

We can have the very best educational system in the world but what matter is this: What are we pouring through it? For example, we can develop the very best water distribution system in the world but more important is the purity of the water that flows through it.

How do you really make people free? Some would like to think it is by vocabulary. Many of us seem to feel you can wave a wand of conversation and change things. We are told to read the Constitution, read the Declaration of Independence, read the Bill of Rights to get the vocabulary in our minds. I was in Germany when Adolf Hitler captured Germany. I listened to his speeches. I read his advertising. The German people marched in lock-step into slavery to the music of "freedom."

Only those who know the Truth can live free. And the only way you will ever know the truth is to get it from One who is Truth - God. By proper relationship of your personal life to God - by your faith in Jesus Christ - you will know the Truth. Then regardless of government, economics, education, wars, or chains, you will be free, even as Christ, the condemned prisoner, was free before Pilate.

RELIGION CAN HELP IN CURING AN ILL MIND

Mental illness is one of our most popular interests and one of our most pressing problems. It is likely that much money and effort will be put into trying to do something about it. There are some things that need thinking about that are not being discussed, in so far as I can determine.

There is no doubt that mental disturbance is an acute problem. However, there is a good deal of disagreement as to what mental illness really is. Because of this disagreement, there are wide differences as to what to do about it.

Much of this difference of opinion rests on the simple fact that there seems to be no clear agreement as to what a human being really is. If you are going to be a good airplane mechanic you must first know what an airplane engine is. If you treat it as though it were an outboard motor the results will not be good.

A great deal of modern psychology and psychiatry leaves out religious faith altogether and much of it treats religious faith as though it were a factor to be eliminated. If man is just a biological animal and if the mind is the servant of the instincts and drives of the body, this approach can be helpful. Freud thought and taught that mental illness was and is the result of cultural (moral and religious) interference with normal physiological processes.

It is encouraging that there is presently a growing movement in the field of psychology toward understanding man as a spiritual being. There is also a growing number of students in this field who are beginning to suspect that mental illness may spring from disturbed spiritual relationships rather than from suppressed physical desires and that it may involve sin after all. This has always been the teaching of the Christian faith and it has lived because it has spoken to the deep need of the human being for abundant life, a life of the spirit which is to be achieved by relatedness or reconciliation or fellowship with God and man, and which begins with reconciliation with God.

Man is created in the image of God and can live at peace with himself only when he is at peace with God. Thus religion represents man's response to God and presents the only basis for any psychology that pretends to understand or help man.

Because I believe this to be true, it concerns me that our fine publicly announced plans to attack the problem of mental illness gather together all kinds of specialists except theologians. Theologians are men trained in the science of God. Theology was once acclaimed as the queen of the sciences. It may well still be. At any rate, it does seem that unless we take seriously man's spiritual nature, our present efforts can lead only to disillusionment and to disaster for all those who so sorely need help.

Religion at its best has always had as its goal the saving of "lost souls" which means bringing them peace and freedom by returning them to a personal relationship of love with God and man -- which is the deepest meaning of mental health.

JANUARY 11   ...BUT he that judgeth me is the Lord.

I Corinthians 4:4 (KJ)

THERE'S ONE WAY AND THAT IS ALL

"According to your faith be it unto you." What did Christ mean? He obviously meant faith in God. But as a nation, we have interpreted it as faith in man. Our traditional optimism - based on man and not on God - is beginning to fade.

Our dreams are rather like withered flowers which we hold in our hand. Through we have sense enough to know they have withered, we don't have intelligence enough to know what to do with them. We use all the catchwords of morality but we are gradually waking up to the fact that we are an immoral people at heart.

After the last war we went out with our pockets full of money and our hearts full of good will. We thought we were going to change the world. We knew how everyone else ought to live. We took for granted they would respond to our ideas which we knew were good. We went out to bring democracy to every man. It was our democracy and we could not understand how anybody could oppose it.

We have suddenly waked up to that fact - after China, Korea, Hungary, and Cuba - that there may be something in this world stronger than good will. There may be something in this world that does not respond to the smiles of do-gooders, or even to the efforts of those who sincerely want to do good. There is a force of evil, sin, that is stronger than our best efforts.

Let's remember the Israelites – God's chosen people - when they were ready to go into the "Promised Land." They had been delivered across the Red Sea and the Jordan River and had had a series of successes. Then they were defeated. The people were scared to death. Their hearts turned to water. Their leaders stretched upon the dust in repentance for sin. The big difference between them and us is that they knew their problem. Their problem lay in their damaged relationship to God in their sin, which cut them off from God.

In our sophisticated day, we feel we are too smart to accept such a simple solution. The Israelites were thrown back - not by a superior force, but by sin. We need to remember this. We are constantly assessing the strength of our enemy when we should be assessing the weakness of ourselves in relation to God.

If we are to solve our problems, personal and national, we must begin with God. Without this our human wisdom becomes foolishness and our strongest efforts turn to weakness.

JANUARY 12 A righteous man may have many troubles, but the Lord delivers him from them all.

Psalm 34:19 (NIV)

POSITIVE THINKING ISN'T A CURE ALL

This year thousands of seniors, high school and college will hear a graduation message. So often the emphasis is on positive thinking. The idea is that if you will believe it can be done, all obstacles will always fall before you. If you will educate yourselves, work intelligently, and apply yourselves, there are no problems in life that cannot be solved.

Believing this, thousands of young people will get married this year under the illusion that emotional experience coupled with good will surely lead to happiness in marriage.

We have taken and distributed to our own use one of the greatest assurances given by Jesus: "According to your faith, be it unto you." This has become the motto of old and young Americans. The only trouble is, we have substituted "faith in man" for "faith in God."

We are teaching our young people to depend on American "know-how" and enthusiasm. We use catchwords of morality without recognizing our basic individual and national immorality. We are asking our young people to move out into the world of many problems and make good on faith in man.

How can these young people look at our nation and believe we have given them the answer? About all the press can say is that these days are the result of "extremely bad luck, poor judgement and bad timing." In plain English, this means we are in a mess and we don't know why.

I wonder how long it is going to be before someone seriously suggests that there is a God in whom America no longer believes - except as a kind of support for selfish pursuit.

We like to blame all our troubles on the Communists. They are so strong and so aggressive. But you can read the Bible from one end to the other and God never discusses the strength of the enemy. The fact is, a man's defeat and a nation's defeat is sin, and sin does not fit too well with our emphasis on positive thinking.

When the Israelites reached their lowest ebb, they knew their problems lay in their personal relationship to God. In this sophisticated day, we are simply too smart to reach such a simple conclusion.

Calvary - not Washington, not Moscow, and certainly not Vienna - is the answer. There is no use coming to Calvary by "faith" unless we come confessing our sin. And if we confess our sin, we must also accept forgiveness. The final step is commitment, wherein we decide that His will should be done, not ours.

This is not offered simply as a better answer than positive thinking. It is offered as the only answer to living a life that means something rather then nothing.

JANUARY 13   **A man there was, though some did count him mad, the more he cast away the more he had.**

Bunyan

MANY NEED HELP YOU CAN PROVIDE

In going about among people, the heart is constantly burdened by the large number who need help. The kind of help that is needed is not usually in terms of the bare necessities of life such as food and clothes and shelter. The help that is needed is for someone to care enough to lend a hand in just figuring out how to meet an emergency or how to meet an unexpected situation or how just to find courage to go on.

At best, life is not easy today even for the strong. It gets to be more than many people can meet when weakness or weariness comes or when one is fighting it out alone. It often becomes all confused because of wrong acts or wrong decisions, but for whatever cause or whoever is to blame, many people need a helping hand. Many who need help may not be easy to help. You can easily figure out that it is their fault. But they still need help.

It may be a young person badly in need of a job that can't be found, or an old couple finding it hard to keep going or an older person who can't find a place to live that is cheap enough, or a person who is lonely and never learned how to make friends or a wanderer who needs someone to talk to even though he may have no real hope of ever becoming different. If you ever really get people in your heart and are willing to stop long enough to see them as they are, you will find some of these needy folks close by. All the government and community programs in the worlds can't meet the personal needs of people. They can't meet your needs and mine.

Jesus said, "In as much as you have done it unto one of the least of these, ye have done it unto me." If you would serve the Lord, these are wonderful days to practice Christian compassion. The hurry and the rush, the ambition and the greed of our day are leaving in their backwash lots of people who badly need a helping hand.

A friend of mine sent me two quotations which are to the point. "This thing of giving," said George F. Burba, "I do not understand any more than you do but there is something about it that blesses us. Those who give most have most left.

"I believe that everyone who dries a tear will be spared the shedding of a thousand tears. I believe that every sacrifice we make will so enrich us in the future that our regret will be that we did not enrich the sacrifice more. Give, and somewhere from out of the clouds or from the depths of human hearts, a melody divine will reach your ears and gladden all your days upon earth."

18

DRAW nigh to God....

James 4:8 (KJ)

HIDING FROM GOD IS TRIED BY MANY

If most of us spent as much time trying to find God as we do trying to escape and hide from Him, we would be a lot better off. After their sin of disobedience, Adam and Eve tried hiding from God in the bushes. Clear and distinct came God's voice: "Adam, where are you?" Adam replied: "I was afraid and hid myself."

Look in your own heart. Do you really want God in the midst of your work and your play? Or are you really hiding from Him in some bushes, hoping He will pass on by without noticing you? A great many of us know exactly where God is. We have found Him or been found by Him and we don't particularly like it. We hide out from Him.

The prodigal son knew where his father was while he was living high, wide and handsome. There are many like him who choose to live as they please and they profess to have trouble knowing how to find God. Usually their trouble is they prefer to hide out from Him.

The rich young ruler found God all right but just didn't like what he found. Lots of men and women busy themselves in their work and in the community in order to hide from God.

Yet God is hard to hide from. He has a way of coming from around the corner in the most unexpected ways. He has a way of finding us in the bushes of our self-deception. God is a seeking God. God is like a woman searching for the one lost coin until it is found or a shepherd leaving all the sheep and going to find the one that is lost. He took upon Himself the form of a man and died a criminal's death that He might miss no one in His search.

Our problem is not to find God. Our problem is to quit trying to hide from Him. Some of us hide from Him in our pretended goodness. We know this is a poor place to hide but we try. Others hide behind the bushes of their good deeds and know they are hiding all the time. Some even dare to hide behind their sins, taking pride in being man. But in their heart they know they are hiding. Some hide in their self-pity and a poor place it is.

If you are having trouble finding God it may be your trouble is not with God but with you. You may be hiding from Him while all the time you hear His voice calling you by name and asking where you are. You may solve your problem by just coming out in the open and honestly facing God who has been seeking you all the time.

JANUARY 15   LABOR to keep alive in your heart that little spark of celestial fire - conscience.

George Washington

THE INNER VOICE HAS A POWERFUL SAY

The most powerful influence in the world is the strange voice within us which demands that we do the right thing. Conscience sits as a spy over our actions and our thoughts and passes judgement on them. Conscience forces us to defend our sins as though they were virtues. We simply do not have the nerve to be mean and to admit it.

However you try to explain conscience, it remains as the voice of God demanding that we do the right thing in everything. Conscience alone can break the power of tyranny by leading man to stand for right, regardless of consequences. Conscience gives meaning to the individual over the mass. Conscience even leads us to accept suffering for our sins and wrongs because it is the right thing to do. No success in business or politics can bring happiness unless conscience approves. Conscience is our only hope for a decent society.

So the most important question is: "How can I know what is

right?"

1. In this quest for your soul's integrity you are assigned to yourself. Unless you face the question for yourself you will not be helpful to others.
2. Finding what is right is always in terms of some definite situation. Theoretical discussions of right and wrong are not very helpful.
3. Seek in the situation the Will of God. Conscience is the prompting of God. You are created by God to find and to do His will. If you do not begin here, you will be lost from the start.
4. Believe that the Spirit of God works on your spirit to furnish guidance. There is no answer to this or to any other human question outside a faith in the supernatural presence of God's Spirit to lead and to help.
5. Paul set forth two principles to help in advising the church at Corinth as to a question of right. He wrote: "Let no man seek his own but every man seek another's good." Be sure your decision helps and not hurts another's welfare, material and spiritual.
6. Paul's second principle was: "Do all to the glory of God." Be sure that you can make your decision and stand before God, unashamedly offering it to Him in worship.
7. Two things are necessary if we are seriously to try to do the right thing. We must be ready to accept God's forgiveness when we fail. We often will fail to do right, but God gave His Son to forgive our sins. Accept Him and His Gift. Then we must believe that God is not defeated by our failures, nor need we be, because He works all things for good to them that love Him.

Some kind of order can be brought out of the confusion of life, personal and national, if we will begin to honestly heed conscience's demand that we do the right thing in whatever decision we face.

JANUARY 16   I have learned the secret of being content in any and every situation, whether well fed or hungry, whether living in plenty or in want. I can do everything through Him who gives me strength.

Philippians 4:12,13 (NIV)

IN TROUBLE WE CAN BE CHALLENGED TO GLORY

Paul, in writing to the Roman Church, said that among the things in which he gloried were the tribulations or troubles of life. This is a hard thing to believe in this ease-loving, pain-killing, tragedy-dodging age. Maybe some of our confusion and unhappiness is caused by our failure to learn the correct lessons from our troubles.

Paul spoke from experience. He was arrested and beaten five times by Jewish police and three times by Roman police. He was stoned once and left for dead. He was shipwrecked three times and once floated around on a piece of driftwood for 24 hours before being picked up. He traveled constantly, often among unfriendly people. He knew hunger and exposure to the elements. He had no home and apparently no family. He knew what trouble was and he found it to be a pathway to glory. Strange, isn't it?

In **FORWARD**, the daily devotional booklet of the Episcopal Church, a man is quoted as saying: "Thank God for all your daily troubles. Be grateful for your family crises, hurt pride, disappointments and thwarted will. Be glad to find in yourself resentment, self-pity, sickness and sorrow. See all these as an opportunity for God to act and thank Him that these troubles bring you to your knees in prayer, so that through prayer, He can strengthen your faith and through the searchlight of His love on your problem, can either dissolve it or show how to resolve it."

Paul says that he found certain wonderful results in the troubles of life. By his troubles he learned patience. Patience is something we all recommend and which usually is practiced and learned under necessity. It is a golden virtue. It endures under strain and it stands

22

fast under testing. Only as we are tested and find ourselves standing up under it do we come to know we can take it. This is something that can come only through trouble. Because we have endured we know we can endure in the future. We thus face life unashamed and unafraid. We find that our troubles are the very means by which we become sure of the love of God because His Spirit makes us strong in the midst of them.

The Christian faith was born of one whose life was marked by trouble and suffering. It has power to enable ordinary folks to find victory in the midst of trouble. No one likes trouble and suffering but they come to all. The Christian faith dares to challenge us to glory in them because they can give life's most precious possession - the assurance of God's love as we find ourselves able to endure them by His Holy Spirit.

JANUARY 17   GOD cannot give us happiness and peace apart from Himself, because it is not there. There is no such thing.

-C.S. Lewis

INNER CONFLICTS ARE EXPERIENCED BY ALL

There is a tug of war within the heart of each of us. We are depressed by our sins and weaknesses and we are impressed by our abilities. Part of the time we think we can't and part of the time we know we can. When we think we can we remember the times we knew we couldn't and wonder if we can.

One group of people tells us to be honest about our weakness and sin and another tells us to think positively. The result is we don't know what to think. We get so confused until often we just are not sure which is the part of us we can trust. This makes for mixed up persons and mixed up homes and communities and nations. We assert ourselves when we ought to be retiring and we retreat when we ought to fight.

One thing is certain: something like the above is in the experience of most of us. The human personality is not nearly as orderly as we pretend when we are on our best behavior. Another thing I believe to be certain: there is no answer for our confusion in man's own wisdom and strength. There must be available an outside power or we are in a bad fix. It is in the good news of the Gospel that God has moved to answer our need for wholeness. It is possible for religion to make the situation worse. Unless God comes to forgive, His coming only spotlights our guilt. The heart of the Christian Gospel is its message of a God who loved us while we were yet sinners. Here is release from our depression over our sin and weakness.

God comes not only to forgive but to enable us to live with confidence. Because He is with us, we live not by our own strength but because He gives us His strength. We substitute the confidence we have in God's power for that we sometimes had in ourselves. This is what Paul meant when he said, "I live yet not I, but Christ liveth in me." Thus our weakness and our strength are united in Him and we are made whole. The tug of war is settled.

It is hard for us to admit that our lives are not sufficient in themselves. We keep trying to believe that some smart person is going to find a way to cure our inferiority and curb our pride. We scarcely dare to believe the wonderful fact that there is available by faith, for each of us, the supernatural power of God which forgives our sin and thus cures our inferiority and which dwells in us to do through us what needs to be done. The answer to our tension begins in our faith.

JANUARY 18   OH, how I love your law! I meditate on it all day long. Your commands make me wiser than mine enemies.

Psalm 119:97,98 (NIV)

THE TOWER OF BABEL AND THE SPACE AGE

There is a story of an ancient people who came to dwell in the land of Shinar. They were of one language and one speech and had evidently developed a rather high state of culture. They were anxious to maintain themselves in security and in peace. So they built a city and a tower whose top reached toward heaven that they might make a name for themselves lest they be scattered abroad upon the face of the whole earth.

One day they had an uninvited guest. God came down to see the city and the tower which the children of men built. He found no reference to Himself. He found men filled with pride, letting their imaginations run wild in things they were doing for themselves. So the Lord scattered them abroad upon the face of all the earth and they left off building the city.

This story of the Tower of Babel has a haunting quality today as we move out into space. There was great jubilation when our astronaut made the safe venture into space. I am sure that the prayers of many people supported him and his family. I am not so sure that there was any real dedication of the feat to the Glory of God. Nor is there much evidence that our space explorations are dedicated to His service.

This is just an illustration of the common mood of our country today. We are terribly concerned over the threats to our security and peace. We are assembling our bricks and mortar to build our towers until they touch heaven. Of course if there is no God and we are dependent on our own efforts, all may be very well. But if we can expect a Guest to come and watch our efforts, a Guest who created us and all we have and are, a Guest who governs it all and who requires that it serves His glory and His will, it is something else again.

25

I keep reading the Bible where, from the beginning to the end, men and nations rise and fall by their relationship to God - God who is holy and loving and demands our worship and our surrender and whose will is man's only sure guide. I keep reading the newspapers and magazines where the record of America unfolds and underneath is an outward show of piety which reads so much like the story of the people who built Babel.

I am deeply troubled, as confusion seems to crown most of our efforts. I wonder if the deepest patriotism is not being manifested by those who are talking to God about it all in prayer.

JANUARY 19   IF we confess our sins, He is faithful and just and will forgive us our sins and purify us from all unrighteousness

I John 1:9 (NIV)

FIRST, YOU NEED TO FACE YOURSELF

There are many problems all around us. Most of us would like to have a part in solving some of them. The interesting thing is that we can. We do our part best when we face ourselves as we are and try first to solve what we see there.

There are racial conflicts in Africa and America. There is one in your own heart which, honestly faced, will teach you how difficult the problem really is. There are moral problems in your community. They are no greater than those in your own life. Here you will find the hardest battle. There is juvenile delinquency in our day. There is delinquency in the heart of each of us. Try to meet it there and you will discover how hard it is to handle. There is the threat of war in our world. There is warfare in each heart that makes it difficult to live in peace with the family and the neighbors. Here is a good place to start your crusade for peace.

Conferences and crusades are popular in behalf of our problems. However, no real progress will be made in any area until reform is started in the hearts of the participants. Intelligent answers are not enough. Information and education won't do the job. No answer by me for someone else is enough. Only an answer I have found for myself, only some victory won over my evil, can make me helpful in solving outside problems. Literally Jesus was right when He said, "The Kingdom of Heaven is within you."

Personal change is the only possible base for social change. You can't make a good society out of bad people. Too many people want other people to do right while they go their selfish way.

If you really want to face a challenge in making a better world, face yourself. You too will know what Paul meant when, facing himself, he cried, "O wretched man that I am. Who shall deliver me from the body of this death?" As you reach out for help for yourself you will also better understand his cry, "I thank God through Jesus Christ our Lord."

You can't wait to help others until you have solved the problem within yourself. However, as you set about to work on problems on the outside, you must remain humbly conscious that you are your own chief problem. This will give to your efforts humility that will commend you to others. Your faith will serve to point others to God as the source of all solutions. Your humility and your faith will make you helpful as a channel of God's wisdom and grace.

In high places and in low we need a lot of problem-solvers who are willing to start with themselves.

JANUARY 20 "AND so I am giving a new commandment
to you now -- love each other just as much
as I love you. Your strong love for each
other will prove to the world that you are
my disciples."

John 13:34 (TLB)

FAITH'S FINAL TEST: LOVE FOR OTHERS

John wrote a letter to some fellow Christians. He was an old man
and he was anxious that his friends understand the heart of the faith.
He wrote, "Beloved, let us love one another: for love is of God and
everyone that loveth is born of God and knoweth God. He that loveth
not, knoweth not God; for God is love."

"Herein is love, not that He loved us and sent his son to be the
propitiation for our sins. Beloved, if God so loved us, we ought also
to love one another - If a man says, 'I love God' and hateth his
brother whom he hath seen, how can he love God, whom he hath not
seen? And this commandment have we from God, that he who loveth
God, loves his brother also."

These words need to be taken seriously by all of us who profess
the Christian faith. There are differences among us concerning many
vital issues of our day. Things are being said and written and passed
around by people who claim to be Christian who are full of the
poison of hatred. Accusations are being made against fellow
believers that are anything but the expressions of Christian affection.

Whatever may be the vocal orthodoxy of anyone guilty of these
accusations, they are in danger of condemnation of God. The final
test of faith is love for the brethren, a concern for and willingness to
seek the welfare of the other person.

These are days when the souls of men are being tested. There will
be wide differences of opinion among good and godly people.
Whatever peace we will have will come from those who manifest the

spirit of Christian love and forbearance, humility and patience - yes, even of sacrifice. God will not be used as a club to hammer our opponents. Any who try to so use Him will finally destroy themselves, while along the way they sow discord and heartbreak.

The Christian faith has a real message for our day. It concerns itself with every problem of each individual and of society as a whole. It offers its one solution, divine love, given by God through His Son and shared by His children with all men.

This gets very practical when we are facing those with whom we disagree. It got so practical with Jesus it cost Him His life when those who disagreed with Him let their hatred loose on Him and He decided to love to the end.

Surely those of us who bear His name are called on to follow Him, lest in professing to be His disciples we find at the end He never knew us.

"By this shall all men know that ye are my disciples, that ye love one another."

JANUARY 21   BE not merely good; Be good for something

Henry David Thoreau

ARE YOU MAKING YOUR LIFE USEFUL?

Each one of us is self-centered. And yet in each of us there is a sincere desire to be useful, to have our lives really mean something to others. In days like this it isn't easy to believe that one man can do much of anything to improve the world. Yet 4,000 years ago Abraham made a decision that not only changed his life, but also changed the life of the world.

His decision was a simple one. It was a decision that faces every man, woman and child and if you make the same decision, it is possible for you to be used.

Abraham lived in Ur - a great city of luxury, wealth and sin. Abraham was concerned and greatly worried. He began to talk to God and to feel quiverings of something he had never felt before. God was beginning to deal with this man. He was going to use him to begin His march of redemption down through the centuries to finally end in Christ.

One day God called Abraham by name. "There are certain things I want you to do. If you will hear, obey and believe me I will make you a great name. And I will bless the whole world in terms of your single life."

Abraham chose to believe. With no proof other than the Spirit of God in his heart, he chose to trust God regardless of cost - and it cost him dearly. It cost Abraham his family, the tradition of his father, his position in Ur. It caused him to become a wanderer. One day it almost cost him his only son, Isaac.

Abraham just launched out and became the "Father of Faith." His kind of faith is the heart of our Christian religion. Our religion is one in which God calls and invites us to become His children. He tells us to believe and that He will bless us and use us.

It will take some real doing to believe the God of the Universe is calling you. He calls to you in the framework of your daily life. He calls you by name and puts His finger on the things He wants you to do.

If you are troubled with your world today, you are walking in the footsteps of Abraham 4,000 years ago. You can be sure God is dealing with your life. Obviously you have a decision to make.

Read your Bible and worship God in your church. God speaks to people there. If you keep reading and worshiping, you will hear Him call and tell you what to do. Choose to believe and hurl your life out in confidence that God will use you if you will follow where He leads. It will demand of you sacrifice. It won't be easy. It will be rewarding as you come to feel yourself a part of God's plan and purpose. You will be useful.

30

YOU WON'T TRAVEL THAT ROAD ALONE

It often seems lonely business to try to do right and stand for the right thing. It sometimes seems almost useless to spend your time doing good to others. We do well to remind ourselves we are not alone. The prophet Elijah dared speak out for God in Israel.

He stood bravely against the men and women who were evil. He included the Queen among those against whom he spoke and acted. As a reward, he was forced to flee his country to escape death at the hands of his enemies. Far away from family and friends, he made this famous lament: "I have been very jealous for the Lord God of Hosts; for the children of Israel have forsaken Thy covenant, thrown down Thy altars and slain Thy prophets with the sword, and I, even I only, am left, and they seek my life to take it away."

God spoke to Elijah and told him that the world was not at an end. There was still work to do. Those who sought his life would be replaced by others and there were 7,000 in Israel who remained true to God. The work of God and man goes on and our part in it is not useless.

If you are trying to make a home centered around God, there are thousands like you all over the world. If you are trying to make life easier for others by the services you render, you are one of a great company at home and abroad. If you are trying to live a decent Christian life you are one of a multitude. If you are giving yourself under God in services to others, seeking to right wrongs, comfort sorrow, heal sickness, banish ignorance, overcome hatred, further the cause of peace, lead men to know God - a vast company marches at your side. In Cuba and the Congo, in America and in Russia, there are faithful souls who have not bowed the knee to evil.

God still works in the world to show His love and His concern and He works through the hands and hearts of men and women and children who serve Him. So often we lose the sense of God's presence and we forget all those who labor as we labor. Our own efforts are often marked by failure and we grow discouraged. We do well to remember that there are still those who march with all who would be good and who would do good. God has not left Himself without witnesses.

Still righteousness shall shine as the light and judgement as the noonday. You are not alone.

**JANUARY 23   FOR life is the mirror of king and slave...
'Tis just what we are and do: Then give to
the world the best you have; And the best
will come back to you.**

-Mary Ainge de Vere

WOULD YOU RATHER BE FREE OR BE SECURE?

One of the things we hear talked about is freedom. We hear a good deal about free nations and a free world and a free America. We had better talk about it for we today have taken and used the freedom we have received without being either grateful for it or faithful in our use of it. We have dissipated the heritage we have received. We are losing our freedom in trying to be like everyone else.

We are losing our freedom by hiding behind government in order to be secure. Sooner or later we must decide whether to be secure or to be free. If we insist on being given security, we can prepare to wear the shackles that go with it.

Government never made anyone free. Free men make free government. We are losing our freedom because of our love of money. Money never made a man free. No slavery is more complete than that which the love of money brings.

Our worship of education can cost us our freedom. Men are saying and writing that education is the foundation of freedom. It is not. It has of itself no power to create freedom. Men use education in this country to enable men to know God. What matters is not education but what is being poured through it. A system for distributing water is good if water is pure and is bad if the water is poisoned.

This country was founded and formed by free men. No government made them free. Government tried to make slaves of them. Money did not make them free. They knew only suffering, privation and danger. Education did not make them free. They created free education because they were free.

They were free men because they knew themselves to be children of God. They had learned what Paul meant when he said, "If Christ shall make you free, ye shall be free indeed." They found that freedom is a matter not of outward circumstances but of inner convictions.

As Jesus stood before Pilate, Pilate was the slave and Jesus was free, free though bound, free even while He died on the cross.

Freedom begins with a man's relation to God. If you would be a free man and if you would serve the cause of freedom here and in the world, you will have to begin at the place of your commitment to Christ as you trust Him for forgiveness and for guidance.

Here and here alone is the source of free government, free business, free education The distance we have drifted from this conviction in our land indicates how near we are to losing our liberty.

33

JANUARY 24   BUT be ye doers of the word...

James 1:22 (KJ)

DOING WILL HELP; IDLE OFFERS WON'T

Cain asked the question, "Am I my brother's keeper?" Paul specifically answers that question: "Bear ye one another's burdens, for this is the law of Christ." In Roman times, those who had contact with Christ helped those who persecuted them, with food in times of famine, with prayers for those who slew them, and with burial for those left by comrades in battle. This was perhaps the most effective witness of Christians among non-believers. The idea of personally helping others was revolutionary in that century.

It isn't easy through our personal lives to be truly concerned for others. It involves inconvenience, time, embarrassment and expense.

Most people claim to be "interested" in helping others. But personal concern is radically different from mere "interest." In the United States millions of dollars are spent every year by federal, state and community agencies. And yet the real problem is that we are prone to delegate our personal concern to impersonal agencies. We are happy to give money to an organization that will help other men. But we are reluctant to make the effort to help men personally.

The great inclination is to pass by the man who desperately needs help like the Priest and Levite in the parable of the Good Samaritan. And we do so with the thought that eventually we may send someone to help, but we are just too busy to stop now.

All of us are guilty of suggesting, "If I can do anything to help, please call on me," rather than just pitching in and doing what we can right now. We suggest that someone call us without any expectation that he will. This statement is typical of the insincerity of concern of our time. How shocked we would be if someone did call us and give us a list of needs.

Our Lord taught us to love one another and to love one another is

34

to be "concerned" with the needs of one another. But how can we become "concerned?" Look up into the eyes of the Lord. Understand that he lived and died for each of us individually. As we look to our Lord, concern comes for all men. It moves into us. We then are moved to do personally what we can.

Christianity in action is - above all else - unselfish in practice. It is a willingness of one man to give completely of himself for another man. The reason is that other men are the "concern" of Christ and all are disciples of Christ.

Thousands of personal needs cannot be met through our charitable agencies. They can only be met by individuals who are concerned. However limited you and I may be in talents, somewhere among your contacts is someone whose life will be made easier if you will today do what you can.

JANUARY 25   CALL unto me, and I will answer thee, and show thee great and mighty things, which thou knowest not.

Jeremiah 33:3 (KJ)

IS THRILLING LIVING PASSING YOU BY?

Do you ever wish your life was more exciting and romantic? Do you dream of princes on white horses coming to rescue you from your narrow prison? Do you imagine having great adventures of which you are the hero? Do you wish you were some great person who seems to go from big event to big event? Or do you find yourself again doing the same old things from day to day, wondering why thrilling life passes you by?

But it need not. Glorious living is made out of the stuff of your daily life. Jesus of Nazareth stands as the greatest figure our world has seen. His life has affected the life of man on earth more than any other. Yet Jesus' life was made up of ordinary days like ours. He grew up in a peasant home with its poverty. He spent His youth working at a carpenter's bench. He grew up in a village and never traveled more than 200 miles from where He was born. He never wrote anything or owned anything. He spent three years as an itinerant preacher. He had fisherfolk for His friends. He walked where men suffer and gave them healing. He touched their lives and gave them hope.

He helped a young bride celebrate her wedding. He watched with a father whose boy was lost. He stood with men who sowed grain and who built houses. He was cut off from family life by His wanderings. Finally misunderstood and rejected, He died as a common criminal. Out of stuff like this God made the life of His Son which has blessed our world.

This is the kind of stuff we try to run away from when God would have us find glory. He would show us adventure in our daily work, in the love of those dear to us, in the kind word to one discouraged, the helping hand to one in need. He would show us the glow of His presence where men suffer as we stand by their side, the comfort of His presence as we walk where men die.

As He walked where we walk, He made it forever difficult because He showed that there was where God is. As we walk where He walked, we find God who was there all the time.

Here is life's real glory, its real adventure - finding in our common way the uncommon path of glory because God walks by our side.

JANUARY 26   HELP thou mine unbelief

Mark 9:24 (KJ)

FAITH CAN BRING COURAGE TO YOU

Some people magnify their problems. They get a sense of importance out of being in a bad fix. If they have an operation it was "just in time." Anything that happens to them is made out to be a major emergency. But there are a good many people who are just about as bad off as they think they are.

Life has a way of closing in on some folks, leaving no visible means of escape. It may be a financial reverse, or sickness, or family trouble. It may be loneliness. It often involves women alone in the world with children to care for. It can be anything which taxes a person beyond his or her visible means of meeting the situation.

It is poor comfort to tell a person facing a blank wall to cheer up, things will work out all right. In many cases they won't in so far as anyone can see. Such advice only makes the depression deeper. It can also hurt rather than help to be too glib about recommending that the person not worry because God will take care of him or her. The feeling that God has absented Himself from the problem is often its greatest burden.

When life brings more pain than you think you can bear, you need help and you need it badly. You need someone to talk to whom you can trust. It is not easy to share pain with another but it is a good place to begin. The person to whom you go ought to be one who is wise in the ways of pain. You need to face the fact that your situation is bad. It does no good to make it less than it really is. Look it squarely in the face. Often we need help to do this.

Now comes the venture of faith: daring to believe that God is in the situation, working it toward solution. Nothing stands still. It helps to strive to believe that God who gave His Son to die for us will freely give us what we need.

Often our chief need at the moment is just courage and strength to go on bearing our burden. It is remarkable how often faith in God's presence, however weak the faith may seem, becomes the means by which we receive courage to go on.

For those who dare to believe and dare to go on there comes a better day. The situation does not always change. Sometimes it gets worse. But there comes strength for the day and always finally comes God's answer.

"God is faithful, who will not suffer you to be tempted above that ye are able to bear, but will with temptations also make a way to escape that ye may be able to bear it."

JANUARY 27   THUS saith the Lord, set thine house in order...

Isaiah 38:1 (KJ)

SINS ARE CATCHING UP WITH THIS NATION

A long time ago the prophet Isaiah addressed his country, which was threatened with military disaster: "And when ye spread forth your hands, I will hide mine eyes from you. Yea, when ye make many prayers, I will not hear. Your hands are full of blood. "

"Wash you. Make you clean: put away the evil of your doings from before mine eyes: cease to do evil; learn to do well; seek judgement, relieve the oppressed, judge the fatherless, plead for the widow."

"Come now and let us reason together, saith the Lord; though your sins be as scarlet, they shall be as white as snow; though they be red like crimson, they shall be as wool."

"If ye be willing and obedient, ye shall eat the good of the land: but if ye refuse and rebel, ye shall be devoured with the sword, for the mouth of the Lord has spoken."

This is the message of Scripture: the judgement and mercy of God. This is a day when we need again the voice of the prophet in the land. We are under the hand of God. Our disordered affairs and military threats to our land are our fault, not Russia's. Our sins are catching up with us.

We have flaunted our luxury in the face of the world. The cocktail party has become the symbol of our life overseas. Immorality is accepted as normal. Public opinion has allowed the moving picture industry by its overseas colonies of movie people and its products at home and abroad to debase the image of our country around the world. With all our pretense at religion, religion plays almost no part in the purpose of the average man's existence or ethics.

The worst thing about it is that no one seems concerned. There is no real evidence of repentance toward God, no evidence of concerned prayer for the mercy of God. No nation can stand which God no longer can use. Once judgement begins, only a turning to God can save us. Lip service only hastens the disaster. We are still guilty. Unless there are raised up prophets whose call to repentance and faith is heeded, we shall fall victims, not of an outside enemy but of our own sin.

Let us pray!

JANUARY 28   THAT we might receive the promise of the Spirit through faith.

Galatians 3:14

TOO FEW SHOW EVIDENCE OF FAITH

Evangelism and missions are by-words in church vocabulary. Books and articles pour out by the hundreds about them. Conferences are a dime a dozen in these vital subjects. And all the time it seems interest grows less and less. Talk has taken the place of action, method has displaced passion and retreat has displaced advance. Buddhists, Moslems and Communists are proving more aggressive than Christians.

I cannot help but wonder if we really are convinced that we have anything to give that is absolutely necessary for our neighbors and for our world. Before you answer too quickly think a bit about it. How often in the past month have you gone to anyone in trouble or in sin and told them that you have something in your faith that will answer their need?

We are hesitant to go to the alcoholic or gossip or thief and offer Christ as the answer. We are afraid it isn't enough. We work up enthusiasm over our old school ties and let everyone know where we stand. By pennants and buttons and flowers we show the school colors. How does anyone know you are a Christian? The early Christians didn't have an education or method but they had passion. They had a story to tell that had changed their lives from hopelessness to hope, from slavery to freedom, from sin to salvation. They had found peace for the heart though their lives were marked by suffering and death.

Evangelism and missions were telling and going and sending men and women who felt Christ to be the most important fact in the universe. Where do you find that today? Suppose you were in Africa or Korea or Cuba just as you are with your Christian faith. What kind of witness would you make? You would make exactly the same kind which you are at home.

Even we who are called Christians look to our good works to save us from the ills that plague us. We give little evidence that we believe Christ is Lord of all of life and that every individual and every human organization must answer to Him. Something drastic may have to happen to us who bear His name if we are going to witness with effectiveness. It sounds almost crazy in our modern day to insist that nothing can be successful without Him - that all efforts of men, of government, of society, of slum clearance, of mental health, are only shadowboxing without Him.

We cannot expect a lost world to take us seriously unless we give evidence of faith that shows the passion of personal commitment. In repentance we must admit there is not too much of this evidence today.

**FEAR thou not, for I am with thee: be
not dismayed; for I am thy God.**

Isaiah 41:10 (KJ)

IT TAKES POWER FROM OUTSIDE

In the newspaper recently the question of how to stay calm, cool
and collected was asked of some philosophers and psychologists.
Possibly no one can give his philosophy of life in a sentence or
paragraph. Not many will make the effort to be profound in an
interview or series of interviews such as was printed in the paper.

It did concern me, though, that not one of those quoted pointed
anywhere to a source of power upon which one might depend for
calmness in perilous times. Most of the answers intimated that you
had to lift yourself by your own bootstraps.

The advice included: "Keep busy," "don't try to be first," "live as
intelligently as possible," "a hundred years from now it will all be
ironed out," "look on the positive side of experience," "it's not life
that matters, but the courage you bring to it," "avoid distressing
situations," "attempt to steer clear of being a pessimist or optimist,"
"have plenty of work to do to keep from worrying about problems
you can't do anything about."

I am sure that each one who gave an answer does not feel satisfied
with the newspaper quotations. I use their answers only as an
illustration of how easy it is to talk about religious things without
even mentioning religion and without really meeting the question. To
be calm, cool and collected in perilous times is a religious question
because it has to do with a man's faith, or lack of it, in God.

Philosophy or psychology cut loose from God is just play-acting.
It results in wisdom that becomes foolishness. It recommends things
man has no power within himself to do. A light bulb gives no light

until the power comes from outside. A river carries traffic only for so long as the source keeps pouring water down the channel. So each of us must receive power from the outside to begin to do the things recommended. We need more than will power.

The whole impact of the Christian faith is toward giving us direction, purpose and power. By faith we are so related to God that His power comes through to us. Thus in perilous times we have confidence and assurance - which may be all the calmness God intended for us to have. Probably God never intended for us to be cool, calm, and collected in the popular sense. This may be why people are always seeking but are never finding a hiding place.

Jesus said, "My peace I give unto you. Not as the world giveth, give I unto you." He gives calmness in the storm, coolness in the heat of battle. This is why the question is ever a religious one and why the answer must seek its roots in the grace of God.

JANUARY 30   ARE we weak and heavy-laden, cumbered with the load of care? Precious Savior, still our refuge - Take it to the Lord in prayer!

-Joseph Scriven, Hymn

AVENUES OF PRAYER NEED MORE TRAVEL

No one will deny today there is a great need for prayer. We like to think of ourselves as the favorites of the Lord. We like to think that we are exceptional in His eyes, and that our prayer should be answered. However, our prayers find acceptance only as they rise from humble and contrite hearts.

Praying is an agonizing experience. It is a matter of vast concern. It is dealing with the great spiritual currents of our world. Prayer is putting yourself in tune with the spiritual powers of God. It is a dangerous and thrilling thing to do. It requires commitment.

1. The first thing to remember about prayer is not to argue about it. Argument is of no use. When men and women need to pray, they are going to pray, regardless of what they have thought about prayer before; regardless of the argument of their friends, there will not be much prayer unless there is a feeling of necessity.

2. We must come to pray as dependent creatures. In our educational system we are taught that we must stand on our own two feet. But you know, the loneliest thing on earth is to stand on your own feet. I know we must bear our own burdens, yet we were never meant to be independent of God.

    We are meant to be leaners. We are meant to lean upon the everlasting arms of God. Once we lean upon God, others can lean upon us, and in turn we can then lean upon them. There is permanence and satisfaction in leaning. The only way ever to be strong is to find the right place to lean. "Jesus lover of my soul, let me hide myself in Thee."

3. We must come to prayer expecting an answer. If you really pray out of need, out of surrender, you are going to get an answer. God bids us to expect an answer.

    If you really seek God's will for your life and your world, you are going to get an answer. But it is an answer that will send you out into the turmoil of the world to live according to the will of God. It will not be an answer that will give you an isolated island of security.

    We should pray that we of the church may become more perfect reflections of the Light of the Kingdom of God. We should also pray that those who control the affairs of the world may be led to seek His glory and to devote themselves to crowning Him King.

    We have tried nationalism, negotiations and the United Nations. Instinctively we know the answer does not lie there. It lies in the church of the Living God and in the avenues of prayer which are open to those who acknowledge Him as Lord of all.

JANUARY 31
TRUST in the Lord, and do good; so thou shalt dwell in the land, and verily thou shalt be fed.

Psalm 37:3 (KJ)

GOODNESS MERITS RECOGNITION, TOO

We are bombarded so much by stories of the world's tumult and disorder, of man's ugliness and sin, that we too easily forget the goodness that is here. In fact, unless we had a sturdy framework of goodness, evil would quickly destroy everything, even itself.

This is being written at the beginning of a day of great beauty. The birds are welcoming the evidences of spring with their merry tunes. The warm air bears promise of budding trees and opening flowers. Already the yards are full of jonquils. The full symphony of spring is about to burst out in full harmony. Surely all this is something to remember in gratitude.

In this frame of nature's glory, there is much of human goodness that reflects the image of God in the hearts of people. The world lives and moves because of faithfulness and goodness of people.

'Tis morning up and down the streets and mothers and fathers get children off to school. Horns blow to announce the arrival of the car group. You can count on it. Men and women go off to work with faithfulness and sometimes with high courage. Women busy themselves with the tasks of home. It is not that all these tasks are thrilling but that they are necessary. In homes without number they are done with unsung faithfulness.

Today and every day there will be those giving themselves beyond the call of duty to the service of their community, to their friends in need, to helping people at home and abroad whom they have never seen.

Recently I saw a group go out to share their faith with people they

44

did not know and to invite them to come and join them, in worship and the work of the church. These were busy people, people tired from their day's work. Yet they went out and there are groups like them everywhere.

All about you there are people who live with honesty, in faithfulness to their marriage vows, with courage in adversity and cheerfulness in suffering. There are multitudes who do resist temptation.

Whenever you see a church building, you see evidence of a company of people who at least are trying with sacrifice and devotion to serve God and man with faithfulness. In city and county and nation there are those who make government possible because they are honest, loyal and faithful.

We are not to forget all these things. In prayer, in participation and in gratitude we do well to keep them in mind. There is a great deal that is wrong with each of us and with our world. There is also a great deal that is right. We need to keep the picture in balance.

FEBRUARY

FEBRUARY 1   **CALL unto Me, and I will answer thee, and show thee great and mighty things, which thou knowest not.**

Jeremiah 33:3 (KJ)

THINK OF THE LORD SPEAKING TO YOU

A friend sent me this prayer recently. It seemed worth passing on. The author is unknown to me. "Think of the Lord speaking to you and saying, 'You do not have to be clever to please Me: all you have to do is want to love Me. Just speak to me as you would to anyone of whom you are very fond.'"

"Are there any people you want to pray for? Say their names to

Me, and ask of Me as much as you like. I am generous and know all their needs but I want you to show your love for them and Me by trusting Me to do what I know is best.

"Tell me about the poor, the sick and the sinners and if you have lost the friendship or affection of anyone, tell Me about that, too.

"Is there anything you want for your soul? If you like you can write out a long list of all your needs and come and read it to Me. Just tell Me about your pride, your touchiness, self-centeredness, meanness and laziness. Do not be ashamed; there are many saints in Heaven who had the same faults as you; they prayed to Me and, little by little, their faults were corrected as they prayed and were forgiven.

"Do not hesitate to ask Me for blessings for the body and mind; for health, memory, success. I can give you everything needed to make souls holier. What is it that you want today? Tell Me for I long to do you good. What are your plans? Tell Me about them. Is there anyone you want to please? What do you want to do for them.

"And don't you want to do anything for Me? Don't you want to do a little good to the souls of your friends who perhaps have forgotten Me? Tell Me about your failures and I will show you the cause of them. What are your worries? What has caused you pain? Tell Me all about it and add that you will forgive and forget, and I will bless you.

"Are you afraid of anything? Have you any tormenting, unreasonable fears? Trust yourself to Me. I am here. I see everything. I will not leave you. Have you not joys to tell Me about? Why do you not share your happiness with Me? Tell Me what has happened since yesterday to cheer and comfort you. Whatever it was, however big, however small, I prepared it. Show me your gratitude and thank Me.

"Are you determined not to run into temptations? Have you made up your mind about bad books and bad friendships? They disturb the peace of your soul. Are you going to be kind to the one that hurt you?

"Well, go along now. Get on with your work. Try to be quieter, humbler and more submissive, kinder, and come back soon and bring Me a more devoted heart.

"Tomorrow I shall have more blessings for you."

FEBRUARY 2   BUT stand thou still a while, that I may shew Thee the word of God.

I Samuel 9:27 (KJ)

KNOWING THE 'WHY' WILL CHANGE LIVES

This column is dedicated to those who don't know why they are doing whatever it is they are doing. If these words can encourage a few of us to face squarely the question, "Why?" and to follow where it leads, they will not be in vain.

I am concerned about the large number of able, attractive, gifted people who are living useless lives and know it. Some of them are quite successful from a business standpoint. The degree of business and social success has little to do with whether a person feels useful or useless. Money is a poor cover for an empty heart.

These people of the empty heart are usually busy people. They are often greatly concerned about their families. More often than not they are good people as the world counts such things. They are often kind people. Actually there is nothing much wrong with them as neighbors and as citizens except that they have no answer to the question "Why?" Because they do not, their lives move in a circle that shrinks in size as time goes on. They keep active in business and social affairs but they are haunted by their hearts.

In almost every instance you will find they have no deep interest in the church. They may stand around on its margins but they don't really give themselves to it. They have reasons why they don't. Nearly everyone who ignores the church feels guilty enough about it to explain it.

The truth is, such people have really never had the courage to face God honestly. The first question of a certain catechism is "What is man's chief end?" and the answer is "Man's chief end is to glorify God and to enjoy Him forever." Each human being is made so that he doesn't function properly unless his first interest is to glorify God and to enjoy Him now and forever. No other purpose will satisfy the eternal in our souls. The eternal is there whether we are willing to admit it or not. We neglect it at the peril of our peace.

I am sure that if any man or woman will honestly seek to find what it means to glorify God in his own life, an answer will begin to come to the question "Why?" Such a person will find the aimless feeling begin to disappear. The business fever will subside. The social round will see less of him; the church will see more of him. His time and talents and gifts will more and more find their way into useful channels. Devoting himself and his gifts to the glory of God, he that has received much will give much and in the giving find the answer to the question, "Why am I doing what I am doing?"

FEBRUARY 3   RISE, my soul, and stretch thy wings, Thy better portion trace; Rise from transitory things Toward heaven, thy destined place.

--Robert Seagrave, Hymn

HOPE OF HEAVEN IS THE SECRET OF LIFE

It is probable that the most powerful word in the English language is the very simple word "home". There is not anybody anywhere of any age who does not have an emotional reaction to the word home. Whether you have a good home or a bad one, there is something very deep in every man, woman and child that makes him want to go home.

We have a homing instinct and the strange thing about it is that it is not satisfied entirely with an earthly home. It is but a reflection of a deeper need for a home in heaven. We were created for eternal life. We were meant to be headed for heaven. Our spirits were created to have fellowship with God, not only now, but throughout all eternity. Deny it as you will, always it haunts. Whenever people think or talk about heaven there is a homesickness somewhere down in the depths of the personality that aches.

You can ignore heaven. You can live without referring your life to God if you want to. You can take your chances. The rain does fall on the just and on the unjust and you can play the laws of averages. You can depend upon the rewards and punishments of this world for your satisfaction. But if you do, there will come a time when life will go dead on you. I care not how attractive you are, nor how much you succeed, there will come a day when it won't make any difference, when the purpose of life dies. Unless heaven is real this world is a dead end. It makes a difference in your whole life whether you are going home.

If you are ever to find happiness in this world it will be thorough the hope of heaven. This hope is the gift of God's mercy. This miracle comes only as you ask God for it, and in His mercy He gives it to you.

This living hope is guaranteed by something that happened in history. It isn't just a dream. It is guaranteed by the resurrection of Jesus Christ, around which all history moves. "If Christ be not raised we are of all men most miserable."

In your life there is nothing permanent but God. Whatever you have is already slipping through your fingers. Life is changing, life is passing, life is dying. Except for your hope of heaven, your life would slip away. With it life is permanent. Our hope of heaven fades not away. It is always here as a lifting power. And that power is what Christ in His Gospel offers by offering the security of heaven which is ours by faith in Christ; by believing that He lived, by believing that He is ours and that heaven is reserved for us.

"In my Father's house," He said, "are many mansions. I go to prepare a place for you." One day He will come back and take you and you will find your name over the door. In the light of that certainty He bids us rejoice in His name.

FEBRUARY 4   CHARITY (love) beareth all things, believeth all things, hopeth all things, endureth all things.

I Corinthians 13:7 (KJ)

BEST OF ALL GIFTS IS THAT OF LOVE

Not long ago I sat in a beautifully furnished home. All through the house there was evidence of good taste and great care. But somehow it did not seem to matter because the wife and mother who had done it all had died the day before. Frankly, it seemed only an empty shell. One day it all had been vibrant and alive. The next day it was just a bunch of furniture.

We forget so easily that material things have meaning only in terms of people. So often we sacrifice our relationship to people in order to have material things only to find out too late that it was the people, after all, who mattered.

Maybe this column is just an appeal to any of you who have someone to love to treasure the gift above all things. It is good to have nice things and to want to have nicer things. But if the process of getting them interferes with the love that binds you to one another, you will do better to let them go. It is fine to want advantages for your children. But if providing them takes you away from your children, you rob them of the only real advantage, which is love.

It is fine to help out in the community. Much good work needs doing. But if it means that you use energies there that ought to be given to those God has given you in love, let someone else do the good work. This is not a plea for selfish living. Where true love is, enough will be given on the outside. It is just a reminder that love is life's most priceless possession and once it is gone, there is nothing that can take its place. Advantages and beautiful things become so much weight to be carried unless they are made personal by love.

50

Love is God's divinest gift. It flows from His own heart unto your heart. Keep your heart open to God in gratitude and in worship. Then before all else, let love have first place. Real love can make radiant the humblest place. No palace is worth having without it.

It is not easy in our day to find the time to cultivate love. Things that seem necessary demand our hours and our energies. Our families and our friends are put off for a more convenient time. And sometimes forever. When that happens life gets desolate indeed. It can make life richer if we make sure we put first things first.

FEBRUARY 5   I THOUGHT on my ways, and turned my feet unto Thy testimonies.

Psalm 119:59 (KJ)

A PRICE IS BEING PAID FOR THIS SECULAR AGE

We are living in a day when very few would suggest that they know what is going on - or why. It is hard to admit that this world is run by God. This is a secular age. "Secular" means we believe in the achievements of man. We place man before God. The fact that the Bible states that God rules nations, nature and man leaves us wondering.

The fact that the Bible - from beginning to end - states that no one can live successfully in rebellion against God or in neglect of God, we have forgotten. Yet isn't it a fact that we have forgotten the very core of the trouble of our time? And hasn't this always been the core of the world's trouble?

It is true the church has been growing increasingly popular in America. But the rest of the world is growing further away from the church. And even in America with our church growth, there seems a minimum of commitment to discipleship. There has been a great lack of any real confidence that we are God's children in God's world.

It is easy to forget God. We are sinners at heart. We respond quickly to the belief that we can handle our own problems. We see wonderful achievements of man all around us. The giant skyscrapers of our time have a way of blotting out the heavens of all time. We have so much concrete. The very sturdiness of it convinces us we have a firm foundation. Big business is so successful. Everything is marvelously organized. There is a feeling - among the common man - that given time, the scientist will solve it all. And if by chance he fails, there is always the "right" psychological adjustment. And, most tragic of all, much of our educational system leaves God out. It doesn't deny Him. It just leaves Him out. It isn't hard to block Him out in this busy, busy world of ours.

If you can run a world as we are running ours and the result is a good world, then God is not Sovereign. The very fact that this world is in its present state is proof enough that God is Sovereign. Whenever we forget Him, the result is chaos! Is there a better word than chaos to describe the times in which we live?

The United Nations was born in great fanfare. But it left God out except in some vague way. It is a beautiful organization. But world peace cannot be brought about from an organization without God. We need to remember that the United States, Russia, Belgium and the Congo are not making history. God is making history.

We need to remember the words of Isaiah: "Behold your God!" Things may get a lot worse before they get better. And they may not get better for a long, long time. Not until men take Him seriously again.

Behind it all God is working His will. And He has only one purpose: that every knee shall bow - and every tongue shall confess Jesus Christ as Lord. That purpose knocks at your heart for acceptance.

52

TRY PLACING BLAME WHERE IT BELONGS

Most of us have a hard time admitting that we are responsible for our troubles. In our modern day we have had a good deal of encouragement from the field of popular psychology to evade responsibility. It is a favorite trick to blame our faults on something that happened to us as children.

Being rejected seems a catchall to blame all misconduct on. Children's bad deeds are due to parent's mistakes. The alcoholic is a victim of circumstance and the immoral person is a poor unfortunate.

Jesus told a story of a man who planted seed. Some of it grew and some didn't. He said the seed was good in each case. The fault was in the soil. He was indicating that we are to blame for much of our conduct. The conscience of most of us backs this up. We do feel guilty for our bad actions and for our failures.

There is a lot of just pure meanness in what a lot of us do - children and adults. It is not possible to rid ourselves of responsibility by blaming it on our past or our parents or environment. The alcoholics may be beyond their own power to help but many of them knew they were playing with fire and still kept on. In dealing with them you perform them no service by treating them as though they were not guilty. They know they are. So it is with most of our moral problems.

You are not going to cure moral problems by medicine or psychology. There is still such a thing as plain evil and the only real remedy for it is to face God to whom we are responsible. An experience of the justice and love of God in forgiveness is the only remedy.

This is not easy to apply. But it is better to work at the true solution than to continue to fool ourselves that bad people can be made good by comfortable surroundings and medical care of any and all kinds and by long-suffering relatives who pretend nothing should be done to make the guilty one feel guilty.

Surely the person needs love but real loves takes account of responsibility and demands that the erring one accept it in order for love to work. God cannot do anything for a person who is not sorry for his sin. Human love can't either. Someone always bears the penalty of sin and in our day too often the wrong person is bearing it. The sinner ought to bear his share of it instead of being excused as a poor victim.

Only then can God's love in Christ, medicated through human heart, redeem. If you are in trouble, the place to start putting the blame may be with yourself. It will make it easier on everyone - including you.

FEBRUARY 7   GOD has promised forgiveness to your repentance; but He has not promised tomorrow to your procrastination.

St. Augustine

HOW LONG CAN THIS GAME LAST?

There is always a straw that sooner or later breaks the camel's back. A child keeps on being aggravating until the roof finally falls in on him. Some one event can start a landslide. It may be that convictions of certain large manufacturers of electrical equipment is the straw that will break our already weakened confidence in American business and the "American way."

It is certainly a fine illustration of the well-known fact that every nation that falls rots out from within. This event has done harm to our "free enterprise" system that communism could not do. It tends to make a farce out of the idea of fair competition.

In many places it has seemed a farce for a long time. The milk people have laws that make it illegal to sell milk below a fixed price. It seemed odd to many that gasoline is sold by competing companies for the same price to the tenth of a cent. "Suggested" prices govern the sale of a multitude of products.

There is in our country a great game of "make believe." It may be near the end of its road. Already it has brought much government control. Pure food laws came because it was the only way to keep people from being poisoned. Meat is government-inspected as a necessity to protect the public.

All this means that we as a people had better examine ourselves. Those convicted are probably no more guilty than many, many others. They are no more guilty than the rest of us who, in many ways of our own, exchange the demands of our conscience for material and social advantages. The problem is one for each business organization and for each individual.

We need to ask some deep questions: What is the purpose of life? What is the place of my life in business? Of my life in this purpose? What are the laws of life that must be obeyed?

Jesus was speaking to all of us when He asked: "What shall it profit a man if he gain the whole world and lose his own soul?" He was giving sound advice when He said: "Seek ye first the Kingdom of God."

I suggest you read carefully the Sermon on the Mount in Matthew 5. As you read, you can hear the drums of doom unless you repent.

The mission and message of the Christian faith is as necessary for us as it was for our fathers. It calls all men to repent and to believe. It calls all of us to obedience. God is not mocked and what we sow, we reap. The truth of this is being borne in upon us.

II Chronicles 20:126 (NIV)

MESSAGE AND FAITH CHANGED THE WORLD

We are living in a problem conscious age. Never have people been quite so concerned with themselves.

1.   There are personal problems. Every publication deals with them - and a good many of them depend on our problems for a profit.

2.   There are social problems. We are in the midst of a world revolution in racial problems. Only God knows where it will come to rest.

3.   We are rightfully concerned with it in the South, but in many respects it is less acute here then in other areas of the world. The people of Ghana are suspicious of the Arabs because they are not black. The Chinese are suspicious of the Russians because they are white.

4.   There are political problems. We have always had a time getting along with each other here at home. But more important today, how can we get along politically with governments and peoples throughout the world? We must find the answer or some trigger-happy fanatic may blow us all up.

5.   There are problems in the church. There is something wrong with our contact with the world. The urgency has gone out of evangelism. We are not quite sure what we are trying to do. We are caught up in a worldwide wave of intolerance. There are enough Christians in Atlanta alone to revolutionize the whole world, yet we are not changing life around us.

But read the New Testament. Nobody is trying to solve any problems. The word is not even mentioned. But there are plenty of personal problems. Peter had sickness in the family. Paul was physically handicapped. They spent a good bit of time in jail. They knew what it was to have their business closed because they were Christians. They saw members of their families killed because they were Christians.

They had social problems. They had slavery. They had poverty beyond the imagination of most Americans. They had immorality that actually destroyed an empire. Temples were built to immorality on the most prominent street corners. They had political problems. Their land was occupied by foreigners. They were treated just like the Russians treated the Hungarians. Yet one finds no discussion of these problems running through the New Testament. It is the simple story of people on the march - out to do something.

They started out to change the world with no resources as we count such things. They had only an absolute personal conviction that Jesus Christ was the Son of God and that "on the third day He rose from the dead." They believed – they knew – they were transmitters of His power. They believed there was no answer to any problem unless Christ was in the center.

Don't dismiss them as flighty idealists. Everything that is dear in our civilization stems from those foolish men and women who went forth – starting with 120 – witnessing to this one conviction. Our problems await a similar group driven by the same conviction.

FEBRUARY 9   **THE man who plants and the man who waters have one purpose, and each will be rewarded according to his own labor. For we are God's workers...**

I Corinthians 3:8,9 (NLV)

DESIRE AND WORK ARE REQUIRED FOR FAITH

Recently I wrote a column on a theme that these are great days in which to be alive. I made the statement that to live greatly you must believe greatly in a great God. Several people have indicated their agreement but have asked the questions:

"How do you come to believe with conviction and commitment in a God who made all things, who rules all things, who makes evil serve His purposes, who saves the lost and restores the sinner, who one day will catch all the world up in His final victory?"

"How do you believe that God has placed us where we are to find our glory in serving Him?"

1. To begin with, you must come to the place where you want this faith more than you want anything else. It will escape you as long as you depend on anything else for support of your life.

2. You must want it because it has become necessary for your life. The confidence which you have placed in your own goodness or your own cleverness, or your own money or social position or your friends or relatives as foundations for life, must have failed you before faith becomes a possibility.

3. You must decide that you are willing to pay the price for it. Faith is a costly jewel. God has revealed Himself in Jesus Christ. Those who seriously seek faith do what they can to know Him in the Bible and in worship in the church. So many people fail to find faith because they are unwilling to seek God where He may be found.

4. Faith is a gift of God. Hence you must ask God for this precious gift. We must pray for it with minds and hearts open to receive what God is anxious to give. Faith is not something we earn or achieve. It is the result of the miraculous touch of the Spirit of God.

5. Having done what we can to know God in Christ and having asked God for faith, we can only wait His good pleasure in giving it. No one can tell you how it will come nor when. You will recognize it as it draws over your soul the transforming power.

6. Finally, you must act on it as it comes. You must dare to live by that which God gives. Only in trusting God as you live will you ever be sure. In trusting Him to comfort your sorrow, to forgive

your sins, to defeat the evil that threatens your life, you will find His strength made perfect in weakness. Often your doubts will get all mixed up with your faith. Act on your faith instead of your doubt.

So, increasingly you will come to live by faith and not by sight and find that it is a great day in which to live.

FEBRUARY 10   ...The whole land is made desolate, because no man layeth it to heart.

Jeremiah 12:11 (KJ)

CONFORMITY'S WAVE WEAKENS THE CHURCH

Nothing hurts us more than to be called "odd." To be odd (to be "peculiar") is to be like an extra glove or extra shoe - cast off. We all desperately fear having nothing to be paired with, to be an "oddball." Today, more than ever before, is an age of conformity.

We wear the same type of clothes, the same hairstyles, and even, to a certain extent, the same facial expression. There is a terrible pressure to be alike. In a nation founded on God for the individual, we have fled from individualism and from God.

The propaganda from business and labor and government tends to see that we think as we should think, buy as we should buy, love as we should love and hate as we should hate.

Unfortunately the church has been caught in this wave of conformity. Today the mark of the church is one of wealth and comfort. The church does not appear "odd" or "peculiar."

The church makes a point of working harmoniously with sociology, psychology and politics. In fact, it fits in so well that you can't tell it from anything else. Yet it still witnesses. But it witnesses in a way not to offend anybody, in a way not to be thought of as peculiar. How strange.

Since its beginning, the Christian church has always lived in tension with the world around it. It has always been composed of "odd" people. It has been swimming against the current. If you are swimming against the current, you may have lost your lifeline. You may have left the stream.

The church has been watered down. It has very little influence today, except indirectly. But we are still the "called" of God. We still have to say to this generation: "There is one God, the God of Jesus Christ." And we must say loudly, with our lives as well as our words, "that no man cometh unto the Father but by Him."

We must be odd and peculiar. We must live our lives as He would have us live if we are to be in the succession of the saints. And maybe once more, we will be found worthy of the gift of the Holy Spirit of God. This is the gift by which the world may again be turned upside down.

FEBRUARY 11   **SO encourage each other to build each other up...**

I Thessalonians 5:11 (LB)

HERE'S A SURE WAY FOR A HAPPIER LIFE

Most people take a secret delight in the failings of other people. We are a bit insecure in our own hearts. We are conscious of our own failings whether other people are or not. It is unfortunately natural for us to relish the weaknesses of our friends. We feel raised a bit in our own eyes if we find another pushed down.

This is one reason for the popularity of books and articles that debunk a popular figure. We feel they have been cut down to size. We like to read articles that point out weaknesses in other people. Bad news makes good reading in the press.

Gossip is popular because it makes us feel somewhat superior to those whose misstep or misfortune we pass on. It is no trouble at all to get the word around about something bad that a person has done. We just can't wait to pass it on. Where the news is about someone of whom we are jealous, we work even faster. Also, there is not much use in repeating a choice morsel of gossip unless we add something to it. The end result is usually far removed from the truth, but this does not greatly worry us.

In all this, we forget that we are judged by the judgement with which we judge for we who judge do the same things. More often than not we pick out our own weakness in our gossip about others. Each of us is a mixture of the good and bad. None of us can stand very close examination by any perfect standard.

The only way we can live together in harmony is in Christian charity. In Christian charity we are willing to regard the other person as better than ourselves. Such charity is born of God's love for us. Only those who understand that God loves them in spite of their unloveliness can ever accept and love people as they are, living with them in charity.

Living in charity with others means we major in their goodness rather than their badness, their virtue rather than their vice. It means seeking to live with others in kindness and in courtesy, without pushing ourselves up by pushing them down.

Living in charity with others has a way of calling out the best in them. They will more often than not respond to kindness with kindness, to goodness with goodness. As we find less to criticize in our neighbor, he usually finds less fault in us.

Listen in on your own conversation and that of your group. See how often we allow unkindness to mar our comments about other people. Jesus said, "All things whatsoever ye would that men should do to you, do ye even so to them."

This is a good place to start if you want to make this world a happier place in which to live.

FEBRUARY 12   JESUS calls us o'er the tumult of our life's wild, restless sea; Day by day His sweet voice soundeth, saying, "Christian follow Me."

Cecil F. Alexander, Hymn

HERE'S A QUESTION TO ASK YOURSELF

When I was in high school my mother put a novel into my hands. It was Charles Sheldon's "In His Steps." I have never forgotten it and it has periodically haunted me ever since. Recently it came to my attention again.

In these days when we are facing reexamination of what it means to live as a Christian, the book may deserve attention. It is the story of a minister of some town's "First Church" and some of its prominent and influential members. One Saturday a man comes to the minister's home asking for help in finding a job. The minister, busy about his sermon, sends the man away with more or less pious words.

Sunday, after he had finished his well-rounded sermon to his fashionable congregation, the man interrupts the service by walking down the aisle to stand before the pulpit. In a humble but direct way he asks the minister and congregation what it means to follow Christ. He tells of his wife's death some months before in a tenement, of how he has not been able to find work, of how few have even encouraged him. He then faints. The minister has him taken to his home where a few days later he dies.

The minister is shaken by the experience. On the next Sunday he tells the story of the man. He repeats the question that the man asked about what it means to live as a Christian. He announces that he has decided to try for one year meeting every decision by asking the question, "What would Jesus do?" He invites any who will join him in such a venture to meet him after the service.

Around 50 came and the book is chiefly the story of certain of those who joined in the venture. It is the story of the publisher of one of the leading newspapers and what his decision cost him. It tells of a young woman gifted with an unusual voice and the strange path in which the venture led her. There is a wealthy young woman who faces the use of money in the light of her decision. There is the railroad executive who follows his conscience to the loss of his position. The book tells how one who turned back lost the way and of how one who was worthless found himself. There are changes in nearly every area of the city's life because of the band who decided to apply to every decision: What would Jesus do?"

The book still haunts me. I can't help but wonder what would happen to a group of modern Christians who for one year would honestly, to the best of their ability, make every decision in the light of the question, "What would Jesus do?"

FEBRUARY 13 **ONCE to every man and nation comes the moment to decide in the strife of truth with falsehood, for the good or evil side.**

James Russell Lowell, Hymn

THE CAUSE OF FEAR IS WITHIN OURSELVES

For years our country has been kept busy adjusting to moves made by Russia. It reminds me of a Western movie where the bad man shoots at the ground around the feet of the good man to see him dance. We have become uneasy and afraid. We need to realize that the cause of our fear and insecurity lies not in Russia, but in ourselves. The cure lies not in ourselves but in God. We are reaping as we have sown. We have sown godlessness and are reaping fear.

Long ago in the days of the prophet, Isaiah, his little nation of Judah was in near panic over the approach of Assyria. The people stopped listening to the voice of God and began to center their attention on the propaganda and rumors from the Assyrian army. Into this situation Isaiah came preaching. He told them God had Assyria on a leash as a man holds a dog. His point was that the course of history is set by God and not by the plans of pagan nations like Assyria or Egypt. The problem of Judah was not Assyria, he told them, but Judah's sins. He told them the cure for their problems lay not in armies and alliances but in repentance and a return to God.

There is a message for us here. Being rid of communism will not rid us of our fears. Before Russia there was Nazi Germany that was to blame for everything bad. Our problems stem from our sins, which cut us off from God. Our answers will begin to come when we get off our high horse and down on our knees in repentance. Books, magazines and the theater parade immorality without inner or outer restraint. Vice rides high in many places. Money comes near to being the measure of all things. Sunday has become a holiday. Marriage has been cheapened.

For us as a people, tomorrow will not be determined by our money and our arms. It will take form on the basis of our faith and morality. The future will be made, if it is to be a good future, by men and women of simple faith and piety.

The answer to our problems lies with God, who in power rules the nations, and in those who know Him and serve Him. We can come to know and trust God only when we are willing to put more time on our Bibles than on the newspapers; more time in prayer than watching TV. He has revealed himself in Jesus Christ and He can be known.

In knowing Him and seeking to do His will in your own life, you will find your answer to fear and your place of usefulness in our confused day.

FEBRUARY 14   **IF thou criest after knowledge, and liftest up thy voice for understanding; If thou seekest her as silver, and searchest for her as hid treasures; Then shall thou...find the knowledge of God.**

Proverbs 2:3,5 (KJ)

THAT SAME POWER COULD BE YOURS

With the rapid changes in our modern day, our eyes have been turned toward the future. Will we shrink from it or meet it head-on? That depends on our inner resources. You can be sure we have our problems. Our wages are the highest in the history of man but there is fear of industrial automation, foreign competition, and higher unemployment. We are spending half our tax dollars on defense; yet we know the Soviet Union can momentarily destroy our cities. We have spent more than any nation in history to help others, but our "friends" seem to be fewer.

None of us knows what the future holds. But that isn't new. Our biggest problem is: Where are we going to get the power to make and take the future? We are living in an age when millions believe the answer lies in us - in better education, better science, better psychology, and more group action. All we really have to do is gather our individual abilities and capabilities together. Nothing more is needed.

Look back with me nearly 2,000 years ago when Christ was gathered in a little room with His closest friends. They had known Him personally. They had seen His miracles. They had seen Him killed and knew Him to be dead. They had seen Him again – alive in the flesh – walking, talking, eating. Death, their real concern, had fallen before Him. And then before their eyes, He was taken up bodily into the Heavens. And they knew it all before Him – first hand.

But they still had problems. Their problems weren't really very different from ours. They had families to support, jobs to do and "crises" to face. But certainly together, they had the capacity and ability to face the future. Or did they? Jesus recognized that, even then, they simply didn't have the power. He advised them to "wait until the Holy Spirit comes." He knew that only with His power could mere men make and take the future. They waited, expected and prayed. And the Holy Spirit descended upon that little band of believers. They got up and went forth into the future with a power not their own. They literally turned the world upside down.

We are certainly no more capable within ourselves to meet the future. No matter how smart we are, how much education or potential we have, we simply don't have enough power. But the same power those first Christians had is available to us. The advice is still there - to believe in Jesus Christ and to wait for the Holy Spirit to descend on us.

That is the power - the only power - with which we can make and take the future. It's available to us today, just as it was at Pentecost - if we want it badly enough. Let's seek the Lord and receive it. Let's turn again to the only source of real power, a power mightier then the sword, the dollar or any form of group action - the power of the Holy Spirit, given to those who wait and expect.

FEBRUARY 15 WHERE there is peace, God is.

Herbert

THE RESULT WOULD BE A MIRACLE OF PEACE

Why is it people don't get along better with one another? Lots of families don't get along with one another. Nearly every business office has its tensions among employees. Neighborhoods have their quarrels. Social clubs divide up sides. Nations can't seem to feel friendly with one another for very long. Even some churches are known to be not all sweetness and light. More unhappiness is caused by people not getting along than by all the natural disasters which come.

Of course, we blame the other person almost without exception. We generally believe there are two sides to every question: the other fellow's side and the right side, which is ours. The truth is that the fault is usually within us. We cannot control how another person acts but we can control the way we act. It is in our power to act in such a manner as to get along fairly well with nearly everyone.

The Christian faith teaches us to get along on the basis of our weakness instead of our strength. We often carry a chip on our shoulder that is easily knocked off by anyone who fails to give us credit for being someone in particular. We defend our position and our importance with passion. We try to hide our weaknesses and we resent anyone who exposes them. Jesus suggests that we admit them and share them. In so doing, we find that we and our neighbors are more alike than we thought.

None of us is as self reliant as we pretend. We desperately need the help and support of others. Admit it. In every conscience there is some burden of guilt. We share blame in every difficulty and it can change things if we admit it.

All of us need affection and encouragement. We need those who love us to share our victories and defeats. Yet so often we are not able to admit it and we push away that which we want most in the world. It will work wonders to admit our need.

Facing our weaknesses and our faults is the first step. The second step is to accept God's forgiveness and His strength. He has promised that His strength is made perfect in weakness. The road to peace with your neighbor leads through finding peace with God.

Having found the answer to our weakness we will want to share this answer with others. Hence we will come to others to serve them, not outshine them. Sharing guilt, we would share a Saviour; sharing weakness, we would have God's strength; sharing our need for affection, we would share His love.

The result can be a miracle of peace and good will among people who get along well with one another.

The steadfast love of the Lord never ceases, his mercies never come to an end: they are new every morning; great is Thy faithfulness.

Lamentations 3: 22,23 (RSV)

IT'S A GREAT ERA IN WHICH TO LIVE

These are great days in which to be alive. Revolution is the byword everywhere. Electricity and all its results are the products of years thorough which many have lived. Transportation has in 50 years changed from the oxcart to jet planes. Home industry has given way to giant corporations.

For centuries, two-thirds of the world's people have lived in poverty. Today they know it, don't like it and intend to do something about it. Science has pushed our frontiers out into what seems limitless space.

We need to stop thinking about everything in terms of problems and to begin living as though life was an adventure. We are so enslaved by the idea of security until we are afraid to launch out and live. We want someone to solve our problems. Problems were not meant to be solved. They were meant to be lived. We need to stop waiting for somebody to tell us what is good for us and to start seeking the good for ourselves. These days of utter change challenge everyone to discover the romance of living. There is an attraction about the unknown future even when the way leads through dark days.

However, you cannot live greatly unless you believe greatly. You need a faith in a great God. You must be able to look out on the stars, to peer into space with all its possibilities and believe that God made it all. This faith must be able to look out over the confusion and disorder of our world and believe that behind it all is God. We must believe that He has a plan for our world and that He is working His plan.

Our faith must be able to look evil in the face, whether it strikes down a loved one or a nation, and believe that God already has defeated its power and that He will make even the evil to serve His Glory. We must believe in a God who seeks to save the lost and to restore the sinner. We need a faith in God that looks ahead to the day when He will catch all the world up in His final victory. Perhaps most of all, we need a faith that God has made us and placed us where we are in this great day to serve Him and in serving Him to find our glory.

Such a God is the God of Jesus Christ. Faith in such a God will send you forth with courage to live with joy in the battle. The very problem you face can be your call to adventure.

FEBRUARY 17   **COMMIT your way to the Lord; trust in him and he will do this: He will make your righteousness shine like the dawn, the justice of your cause like the noonday sun.**

Psalm 37: 5,6 (NIV)

CHURCH DISCIPLINE IS THE TELLING FACTOR

A friend recently said to me that unless the church spoke out with a clear voice in our present troubles it would lose out. Strangely enough there are those who seem to feel it has said too much already. It all depends on your point of view.

I am not sure the church furnishes its best leadership in making pronouncements on politics and economics and race. These are at times necessary, but unless we as the church are the kind of people we tell other people to be, we are not likely to have much influence.

The church furnishes its most telling leadership when its ministers and members have a quality of life as a group and as individuals which is truly Christian. The church has been at its best when, under difficulty, it has dared to live in love toward all men and with courage before all opposition.

This quality of life is possible only through Christian discipline. Perhaps the clearest voice the church today can utter is a call to the people who make up the church to be faithful to the disciplines of the church. Discipline is the faithful doing of what is required to reach a desired goal. Certain disciplines are required to become a musician or an artist or an athlete. If you are going to be a Christian filled with the spirits of good works, certain disciplines are required.

1. Attendance of public worship is the first of the disciplines of the church. Here God meets His people in power. As we worship together, God moves to touch each life with forgiveness of sin and strength for the day. In worship we find ourselves a part of the family of God and thereby members one of another. It is doubtful that any person who willfully and regularly absents himself or herself from public worship can feel very confident of any saving relationship to God or to man.

2. A second discipline is the study of the Bible. Only thus can we know what God's Word is for us in our lives. You won't find the same answer in the average book or magazine. Every church furnishes guidance and special opportunities for Bible study.

3. The effort to take seriously the stewardship of our time, ability and money is a third discipline. All you and I have and are has been put into our keeping for a while by God, the Owner. All of it must be used for His glory. He requires a fair part of our time, ability and money for His church. It requires real discipline to be faithful to His requirement.

Where the church is composed of those who are faithful to these and other required disciplines, it will show forth a quality of life that will give new power to its witness before men.

FEBRUARY 18   I BOW my knees unto the Father of our Lord Jesus Christ, of whom the whole family in heaven and earth is named.

Ephesians 3: 14,15 (KJ)

THIS IS A TIME FOR ALL TO PRAY

Surely this is a time that calls for prayer. Anyone and everyone that can pray at all ought to be praying. Little children will do well to add their voices. Maybe shut-ins can do more for us than anyone else. One thing seems certain: the situation is out of the control of the wisdom and ability of men.

Yesterday's image of modern man as a well-educated, capable person calmly sitting down to think through a situation, then talking it out with other smart people and then pressing a button and ordering the answer carried out is gone.

Suppose you had absolute power and authority – what would you do about the race problem, or about the situation in Russia or China? What would you do about inflation or the flight abroad of gold or unemployment or crime or the immorality of our day which hides behind such terms as "freedom of speech" and "adult"? What would you do about your own "split-level" personality, your discontented and frustrated life? Have you heard or read of anyone who knows the answer to even one of these problems?

These are all problems of people one by one. In them, men, women and children live, suffer and die. These are all problems of people whom God loves and for whom Christ died that they might have abundant life. What do you suggest that will help make this life real to all this suffering mass of men?

In our ignorance and weakness, it is probable that the best thing we can do is to pray about our world. We can pray that God who

71

made our world and loves it will move to redeem it from its evils. We can pray that He will give to men wisdom, guidance and strength; that He will raise up those filled with His Spirit who will rally around them the weary spirits of men. We can pray that there will come a real revival of integrity of character, of hope to our hearts, of clarity to our minds, of faith to our souls.

It can well be that the weakest prayer will be stronger than the largest bomb. Maybe this was what Jesus had in mind when He said, "Except ye be converted and become as a little child, ye shall in no wise enter the Kingdom of Heaven." Certainly this is what Paul meant when he wrote that "supplications, prayers, intercessions and giving of thanks be made for all men, for kings and for all that are in authority, that ye may lead a quiet and peaceable life in all godliness and honesty."

The fear of the Lord is still the beginning of wisdom and this wisdom comes best in the prayer room and in the prayer meeting.

FEBRUARY 19   **BOOK of books, our people's strength,**
Statesmen's, teacher's hero's treasure,
Bringing freedom, spreading truth,
Shedding light that none can measure.

Percy Dearmer, Hymn

HERE'S WHY MANY DON'T READ THE BIBLE

A young matron recently told of her grandmother who left as the chief impression of her life her devotion to the Bible. She had read it through 17 times. It was her constant companion and she reared her family in its strong shadow. The young matron asked the question, "Why don't people read the Bible today as the older generation did?"

I have an idea that the main reason people don't read the Bible more faithfully is that they don't feel any need for it. They are just not going in the same direction. The Bible does not talk about things they are interested in. It actually offers little help for the ambitions and desires of the average person.

The Bible is concerned with the world of the spirit and most of us are too busy with the material world to care for the spiritual world. One world at a time is a popular motto. The Bible talks of heaven and most people are not much concerned about it. The Bible talks of hell and we just don't want to think about it. The Bible is a handbook for pilgrims traveling through this world and we are interested in staying here.

The Bible talks about sin and we like to think we have gotten beyond such outdated words. It talks about being saved and the average person doesn't know what the word "saved" means. The Bible's chief interest is in reconciling man to God and our chief interest is in getting along in this world.

The Bible talks about obedience to Christ as the guide for our daily life. We are chiefly interested in following whatever will help us make money and be socially popular.

When you think about it, it is not so strange that people don't read the Bible. They don't need it for what they have in mind. It serves only to disturb us in our desires and ambitions. We would rather leave it alone.

Perhaps it won't be widely read again until conditions drive us to see that the direction we are going leads into a blind alley, that only the pilgrims on the way to heaven are on the right road. Only those who have been driven by circumstances to understand that they are lost will faithfully read the Bible to learn what it means to be saved. When we are forced to see that getting along well in this world depends on being reconciled to God, we will really read the Bible.

Only thirsty people drink water. Only needy people seek help. Only those who find they must have an answer to life's divine origin, meaning and destiny will read the Bible as an older generation read it.

FEBRUARY 20   ...WE wait for light...

Isaiah 59:9 (KJ)

LIGHT IS AVAILABLE FOR THE NEXT STEP

Not many people walk with lanterns anymore. Some probably never saw one. In the good old days, people in this country never went out at night without one. The lantern gave out a small circle of light that lighted the next step or two ahead. It would usually take you where you were going and bring you home again.

The Psalmist must have had a lantern in mind when he wrote: "thy word is a lamp unto my feet and a light unto my path." In his day there were no flashlights to pierce the darkness far ahead. Only light enough for the next step. That is what God promises us – light enough for the next step.

We often want too much information about the future. We face a decision and demand to know how it will turn out before we are willing to act. We want a blueprint of the future before we are willing to venture. Life just does not provide these. We are ignorant of the future. Life itself is a gift that can be withdrawn anywhere along the journey. Strange turnings we cannot anticipate or control mark our ways. All we really ever can have is light for the next step.

In most of our problems and troubles, it is possible to know what to do next. God does give us that. It may be a very small step. It may seem too small to bother to take but unless you take it, you will not get very far along the way. This is part of the philosophy of Alcoholics Anonymous. You cannot handle the future but you can handle the day you have. You may feel unable to change your life but you can do the thing that is at hand.

When tragedy and sorrow come, some people fall down under the threat of the dark future. They feel sure they cannot go on. But certain simple things can be done such as eating something or going for a walk or meeting the ordinary demands of the moment. These steps can be the key to the future and strength for these simple steps usually comes.

We get disturbed over the problems of our day but fail to do what we can to solve them. We are concerned over race prejudice and fail to deal with it in our hearts. We talk about the breakdown in morals and are not careful about our own thoughts and actions. We talk about the national debt and are careless about paying our own bills. We decry alcoholism while sipping cocktails.

The place to start changing things is where you are. Take the next step and keep walking. Christ says: "Lo, I am with you."

FEBRUARY 21   **PRAYER is a preparation for danger; it is the armor for battle. Go not into the dangerous world without it.**

Robertson

A TABLE OF CONTENTS HELPS IN OUR PRAYERS

This is an attempt to speak to the person who finds difficulty in knowing what to pray for. These suggestions are such as will be found in any book on prayer. They come from the experience of the church through the ages.

1. As you come to pray, let your mind dwell on the greatness of God. Let your mind's eye see Him on high and lifted up, full of glory. In prayer we are in the presence of One who is Creator of the entire Universe and who guides it in its course. Take a little time to bow in reverence before Him to whom you come.

2. Before you rush in with your needs, stop a moment to give thanks for what you have received. It may surprise you to find how your past is marked by God's faithfulness. It may even help

to take a pencil and paper and write down your blessings. Don't let troubles blot out your gratitude. It is one of the keys to happiness and to effective praying.

3. As you bow before the greatness of God and remember your blessings in gratitude, the confession of sins follows naturally. All of us are conscious of failing to do what we ought to do and of doing what we ought not to do. It is a cleansing experience to be honest with God about ourselves. As we confess our sins to Him in sorrow and in faith, there comes the assurance of His pardon. Here we find the answer to our problem of guilt.

4. Then we move to petition, to our quest for grace to help in our time of need. We seek God's presence in the midst of our lives. The prayers of the ages are filled with words asking for help: forgive, deliver, guard, defend, strengthen, bless, comfort, relieve, spare, guide, direct.

5. Our petitions include everything we need in body, mind and spirit. Ask for anything. Nothing is too small and nothing is too great. We will not be given all we ask as no child receives all he asks of his father. But God invites you to talk over with Him everything that is in your heart.

6. One of the greatest privileges of prayer is to pray for other people. In a flash we can cross the world and hold up to God people about whom we are concerned. We can pray for definite results: for those being destroyed by evil, for the sick, for those who sorrow, for our loved ones, for our enemies.

7. As you move toward the end of your praying, commit yourself to God as a channel He can use. You may be surprised how often He uses you in the answer which He gives to your prayer.

8. The Christian ascription to all praying is in the words, "In Jesus' Name." For the Christian there is one mediator between God and man. We come to God through Him. Not only so, but in these words we submit our prayers to His will to work in our lives and in the lives of others as He sees fit.

Romans 12:12 (RSV)

IN PRAYER, FOLLOW WHAT THE HEART SAYS

Prayer is a thing we all have in common. In some form, at some time, everyone prays. The human mind often questions the value of prayer but unbelief has never been able to stop the heart from praying. Every time you and I pray, the heart asserts certain things to be true.

1. Every prayer confesses a faith in the unseen world. We believe that behind this material world there is a world of the spirit that gives meaning to all we do.

2. In prayer we take for granted that at the heart of this unseen world there is a personal God. Some person will ask, "What do you mean by 'personal'?" You won't be able to answer. You can't really answer the same question about yourself. You just know you are a person and the heart knows God is a personal God with whom you can talk and who talks to you.

3. The human heart assumes in prayer that this personal God is interested in us one by one, by name, as a father is interested in his children. It is easy to find reasons to doubt this but when the heart prays it takes it for granted – despite all the reason the mind can give against it.

4. The human heart prays in the conviction that this personal God hears and answers our prayers. We hear men say God is a prisoner of His own laws and cannot act. We believe He can and does act when we pray. We hear that prayer is the reflection of our own needs. It is, but also our heart assures us that God is there hearing our prayer.

The strongest assurance of prayer's reality comes in the midst of experiences which outwardly seem to contradict its reality. We pray for health and become sick, we pray for a loved one's life and death comes, we pray for light and find darkness. Yet when life is broken by tragedy, God usually shines brightest through the breaks God often seems nearest when our condition is at its worst. This is not a matter of debate. It is a fact witnessed to by many people.

An assurance for the intuitions of our heart concerning prayer is that the unseen world is real, that God is a Person and personally interested in us and that God works at the behest of our prayer. God revealed Himself in Jesus Christ. Christ took for granted the unseen world. God was His Father. Christ dealt with people one by one at the point of their need and changed their circumstances. He spoke and the storm stopped. He said, "He that hath seen me hath seen the Father."

The only way you will ever be sure about prayer is by praying. God invites you to trust the faith of your heart and to pray without ceasing. So shall you come to know.

FEBRUARY 23   I can do all things through Christ which strengtheneth me.

Philippians 4:13

FAITH IS THE ANSWER TO A DOWNWARD PULL

We bring most of our worst troubles on ourselves. This is one of the sad truths about life. Jesus looked at Jerusalem. It was going to be destroyed and people were going to die. He said: "O Jerusalem ... how often would I have gathered thy children together as a hen gathereth her chickens under her wings, and ye would not."

We usually know we are hurting ourselves and just can't stop. There is a peculiar twist in human nature that makes us go on destroying ourselves.

We want to be happy, yet we do things that make it impossible. We want to be useful and helpful, yet we persist in being self-centered. We want a happy home. We know what is necessary for such a home, yet we do the opposite. We are sharp with our loved ones when we meant to be gentle. We nag when we know we should encourage. We win love by thoughtfulness and kindness and lose it by selfishness and harshness. This peculiar twist runs all through our lives. Anyone dealing with people must take it into account.

In many a heart there is the cry of the Apostle Paul: "Who shall deliver me from the body of this death?" Dr. G. Roy Jordan tells in his book "Religion That Is Eternal" of an experience of Muriel Lester, social worker of Kingsley Hall. An old East End woman of London was charged with breaking her promises and doing wrong. When evidence of her failures were forthcoming, she exclaimed: "Oh Miss! I'm as good a woman as God ever made. Only I can't live up to it."

None of us can. The easy answers just don't work out for us. The rules for the good life read well but something happens as we try to carry them out.

There is still only one answer: "I thank God through Jesus Christ our Lord."

FEBRUARY 24   REMEMBER to keep the Sabbath as a holy day.

Exodus 20:8 (LB)

HERE ARE WAYS TO KEEP THE SABBATH

"Keeping the Sabbath" is a subject with an old-fashioned flavor. It seems that this generation is trying to rewrite the recipe. The Old Testament stresses that the keeping of the Sabbath is one thing that will insure stability. Also, it is in the fourth commandment as given to Moses.

Jesus is talking about Sunday. He said the Sabbath was made for man - not to do as he pleases, but to become what he can become: to be able to stand up to life, to develop order and harmony, to have faith in God. All of these are things which help us gain stability. We are a tired people on a treadmill going nowhere. We are using up all of our energy without renewing it from the Divine Power.

Perhaps it is harder in our times to keep the Sabbath. The indirect effects of our material progress certainly have something to do with it; our occupation with the telephone, television, automobile, airplane, speedboat, golf course and many other things, use our time. Mainly however, it has been due to the consistent attack upon the idea of the Sabbath. Its chief point is that we shouldn't be denied our freedom. In short, those who want to keep the Sabbath are usually pictured as a narrow little group that is trying to rob you of pleasure.

How to keep the day? Each individual may keep it differently, but it rests in certain principles. First, it is the Lord's day, the day on which He was raised from the dead. We celebrate it as such. It is a weekly reminder that someone died for us. This realization can do something to and for us. Second, it is a day simply for rest. We can lie down without feeling guilty.

Third, it is a day for living in the home, a day in which through some joint activity the family may be bound together, may come to know one another better. Fourth, it is a day of worship when believers worshipping together experience the power of God. Private worship is necessary, but when public worship is intentionally skipped, somehow private worship suffers.

Fifth, it is a day for doing good, a day in which, within the circle of your life, a kind word or deed by you makes the difference in the entire outlook of someone else.

The Sabbath is one day in seven, a day in which to renew the power from the only Source from which true power can come. We were meant to receive power, but we must go where it is. In keeping the Lord's day we find stability for the other six days and it is through the loyalty of the people who keep it that God will save our day and give us a better tomorrow.

BUILDING CHURCHES IS GROWING

Everywhere there are new or enlarged church buildings. In the midst of a day when people seem to have gone crazy over money and sex, it is interesting that men still build churches. Not only are they building but also they are sacrificing to build of their best. This is something to think about when you are tempted to grow hopeless or cynical about these modern times.

We are building our churches because we are not willing to surrender our souls to the material things that surround us. Our church buildings stand as silent sentinels over city and town and countryside. They point to God whom we often follow only afar off but whom we are determined to keep in our lives.

Around our church buildings gather our most precious memories. Many a heart has a sacred spot for the little church in some far away wildwood where as children, God was first worshipped. Memories of father, mother and children gathered in the church to worship and to hold the ship of life steady on its course. I knew a physician once who would travel 600 miles to a little country church. Here he would come to kneel and pray beside the memories of his past when life got too difficult.

The church building is a silent sentinel keeping guard over the best that is within us. By its very presence it reminds us that to do right is better than to do wrong, to act kindly is finer than to hurt another, to live purely is better than to soil our lives. We are reminded to be holy as He is holy.

We can go into an empty sanctuary to pray and find a sense of

God's presence which speaks to the burden of the heart. When we marry, we want to do so in church. All through our married life, the building itself has a place in our dreams. We bring our babies to church to renew our covenant with God in their baptism. We turn to the church for comfort when the angel of death has come for a loved one. Because God's comfort meets us there, the building is always precious in memory.

When you see a church building, take heart. As long as men build churches, faith lives. As long as faith lives, evil that seems so strong will be defeated.

Here is encouragement for all of us.

FEBRUARY 26   **...GOD'S truth - the kind of truth that changes lives...**

Titus 1:2 (LB)

A PERSON'S RELIGION MAKES A DIFFERENCE

A man's religion makes him what he is, but a good many people do not believe this. In election campaigns people get so concerned over other issues until they almost convince themselves religion does not matter. It does. You and I are what we are because of what we believe or do not believe about God. Religion makes a difference in politics and in business and in society in general.

If you can find out what a man's real religion is you can pretty well predict what kind of public official he will make. If he worships the false god of power or of money or of personal prestige, he will easily sell out for gain. If he is a devout Christian you can usually count on his honesty.

If you are hiring a man or woman to work for you, you will do well to know his religious commitment. If he is a Christian, he will be one kind of person. If he is a Moslem he will be a different kind of individual. If he is a pagan, you will find his lack of religion shows in his work and in his relation to other employees. There is legislation in some states making it against the law to decide for or against hiring a person on the basis of religion. This shows how far we have strayed in deciding religion does not matter.

Faithfulness, honesty, patience, consideration, loyalty, courage and wisdom do not just happen. They are the fruits of character. Character is the result of a man's religion. A man's religion determines how he pays his bills, how faithful he is to his marriage vows. It sets the whole moral tone of his life.

It is no accident that most workers and contributors to worthwhile community projects are people supporting and sustained by the churches. A nationally known fund raiser told me once that 85 to 90 per cent of all money given to community projects came from active church people.

Voices are being heard all over our land expressing concern over low moral standards. There has been publicity over scandals in the new national road building program. Appeals to the low in us have become common in the amusement world. There is nearly always evidence somewhere of apparent dishonesty in government.

It can well be that we are reaping the results of believing that a man's religion does not matter. It matters so much that all efforts to reform men or society will fail unless they begin with each man's personal relation to God...which is his religion.

It is high time that each one of us began to take our religion seriously in our own conduct. We will do well to concern ourselves with efforts seeking to relate men to God properly.

FEBRUARY 27   IT is good to praise the Lord and make music to your name, O Most High, to proclaim your love in the morning and your faithfulness at night.

Psalm 92:1,2 (NIV)

HEROES, HEROINES ARE BESIDE YOU

I want to pay tribute to four heroes and heroines I have known. You won't find any marble statues or bronze tablets to their memory. Their heroism is known only to God and to some few who have gained strength from them, but they are typical of the people who hold our world together.

1. He was a lawyer, no longer young. He had a name for integrity in his town. The bank was in trouble. They asked him to become its president. He accepted, hoping he could help, but the bank failed. Many lost their savings. He had only small legal liability but because people had trusted him he sold all he had except his home to help make up the loss. As long as he lived he gave most of his earnings to those who had lost money in the failure.

2. He was in the prime of life and suddenly cut down by a fatal disease. He said, "God has given me a full life. This is all right." For some two years he went on. His courage never wavered and his cheery spirit never seemed to die. Strong men went to comfort him and came away comforted and made strong. From the deep wells of faith he was sustained and sustained others in the process.

3. She was a young woman busy with her three children and her husband and her active social life. She seemed almost a social butterfly. One day without warning her life collapsed about her. There was business failure. Her husband found his answer in alcohol. She went to business school, moved into a cheap

84

apartment, went to work. Her smile seemed never to fade. No complaint was ever heard. Year in and year out she carried the load. No one but God really knows how she did it, or how countless other women who work and raise children do it.

4. He was just an ordinary man. Once he had dreams of doing big things but it never worked out. There was always just barely enough money for his wife and children. They did not appreciate it or him very much. They were really ashamed of him and often his wife apologized for him. The children didn't pay him much attention as they got older. But he went on supporting them, if not supported by them. He was never bitter, never critical never demanding and never seemed to notice their demanding or their slights. He quietly died one day and I am sure his crown was a bright one.

There are heroes and heroines all around you – men and women doing hard things faithfully and cheerily. In your rush, take time to note some of them. They have found the secret of life. They hold our world together. They are the faithful ones, sustained by great faith in a great God. They are the ones we depend on.

FEBRUARY 28 **THE very reason all these terrible things have befallen you is because you have...sinned against the Lord and refused to obey Him.**

Jeremiah 44:23 (LB)

SIN IS STILL SIN DESPITE ITS MASKS

Some people think that sin is like styles that change; that with progress towards modern sophistication, sin can be said to have passed away with the Victorian era. As a result, we have a new definitions for plain old sin. We call it misfortune, or we call it disease.

We say the alcoholic has a disease, and well he may have, but at heart he is guilty also. There are others who in the dark of sleepless nights know they are also guilty: the loose moralists who bring vice from the gutter and put it on motion picture or TV screens; the simple adulterer; the malicious gossips; the people who get rich very quickly without worrying about how – and many others.

We feel that if some of these sins can be covered with enough money, enough business and social status, enough style, they won't matter too much. The truth remains, however, even though the alcoholic may support himself in luxury, he is the same character as the stumblebum in Monday morning's police lineup. No matter what we call it, stylish or not, the essence of our illness is still sin.

And we are all sinners. No day passes but we sin in some way. For nothing, short of perfection, is without sin. The rub comes in simply admitting it.

Now the heart of the Gospel is that Christ came to save sinners. Not as a Master Psychiatrist – though the Gospel is helpful in giving stability to the mind and in healing sickness. He really came to stir us up and to hold our faces before Christ's cross so that we may see that we are sinners. The chief message that Christ sends through His Gospel is there is forgiveness of sins no matter how black they may be. And make no mistake about this, God loves the admitted sinner even more than he loves those who think their own goodness will save them. To the dismay of the "important" people of His day, He spent the greater part of his ministry with those of ill repute.

He is asking us to wake up to the fact that our best still doesn't commend us to God, and until we see that Christ had to die for us we can never understand that this sacrifice is Supreme Love.

We can't save men by condemning them. They know they are guilty. What we need is an experience of Christ's love so that as instruments of God we can convince men and women that God loves them and that with forgiveness of sins comes a fellowship with God and a human fellowship with other sinners who are also saved through God's grace.

The words "sin" and "saved" have been the objects of pathetic jokes in some circles, but if we are going to live with any real peace in this world – and certainly in the next one – we had better accept them. Confessed sin, forgiveness and love must not only be preached from pulpits, they must be lived by Christians so that Christ may be seen living in them.

MARCH

THIS JOB TAKES MORE THAN ARMED MIGHT

Our nation has begun to be stirred up. We seem to be determined to get stronger. We are tired of being pushed around. Suggestions are a dime a dozen. Most of them have to do with military and economic measures. Yet there is something being left out and without it military and economic measures will prove useless.

History and the Bible agree that nations rise and fall because moral and spiritual strength or weakness flow from the relationship of a man or a people to God. This is one thing Roman Catholic and Protestant faiths should be able to agree on. If rivalries between them and between different branches of them make it impossible to have a clear voice calling men to God in our land, we shall all fall together.

No amount of military strength and no amount of wealth can keep us from dealing with God. God very easily makes mockery of man's strength and turns his wisdom to foolishness. In our day of scientific knowledge, wise men are in short supply. We need in our land the voice of the prophet again, calling men to God. It is a matter of life or death.

The way to God is clearly marked:

1. Confession of sin is the first step. Isaiah began his ministry by confessing that he was a man of unclean lips and that he dwelt among a people of unclean lips. We are stronger, and not weaker, when we confess our sins. We do not have clean hands and we make ourselves ridiculous by pretending that we do. Greed,

immorality and godlessness are too much a part of us.

2. Repentance is the second step. This means we turn from our sins and turn toward God. Only the most optimistic can see any real desire in our land to turn from sin and turn to God, seeking His forgiveness and His strength.

3. Forgiveness is the third step - accepting the forgiveness He gave His Son to offer. Here is the grace of God offered to us to reconcile us to God so that His power may be in us.

4. Obedience is the fourth step. Only those seeking honestly to do His will can know His power.

All efforts of man without God can lead only to tragedy. In these days, this truth needs to be shouted from the housetops. It is the central truth of the Bible. You will find it inscribed in man's history. It will be true in man's future. With all our striving after a renewal of our strength, we will do well to begin at the beginning, which is the fear of the Lord.

MARCH 2   **CLEANSE thou me from secret faults. Keep back thy servant also from presumptuous sins; let them not have dominion over me...**

Psalm 19: 12,13 (KJ)

SOME TEACHINGS JUST AREN'T SO

Some of the things we teach children are not true. Among the many things that come to my desk is a monthly paper of the TNT Club of St. Luke's Episcopal Church. It is edited by Mrs. Vernon H. Shearer. She had an article in one edition which seems worthy of wide reading. With her permission I am reproducing most of it.

"Much theology and basic truth are to be found in a number of books and stories written for children. But in addition to these are many more which are built upon false premises.

"Ever with us are those who assure the small folk that they can do anything they set their minds to, and that if only they want something badly enough, they can bring it about. This philosophy, duly absorbed and put to work, is probably responsible for more nervous breakdowns, stomach ulcers, and cases of hypertension than can ever be proved.

"The devil thought it up, of course. No sooner was man made and living in harmony with God and himself than the devil got busy. What could he do to wreck this relationship? He could not attack God directly and expect man to help him. He would have to devise some means of appealing to man's pride in his own intelligence, some clever, pious way of perverting the gifts of God to use against God, and man would have to be fooled so that he would not suspect what he was doing.

"So the devil suggested that man should try to become like God. In that way, he could do anything he set his mind to. In the beginning, of course, man understood that the only one who could do anything He set His mind to was God, Himself. But as soon as the idea caught hold that he could subjugate anything to his own determination if only he was determined enough, then man's understanding of his dependence upon God was a thing of the past.

"So subtle was the whole thing that he really had no notion of what he was doing. He was going regularly to church, keeping the laws, and on the whole, the things he set his mind to were very fine things.

"Man has a very hard time accepting the truth that there are some things he can never do...because he cannot be God. This is infuriating! And man fights it every way he can. He writes stories and makes speeches urging little children to decide what they want to do and then do it.

"Yes, there is truth to be found in some stories for children and there are honest lies to be found in fiction, too – lies written in sincerity and, unbeknownst to the writer...with the devil's help. For if Satan can ever convince every man on earth and in Heaven that he can do whatever he desires, it will be a great day for the devil. It is another way of saying that God is obsolete.

"And what could please Satan more?"

MARCH 3   MY God will meet all your needs according to His glorious riches in Jesus Christ.

Philippians 4:19 (LB)

HELP IS AVAILABLE TO CARRY THE LOAD

"I'm the tiredest man you ever saw," he said as he sat in a chair opposite me. He was tired of trying to lift himself by his own bootstraps. My friend is typical of most of us.

We have taken the "do it yourself" craze seriously and we apply it to everything. We try to forgive our own sins and overcome our own mistakes. The result is a burden of guilt that will not go away because we have forgotten that God promises: "If we confess our sins He is faithful and just to forgive us our sins and to cleanse us of all unrighteousness."

We insist on carrying our own burdens and they wear us out. We forget that God insists: "Cast your burdens on the Lord for He careth for you."

We insist on solving our own problems and we quote such proverbs as "A sound mind in a sound body." We beat our minds and bodies in our search for wisdom and spend our energies in the effort. Our problems only increase because we forget that we are warned: "If any of you lack wisdom, let him ask of God that giveth liberally to all men...and it shall be given him."

We have to make a living, care for our families, do our part in the community and we grind our lives away carrying the full load on our own shoulders. We never really take seriously the promise of Christ: "Seek ye first the Kingdom of God and His righteousness and all these things shall be added."

God never meant for us to live in this way. We are overstrained because we are carrying loads never meant for us. In the beginning God gave man responsibilities but he walked with man to support him day by day. It was man's first sin in Eden when he decided to go it alone. We still sin Adam's sin and we still suffer Adam's penalty – weariness and disaster.

Yet God still offers you His forgiveness and His wisdom and His strength. In Jesus Christ He comes to you and to me and offers Himself personally in forgiveness and in strength for the day. The best prayer you can have made for you is "that ye may know the exceeding greatness of God's power."

We are not made to go it alone. It is not easy to believe God nor is it easy to trust Him. But it is the only way to escape that day when you will say with my friend, "I am the tiredest man you ever saw."

MARCH 4   **THEREFORE, if anyone is in Christ, he is a new creation; the old has gone, the new has come! All this is from God...**

II Corinthians 5:17,18 (NIV)

WHAT YOU BELIEVE SHAPES YOUR LIFE

If you cut a flower from its roots, it will soon die. In the same way, if we – as individuals or as groups – cut ourselves off from God, we show signs of death. It makes all the difference in the world what you believe about God.

Fear and insecurity are the marks of our day. Confusion and disorder are the steady theme of our efforts to get along with one another. The remedy for our troubles will continue to evade us as long as we evade God.

There is every evidence that we are trying to live in this day as though God does not matter. We are trusting in ourselves and in our own resources. Any daily newspaper tells the results.

What you and I really believe about God determines our whole lives. It molds attitudes and forms character. It determines what kind of homes we have, how we pay our bills, and what kind of citizens we make. It gives direction to life in this world and in the world to come.

If a person believes that this vast world was created by God, he can live in this space age with confidence. Nothing will be found by science that will be beyond Him who created it out of nothing and for His glory. If you believe God rules His world you will be able to live in it without fear. There is enough going on to make any man afraid unless his faith is anchored in God who controls it. Such faith does not make it possible to understand how or why evil and tragic things happen. Yet there comes a strange confidence to the heart as you look into the face of God as revealed in Christ, knowing that this God who keeps His world under His control neither slumbers nor sleeps.

It makes a difference if you believe in God to whom you personally are morally responsible. If you know yourself to be under the judgement of a holy God for all you do, you will take seriously the promptings of your conscience. This is the only foundation for right conduct in men and in all organizations of men.

It makes all the difference in the world that you believe that God loves you in spite of your sin. We know ourselves to be guilty before God. It makes a difference to know that a loving God comes offering forgiveness and cleansing through His Son whom He gave to bear our sins. Only those who have found the freedom of divine forgiveness can truly live as free men.

As we see the power of evil in our own hearts and in the world about us, it is easy to become discouraged and cynical. It makes a difference in our fight to really believe that the victory of God over evil is already assured. When Christ died and was raised from the dead, He broke the power of evil forever. One day He will return and make this victory visible to the whole universe. Those who have faithfully shared His fight and taken part in the fellowship of His sufferings will share His victory.

All this is what the Psalmist had in mind when he wrote: "I will say of the Lord, He is my refuge and fortress: My God, in Him will I trust.

FOR the eyes of the Lord range throughout the earth to strengthen those whose hearts are fully committed to Him.

II Chronicles 16:9 (NIV)

THE SOURCE OF POWER IS OFFERED TO YOU

Everyone today is looking for power to live by. Many books tell us how to meet our day with strength and courage. Psychology is widely read because it promises help for a tangled state of our lives. The candidates for President are offering their plans to make the United States stronger and richer so that we may have more power to live by. Much of what they propose is popular.

The fact that so many different offers are being made poses the question, "Where does power to live by really come from?" "What makes people and nations strong?" "Is a nation really made strong by military forces and money?" The popular answer is "yes."

There is a growing suspicion that it is the wrong answer. More money, more arms, more training may only make our situation worse. They really have little to do with giving us power to live by.

Living power is a moral and spiritual force. The theme of the Bible is power. But it puts very small value on the physical and mental powers we have come to depend on. It talks about strength being made perfect in weakness. It teaches that a king is not saved by the size of his army. Money is treated as a stumbling block to power - not a stepping stone.

Power to live by comes from the presence of God in our hearts and lives. It is a gift of God and not the result of human effort. Our minds and bodies may be developed to the ultimate and we still won't be able to live out our days in real power unless God is working in and through us. Our nation can develop the most potent missiles and best fighting men, but it will fail without the power of God.

Power to live by is "closer than breathing, nearer than hands and feet." It is as close as a look toward God in prayer that He gives us faith. It is the marvel of the Christian faith and the hope to all that "He giveth power to the faint and to them that have no might He increaseth strength."

MARCH 6   **OBEY the laws then, for two reasons: first, to keep from being punished, and second, just because you know you should.**

Romans 13:5 (LB)

ARE YOU OBEYING YOUR CONSCIENCE?

Did you ever try to fully obey your conscience for a whole week? Or even a day? If you have not tried it, a test run may show you what you're up against. This obeying of conscience is not half as easy as you might think. It is likely that if you try very hard over a period of time you will not always be popular with your group. You may feel as if you don't belong, for you won't be doing what "everybody else" is doing. Some feel it will even make you mentally sick to think too much about conscience.

Let's look at an example we all recognize: There are those who don't consider it right to drink alcoholic beverages. However, alcohol is served at many social functions and young people are being taught to "handle it" as one of the social graces. Many of these young people actually disapprove; but it is difficult to stand alone. Most business contacts seem to demand a cocktail hour, and one that is coming more frequently during the day. Actually, chances for promotion or making a sale can be seriously affected if your conscience is too rigid.

Now, what really is conscience?

Volumes have been written in an attempt to answer the question and no one can ever fully explain it without dealing with God. Everyone agrees that it is important for it is an inner voice which, somehow, everyone knows speaks with authority.

Conscience says to each of us, "I ought - or ought not" and no amount of clever mental dodging can silence this voice. You may try to explain it away but it is still there. It pronounces you guilty when you disobey it and you get a glimpse of true goodness when you obey.

In fact, the very laws of our land cannot be enforced unless they are approved by the conscience of the people. Conscience speaks with authority because it is the authority of God. We know we are in the presence of God when conscience speaks and we cannot escape the feeling that in its commands we are being told the will of God.

God is our Maker and having made us He must have a way of speaking to us and guiding us. In our battles with conscience, we are having a person to person argument with God. David sinned very badly in his scheme to take another man's wife, but his conscience drove him to admit, "Against Thee, and Thee only, have I sinned and done this evil in Thy sight." Of course, he had sinned against people; but more, than this, he had sinned against his Maker.

We know what is right – most of the time. Before you blame troubles on someone else, examine your own conduct in the light of your conscience. Then ask God to help you – one day at a time. You may be in for a surprise if you obey. But one thing is certain: you can't find true happiness until you live at peace with the God who made you and knows you.

MARCH 7   MY grace is sufficient for you, for my power is made perfect in weakness.

II Corinthians 12:9 (NIV)

HELP IS AVAILABLE WHEN SORROW HITS

There are ties that bind all of us together. One of these is sorrow. I have sat beside an Arab in a Palestinian cave mourning with him the loss of his mate and I have been in a mansion where death had come for a beloved wife. The heartache was the same. Where men mourn their departed loved ones, they walk very closely together.

Certain things have proved helpful to those who walk in the "valley of the shadow."

When sorrow comes, it is no alien intruder. Sorrow is at home not only in our world but in the heart of God. He gave His Son to die. He was in Christ reconciling the world to Himself as the cry rang out in Gethsemane; "My soul is sorrowful unto death."

Sorrow is not only at home in the heart of God but it is the common experience of men. It is a part of life and must be lived by us all. The tapestry of life has woven through it many dark threads. Many who sorrow feel they are the victims of something strange and unnatural. It is not so. Sorrow is one of the precious ties that bind our hearts to one another and to God.

You and I really choose sorrow for ourselves. It is the other side of the coin of love. The day you commit yourself to love another person, the day you receive love unto your heart, that day you choose to walk on in sorrow. If you love, one day you must lose that object of your love. Surely knowing this to be true, you would not refuse love. Sorrow is the expression of love that has lost the object of its affection.

Perhaps the key to comfort in sorrow is surrender. First we must surrender our loved one to God who is able to keep that which we have committed unto Him.

Comfort comes as we strive to believe that all things work together for good to those who love God. Believe it against all the outward evidence. Believe it because God says so. Believe it because God guarantees it by the death and resurrection of His Son.

Comfort also comes as we face frankly our questions and our doubts. God knows that everyone has these. One of the most frequent questions is: "Why does this happen to me?" It sounds blunt but the best answer I know is: "Why should it not happen to you or to me?" It happened to the Son of God. It happens to everyone else. Why should you and I escape? In your sorrow, you hate the company of God and of all mankind.

These are way stations along the road to comfort. They have helped many people along the way of sorrow to find the presence of the Master. This is part of the Christian's victory that overcomes the world.

MARCH 8   **LET us then approach the throne of grace with confidence, so that we may receive mercy and find grace to help us in our time of need.**

Hebrews 4:16 (NIV)

SEEK FIRM PLACES ON THE MARSHY ROAD

Walking through a swampy area is a matter of finding firm spots on which to step. Some spots look firm and are not. Experience is needed in judging where to walk. Life can be like a swampy road. One needs carefully to pick out the right places to stand.

Today, as much that looked like secure footing turns out to be sinking sand, we need to be sure of where we step. We constantly search for firm footing for our lives and so often are disappointed. The temptation to seek it in material security is almost impossible to resist. Money becomes the measure of our ambitions.

Yet not many people achieve financial security and some of the most insecure people in the world are those who have money in abundance. We gather all kinds of gadgets but are no happier for them. We place our hope in health and lose it. We anchor our security in our family and the years break our circle. We end up lost in our world of abundance.

Certain things do work out as supports for life – as firm ground on which to stand. There are certain things that never let you down.

Doing what our conscience, under God, tells us is right is one of them. There are times when our conscience may mislead us due to ignorance or to a faulty relation to God, but we will not go far wrong if we seek honestly to follow its guidance.

Doing the kind thing at all times is another firm place on which to stand. It sounds easy, doesn't it? Try it in all your conversation about other people. Be sure by word and deed you are kind at all times in your home. As you drive in traffic, be sure you are kind one to another. In your shop or office, seek out the kind thing to do and say.

Most important of all is to worship God regularly in the heart, in the home and in the church. The electric light bulb burns only as long as it is connected with an outside source of power. It is made that way. So are we. The heart starves and grows cold and hard unless it is kept in touch with God by regular worship. God is love and the home continues to be warmed by love only as it is kept in constant touch with God. In the worship of the church, our lives are touched by Him in a way possible nowhere else.

Out of simple faithfulness great lives emerge. There is not much you and I can do to solve the large problems in any direct way. Most of us have no direct contact with places where great decisions are made. We probably would not be very helpful if we were. However, we can find our own answers and our own places of usefulness by doing what we can. We can obey conscience, act kindly and worship God.

You will be surprised what a difference it makes to you, to your family and even to your world. In our desire to change the world, let us start with ourselves.

MARCH 9   **JESUS answered, "I am the way and the truth and the life. No one comes to the Father except through me..."**

John 14:6 (NIV)

HE CAME TO SAVE THE WORLD'S SINNERS

The figure of Jesus Christ remains the most attractive of all those who have walked our earth. This is true because He came to seek and to save the lost. This includes the majority of us and He came to identify Himself with all those who are lost in one way or another. He said, "The Spirit of the Lord is upon me because He hath anointed me to preach the gospel to the poor. He hath sent me to heal the brokenhearted, to preach deliverance to the captives and the recovering of sight to the blind, to set at liberty them that are bruised, to preach the acceptable year of the Lord."

Running all through the Gospel story is the fact that the common people heard Him gladly. They heard Him gladly because He was one with them and because He bore their sins and griefs in His own heart and in His own body. As He did, they found release and relief.

His only home was with the homeless for He had nowhere to lay His head. He touched the sick and they were made whole. He gathered around Him those whom society rejected because of their sin.

He faced those for whom religion was just a protection of position, or a support for comfort, or a tool for profit or cushion against discomfort and told them they really had no religion.

He dared to live in love toward all people, even toward those who hated Him and planned to kill Him.

It never occurred to Him to wonder whether it would work as we count such things. He did what He did because it was the will of His Father in Heaven. He came to save the lost and the lost can be saved only by knowing where they are.

He knew that you run the risk, humanly speaking, if you come into contact with sickness. He knew that if you mingle with evil men in love you probably will get hurt. He knew that if you try to love selfish men you probably will get crucified one way or another, but He also knew that contact is the only way to heal the sick and save the lost. He knew also that when you thus take men's evil on yourself, you are nearest to redeeming them.

If you are lost, the pressure on your hand is in His, seeking to lead you home. If you are sick, His hand is on your brow. If you are set in your evil way, He is with you in love, willing to take away your hatred and redeem you by His love.

He offers tribulation to any who will follow Him - the tribulation of bearing the burdens of others. He offers a cross, the cross forged by those who still refuse love and who will be redeemed only by love.

MARCH 10   **NO one who has not tried it would believe how many difficulties are cleared out of men's road by the simple act of trying to follow Christ.**

Alexander Maclaren

A TURN IN THE ROAD SLIPS UP ON YOU

There come to all of us those times when we must make a sharp turn in the road. We go for a long time in our routine way of living and suddenly the routine way is no longer there. On one occasion such a turn in the road came when I walked in a room and turned the light out. Here is the story.

Since her mother's death more than four years before, she had been the mainstay of the home. She changed her college plans so she could stay home. For four years she was a day student at the university, taking an active part in its academic, campus and social university, taking an active part in its academic, campus and social life. She was the center around which the home revolved. She was loyal to the church in its services and its work. In addition, she kept her ties strong with the young man she was to marry.

The days went by in orderly fashion and life moved along a fairly straight road. The weeks turned to years and suddenly there was the realization of a sharp turn ahead.

The date was set for the wedding. It was to follow the high school graduation of the younger sister and her own from the university. There was much stir as these events rushed toward us and the turn in the road still seemed far away. Things were still the same in spite of the coming change.

Then came the wedding. When it was over and the last guest had left the reception, we came home. She had left the light on in her room when she left for the church. I went into the room and stood there. I turned the light out and there in the darkness I saw clearly the turn in the road.

Despite the sharpness of the turn, I think my chief emotion was one of deep gratitude for the family love that marked the road behind us, a love that has been ministered by each and to each as we traveled along. Surely the love of God has been given to us in abundance.

I was grateful also that even though we shall be out of sight around the turn of the road, we shall walk together because we walk with Him. I am grateful for this kind of home and I covet it for you. There may be something other than God's love that will provide it but I have never seen it in my experience.

It may so often seem unimportant to be faithful in worship when the joys and the sorrows, the strains and tests, are sheltered under His care. It may seem unimportant to be faithful to the worship and work and service of the church, to keep your children under its care and teaching. But God is faithful. At the turns of the road you will be able to look back with gratitude and to look ahead with courage.

Psalms 27:11 (NIV)

CHRISTIAN LOVE FACES MANY TESTS

As we deal with the events occurring around us, we face times of testing. This is particularly true for those of us who bear the name of Christian. Bearing the name is mockery unless we are obedient to Him whose name we bear. Obedience means acting in every situation as we believe He would have us act.

I believe most of us know pretty well how we should act in most situations. Too often our pretended ignorance is a cover-up for an unwillingness to respond as we know we should. We would rather debate than obey. In this and in all situations, the Christian is left with his or her own conscience. No one can finally tell another what he ought to do.

These are good days to face our discipleship and to find out whether our actions flow from our faith or from outside social pressures. Love and forgiveness are the cardinal points in Christian obedience. The Lord said: "By this shall all men know that ye are my disciples, that ye love one another." However, love is not the easy thing we often try to make it. It comes hard. It is not easy to act in love toward those with whom we disagree or who are just unlovely.

Such love can be given only by those who are conscious of being loved by God in spite of the fact they are unlovely. "We love because He first loved us." Because Christians claim to be loved of God, they are expected to show love in relationships. Unless our professed love is grounded in God's prior love, it will turn to selfishness.

Where our love for others is the expression of gratitude for God's love for us, it leads us to seek the welfare of all with whom we come into contact. If we are Christian, of whatever race, we will seek the welfare of others. I am confident that most people really know what

102

this means for them in any given situation. You can evade doing it by arguing about it but not without a sense of guilt for your failure. Often the very heart of our argument betrays our guilt.

Since everyone must finally make his own decision as to God's will for him, room must be left for this private decision. There will be deliberate disobedience of God's commandment of love by some. Others will fail to respond to the need for love out of ignorance or for what honestly seems to be good reason. Hence there must be extended the hand and heart of forgiveness to all who fail to show love. Thus and thus alone can there be reconciliation. Such forgiveness will not always be successful in healing divisions but it is the only way.

These are good days to practice our faith.

MARCH 12   THE MOST important thought I ever had was that of my individual responsibility to God.

Daniel Webster

CHALLENGING WORDS ARE IN THE PLEDGE OF ALLEGIANCE

We saw fit some years ago to change our pledge of allegiance to the flag to include the words "under God." We bear witness to the world that we are a nation under God. This is important and it is good. It is also dangerous. The Lord once said: "Why call ye me Lord, Lord and do not the things I command? Not everyone that saith unto me Lord, Lord, shall enter into the Kingdom of Heaven but he that doeth the will of my Father in Heaven."

For anyone to be "under God" and for a nation to be "under God" certain things seem to be self-evident. First, there must be a knowledge of God. If God is worth being under, He is worth knowing.

Theology is the study of the nature and work of God. The Bible is the chief textbook about God. There is a wide difference between knowing about God and knowing God. If we are to know God we must add to our knowledge about God, praying that the Spirit of God will meet our spirits so we will know Him personally. We must associate ourselves in worship with others who know Him if our knowledge of Him is to live and grow. It takes time and effort to know about Him and to know Him. I do not believe that the average American is viewed as a Bible studying, praying, worshipping individual.

The second thing that seems self-evident is that if we are really "under God" we will be obedient to His will. As individuals, we will seek to follow Him day by day in all our decisions and actions and as a nation we will seek to order our affairs under His hand.

There is too much going on contrary to His will to feel very confident that obedience to the will of God is the compelling motive of our lives. Business dishonesties, government scandals, declining moral standards, increasing use of alcohol, the growing disregard of Sunday as the Lord's Day, sex exploitation in all phases of life – all these things and more make it doubtful that the main stream of our people direct their lives by any real commitment to God.

If we were really "under God" we would be a much more humble people. We would see, if we knew Him and took obedience seriously, that our very sins would make any favor God shows us as an act of divine mercy. We would come to understand that what we deserve is judgment, not favor. We would learn to be grateful for His abundant blessings rather that using them as a "grab-bag" to satisfy our selfish desires.

There is more to being "under God" than putting it in our pledge of allegiance.

MARCH 13   I have read in Plato and Cicero sayings that
are very wise and beautiful; but I never read
in either of them, "come unto me all ye that
labor and I will give you rest."

Augustine

SIMPLE LOYALTIES CAN SLICE THROUGH CONFUSION

The Christian Gospel is designed to help us live. But because life today is so fantastically complicated, we are not inclined to believe the gospel can help. We are all faced with so many different kinds of responsibilities. Each of us gets up in the morning with 1,000 things to do. One-half of them are not related to each other.

We are victims of different moral demands. As individuals we are taught that certain conduct is right. Then we move out into the social world and here we often find that those things which we are taught were not right, are accepted. We are confused with it all. We find ourselves going along with the social order, but the net result inside is a split conscience.

Nearly all of us are guilty of assuming that bigness is the great thing. We get involved in the worship of bigness. We pretend – at least – that it is right. But inside we are quite frantic. We can't handle the bigness; the personal concern has been squeezed out of it except in vocabulary.

Every generation feels it is a peculiar generation insofar as trouble is concerned, and so many of us are inclined to dismiss Christ because we feel He lived in a very uncomplicated age. That is not true. The Roman world was difficult, more difficult than ours. It was a regimented world - more regimented than ours. Business then was as complicated as it is now, and the social problems then make our social problems look pale.

Jesus came along doing very simple things. I don't think He did anything "important" in His life, from the world's viewpoint. There was not anything complicated about His life and the very simplicity of it made it – then and now – so terribly hard to believe.

There are two simple loyalties in this complicated world that will give us security and rest. They will not assure us an easy life but they will give us a confidence at the heart of our lives.

1. Simple loyalty to worship. God made us for Himself. One reason we get so nervous today is we don't take time to worship our Father. We can't be physically strong without taking food and we can't live secure within our own souls without worshiping God.

2. Simple loyalty to love. There is the simple loyalty of Christian love that binds men, women and children together in the home and in the world. Life is complicated by our failure to be loyal to love. From giving and receiving love, life gives and receives strength found nowhere else. If you are loyal to love, you are going to find life a little less complicated. Love does not mean going around romantically loving everybody. It does mean that you at least seek the welfare of everyone.

If your life is complicated, start concentrating on the simple things that count. And a good time to start is this morning.

MARCH 14   THE work praises the man.

Irish Proverb

A TREND OF TALK NEEDS REVERSING

The favorite topic of conversation is people. The chief interest of most of us is our own excellence. Next in line are the faults of others. Listening to group conversations you hear an abundance of such expression as: "I told him..." and "He came to me and I let him understand..." The "I's" have it in most our conversations and we are always interested in reciting or hearing recited the sins, failings and misfortunes of others.

We just never grow tired of these two topics. The result is we bore our friends by talking about our good points because they are frustrated by not being able to tell their experiences wherein they are the heroes. Or we make life more difficult for others by keeping alive their unfortunate circumstances.

Life can be made much happier for ourselves and others by just reversing the process. If we could only be more conscious of our own failings and our own sins and let our conversation dwell on the excellences of others instead of their failings, all our relationships would be better.

There is an ancient proverb that says, "Let another praise thee and not thine own lips." We might do well to take it more seriously. If you and I will deal with others out of humility born of an awareness of our own frail natures, we will find a much more favorable response than if we try to impress with our self-acclaimed virtues. Certainly we will help others more by remaining quiet about their failures than in airing them with our friends.

This is what Paul was talking about in his hymn of Christian love found in I Corinthians. "Love vaunteth not itself, is not puffed up...seeketh not her own...thinketh no evil...rejoiceth not in iniquity..."

It could be that our whole moral tone could be changed if we took these things seriously. Actually the faults of others won't hurt us. Our own faults will destroy us unless we recognize them and repent and change. John Wesley is credited by many with changing England. The heart of his movement was the meetings where small groups talked about their own sins and sought help from one another.

The only way we are really going to combat the threats to our way of life is to deal with the sins and faults of our way of life. We simply can't do it by thinking about evils of the enemy or of the neighbor. All our talk about our own excellences as a person or as a nation will prove idle chatter unless we begin with ourselves to be sure we possess what we claim to have.

Only those who walk humbly with God, grateful for His grace, can honestly face their sins in a healing way and their neighbors and enemies with reconciling power.

MARCH 15   PRAISE can be your most valuable asset as long as you don't aim it at yourself.

O. A. Battista

THE ROAD TO HAPPINESS IS PAVED WITH BELIEF

I have a friend who prides himself on being a "realist." He always finds in people and in circumstances something to distrust. He does not believe in life. He is sure that everyone he meets has some "angle." He expects every circumstance to go wrong. His cynicism gives him an air of superiority.

He feels he is wiser than his "simple" friends who are foolish enough to trust people and to believe that life can be good. The result is that he cuts himself off from people and he never enjoys anything or anybody.

The secret of happy living is to believe in people and in life. A married couple finds happiness only as they believe in one another's love and goodness. In this faith they open their hearts completely to each other. You can get happiness only by taking that chance.

Parents can find joy in their children only by trusting them and by believing in their ability and in their goodness. Young folks are smart and they tend to respond to the attitudes of their parents. The people we meet day by day usually respond to our attitude toward them. If we give ourselves to them in trust and in confidence they will return trust and confidence. If we depend on their goodness, they will usually try to measure up. If we are suspicious and critical, they will withdraw and will tend to give us reason to be critical. Expect the best in others and you will find them trying to give their best. This is what Jesus had in mind when He said: "Therefore all things whatsoever ye would that men should do to you, do ye even so to them."

The same principle applies to the circumstances of our lives. More often than not they turn out as we expect them to. If we are cynical about life, it will give us reason to be. If we really believe that things will work out for good, they have a strange way of responding. The miraculous thing about life is that even the tragedies of life often later lead to good when we receive and act on them in faith.

In order to believe in people and in life, you must begin by believing in God. If you trust Him with your own life, if you believe that He forgives your sins and gives you wisdom and strength, you can trust others. When they fail to measure up, you can trust that to God also.

You can trust circumstances when you trust God to work all things for good to them that love Him. To believe in people and in life is the road to happiness.

MARCH 16   **YOU can't build a reputation on what you are going to do.**

Henry Ford

PEOPLE, NOT PLANS, STILL COUNT MOST

The Christian faith has always insisted that transformed lives must come before transformed communities. For the last 25 to 30 years this idea has seemed ridiculous. In recent months, however, it has become slightly more popular. Traditionally we have thought that if we had a good plan, we might expect to have reasonably good success - that if our program was well worked out we might expect the result to be good.

We live in an age when people have developed grandiose programs. In our age, we have sought to reform the world by

109

idealistic schemes. We have taken for granted that there would be people there who would respond to plans, carry them out with integrity, feel gratitude and form characters in keeping with our efforts. Well, it just has not worked out that way.

We have found that bad people make programs turn out badly. We have found that bad people generally produce bad results; and that good people generally produce good results. We have found that neither program nor plan is as important as people. And we have been shocked by the power of the bad individual to corrupt the best-laid plans.

The hope of the world lies in people and somehow we are beginning to believe this again. The Saturday Evening Post carried an editorial about the loss of integrity in this country. The editor of Newsweek spoke to a group of America's outstanding businessmen. He discussed a questionnaire that had been sent to many thousands of people asking them this question, "What do you think this country needs most?" He said the most common answer was, "a rebirth of moral integrity."

How do you get moral integrity? It is important to know the answer. How do you make good men? This is something we had better take seriously. The Scripture – from beginning to end – insists that you make good men by making men Christians.

Good men are made by God as men of faith are moved by the Spirit of God and are molded into the likeness of Christ. The efforts of your church have become basically important in this day. As you go out from your church to invite people into the full discipleship of Jesus Christ, it becomes important that you understand that you are offering, among other things, the one answer to the problem of how to make good men.

MARCH 17 Redeemed by the blood of the Lamb, His child, and power I am.

Fanny Crosby, Hymn

AN ANCIENT QUESTION BECOMES MODERN

The ancient question was, "What must we do to be saved?" The question is becoming modern again. We have known the question, but for most of us it has far more theoretical meaning than practical urgency. This is because we have really thought – deep in our hearts - that either we were already saved or were well on the way. We have trusted in certain things to save us. Only recently have we begun to suspect that they are not enough.

God said to the ancient world that a king is not saved by a multitude of men and that a mighty man is not saved by much strength. But we have actually believed that we could surround ourselves with physical power - and this physical power itself would save a people or a person.

We have suddenly been shocked awake by finding ourselves weak in the midst of strength. In spite of all our arms, we are being pushed around as a wind pushes a straw. We are beginning to suspect that something more than physical strength is necessary – and that the ancient wisdom of God is actually true!

The Lord himself said that a man's life does not consist in the abundance of things he possesses. We have read that and we have accepted it as a true saying of the Lord and we have gently laid it aside without believing it at all. We have built our modern economy on the simple confidence that a man's life does consist in the abundance of things that he possesses.

We have built our economy - an economy of abundance -on the idea that the standard of living determines the degree of happiness of a people. We believe the economic standing of a person or a community determines the health, strength and happiness of that person or that community. With almost the same devotion, the Americans and Russians believe it, but we are beginning to wonder.

We have also believed that we could be saved with manipulations of the human mind from the human standpoint. We actually believe that education and psychology somehow can produce a good life and abundant living. They have become gods before which we have fallen down in adoration and worship.

We have thought that by these things we could be saved. Yet we find our nation going to pieces morally, without any single standard of moral conduct which people are willing to admit as having authority. We are beginning to suspect we are lost.

We are about to understand that for the sins of men, there comes death. Only through the grace of God received by faith in Christ is there hope and the promise of life.

MARCH 18   **AND now, brethren, I commend you to God and to the word of His grace; which is able to build you up, and to give you an inheritance among all them which are sanctified.**

Acts 20:32 (NIV)

DENY FOOD TO THE SPIRIT AND FACE DISASTER

Jesus said, "Man does not live by bread alone but by every word that preceedth out of the mouth of God." This is a true saying and worth believing by everyone. Nobody doubts that we need material things. Nobody doubts that we live in a space age. There are problems connected with earning a living and of adapting to a space age, but there is a greater problem: how do you pursue material things without ruining your life?

The spirit of man – the person – the personality - the thing you mean when you say "I" – how do you feed it to make it strong and brave and wise and loving and good? It is not hard to realize that if you stop eating food the body becomes weak and unable to meet the demands of the day. We even understand that the wrong kind of food finally will ruin the body and make it weak. Likewise, the demands of the day will kill the body unless we feed it properly.

Exactly the same thing is true of the spirit. Fail to feed it or feed it the wrong kind of food and soon the demands and temptations of the day will destroy you. This is what worship is all about. Worship feeds the spirit. Worship feeds the soul because it brings man into surrendered contact with the spirit of God who is the source of strength for the soul.

Jesus said, "I am the bread of Life." Here is the word of God...the word of God that is the true food of the spirit of man. In worship, this Word is given to those who by faith receive it.

Without worship the spirit grows lean and hungry. The individual finds earning a living unsatisfactory. Marriage loses its glow. Play is not much fun. Love dies and our relationships become marred by jealousy and hate - we become lost.

If you are a man or a woman trying to make a life or a couple trying to make a home in this Lenten season when worship is in the public eye – decide to open your lives in worship to God by faith in Christ. God's Spirit will then feed your spirits and the fruits will be love, peace, joy, patience, gentleness, goodness, faith, meekness and temperance.

MARCH 19 YEA, though I walk through the valley of the shadow of death, I will fear no evil: for Thou art with me; Thy rod and Thy staff they comfort me.

Psalm 23:4 (KJ)

LENTEN SEASON IS A GOOD TIME TO FACE YOURSELF BEFORE GOD

The Lenten season is widely observed. Directly or indirectly, most Christian groups give attention to it. Particularly is this true of the last week in which the death of Christ is especially remembered. It is a time when we are given opportunity to slow the rush of life, to turn aside from some of our ordinary pleasures, and to give more attention to the spiritual realities of life.

We do well to stop ever and anon and face ourselves. Within the heart of each the struggles go on which make or break life. The things that happen, good and bad, are the results of battles won or lost in the souls of men.

Armaments and money are just tools men use to express what is in their hearts. A man of 45 makes his bitterness toward a certain group the ruling passion of his life because as a boy of eleven he saw his adored father humiliated by representatives of the group. A man with money and health and position takes his own life because he lost the inner battle of his own soul.

In each person, the struggle goes on between good and evil, darkness and light, purity and immorality, honesty and deceit. The Lenten season calls us to reflect on the inner realities of our own hearts. The writer of the Proverbs sums it up: "Keep thy heart with all diligence, for out of it are the issues of life."

We are reminded in the Lenten season that the evil in our hearts

114

and in our world is too strong for man to handle in his own wisdom and strength. The heart of its message is that God has entered the human scene to battle with evil and to overcome it. He comes to each individual and offers Himself as a participant in the battle you wage in your own heart. He invites us to believe in Him as He comes in Christ; to repent of our sins, to accept His forgiveness, to trust His strength, to share His victory.

Only as we put on the armor of God will we find victory in our inner struggle. Only those offering the armor of God have the resources to drive back the evil that shows itself in all the problems of our day.

You will do well to take advantage of the Lenten season to face yourself before God.

MARCH 20   ...AND LET him that is athirst come...

Revelation 22:17 (KJ)

WHAT GOES INTO THE GOOD LIFE?

Closer and closer comes the day of decision. The lines are tightening between the forces of materialism and those of the spirit. We are going to be forced to decide what we believe about the ancient word, underscored by Jesus: "Man shall not live by bread alone."

Time and again we read that the underdeveloped countries need roads, housing, schools, hospitals, industries. Here in our own country we have all these things and are feverishly building more, yet we are not saved. No one questions the need of those things, but the real question is if they are the secret of the good life?

If so, we need to set up a new religion. We need to go back to the gods of Greece and Rome with their images and their temples and their priests. Communism is at least consistent. Communists have made a religion out of their faith in the material as the secret of the good life.

Surely we need to help nations find and develop new strength, but do we have nothing to export except roads and houses and schools and hospitals and industry? Is it possible that the largest temple we have to build for our friends is to the god named "standard of living?"

The poverty of our spiritual life is showing. We have no national dedication to any unifying spiritual force. We have no God we can present to the world and say: "Here is the secret of our greatness." We have not attained the good life by the things we seek to give others.

It is high time we come to a decision as to what we believe. Have roads and housing and schools and hospitals and industries made you satisfied? Or is there a necessity deeper than all these, a necessity for God? Until we export our faith in God it may be better that we export nothing at all.

A return to God begins with you and me. You cannot serve God and mammon. We have tried it long enough. Any newspaper will show you the results of trying. Elijah's question to Israel is very modern: "How long will you go limping with two different opinions?" Read I Kings 18.

MARCH 21   WHY are thou cast down, O my soul? and why art thou disquieted in me?

Psalm 42:5 (KJ)

TAKE TIME TO THINK IT OVER: JUST WHAT ARE WE LIVING FOR?

I have been spending some time with a clergyman of national stature. Dr. John Sutherland Bonnell was minister of New York's Fifth Avenue Presbyterian Church for 25 years. He is known to thousands through radio and television and the many books of which he is the author. He is a recognized authority in the field of Christian counseling. At the center of his concern is his conviction that we have lost our sense of direction, our purpose for living.

Sometime take off an hour or two and ask yourself where you are going. Get off by yourself and try to express clearly the real purpose you have for your life. What is it that ties together all the busy round of the day and gives it meaning? Go further. What are we trying to do in our community, and in our nation? What is the purpose of our efforts to help other nations?

We have lost our sense of direction because we have lost confidence in the things that we have accepted as our purpose. We have made money too much a goal. Our young people have been taught that the pursuit of a higher standard of living is the answer to a higher level of living. We are being caught in the Biblical warning that the love of money is the root of all evil.

We are making education in material skills too much a goal or purpose of living. We forget that Germany was the symbol of education in the old Nazi days of that land. We are told so often that other countries are ahead of us in education. We are haunted by an old Biblical word: "The fear of the Lord is the beginning of wisdom."

We are enamored with health as a goal worth living for, yet too many people in good health live bad lives. Money and education and health are good in their places as servants of a worthy purpose for life, but they make poor masters and as masters they make poor lives.

We have lost our sense of direction because God has been lost from the center of our lives. We are so made by God that the only purpose that will hold life together and give it proper direction is to serve His glory and to do His will. This is true for each one of us and for all of us together as a community and as a nation.

If you are leaving God out of your life and out of your family, you are having a problem of direction and purpose. Unless we as a people rediscover the secret of dependence on God as the purpose of our existence and as the guide for our affairs, our problems have only begun.

Go off by yourself and think it over. Where are you going? What are you living for?

**MARCH 22   THE GOOD man does not escape all troubles
- he has them too. But the Lord helps him in
each and every one.**

Psalm 34:19 (TLB)

PRACTICING FAITH IN PRIVATE PLACES

This Lenten season fixes the attention of the world on the crucifixion of Jesus Christ. It is relevant to everyone who hears about it, because Jesus Christ invites every person to follow Him. Strangely, He says, "If any man will come after Me, he must take up his cross and follow Me." So being a follower of Christ involves not only benefiting from the cross of Christ, but also bearing one of our own.

Jesus made His cross inevitable in the very beginning of His ministry by deciding to be true to the will of God in all His decisions. Just after His baptism, He was led by the Spirit into the wilderness to think through the life that lay ahead of Him. Satan met Him and sought to turn Him aside from the will of God.

Jesus was hungry, and He was met with the temptation to use His powers to provide bread. It seemed reasonable to assume that man's first need is to have his physical requirements met. Jesus said that man needs first to be fed spiritually by every word that comes from God. You solve man's real problems only as you begin with his soul. Believe and practice this today and you can head yourself toward a cross.

Jesus was presented with the assurance that He could win men if only He would compromise with the demands of the world. Jesus took a long step toward the cross by deciding that only God would be served in obedience. If you are willing to make all your decisions in your political, business and social life in obedience to the will of God, you will come to understand the cross.

118

Jesus was invited by Satan to use His power to prove God's presence by spectacular displays rather than in day-by-day obedience in the ordinary circumstances of life. Jesus put the temptation behind Him and the cross before Him. It is tempting to make a display of our faith in public while privately following our own selfish and sinful ways. To decide to prove our faith in the private places of our lives is to step with Jesus on the way to the cross.

He received the crown after He bore the cross. The disciple can do no less. The decision to do the will of God is the first step in following Christ through Calvary to the Resurrection.

MARCH 23   **WHAT we are is God's gift to us. What we become is our gift to God.**

John Kobal

JOBS THAT SERVE DON'T PAY WELL

Once I was talking with the head of a large technical school. The subject of the talk was the shortage of engineers and of men and women trained to teach them. He said we needed somehow to lead young people to want to make the sacrifices necessary to fill the places of need.

The head of a fine school for children with learning difficulties told of the great difficulty in finding teachers dedicated to this kind of service. There just don't seem to be many who want to do this kind of thing.

There is constant complaint that there are not enough schoolteachers to supply the demand. We are told that it is largely a matter of the appeal of jobs that pay more.

It is hard to fill jobs in the various welfare and health agencies that serve people, because competent people find better paying jobs elsewhere. Churches are always short of candidates for the ministry and mission fields.

In keeping with our modern worship of money and security we are told that the trouble is we don't pay enough in these and kindred areas. This says that money is the proper motivation for the commitment of your life to the service of others. I do not believe it. I believe that young people would respond with enthusiasm to a rebirth of idealism. The jobs and professions that really serve mankind never have paid well and never will. This is as it should be, for money has a deadly effect on one's desire to serve. Men are motivated to serve others by something far deeper than money.

We need to invite young people into those things that serve humanity by reminding them they probably won't make much money; they will probably have to work far harder than most people who make money, they will know insecurity, they will often know ingratitude from those they serve and they will be forced to accept a discipline of living that will exclude many of life's pleasures. Not many will know any acclaim for their labors.

What do you offer by way of inducement? Sacrifice with the joy of knowing you have added something to the happiness and welfare of others. You offer a chance to be a servant of God in His concern for and ministry to men. This is the heart of it all. God calls men and women to serve Him in these fields, where money is always short. He gives in return the inner approval of the spirit. He promises His presence and He promises to supply the needs of those who serve. This is as true of a scientist as of a preacher.

MARCH 24   **WHEN I survey the wondrous cross on which the Prince of glory died, my richest gain I count but loss, and pour contempt on all my pride.**

Isaac Watts, Hymn

IS THE MESSAGE OF LENT STRANGE TO YOU?

The Lenten season has a strange place in our modern world. The main events it celebrates are out of harmony with the accepted standards of our people. The world pauses to allow them to pass by and then rushes on its way. It is as if a man stood by impatiently waiting for a parade to pass before rushing to his next appointment.

Lent speaks of suffering and death. We seek to escape suffering and we ignore death as best we may. Lent tells of earthly failure as the door to heavenly treasure, but we often strive only for earthly success. Lent speaks of One who had nowhere to lay His head and we build ever more stately mansions.

Lent speaks of sacrifice and we hardly know the meaning of the word. Lent has the awful reality of sin as its background while we no longer take it seriously. Lent speaks of saving yourself by losing yourself and we have no intention of getting lost in the shuffle if we can help it. Lent tells of One who gave Himself that others might live. To many this is sentimental foolishness.

The season speaks of love and faith and hope. We live in a day that better understands hate and works and despair. Lent speaks of living and growing in the world of the spirit while we think of growth in terms of statistics. Lent speaks of the eternal value of the least person while we think of prestige and position. Lent speaks of how God sent His Son to redeem and save us and we think we can do it ourselves.

One can only wonder when we will begin to understand how false our values really are. We cling to our faith in ourselves in spite of everything. Any edition of the newspaper ought to make us stop and think. If ever failure was written in large letters over the efforts of man it is today. The Tower of Babel (Genesis 10:1-9) is being re-enacted. Who would have thought that the tribesmen of Africa would be rocking the world or that various countries would become a time bomb set at our door, or that the bright face of our business success story would be so tarnished, or that the race question would become so hard to manage?

It could be that God seeks to show us truth in the Lenten message. Maybe suffering and death are the way to life, failure the road to success. It may be true, after all, that love is stronger than hate, the spirit more important than the world. The evidence is strong that we do need God's Son to redeem and save us.

We do well in this season quietly to ponder the message of Lent.

MARCH 25 **TODAY are you trying to find out the future by consulting witches and mediums? Don't listen to their whispering and mutterings. Can the living find out the future from the dead? Why not ask your God?**

Isaiah 8:19 (TLB)

LENT: A TIME TO EXAMINE ONE'S SELF

This Lenten season is a good time to read the old Bible story of the building of the tower of Babel. It is the story of a people who thought they were smart enough and had resources enough to build themselves a city. They planned to erect a tower that would be high enough to anchor it in the heavens. They would make a name for themselves. The result was they got so confused they no longer understood one another's language. They forgot the ancient bit of wisdom that unless the Lord builds the city, the builders labor in vain.

Lent is not very popular today, because it has at its heart a reminder that we human beings are not able to build anything good by our own efforts. Most of us seem determined to do it ourselves. We have the ability and the resources, so we think, to build character by education; our cities by towering buildings; our nation by politics and our world by diplomacy. We hide our heads in the sand ignoring two basic facts: we the builders are sinners and we are sure to make mistakes.

We need a Lenten season to call us to see ourselves as we are, to bring us to repentance and to remind us that we need God's forgiveness which He offers in the cross and resurrection of Jesus Christ. We need a season like Lent to remind us how weak we really are and how much we need the power of God to save us.

Lent is a good season to stop blaming the other person or the other race or the other nation for our confusion. It is a good time to confess our own sins and our own foolish conduct and to turn humbly to God.

Whether you build a life, or a home or a nation, you labor in vain except the Lord builds the house.

MARCH 26   FOR I admit my shameful deed - it haunts me day and night.

Psalm 51:4 (LB)

WE BELIEVE IN SIN -- IN OTHER PEOPLE

The Lenten season is traditionally a time of prayer and self-denial. It has as its purpose the proper preparation of our hearts for the message of Easter: "He is risen!" It is a time when people are made aware of their sins and shortcomings. Some have said that we no longer believe in sin. This is not true. We do believe in sin - in the other person's sin. We are not willing to blame ourselves when things go wrong. Always someone else is to blame.

If young people go wrong, it is the fault of the parents or the pressures of our day. If a person becomes an alcoholic, there must be found some reason that will relieve him or her of personal blame. If a home breaks up, a dozen reasons are given to excuse the actions of all concerned. If a man or woman is immoral, it is but a reflection of our troubled times. When we can find nothing else to blame our troubles on, we can always point to our enemies or the government or the courts.

This Lenten season is a good time for all of us, young and old, to face the fact that regardless of circumstances, we are largely to blame for our own troubles. Each of us brings most of the difficulties we have upon ourselves. We do what we ought not to do and we fail to do what we ought to do.

We will not make much progress in meeting the problems of common dishonesty, of immoral living, of cruel attacks of men on our city streets and on far-flung battlefields, until we each begin to take seriously our responsibility before God for his own actions.

Psalm 51 is the record of a man who had done a great wrong to another man. He found that it brought him into the presence of God. Burdened by great guilt, he made his confession and sought and found forgiveness and release from his burden. I commend the reading of this Psalm if you are fighting a losing battle with guilt over some wrong you have done. You will find the writer speaking to your own need and you will see the deeper meaning of the Lenten season.

MARCH 27   **MY GRACE is sufficient for thee: for my strength is made perfect in weakness.**

II Corinthians 12:9 (KJ)

THE EASTER SEASON CAN BE SUMMED UP IN THE WORD 'GRACE'

Perhaps the message of the Easter season can be summed up in the single word "grace." It is not a familiar word in our common language. Properly understood, it may not be a popular word in our self-sufficient generation. We live in a do-it-yourself day. We are a bit impatient with the idea that we cannot do for ourselves what needs to be done. If we cannot do it, there is someone who can teach us how. We evade the idea that we cannot do certain things for ourselves and that no human wisdom or ability can teach us how. This is thought to be weakness, but it is also the truth.

We are weak. The strongest and wisest person is weak. All men pooling their human wisdom and ability are weak. Because we are weak we make a mess of our do-it-yourself projects, whether it is building a life or building a nation.

It is to our weakness and to our failures that the Easter season speaks. It speaks the word "grace." It says that God is personally and actively involved in our lives.

There is a fatal flaw in human nature. It is called in religion "sin." We are not able to make a good life by ourselves. We cannot make a real home by our human efforts. Something goes wrong and the glow dies. We cannot make a good community by our own efforts. The bad things people do are continually fouling up our best efforts.

Grace is God saying: "My strength is made perfect in weakness." Although we are undeserving, God moves toward us to save and to help us. Grace comes to us in His ordering of our lives. Look back into your life and you will be impressed with the fact that so often good things have come through no effort of yours, sorrows have been turned to blessings, defeats into victory.

Grace comes in the midst of the day's burdens and responsibilities. There is strength for the task, comfort for the sorrow. Grace comes most powerfully in the consciousness that in the cross our sins are forgiven and in the resurrection we have new life. The fatal flaw is overcome and by His grace we are enabled to win victories in our struggle to build good lives and good communities.

The measure of the Easter season is that of the angel at Christmas: "Emmanuel, which is, being interpreted, God with us."

**SO, dear friends, carefully avoid idol -
worship of every kind.**

I Corinthians 10:14 (LB)

WE MUST KEEP AWAY FROM IDOLS

An idol is something we worship instead of the true God. Writing to some Christians, an ancient writer, speaking of Christ, said: "This is the true God and eternal life. Little children, keep yourselves from idols."

Rome had problems. Paul describes them in his letter to the Romans. The list sounds quite modern. "Being filled with all unrighteousness, immorality, wickedness, covetousness, maliciousness, full of envy, murder, debate, deceit, malignity, whispers, backbiters, haters of God, despiteful, proud, boasters, inventors of evil things, disobedient to parents, without understanding, covenant-breakers, without natural affection, implacable, unmerciful."

God's word says in this same chapter that these problems were due to worship of idols. "Professing themselves to be wise, they became fools and changed the image of the incorruptible God into an image made like corruptible man."

The problems that plague us are due to our worship of idols. For many, the state becomes an idol. For these, the decrees of the state are right. For others power is an idol. If it makes us strong it is right. Some have pleasure as a god. If it is fun then it must be right.

In Rome's day, the Christian church was sent to tell men of Christ, saying: "this is the true God and eternal life." God honored that witness by changing men, creating a new society and raising moral standards to a new high. Freedom and human dignity are the fruits of this witness. Our democracy can grow only where this witness is maintained.

Any effective approach to our present mushrooming problems awaits a revitalized church sent to witness to Christ as the true God and eternal life, warning men to keep themselves from idols.

MARCH 29   AND how does a man benefit if he gains the whole world and loses his soul in the process?

Mark 8:36 (LB)

SICKNESS OF SOUL TAKES A HEAVY TOLL

Reading a magazine recently, I ran across the following statement: "Five nations lead the world in alcoholism, a high divorce rate, juvenile delinquency and mental illness. These are the United States, Switzerland, Britain, Denmark, and France." These are evidences of a sick society, caused by sick people. The sickness is a deep moral sickness.

It is comforting to our ego to call alcoholism just an illness. Of course, it has physical characteristics, but it is dangerous to surround the alcoholic with the comfortable assurance that he is sick in the same sense that a man with cancer is sick. It is dangerous to allow the boy or girl who flagrantly violates the law to think he or she is the helpless victim of inept parents or of a bad environment. The boy or girl knows better.

It is dangerous to allow men and women to think they can break a marriage by a court order and be free. Marriage is a merging of personalities and broken roots will fester for a lifetime. It is dangerous to believe that mental illness is subject to psychological manipulation on a completely secular basis.

The human being is a vast, complex creation. The body and the mind and the soul are all involved together. They are unified and given direction by that mysterious being we identify when we say

"I." This mysterious "I", which is each of us, roams the universe. The "I" uses the mind and the body.

Most of all, this "I" has dealings with God. Created in the image of God, the "I" is restless until it rests in God. This search for peace with God is in the realm of the soul. It is here that morality and conscience hold sway.

If you satisfy the body and the mind and fail to satisfy the soul, you starve the "I." No longer is there a resting place for the soul or a guide for conduct. You have alcoholism, delinquency, divorce and mental illness.

These are the inevitable results of a secular society, a society without God. These are insolvable problems except in the framework of commitment to God by faith. At their heart is our sin. Guilt is dominant in these evils. Guilt is the emotion of personality, the "I," which is cut off from its home base.

Whatever needs to be done to cure these ills must offer forgiveness and new life. This is what the crucifixion and resurrection of Jesus Christ means. Here the "I" finds acceptance with God, moral integrity and unity of purpose. So the sick are made whole. Only whole people make a whole society.

MARCH 30   NOW faith is the substance of things hoped for, the evidence of things not seen.

Hebrews 11:1 (LB)

FAITH LIGHTS THE PATH OUT OF A BLIND ALLEY

At one time or another, all of us come to the place where we face the loss of something that we believe necessary to our happiness. Our prayers for escape are useless. This experience comes to different people in different ways. There may be loss of health or a job or of a loved one. It comes to some in failure to receive deserved recognition. No one escapes. It is part of life as it must be lived. The experience of Jesus in Gethsemane will be helpful to any who would find a way through such an experience with hope of victory.

Jesus faced death at the hands of His enemies. His life was to be cut short in His younger years. He had given His life in service to others. What He faced seemed poor payment for years dedicated to helping others. From the disaster that faced Him, He won his greatest victory.

1. First He kept close to his friends in His great need. He did not have many. There were just three that went with Him to this place of prayer. We need our friends when we face the crisis of our lives. He asked the three friends to watch with Him as He wrestled with His problem in prayer. All of us can witness to the help our friends have given us in our dark hours.

2. It will help us to remember that Jesus prayed to escape His situation. This is what we all do, and it is right that we should. Jesus said to God that He was in agony over the unhappy prospects. God understands our pain and would have us be honest with Him about it. No one faces loss without suffering.

3. In His agony, Jesus was alone with God. He withdrew a short distance from His friends to face His problems alone. There is a space between us and others not even our closest friend can cross. Here we are alone with God.

4. In His prayer He won His victory in surrendering His whole problem to God. "Not my will, but thine be done" was the key to His peace. This was the surrender of faith and not of despair. He surrendered to God whom He believed could take the death that evil men would bring to Him and use it for good. The resurrection proved that His faith was justified. It also proves that it is the way of victory for us. We are not asked to give up. We are invited to take our loss and hold it up to God in the confidence that He will make it the means of blessing to others and to us.

MARCH 31   **ALL who are oppressed may come to him. He is a refuge for them in their times of trouble.**

Psalm 9:9 (LB)

EASY LIFE WASN'T PART OF CHRIST'S PROMISE

The Gospel of Jesus Christ is thorny and its flowers are hidden among the thorns. We often miss the flowers because we hate to get our hands pricked. Someone has said that when the Lord lays His hands on ours, He leaves blood on them and when we follow His footsteps He leaves bloodstains.

This is a far cry from much of our modern religion. This may explain why much of it is so powerless. It is a far cry from what Jesus taught. He said strange things to those whom he invited to follow Him. "If any man would come after me, let him deny himself and take up his cross and follow me." He told a rich man: "Go thy way, sell whatsoever thou hast and give to the poor, and thou shalt have treasure in heaven: and come, take up thy cross and follow me." He said: "For whosoever will save his life shall lose it; but whosoever shall lose his life for my sake and the gospel's the same shall save it." "If any man will be first, let him be the servant of all."

In His list of happy men, Christ named the poor, the meek, the mourners, the persecuted, those who seek righteousness, the peacemakers. He said he came not to bring peace but a sword. He said His followers would suffer tribulation in this world. He warned all who would follow Him to love their enemies, to bless those that curse them, to do good to those that hate them.

Where do you suppose we got the idea of religion as a cushion against trouble or the giver of physical comfort and ease? Actually the Gospel is a shocking thing to those who love comfort without a cross.

130

It is made to sound so easy to follow Christ as Lord and Savior. Yet all that Martin Niemuller was doing in his fashionable Berlin church was preaching the Gospel, saying that Christ is a higher authority than Hitler. It cost him six years in a concentration camp.

Taking our discipleship seriously can still bring collision with our society. Many are finding it costly in countries dominated by communism. It is a burning issue in the racial tensions all over our country. It can be costly in daily decisions of Christians who are involved in social life, in business, in politics.

The main thing I am trying to say is that when it does get costly, we are in the line of march of the followers of Christ in all ages. The power of God is always the greatest when the going is the roughest.

APRIL

APRIL 1 **NOW ye are the body of Christ, and members in particular.**

I Corinthians 12:27 (KJ)

THE CROSS HAS THE POWER TO END HATRED

There is a danger that we are going to be engulfed by hatred and enmity unless we find an answer to it. The fire is spreading rapidly in individuals and in groups here at home and all over our world. It destroys marriages, it divides neighborhoods, it inflames groups of different nationalities and races.

What is the answer? Education can do certain things but it is naive indeed to believe it can lessen the hatred in a human heart. Others offer economic answers: abolish poverty, divide the wealth and men will live together in peace.

We will all do well to consider afresh the Christian answer. Paul exhibited enmity toward all not of his clan and race and nation. Education and economic security and privilege had only fed the fires of his hatreds.

Then one day he met and accepted Jesus Christ in a personal encounter. He found himself reconciled to God by the cross of Christ. He discovered that the fires of his hatred were put out and that the walls which divided him from others were destroyed. He found that in Christ, enmity was destroyed and that God made a new man of him. He found that God made of believers a fellowship of those bonded together by love. In this fellowship the barriers that divided men and women, rich and poor, educated and ignorant, Jews and Gentile, were abolished.

In spite of all its failures and in spite of all the criticism hurled at it, the church today is the one hope against the enmities of your day. The church as you and I know it fails often enough to deserve criticism. However, more perfectly than anywhere else on earth, it does show forth the power of God in Christ to destroy the barriers that divide men.

In the church, men and women find harmony in marriage and the rich and poor, the ignorant and the educated and men of different races live and work together in peace and with mutual love and respect.

APRIL 2   **FOR whosoever exalteth himself shall be abased; and he that humbleth himself shall be exalted.**

Luke 14:11 (KJ)

EVERYONE MUST OBEY AUTHORITY

Sooner or later authority will become a popular subject for general discussion. We are on a freedom "binge" when everyone seeks to do that which is right in his own eyes. What is more, a great many feel they have a right to do so. One wonders where all this assumed right to do as you please came from. It didn't come from the world of science which is so popular. Here obedience to established law makes any accomplishment possible.

Obedience to discovered facts makes possible the conquest of space. Gordon Cooper would never have been successful if any one of a host of involved people had decided to do as he pleased.

It did not come from any honest study of success in any business or profession. No one ever became a success in any line of endeavor by doing as he pleased. Behind every good artist or musician are hours and years of rigid obedience to the authority of accepted discipline.

It did not come from any unbiased study of home life anywhere in the world. The homes that are fruitful in happiness and in character are those where authority is established and accepted and obeyed.

It has not come by any proof that the person who does as he pleases is a happy, well-adjusted individual. The most miserable person in the world is one who is free to do as he pleases.

It has come because we continue to be guilty of Adam's sin. Under authority of God, Adam had everything. Free of this authority, he had nothing but trouble. The temptation convinced Adam and Eve that authority sought only to keep them from being as wise as God. They were tempted to believe that God was lying when He told them they would find disaster and death in freedom to do as they please. They found God was right, but it was too late.

We were created to live under authority, not to be free. At the heart of each of us is the divine "I ought to obey." All proper authority rests in the authority of God and in our obligation to obey Him. We are members one of another, subject to authority in nature, in our country, in our business and in our homes. Within us is the Voice of God calling us to obey the authority over us.

When human authority forgets its responsibility to God, disaster follows. When those under authority rebel against proper authority, disaster also follows.

We need to belong to God and to one another. The key is

obedience to God's authority.

APRIL 3   **BLESSED** is he whose transgression is forgiven...

Psalm 32:1 (KJ)

ADMIT WRONGS, HEAL DIVISIONS

Everybody is so right to hear them tell it. The walls between people and races and nations are built ever stronger by the fact that no one is willing to admit any wrong. We are always ready to defend our position and to attack the opposition. This is true in our families, between races and among nations.

Yet this is not the way we really feel. All of us know that we are wrong in much that we do and think. No one is free of guilt. What a relief it would be many times if we could just say: "I was wrong and I am sorry." For some strange reason, this is considered weakness.

There are few, if any, misunderstandings in which either party is entirely free of fault. So often one is hoping the other will give some indication of being even a little bit wrong so that he can respond with: "I was wrong, too." When neither has the courage to do it the breach is widened and the pain increases.

One thing that makes confession difficult is that we have forgotten that it begins with confession to God. David seriously wronged another. He began his effort to make things right by turning to God and saying: "Against thee and thee only I have sinned and done this evil in thy sight." When we do wrong it always involves other people, but it means that first we have fallen short of what God requires of us.

In this day when there are so many divisions between people, the greatest service the church could render is to call people to repentance and confession. Perhaps there is no real hope for much

134

improvement until our hearts and our homes and our churches are places where we make an open confession of our sins.

This would bring peace to many a troubled breast. It would heal many a broken home. It would heal many a neighborhood quarrel. It would give a healing touch to our growing racial tensions. Confessing our sins will not solve everything, but it will give an atmosphere in which contact and communications are possible.

It is good and necessary to stand for what we believe to be right. It is good and necessary that we seek the forgiveness of God and of man. There is a strange and wonderful reconciling power in the confession of sin. It opens the gates of healing. It is the mark of strength, not weakness. It is the open door to peace.

Try it in your own situations. You will be amazed at its results. You will become a witness to its power. Thus you will become a part of the answer to our divisions.

APRIL 4   **"I have lived sir a long time, and the longer I live, the more convincing proofs I see of this truth -- that God governs in the affairs of men."**

Benjamin Franklin

CONVICTION GIVES A UNITY TO HISTORY

When I was in grammar school and high school, geography was a dry recitation of locations and products, none of which mattered much to the teacher or to me. History was more interesting but did not matter much more insofar as my daily life was concerned.

Today they are teaching geography and history in a different way. It is forced on us by the kind of world we live in. You cannot understand what is happening in Washington or in Atlanta without knowing what is happening in Asia or Europe or Africa. You cannot understand what is happening in these places without knowing their geography and their history.

It is a chaotic world and history is being made in strain, in tensions, in bloodshed, in rivalries. In every place there are men of good will who devote themselves to human betterment. Too often their efforts seem to be overcome by the very conditions they seek to improve.

However, the Christian can live as a part of it with confidence. In the resurrection of Christ we have assurance that there is a God of power and of love. Christ said: "All authority is given unto me in heaven and in earth." Through all the apparent disorder of history, there runs the steady stream of God's purpose to lead us to the point where "every knee shall bow and every tongue confess Him Lord to the glory of God, the Father."

One of the convictions that comes from the Easter message is that we can read our daily newspapers, certain that at the heart of all that is happening is the God revealed in Jesus Christ. He is at the heart of it all, guiding it and governing it, making evil to praise Him, even as He made the evil of the cross to praise Him by the resurrection of Christ from the dead.

This conviction gives to all history a unity. It gives hope to all who serve the common good. It gives to each person who serves, the purpose and will of God a place in history that has meaning.

APRIL 5   **...ALONG unfamiliar paths I will guide them; I will turn the darkness into light before them and make the rough places smooth.**

Isaiah 42:16 (NIV)

OUR REAL CROSSES ARE NEVER LIGHT

Jesus made a decision which he knew would lead to His being

rejected and finally crucified. He decided to do the will of God at any cost and to see it through. It is not too hard to decide to do the will of God when there are no pressures on us. However, there comes a time when we have a decision to make in the face of unpleasant consequences.

Jesus faced the results of His commitment to God's will as His enemies began to close in on Him. They were plotting in Jerusalem to kill Him. He had made His decision to give His life for the world.

The hardest decision in the world is to go through with a course of action we have chosen. It was hard for Jesus. In the Garden of Gethsemane, He struggled to the very end. We read He was "sore troubled and very heavy." He fell on the ground in agony of spirit. He prayed that some other way than the cross might be found. He sweated drops of blood. Finally in one mighty effort He found peace: "Not my will but Thine be done."

It was only through the cross that the resurrection was possible. Thus life became men's possession through death. Hope found its solid foundation in the fact that He decided to see it through and lived again as our Hope.

Here is our encouragement to see through to the end our engagement to live as God in Christ would have us live. There come times when it seems a losing game. There are other times when it does not seem important. There are other times when we do not have the strength to face it, or so it seems. Sometimes the only answer is just to trust in God. Here we follow Christ and take up our cross and follow Him.

We do it with Christian hope because He did it and found it led to the glory of resurrection. This is our assurance that however difficult the decision to see it through and however weak we feel, we will find it is the way to strength and victory.

On Good Friday we remember Jesus' crucifixion. It was the result of decisions made years before. We do well to remember also that He invites us to join Him in the decisions that led Him there. He promises that because He lives we shall live also, and that this is the victory that overcomes the world, even our own faith.

APRIL 6   ...WHEN I see the blood, I will pass over you...

Exodus 12:13 (LB)

THE LORD'S SUPPER IS THE CORE OF FAITH

The heartbeat of the Christian faith is the Lord's Supper. Here the death of Christ as the Lamb of God sacrificed for the sins of the world is remembered. This memorial supper goes back for its roots into Jewish Passover where the lamb is sacrificed in memory of the deliverance of the children of Israel from Egypt.

The Lord's Supper is not only a memorial, it is a channel of the power and the grace of God to those who take part in it by faith. The Cross of Christ is set at the very crossroads of human life. It does for all men certain things without which human life would be hopeless.

1. The Cross of Christ where He took upon Himself the sins of the world is our assurance that evil will be defeated. Cruelty and selfishness and moral degradation are in power everywhere. Call the roll of nations and you list the places of the earth where men and women suffer under the weight of these things. Men without God see little hope for the things of peace and goodness and truth. Only those who believe that God in Christ was reconciling the world to Himself can be sure that God did so love the world and has in Christ, defeated evil which rises only to fall on its own sword.

2. Each one of us is an empire within himself. In you and in me, all the forces of evil swirl and contend for our souls. selfishness and greed and immorality are strong within us - too strong for our own power. Guilt builds up and the older we get the more helpless seems the fight. The Cross of Christ where He bore our sins in His own body is our only hope of victory over our sins and the guilt they pile on us. Here we find the power of God working in us by faith which keeps us from being devoured by

our sin and which relieves us of our burden of guilt.

3. A third assurance of the Cross comes to those who seek to do the will of God and to do good to men and find that it does not work out in terms of response and success. Serving people can often seem a fruitless job. Honestly trying to do what we believe God would have us do can bring us into hard places. Christ found it brought Him to the Cross. His assurance is that victory and success come even through the outward failure of our efforts. If He had not suffered and died in the line of divine duty we never would be able in our efforts to do His will.

Wherever the Lord's Supper is observed, the hearts of men are made strong by the assurances of the presence and the power of God through the death of His Son.

APRIL 7   I see His hand of mercy, I hear His voice of cheer, and just the time I need Him, He's always near.

Alfred H. Ackley, Hymn

THE IMPORTANCE OF CHRIST'S PROOF

The question in the book of Job haunts the human heart: "If a man die, shall he live again?" The affirmative answer of the Christian faith sheds light over all the earth and gives hope and assurance to the questioning heart of men. This affirmative answer is one in fact, not theory. One has died and returned from the dead. It happened once for all and for us.

This is the great cornerstone of faith and hope of the world. Paul spoke truly when he wrote: "And if Christ be not risen, then is our preaching in vain, and your faith is also in vain. If in this life only we have hope in Christ, we are of all men most pitiable. But now is Christ risen from the dead and become the first fruits of them that slept."

A whole new dimension was given to our life by the resurrection of Jesus Christ from the dead. This is the dimension of eternity. All of life is now lived in the light of the fact of life after death. Because He lives, we shall live also. When death has taken its toll we shall live and face the risen Christ in mercy or in judgment. What we do and how we live has reference to this world and also to the world to come.

Because He is risen, our human efforts are not bounded by the grave. We do not have to do it all in the few short years of our lives. Our labors in the Lord are not in vain because He lives and will preserve and perfect our efforts by His own power.

Because He is risen we do not walk alone. We have his promise that he is with us to the end of the way. Countless millions witness to the truth of this promise.

Because He is risen, we can believe that he is working all things for good. In the comic strip called "Peanuts," Lucy is fearful the rain will flood the world. Linus reminds her of God's promise not to let it happen. Lucy says: "You've taken a great load off my mind." Linus replies: "Sound theology has a way of doing that." And it does. No one can understand the tragedy of so much of life. It takes a load off the mind to believe that the living Christ is in the midst of it.

Because He is risen, we can face the death of our loved ones with hope and courage. He comes again to receive them unto Himself that they may be where He is, and we can die in the blessed assurance that we will be with them in the living Christ.

YOUR HOPE STEMS FROM HIS CROSS

The crucifixion of Jesus Christ has brought hope and healing from the day it happened until now. There is no human explanation large enough to explain the depth and vastness of its influence. Christ died at the hands of His enemies. That should have been the end of it. It turned out to be only the beginning.

People beyond number have stood before the cross of Christ, burdened by their guilt. They have confessed their sin in faith and have received forgiveness. Literally, the burden of their sins has rolled away. They have become new creatures, cleansed in soul, renewed in mind and refreshed in body. History, biography and present day witnesses testify to the reality of these things.

The cross of Christ has given a new meaning to suffering and death. Because His suffering has become the door of hope to all men, His followers have, in all generations, accepted suffering and even death as means of bringing life and hope to others. They have actually found joy in the fellowship of His sufferings. These have followed where He led, not counting the cost. The martyrs under Roman oppression sang on the way to execution. Christian missions is the story of men and women enduring all manners of sacrifices and sufferings for His sake. During World War II more than 2,000 German pastors went to jail, choosing to obey God rather than man.

In the cross of Christ rests our confidence that evil cannot finally win. He took on Himself the worst man can do. There was at the cross all manner of evil man can devise: jealousy, hatred, betrayal, desertion, indifference, cowardice, lying, cruelty and legal injustice. These and other marks of man's evil, gathered to kill Him. He was helpless in the hands of the religious and civil powers of His day. He

141

took it all on Him and then used the death they inflicted as the very instrument of his victory. Raised on the third day, it is His death that has given to mankind hope of final victory over all evil. He defeated the powers of evil and offers His victory to all men.

So we can look the evil that is all about us straight in the face and believe it is already defeated. However strong it may appear, whatever of good seems defeated today, we may be sure that the evil must lose and the good must finally win.

In the confidence of sins forgiven and evil's power broken, we can meet our days with courage. He carries our sins and bears our burdens and assures our victory. This and this alone is the secret of confident living.

APRIL 9　　　　**THERE is pow'r, pow'r wonder-working power in the precious blood of the Lamb.**

Lewis E. Jones, Hymn

THE MEANING OF GOOD FRIDAY

On Good Friday there are millions of people all over the world who remember that Jesus Christ was crucified between two thieves by the order of Pontius Pilate. Strange indeed that it is called Good Friday. Certainly there seemed nothing good about it when it happened. Jesus had prayed to be allowed to escape the death that stared Him in the face. His friends grieved over it, but most of them withdrew from Him.

With two or three exceptions, no one came near Him except to increase His agony by their insults. He who had come to serve and to save man died as a criminal, practically alone.

Yet, because on the third day He was raised from the dead, this black day has come to be called "good." This can be explained only by what the death of Christ has come to mean to believers and even to unbelievers.

By His death on the cross, a way is opened by which we can be reconciled to God. We are created to have a holy, happy, faithful and fruitful relationship to God. No man can live at peace with himself or with his neighbor when this relationship is broken, yet it is broken by our sin.

Because in the death of Christ men have found God loves them as they are and receives all who come by repentance and faith, black Friday has become Good Friday. It meets man's deepest need: Forgiveness of sin. He took on Himself the final punishment that we deserve and cleansed us of our guilt.

It is Good Friday because it is the sign of hope in our struggle against all the world's evil. God has taken it on Himself and defeated it in the cross and in the resurrection.

Good Friday and Easter are God's guarantee that our problem can be solved and our evil conquered by God's gift of the Spirit to those who find forgiveness at the cross.

APRIL 10 THANKS be unto God for His unspeakable gift.

II Corinthians 9:15 (LB)

THE MESSAGE OF EASTER IS A BLESSING TO ALL

On Easter, we remember the faith of Christians that the grave was not able to hold Christ and on the third day He was raised from the dead. One has come back from the dead. The question, "If a man die, shall he live again ?" is answered with an earth-shaking "Yes." Here is victory over death.

The resurrection of Christ is man's fairest possession. Here the grip of death, which fastens itself on all human hopes and dreams, is broken. "If Christ be not raised from the dead, we are of all men most miserable." Paul wrote this to the Christians in Corinth. It is still true. It is the fact that gives meaning to our faith. We trust the death of Christ for forgiveness of our sins. His resurrection proves our trust is not in vain.

We lay our dead away in hope of life beyond the grave and His resurrection is our confidence that our hope moves toward fulfillment. We give ourselves in His service and because He lives, our service is filled with His power.

Even the unbeliever lives by the power and blessing of the resurrection of Christ. Any faith in a good future is a fruit of the faith of Christians in a living Lord who rules history and whose glory is its final goal. Hope for tomorrow, wherever it is found, is a spark from the fire of Christian faith.

Sacrificial concern for those who suffer and for those in need is a reflection of the concern of Christ who died to save men and who was raised that they might live. The history of medical care and of education in the early days of nations across the world is largely the history of men and women who sought to serve their fellow men for Christ's sake.

The chief bulwark of morality, integrity and law in any community is the church that witnesses to a living Christ. Wherever women hold a place of honor in the social order, they are in the presence of the far-flung influence of Him who was raised in the third day.

The very surge of the poor and downtrodden across the world is witness to the work of Christ whose disciples have gone everywhere proclaiming the eternal worth of the humblest soul.

The Christian faith in the resurrection of Jesus Christ taps the deep springs of our being. It speaks to all the longings and aspirations of the heart. It comes to man in his sin and degradation and confusion with a word of eternal hope. It opens the alleys. It gives an unconquerable power to daily living and destroys forever man's last enemy - death.

Christ is risen! This is humanity's gladdest cry!

HE has also set eternity in the hearts of men...that everyone may eat and drink, and find satisfaction in all his toil - this is the gift of God.

Ecclesiastes 3:13 (NIV)

THE RESURRECTION: SYMBOL OF ETERNITY

At the conclusion of Paul's great statement about the resurrection, he says: "Therefore, my beloved brothers, stand firm and immovable, and work for the Lord always, work without limit, since you know that in the Lord your labor cannot be lost." To everyone who seeks to do right and to labor for the common good, there is the assurance that God is involved.

In the death and resurrection of Christ, God made sure that evil cannot win, and He overcame the power of death to destroy your life. He forever placed human life in an eternal framework. Here is the antidote to the pessimism of our day. We are bombarded from all sides by evil and tragedy. It is easy to feel there is nothing one can do to change things.

For most of us, the most difficult battlefield against evil is in our own hearts. It is hard to escape defeat at the hands of the temptations that come at us. We struggle to do what is right and so often fail. Our hope lies in God whose grace and power will see us through if we labor by faith in the Lord.

In this faith is the source of encouragement for all parents who take seriously the rearing of their children. You do what you can but are conscious of how feeble your efforts can be. It is a different matter entirely when you enter into a covenant with God and discover His presence giving your efforts the blessing of His Spirit.

In this faith is the foundation of hope for all who would serve their fellow man. It is not easy to help other people. One can get discouraged. Many grow cynical in the process. It is a different matter if you are sure God loves those you seek to serve and is working through you and in them. You can do your best and trust results to Him.

God alone can heal. It is God that changes lives and corrects conditions. In Christ he commits Himself to these things. We can rest in that hope.

For all who seek to be and to do good, the crucifixion and resurrection of Christ are God's assurance that their labors in the Lord cannot be lost.

APRIL 12   GOD did not send His Son into the world to condemn it, but to save it.

John 3:17 (LB)

THE IMPORT OF EASTER: CHRISTIAN HOPE

Easter has come and gone. What has it meant? What does it mean? In a word, it means Christian hope. Once I went to a distant city to have part in the funeral of a friend of mine who had been the pastor of one of the churches there for 10 years. He was a loved and useful man who died suddenly at the height of his usefulness. The center of the hope of his congregation, his family and his friends was the message of the living Christ.

The Christian hope dares affirm the eternal meaning of the things of this earth. Surrounding the death of this man was the fact of eternal significance that he was with Christ in glory. In the midst of grief at his passing, there was the assurance that he was taken in God's own time and for purposes hidden from our eyes but divinely good nevertheless. There was the assurance that his service in and through the congregation and the city would continue to bear fruit because the Spirit of God would continue to bring to fruition the seeds he had planted.

146

In their Christian hope the family found the assurance of God's presence to comfort them in heart and to strengthen them in body. The wife was just home from three weeks in the hospital, yet the ministry of the Spirit was present for all to see. In this hope there was the assurance that however lonely and difficult the future, the living Christ would open the way here on earth and one day bring reunion.

There was the assurance that good is stronger than evil and that there is the Spirit of God in our world to guarantee the final victory of the kingdom of God.

This meaning of Easter permeates our world. Those who know Christ as Savior and Lord depend on His life to encourage them on the way. Even secular optimism, which believes in the worthwhileness of efforts to do good, has no sound basis outside the Christian hope founded in the resurrection of Christ.

In the death of a good and godly man, all these things come into focus and we see and feel them in all their reality. We are encouraged to give ourselves to our own struggle in the assurance that it is eternally worthwhile and will be a part of His final victory over all that is evil. It also gives us assurance that because He lives we shall live also and one day be with the Lord where He is.

APRIL 13   ...IT is He who makes us victorious through Jesus Christ our Lord.

I Corinthians 15:57 (LB)

THE RESURRECTION TELLS US THAT EVIL CAN BE DEFEATED

There are certain convictions that come out of Easter's witness to the resurrection of Christ. This witness is emphasized each Sunday. It is sorely needed in our lives. Because Christ was raised from the dead, the Christian knows certain things. He knows that all things were made by God and that behind all creation is a God of love and mercy. He knows that all men are made in God's image and are objects of God's love and mercy.

The Christian knows a third thing. He knows that evil cannot finally win because of the resurrection of Christ. At the cross, human evil concentrated its power. Here was gathered the cruelty, deceit, injustice and greed of the world. Because the cross of Friday was turned into the empty tomb of Sunday, we enter the battle against evil knowing that we are on the winning side, in spite of appearances to the contrary.

"This is the victory that overcomes the world, even our faith." Here is your encouragement as you fight temptation in your own life. It is not nearly as easy as it sounds to do the right thing, to tell the truth, to treat others as we know we should. It is not easy to withstand within our hearts the temptations of the world, the flesh and the devil. We would give up the struggle without the assurance of the victory won by Christ and promised to us in the end.

Evil seems strong in our world. Godless political systems march across our world with cruelty and without regard to honor. Selfish interests trade in the weaknesses of human nature for profit. Hate often seems stronger than love. Physical force moves roughshod over those who would live by love.

The resurrection is our one assurance that those who oppose the evils of our day are on the winning side. It is proof that love is stronger than hate, that kindness finally conquers cruelty, that truth triumphs over deceit.

There is a confidence in both the believer and the unbeliever that the struggle for God and for decency is worthwhile. This confidence finds its one sure foundation in the Easter message. The future belongs to God and to those who serve Him.

COME unto me, all ye that labor and are heavy laden, and I will give you rest.

Matthew 11:28 (LB)

GOD IS WITH US IN TIME OF NEED

As we get further from the Easter season, the stress of living often moves us further from its message. We need to be reminded often of what God did for us in the resurrection of Jesus Christ from the dead.

One of the most amazing assurances that come to us is that God cares for us one-by-one. It is easy to lose this confidence if we do not keep our heart fixed on the revelation of God in Jesus Christ. The bigness of the universe and the mass movements of our day attack our confidence that we are known to eternal God by name. It is in Christ that we can know that God is personally interested us all.

God loves us just as we are. We often have a hard time loving ourselves because of what we know about ourselves.

Often we evade other people and try to evade God because we feel unworthy of their acceptance. Even as we are, God comes in Christ and, calling us by name, invites us to come and to accept forgiveness. Accepted by God, we can face ourselves and others unafraid. With all our shortcomings, he says to us: "Come just as you are."

This is the assurance that the God of the universe hears us when we pray. God is available. The whole Bible is a record of God's dealings with individuals and with two-way communication between God and people. Christ made this plain by His words and by His actions. "Ask and ye shall receive. Seek and ye shall find. Knock and it shall be opened unto you."

For those who pray in faith, there comes the assurance of answered prayers. The answers are not always what we want, but they are the answers of God who personally cares for us in love.

In Christ we have the assurance that God is with us in our sorrows in a very personal way. He ministers to us in our needs and meets us in our crises. His words: "Fear not, I am with thee," have carried many a troubled soul through the deep waters.

In the certainties of faith there is power to live in a day like this.

APRIL 15   BLESS the Lord, O my soul; and all that is within me, bless his holy name!

Psalm 103:1 (RSV)

'A GOOD THING TO GIVE' --- WITH OUR LIPS AND OUR LIVES

The following is taken from the "St. Luke's Messenger," a publication of St. Luke's Episcopal Church: "It is a mighty easy thing to get into the habit of accepting all the blessings of life and never feeling any gratitude toward the God who bestows the blessings. In the training of our children we know how hard a thing it is to instill in them this same spirit of being grateful for the things that we and others give to them.

"Over and over we find ourselves asking them: 'Well, what do you say?' And at last there comes a 'Thank you.' We keep on with this over the years because we know that 'thank you's' are one way to keep our children from taking things for granted. We know the Psalmist was right when he wrote, 'It is a good thing to give thanks.'

"Gratitude to God is the way that we may saturate our souls with the spirit of His love. 'Yea, 'it is a good thing to give thanks unto the Lord – 'yea, a joyful and pleasant thing it is to be thankful.'

"'Yea, it is a good thing to give thanks unto the Lord' - not only with our lips but in our lives. It is one thing merely to mumble thanks with a word, it is quite another to put our gratitude to God into terms of actions. It is only when our gratitude to God is reflected in the things we do that we develop within ourselves that Christ-like concept of living this life in terms of responsibility toward God.

"All of the life of our Lord and all of its teachings are based upon the fact that this life we have is a gift of God. All that we have and all that we are and all that we hope to be are blessings bestowed upon us by the Lord our God.

"The only begotten Son of God makes no bones about this matter. He speaks quite bluntly that we shall one day be responsible to our heavenly Father for the way in which we have used our time, employed our talents and shared our treasures.

"What we are saying is that we need to think through thoroughly our sense of responsibility to God, and His Church, to ourselves and our fellow men. Do we really think of all life in terms of stewardship to our heavenly Father? Is our life and all that is in it simply our own to be used for ourselves as we see fit? Or is our life held in trust from the God who gave it to be used in His service according to His holy will?

"Yea, a joyful and pleasant thing is to be thankful - not only with our lips but in our lives."

APRIL 16   ...HOLD these virtues tightly. Write them deep within your heart.

Proverbs 3:3 (LB)

LIFE IS SHAPED BY OUR BELIEFS

I once read a book called "Psycho-Cybernetics." The author is Dr. Maxwell Maltz, a plastic surgeon. The word "cybernetics" was a new one for me. It has to do with the image you have of yourself. The theme of the book is that the resources of your personality work almost automatically to produce the self-image you have.

The book is a study in psychology of what the Bible means when it says: "As a man thinketh in his heart, so is he," and "Keep thy heart with all diligence for out of it are the issues of life."

Dr. Maltz apparently became interested in this whole matter when he noticed radical change in personality brought about by a change in a person's idea of himself through plastic surgery. Changed appearance caused changed personality because the person thought of himself differently.

Jesus touched lives and gave them a new idea of themselves and miracles occurred. We are so made by God that our minds, bodies and souls respond to what we believe. The goal we have for ourselves makes us what we are.

This means that it is of first importance what we believe about ourselves. If we see ourselves as victims of circumstances, then we will be. If we believe we are victors over the problems of life we will become conquerors.

But we cannot lift ourselves by our own bootstraps. Life will always be too much for a person who depends on his own strength. The weakness of our own natures and the difficulties of life will combine to destroy self-confidence.

The Christian faith meets each person at this point. In Christ, God offers us the opportunity to become the children of God, joint heirs with Christ. He comes to us with forgiveness for our sins and strength for our weakness.

Here is the self-image that draws forth all our energies in a way that enables us to live with confidence and with victory. Believing yourself supported by God, you can meet heavy responsibilities with the assurance: "I can do all things through Christ who gives me strength." You can meet trouble with the support: "If God be for us, who can be against us." You can meet sorrow with the comfort: "My peace I give unto you."

If you believe the right things about God, you will believe the right things about yourself and all you need will be added unto you.

APRIL 17   ...THE tongue of the wise brings healing.

Proverbs 12:18 (NIV)

TRY CONSIDERATION TO EASE TENSIONS

Once I heard a talk made by Mr. Lee Talley, then chairman of the board of Coca-Cola Company. He closed it by quoting some words of R. W. Woodruff. These words are so true and can be so helpful. I am passing them on with Mr. Woodruff's permission.

1. "The five most important words in the language are: 'I am proud of you.'

2. "The four most important words in the language are: 'What is your opinion?'

3. "The three most important words in the language are 'If you please.'

4. "The two most important words in the language are: 'Thank you.'

5. "The least important word in the language is: 'I.'"

We get so involved in the "I" until we forget the other four statements. You can make life so much happier for yourself and for others if you will try to bring to others the same consideration you desire for yourself.

1. We hunger for commendations from others. It is like water on a dry ground. Where honest effort is made, life can be made beautiful by a few words of praise.

2. Everyone feels he has some contribution to make. Few things deflate one quite so much as being ignored. We really are not determined to have our way, but we do want to have our say.

153

This is true in the family, in business, in the social group.

3. Courtesy is the lubricant of human relations. The greater your authority and prestige, the more necessary it is. We usually know we must do certain things. There is a difference in doing them because we must and in being allowed to choose to do them. "If you please" opens the door for us to respond freely even to a necessary command.

4. "Thank you," sincerely said, throws bridges of loyalty and affection across most gaps that separate people. One wonders why so little appreciation is expressed. It is easy to do and is so wonderful in its effect.

All these things you want for yourself. The place to begin is by giving them to others. There are lots of problems today in personal relations. If you are involved in tensions with other people, try giving up the demands you are making on others. Try praise where praise is due, give consideration to others, practice courtesy and express your gratitude.

You will be well on the way to loving your neighbor as you do yourself. The results will surprise and delight you.

APRIL 18   THE great Easter truth is not that we are to live newly after death - that is not the great thing - but that we are to be new by the power of resurrection...

Brooks

REFORMERS SEEK ACTION, BUT THE CHURCH HAS A DEEPER MISSION

It is not unusual for those interested in our social problems to complain that the church is not taking its proper place in seeking solutions. There is, of course, some truth in what they say. But there is not as much truth in it as some think. There is among many reformers a grave misunderstanding of the real nature of the problems and of what the church was established by Christ to do.

The church is built on certain convictions that bring it into conflict even with men who honestly seek to solve our problems of race and poverty. It seems to be self-evident to many that the church ought to give itself to any cause that men count good. The trouble is that the church sees the problems as too complicated for human wisdom to solve simply by getting men of good will together on them.

The church does not believe that it is possible to solve any human problems until there has been a change in human nature. Pride and self-interest defeat our best efforts. Sin poisons the best intentions. Until the previous problem of man's relationship to God is solved, every effort to solve his racial and economic problems will result in further problems.

It is at this point that men of good will grow impatient with the church. Their impatience is easily understood. Their cause seems so good. Talk about a prior necessity for a proper relationship to God can seem irrelevant.

The church insists that man must be reconciled to God because of the nature of man. Only as God makes men whole by the cleansing power of the shed blood of Christ can His grace operate in men and in the good efforts of men? Where men seem to bring needed reforms without the required cleansing, the church is concerned because it knows failure to be certain. The fear of the Lord is still the beginning of wisdom.

Churches must manifest the love of Christ. Where this is not a fact, judgment by God and man is in order.

But the first task of the church is to proclaim the Word of God: "For other foundation can no man lay than that is laid, which is Jesus Christ."

HOW CAN WE CURE OUR LONELINESS

Loneliness can be fatal to human happiness. It causes mental breakdown, moral collapse, cynicism, despair and, sometimes, suicide. Loneliness is not the same thing as being alone. Many people who live alone are not lonely while many that live with others are afflicted with desperate loneliness. Loneliness is being cut off from people to whom we must belong. It is a sense of isolation, of not belonging.

Some married couples live together with a wall between them. Each is lonely.

A young person is cut off from being a part of his crowd by a wall of misunderstanding. In the midst of a group, he knows crippling loneliness.

Two soldiers in a foreign land get letters from home. The wife of one tells him of her love. The other letter tells the second soldier his wife is divorcing him. The first is alone and there is pain, but he is not lonely in the deep sense of the word. The second has his whole life undermined by loneliness.

Loneliness that destroys has a deeper cause than being alone in the big city or being just a cog in a big business machine. Death that robs us of a loved one brings continuing pain but not necessarily the kind of loneliness that destroys mental balance and moral stability. Children of divorced parents almost always are damaged by the loneliness of feeling rejected or deserted. This almost never happens where parents are lost in death.

Loneliness is caused by our separation from God. We were

created to belong to God and to none other. We can truly belong to one another only as we belong first to God. Dr. Norman Vincent Peal is quoted as saying he never saw a true Christian who was lonely.

In being reconciled to God by faith in Christ, we come to know that God loves us. In this assurance we are able to love others and we are not alone.

Givers of advice often tell those who feel lonely to go to church. This is a good counsel if they find there reconciliation to God. Having found this, they will find fellowship of people bound with them in a common faith and a common affection.

The church often fails to break through the walls that separate but it remains the only cure for loneliness because here alone man faces God's love, offering to remove all barriers between God and man. Only as these barriers go down can all have fellowship one with another across all the human barriers of pride, class, sex, and race.

APRIL 20   OUR Lord has written the promise of the resurrection not in books alone, but in every leaf in the springtime.

Martin Luther

ASSURANCES FLOW IN EASTER'S WAKE

Easter has come and gone. The words "He is risen" have echoed around the world. It is a fair question to ask: "What difference does it make?" Surely anything that strikes such a worldwide response has deep meaning for people. Unless it struck a chord deep in the human heart, the observance of the season would have died long ago. Anyone interested in people must be interested in seeking to discover the reason for the response of the heart to the resurrection of Jesus Christ.

Simply put, the resurrection is the proof that Christ is the perfect revelation of God. If the cross had been the end of the story it would have left us lost indeed. Easter is the celebration of the great central fact of human history, the victory of life over death, of goodness over evil. Here in Christ we can know what God is like. Because this is true, there are some badly needed assurances about our world and about people. The first assurance is that we are at home in this universe. The Christian can sing with confidence: "This is my Father's world."

We live in the space age. The limits of our knowledge of the universe are being expanded every day. Many seem afraid of what may be found by exploring the mind of man. The bigness of it puzzles the best minds and leaves most of us in ignorance.

The Bible begins by reminding us that God made it all. In Christ, we see the kind of God who is at the heart of it. "All things were made by Him, and without Him was not anything made that was made." The everlasting arms of a loving God are around all that ever will be found in space.

Here is an invitation to the best minds of men to seek out the secrets of the universe in the assurance that they are good secrets. When all that man can do is done, we shall have only touched the hem of His garment. When man has landed on the last star, he will find a loving God waiting there to explain its mysteries.

Here is the assurance that nothing will be found that in science is beyond the control and care of the God of Jesus Christ. We will not understand much about the vast areas of space, but in Jesus Christ we can know the God who has it all in His keeping.

This is one conviction that flows from Easter.

APRIL 21 YES, each of us will give an account of himself to God.

Romans 14:21 (LB)

ACCOUNTABILITY IS THE FOUNDATION

Thomas Carlyle was asked what was his greatest thought. He replied: "My accountability to God." When David had sinned grievously he turned to God and said: "Against thee and thee only have I sinned and done this evil in thy sight." He was not unmindful of the damage he had done to those against whom he had sinned. But the fact that he had violated the holiness of God was so overwhelming that it momentarily blotted out his responsibility to men.

This thought of our accountability to God has been weakened in the secular day. Until it is restored, our moral decline will continue. We are made to have dealing with the Eternal. The moral law rests in Him as its Sustainer. We are under the divine eye, and we face an accounting before the judgment seat of Christ.

As you read this, can you honestly say that it does not find some response in your own heart? Where else is there foundation for the spirit within each of us which whispers: "I ought to be right?"

We have a great many moral problems. Let it always be remembered that these are problems of people, one by one. Some suffering soul is involved in every statistic of misfortune or sin. In each one of us, there is an inborn sense of responsibility. Even a denial is a sign it is present.

This sense of responsibility finds no resting-place until it rests in God. "I am accountable to God for all my actions" - here is the only motive that will keep us striving to do and be good. Here is the only possible foundation for community life that demands for each individual a conformity to moral law. The fact we are accountable to God is the only support for the demands of society that laws be kept.

This is our only safeguard against the tyranny of man-made law. When obligations to human demands violate our obligation to God, human law must be resisted at whatever cost. This is why political dictators always fear the church.

We are accountable to a God of judgment and mercy. If there were only judgment, no man could live with hope. It is the good news of the Gospel of Jesus that God is slow to anger and plenteous in mercy.

Our accountability to God is the frame for all our existence. Here is our security and our peace: "For we shall all stand before the judgment seat of God."

APRIL 22 **STAND up, stand up for Jesus, ye soldiers of the cross; Lift high His royal banner, it must not suffer loss.**

George Duffield, Hymn

AFTER ALL THESE YEARS, OUR WAY OF LIFE IS HELD TO BE UNLAWFUL

The Supreme Court has ruled that it is illegal to recite the Lord's Prayer and to read God's Word in the public schools. A new law has been made, not by Congress nor by the will of the people, but by a court quoting a section of the Constitution which says no such law shall be made.

It is a strange thing to some of us that it is now possible to put a man or a woman in jail for reading a passage of Scripture and saying, "Let us pray." We have been properly indignant over the suppression of religion in Communist countries. Now the reverent worship of God is banned in one of the most important segments of American life.

One almost hesitates to think where this will lead. At any rate, it is the end of an era. Those who write history can start a new chapter. Officially now, Americans who are a part of government functions must be neutral about God. This is a new direction for our country.

There are differences of opinion, and it is time for opinions to be expressed. It seems to me that to be neutral about God in education is as if a man wires his house for electricity and is neutral about the connection to the source of power. To be neutral is either not to care or it is an attempt not to get involved.

Not to care about God is fatal and every human institution is involved with God by the very fact that God exists. In Him is our only source of power and of meaning for our lives. Our relationship to God is our only support for our belief in the sacredness of personality, in human rights and in liberties. From God and His word we have received our convictions of what is moral and good. In God alone we find the final goal of all our striving.

It is the place of the home and church to teach religion. However, it is required that every man and every human institution acknowledge God. Neutrality toward God makes as much sense as neutrality toward breathing.

This legal decision will raise basic questions for every citizen who cares for his children and his country. It will disturb the mind and heart of every school administrator and teacher who regards his position as a trust from God. It will justly alarm all who believe no human institution can long endure while trying to be neutral about God. It will make almost impossible any school effort to build character. A man's character is the result of his religion and of the God he worships. You cannot have the Christian ethic and be neutral about the God of Jesus Christ.

For years, the American way of life has been a fruitful relationship of education and worship. This way of life is now changed. The results will be interesting to watch.

This is a time when we do well to pray for our country.

APRIL 23   WHAT does the Lord require of you? To act justly and to love mercy and to walk humbly with your God.

Micah 6:8 (NIV)

FOR JESUS, WE MUST FIGHT OUR BATTLE AGAINST COMPROMISE

The account of Jesus' temptation by Satan in Matthew 4:1-11 is of value to us. Here you have Christ and Satan contending for the souls of men. It is hard for us Americans to think in terms of the spirit, to believe that life is not determined by material things. We give lip service to the facts of the spiritual world but do not really take them seriously. Yet what will happen tomorrow has already been determined by the battles won or lost in our souls.

It is the heart of the Christian faith that if you seek the Kingdom of God all material things fall into place.

It is this affirmation of faith that is fought out in the temptation of Jesus. This is a real struggle as Jesus is attacked by the personal enemy of all good. It follows the high moment of His baptism when he fully committed His life to do God's will.

This is true to life. When you commit yourself as a servant to the Kingdom of God, when in a moment you see your business, your social life, as channels whereby you will serve God - at that moment the tempter strikes. All of us know what it means to be tempted, to try to do right and yet be pulled to do wrong, to try to love God and finding yourself hating God. It is hard to set yourself a high goal and follow it.

We are tempted, as Jesus was, to take care of ourselves. How can you serve God if you do not use your abilities to provide for yourself? Jesus made a point for Satan and for us, that man does not live by bread alone. If we obey God, He will take care of us. We live by every word that comes to us from God.

162

As Jesus set out to win men, Satan suggested that He could be sure of popularity by compromising with evil. Jesus replied: "Thou shalt worship the Lord thy God and Him only shalt thou serve."

In our own battle, we need to decide whether we believe Jesus or whether we believe it is better to compromise. How many times do you and I say, "I do not really approve, but-." Too many of us are more interested in what we get by our compromises than in being true to what we know Christ would have us do. How can we have moral stability in this way?

The only way you and I are going to help build the Kingdom of God is in our own lives where we live and work and play. Here we will win the battle against Satan and serve our day.

This battle goes on in every person. It is not a psychological struggle alone. It is part of the battle between Christ and Satan, Heaven and Hell, good and bad. Because Christ won we can win since He, having suffered, is able to help us if we will trust Him when we are tempted.

APRIL 24   **DO not set foot on the path of the wicked or walk in the way of evil men...turn from it and go on your way.**

Proverbs 4:14,15 (NIV)

REAL FREEDOM MUST BE SLAVERY TO AN ABSOLUTE MORAL STANDARD

Sooner or later, we who are free Americans are going to find it necessary to quit being so free. No one remains free very long. You either restrict yourself or you will be restricted by others. Freedom to do as you please never has existed as either possible or desirable for anything but the briefest time.

If we are going to remain free to choose that to which we give ourselves, we must have some absolute moral standards to which we are committed. Not only must we have them, but we must be willing to be true to them at any cost. Only thus will we escape the outward control of the social or business or government group.

Almost overnight we find ourselves without any standards of morality which are generally accepted. The Ten Commandments have become optional. The courts and the community appear more interested in an idea of personal freedom that permits the community to be flooded with immoral things than in holding to some absolute standard of right and purity.

The Bible is being bowed out of public places such as schools and courts. What then will you use as a standard for measuring character? You must have something.

Scorn is usually poured on church groups that speak out for moral standards. But what do you suggest in their place? The American Way - what is it? Jesus told some disciples that if they followed Him they would know the truth and the truth would make them free. Freedom is slavery to the right absolute moral standard.   This standard is not any code or any constitution. It is a person - Jesus Christ. He is the Word of God. He demands absolute obedience.

Here is the only freedom man can know - slavery to Christ. Deny this and sooner or later you will become the slave of man. In this obedience there is guidance in morality, business and politics. There is also freedom from all who would enslave you.

If we are interested in freedom and our American way, we had better start with some absolute standards. These standards will come alive for us only in the realm of personal loyalty - only as God becomes personal to us can we really give ourselves in obedience to Him. That we might personally respond, He came personally in Christ. He is our absolute standard for conduct.

Our freedom is a freedom to choose or reject Him. Rejection involves a loss of any absolute standard and final slavery to some human authority. Acceptance results in freedom to grow in character, wisdom and usefulness as we live to do His will.

COMMIT to the Lord whatever you do, and your plans will succeed.

Proverb 16:3 (NIV)

YOU CAN'T DO GOOD JUST BY DOING GOOD

Do you ever get really tired of doing good? Do you ever wonder why doing good often does not seem to do more good or bring more joy? There is the young person who goes into his life's work to serve others: church work, social service, medicine, or any worthy calling. Too often something happens to the ideal and discouragement gives way to cynicism. In many cases, the occupation is changed or made to serve self rather than others.

This desire to do good is deep in all of us. It is appealed to by all kinds of community enterprises. Thousands of volunteers give time and money to good causes. It does look as if more good ought to be done. It also looks to many that there ought to be more joy and less weariness in doing good than is often the experience.

It may be that we have forgotten the simple but deep truth that the good you do and the joy you get depend more on your inner life than on what you do. Really, you don't do good by doing good.

This is what Paul is saying in the famous chapter on love in I Corinthians. "I may speak in tongues of men or of angels, but if I am without love, I am a sounding gong or a clanging cymbal. I may have faith strong enough to move mountains; but if I have no love, I am nothing. I may dole out all I possess or even give my body to be burned, but if I have no love, I am none the better."

The true value of deeds depends on the goodness of the inner life and on what you are, rather than what you do. If the heart is right, the smallest deed is of great worth. If it is not right, no outward effort can be worth very much in true good or inner joy.

If we are to be of value, the instrument we use, our own life, must be clean, steady, strong, loving and faithful in the things that are best. There must be true communion with God who is the author of all good to make it so. At best we can be only channels of good - His good. Only if the channel is clear can we be used.

If you want to do good and to find joy in it, there is the demand upon you to keep close to Him in worship and in obedience to things He points out as His will for you. Make way in your life for His light and love. The results in your days and hours will be great in usefulness and in joy.

APRIL 26   **GOD is the Master Builder, His plans are perfect and pure, and when He sends you sorrow, it's part of His plan for you.**

Helen Steiner Rice

IN TIMES OF SORROW, WE NEED WELLS DOWN TO GOD'S COMPASSION

Sometime ago a family went through deep sorrow. One of the family was stricken by a fatal disease and died. There came into my possession a prayer which was used during the terrible days of agony and pain. It has been helpful to me and I pass it on, believing that it can help others in similar circumstances:

"Fix my affections on Thee, O my God. Unless Thou dost keep me I am lost. All my circumstances are beyond my control. Thou and Thou alone art my hope. Therefore, fix my affections and my trust in things of Thy power, purpose, presence, love. Help me to say, 'Thy will be done.'

"Give me a genuine desire for what Thy heart desires. Make me want what you want rather than what I want. Give me the grace of surrender.

"Make me content with the simple, miraculous, daily gifts of Thy hand: family, love, nature, people, health, job, etc. Make me loving to those who depend on me for love. Help me to see and respond to every need for love and appreciation I run across, however hidden.

"Lord, forgive me generally and specifically for my unbelief, fear, pride, selfishness, sensuousness, unrest, lovelessness, ingratitude, hypocrisy. Make me kind in word and deed, generous, honest, patient, uncritical, grateful to God and to people.

"Make me Christian enough to relax. Guide me, O Thou great Jehovah. Give me wisdom and grace to follow procedures which will bring assured guidance from Thee. Deliver me from selfishness and self-seeking which leads me to protect my own security, inner and outer.

"Fix the facts and language of the Bible in my mind, the spirit of the Word in my heart and the living Lord on the throne of my being.

"Take care of our children. Give me grace to surrender the children, myself, the future, to the God of Jesus Christ.

"These needs being met by the grace and power of Jesus Christ, make me a worthy follower of Thine. Let me do and say what needs to be done and said, and only that. Help me to desire to worship Thee and give me Thyself in it. Make me genuinely interested in other people and help me in all things to realize the real presence of the resurrected Christ."

Beneath all the exterior show of our lives, we struggle constantly with the simple realities of existence. Among these are the priceless gifts of love and affection. Where there is love, one day inevitably there will be loss. At such times we need deep wells down to the compassion of God, that the living waters of His comfort may flood our souls. Prayers like this are such wells.

APRIL 27 **DO not let this book of law depart from your mouth; meditate on it day and night, so that you might be careful to do everything written in it.**

Joshua 1:8 (NIV)

NO NATION OR PERSON ENDURES EXCEPT BY MORAL INTEGRITY

The Prophet Amos was a preacher of judgment. He did not last long as a popular preacher because he made his own people, the people of God, face the fact that they were under God's judgment. His preaching had three points: 1. Every living person owes God obedience. 2. All disobedience comes under the judgment of God. 3. There is no hope for any man or nation except in repentance to return to God.

Too many people seem to have the idea that because they are "saved" they can act as they please. They forget that they are judged for their sins. They do things they know are wrong. Conscience prods a little but they feel it doesn't make too much difference because they are Christian and God will make allowances.

They forget they cannot have God's blessing unless their faith bears fruit in their conduct. Amos told the people that because they did not produce the right kind of conduct they were going to be destroyed.

They were going to be destroyed because they had lost their moral integrity. They lost their moral integrity because God was taken from the center of their lives. They were worshippers of themselves.

No person or nation long endures without moral integrity. Moral integrity is the fruit of living in obedience to God. There is no abiding character without religious commitment, Education will not produce character. Taken by itself, the word character has no meaning. It requires an adjective, which describes the kind of character you mean. You develop a Christian character or a Moslem character or a Communist character or any other kind, according to what your commitment is. Education is but the tool of the commitment.

Juvenile delinquency is not a problem. It is a symptom of a problem; the problem of homes and society divorced from God and Christian commitment.

Corruption in government and business is not a problem but a symptom of the problem of men and institutions which try to live without having God in the center.

These things are God's judgment on us for trying to live without Him. Unless there is a return to God, these and other symptoms will destroy us. All our huge welfare programs, all our social and business and political planning, will fail to save us unless people, families and institutions become concerned again with the prior question of man's relationship to God. Out of this concern comes obedience to God's will. From this comes moral integrity and wisdom for the day.

"Seek the Lord and ye shall live." This was Amos' word to his generation and to ours. We need to become aware again that in all our difficulties we are dealing with God. By His judgement He seeks to lead us to Himself that by His forgiving grace we may be saved from the results of our sins.

APRIL 28   **I will lift up mine eyes unto the hills from whence cometh my help. My help commeth from the Lord...**

Psalm 121:1,2 (KJ)

LIGHT WILL APPEAR THROUGH DARKNESS

Sadness, loneliness and depression are emotions we all know or have known. No one escapes conditions and circumstances that seem impossible to endure and live through. "I do not see how I can go on" is an expression many of us have thought, if not said. We pray for comfort and our hearts well nigh break.

We read our Bible and the assurances seem almost mockery. The Psalmist says: "I sought the Lord and He heard me and delivered me out of all my troubles." We say we would give anything to share his certainty.

There are certain landmarks that, followed, will help lead you out of your darkness.

1. If you are in earnest in wanting to find an answer to your dark emotions of fear and loneliness and depression, you may be sure the answer will come. Your circumstances may or may not change but your reactions will. Time does not heal, but God uses time to heal if you will let Him do it. You have only to talk with people who have felt as you do to find that this is true. The assurance that your case is not hopeless is in itself helpful. God will, with the trial, make also a way of escape.

2. The giving of thanks will help bring light to your darkness. Think with God about what you have had and not about what you have lost. Whatever the cause of your trouble, there is much to be grateful for. It may be of value to make a written list.

3. It will give some comfort to seek to discover what God would teach you in your unhappy experience. You can be a finer and more useful person because you are being tested by fire. Certainly you will be more understanding of those who walk where you walk. No experience of life is wasted in God's economy. Strange strength will come to you as you ask God to use your circumstances to be of service to others.

4. Perhaps the secret door through which healing comes is that of surrender. You cannot handle your situation in your own strength and wisdom. You can surrender it to God in whose hands the future lies. In your surrender you can ask for light to see the next step. Asking, you shall receive not only light but also strength to take the step.

Our Lord has promised: "Lo I am with you always." If you will cling to this promise you will find that your way leads upward and outward. You will join the host of men and women who say with David: "Yea though I walk through the valley of the shadow of death, I will fear no evil, for Thou are with me." The Lord heard David and saved him from all his fears."

APRIL 29 **THE Lord is close to the brokenhearted and saves those who are crushed in spirit.**

Psalm 34:18 (NIV)

WHY DOES GOD LET TRAGEDIES HAPPEN?

There is no satisfying answer to the question: "Why?" No one ever fully understands tragedy. Certainly it is a common bond that ties all of us together. We join hands with those who suffer everywhere.

We must choose what we believe about the events of life that come upon us. Sooner or later, they force themselves in on us in stark reality. I choose to believe, as do most of you, that such things are not left to blind chance or impersonal fate. I believe that at the center of all life's circumstances there is God ruling and overruling even the evil things of life for His own purposes of eternal life. Such a faith does not give all the answers we would like. It does hold life together and gives to it dignity and meaning. It does make it possible to go forward in strength and in confidence.

Even as God took the stark tragedy of the cross where Jesus died and has made it a source of blessing to countless millions, so He can and will take our tragedies and use them to enlarge our own lives and to bless the lives of others.

He can use any sad event. When we are deeply stirred by emotion, there is laid on each of us an obligation to discover what we can do with our own lives to make them more useful. The Psalmist in the 90th Psalm thought of the brevity and uncertainty of life. He compared it to the grass which groweth up in the morning and in the evening is cut down. This was his prayer:

171

"So teach us to number our days, that we may apply our hearts unto wisdom."

This may well be our prayer. We are continually reminded of the frail grip we have on life. Any day may be our last day with those we love. We do well to be sure that we are not putting off until tomorrow our proper response to the privileges of this affection. Today, we have the opportunity to be the kind of person we know we should be, to do the good that offers itself to be done.

We can honor our friends best by a renewed resolve to live each day in gratitude to God as though it were our only chance to live in love and in service to our families, to our friends, to our community and to our God.

This day, we can express our gratitude to God for these who have lived among us, for the warmth of their affection, for what they have meant in making our world a finer place in which to live. The roll call of the dead is that of leaders in many areas of this city. Others will take from their hands and hearts the vision and the dedication which were theirs. They will live in memory as builders of our community. This memory will be a living encouragement to those who follow after.

APRIL 30 THE soul would have no rainbow if the eye had no tear.

Unknown

KINDNESS ARISES OUT OF MISFORTUNE

It is never possible to understand tragedy. However, it is possible to mark some of the good things that arise out of it.

Human kindness comes to the front. People do lay aside their own interests and their own pleasures and even their own problems to stand by those in distress. Few there are who have walked the dark road of suffering who have not been lifted up and literally carried along by those who stood by. There has been poured out a flood of kindness and affection.

The secret of the help such concern brings lies deeper than the things that are said and done. There is a ministry of spirit to spirit in a mystic interchange as heart touches heart. Such relationships become channels along which God's presence comes in deeper reality. As human affection offers itself in comfort, God's comfort flows through. We are helped to know the peace of God that does pass understanding.

Many hurt hearts have been made grateful in these days by kindness of people. For this good thing we can all give thanks.

There is a second good thing that can come from tragedy. Many of us have realized anew the uncertainty of life. All of us have been reminded how quickly we can lose things we value most. I am sure that there have been many who have stopped to think seriously about their own lives.

We have been given time in which to live. It is likely that there will be many who will resolve to use such time as is left to better purpose. Our inner self constantly calls us to greater faithfulness in our obligation to God and to people. Many who followed comfort and pleasure, will pay more heed to the call to noble living.

No one can tell another where such a call to faithfulness will lead. Each will know for himself and for herself. For most of us, our problem is not that we do not know. It lies in our refusal to obey the call to be our best and to do our best. Such a sense of loss as has come to us all will send us to examine how well we are fulfilling our obligations to God, to family to friends, to the community.

It is easy to get so involved in our own affairs that we fail in our kindness to others and in measuring up to the best within us. Whatever the meaning of tragedy is, it does shock us awake and set running the streams of concern and conscience.

It must be our prayer that ours shall continue to be a community of kinder and better and more useful people because tragedy has come into our midst.

MAY

MAY 1   **I, even I, am He who blots out your transgressions, for my own sake, and remembers your sins no more.**

Isaiah 43:25 (NIV)

WE ARE LOVED, FORGIVEN AND SAVED BY GOD'S PERSONAL INTERVENTION

The Christian gospel is the Good News that Heaven has come to earth.. God has invaded this wandering planet in space. Here on this earth the Divine Fire has been set to purge, cleanse, try and destroy. However big the universe seems, the fact remains that God has come - in the form of man - for the purpose of dealing personally with you and with me, whom He made in His own image.

The man who set the fire burning was a man named John whom we call "John the Baptist." He was the man, chosen for all Eternity, to set the fires burning - the fires of God's own coming into the world. He was the man, pointed to back through the centuries, as the one who would prepare the way.

As the Prophet Isaiah had written centuries before, "The voice of one crying in the wilderness, 'Prepare ye the way of the Lord, make His paths straight.'" This is what life is all about from that point to this point and continuously until Christ comes again: "That all flesh shall see the salvation of God." The meaning of the world does not center in the United States or Russia - or in any summit conference. Those things are almost incidental, and they are absolutely incidental except as they serve His coming purpose.

As the word of the Lord came to John in the wilderness, you can hear the booming surf of the Kingdom of God. You can feel the tension of the New World - waiting to be born. John came baptizing and preaching - laying the fire; preparing the way.

Do you know what John said? What did he say that was so

important that people hurried from all parts of the country to hear? What did he say that was so important that he lost his life because he said it?

All he really did was open the consciences of men to their God. With Christ, the Kingdom of God had come. It is still here. It is moving in and on through our material lives. None of us is simply dealing with each other. We are also dealing with the effect of God having come to this earth - with the power of God that comes and deals directly with the human heart and with any human situation.

As so many of us stumble along our way, it is terrifically encouraging to remember that we are not "caught" in this world. We are not subject to the blind laws of a blind chance. We are held and protected by the regularity of God's creation.

We are loved and forgiven and guided and finally saved by the direct personal intervention of God Himself. And the message of the Christian faith is the same as in centuries past. "The time is fulfilled. The Kingdom of God is at hand. Repent and believe the Gospel."

MAY 2   THE real measure of a man's wealth is what he has invested in eternity.

Unknown

PRIVILEGE, MONEY CAN BE MAN'S WORST PERILS TO PEACE, ETERNITY

The standard of living has become the god of the world. It is true in America as well as Russia. We are constantly trying to live better but the word "better" applies mainly to money rather than morals. We call a man with money a success and a man without money a failure. We raise our children to make a good living rather than to live the good life. We are more interested in their social contacts than in their contact with God.

In our obsession with things, we do well to at least hear from another side of the question. Jesus Christ has a good deal to say about people who majored in their standard of living. He said, time and again and in many ways, that money is man's greatest danger. He said that a man's life does not consist of the abundance of things that he possesses. He told a story of a man who could think of nothing to do with his accumulating possessions but hoard them in larger bins. He noted that the man was to die a lost soul.

He said it was as hard for a rich man to enter the Kingdom of Heaven as for a camel to pass through the eye of a needle. He told of a rich man named Dives, who lived as though the beggar Lazarus did not exist, and it cost him his soul. Jesus never said it was wrong to have money. He did constantly point out that it easily generates pride and conceit, which destroy the soul. A dollar gets between a man and God more easily than anything else does.

Nearly every nation that has fallen in history has first rotted out inside because of the life of ease and luxury which destroys character. Communism made its greatest stride where men and women of privilege and money failed to see the poor at the door.

Paul said the love of money is the root of all evil. In our land we do well to think about this whole matter. Life is more than food and raiment. Real life exists at another level altogether. It exists at the spiritual level of love and mercy and kindness and truth and beauty and honor. Those who seek these things first may never make much money. To those who seek the things of the spirit, money ceases to be a major concern.

No one denies the value of material things in their place. Their place, however, is second to spiritual values. Christ's admonition, "Seek ye first the Kingdom of God and His righteousness and all these things shall be added," is the only true guide to abundant living. To build your life, your family, your nation on a material standard of living is to ensure failure. To surrender all to God to be used according to His will is to find the way of life.

176

MAY 3   WELL done is better than well said.

Ben Franklin

LIP SERVICE ISN'T ENOUGH - WE MUST LIVE BY OUR IDEALS, TOO

There is much concern today over the various threats to our way of life. Everyone seems to agree that we ought to know more about the enemies that threaten us. However, you do not build character in a person by attention to the things that destroy character. You build character by giving yourself to those things that are builders of character. You also build a society and a nation by loyalty to the things that make people strong.

Lip service to spiritual values and high ideals without commitment of life only helps our enemies destroy us as individuals and as a people. Hence, it is important that anyone who is really interested in being helpful today take seriously the things that are positive.

The Hebrew prophet Micah spoke to this point. His people were faced with strong enemies. Their situation was more dangerous than ours. Assyria was a conquering world power knocking at their gates. What was worse, there was among people general moral decline and dishonesty was rampant in official life. Family life was breaking down and immorality was growing. Micah told his nation - and is telling us - that there are certain moral laws underlying the structure of society. To ignore them is to make sure the structure will collapse.

Micah made it plain that religious observances without moral living is of no value. "Will the Lord be pleased with thousands of rams or with ten thousands of rivers of oil? He hath showed thee, O, man, what is good: and what doth the Lord require of thee, but to do justly and to love kindness and to walk humbly with thy God? (Micah 6:7,8)

The deepest and most profound patriotism is found among those who try to do right, who seek to deal kindly with all with whom they come into contact and who trust God and worship Him faithfully. Here, character is built. Upon such character, and only upon such character, is a strong nation built.

Each one of us is in the front lines in the battle for survival. This has always been true. But the real battle is in the soul of each of us. If we lose our personal battle, we make it harder for the victory to be won, regardless of what we do otherwise.

Somewhere among us there must arise a new crusade. It must be a crusade to make central in all our thinking and doing, as individuals and as groups, the hard matter of doing the right thing, of dealing kindly with all people and of walking humbly with God.

Unless this crusade meets with success all others will fail.

MAY 4   BE joyful in hope, patient in affliction, faithful in prayer.

Romans 12:12 (NIV)

IN WEAKNESS, A CRIPPLE IS STRONG

There is in my possession a little rolling pin carved out of mahogany. It is about one and a half inches long. It is the gift of a man I recently met. He lives in a home for the aged and is partially helpless. It is not an attractive place. Years ago it was a TB hospital; then it lay idle. Now it is a rest home. The ancient wooden cottages with connecting covered walks present very little in the way of beauty.

The man who gave me the little rolling pin is probably around 50 years old. It is not easy to tell because he is crippled and completely confined to a wheel chair, his legs being useless. He has no immediate family. He showed me a lamp he is carving from a piece of mahogany bedpost. There were small ships carved out of a large piece of driftwood someone had brought Him. All this is the more remarkable since my new friend is completely blind in addition to his other handicaps and difficulties.

On being introduced, his happy spirit almost startled me. It was raining outside and drab within the room. Literally, he radiated sunshine and good cheer. You got the impression that it came from the center of his being. As he talked and showed me his carvings, he made me feel completely at ease.

I told him how remarkable his work was. I really meant his spirit was remarkable. His reply was that he really didn't do it all. God did. He went on to say that God has promised us always a way of escape from the trials that come upon us and that this gift of carving is God's fulfilling the promise to him.

Every Sunday friends come and carry him, chair and all, to a church. He had never moved his letter to the church because he was afraid that people would think he was seeking sympathy. One day he was convinced by a friend that his way of living in the midst of difficulty was giving to others more than anyone could ever give to him.

I am grateful for meeting this man. We live a long way from one another and shall probably not meet again. But I shall keep this little rolling pin with its message of the power of Christian faith to supply our every need. At times nearly all of us need encouragement in faith and in well doing. At such times, we are especially grateful for those who, under the pressure of great trouble, have lived with radiance and victory because they trusted the Lord.

If there is someone upon whom you have leaned because in their weakness they were strong, be sure and tell them so if it is not too late. It will add to their happiness and to your own.

This column is in tribute to all of you who, in any kind of darkness, let your light shine before men.

MAY 5 THIS is what the Lord says to you: "Do not be afraid or discouraged for the battle is not yours but God's."

II Chronicles 20:15 (NIV)

WE PLAY OUT OUR LITTLE ROLES TRYING TO HIDE THE BATTLE WITHIN

Are you having any luck living as you want to live and being the kind of person you want to be? We put on quite a front for people we live among. We play out our little roles, trying always to hide the battle that rages within. Because the other people also put up a front, we take for granted that they fight no battles. All the time they take for granted that we glide smoothly along. So we are cut off from talking honestly with one another and we fight our battles largely alone.

You have heard much about living by law. "Law-abiding" has come to be a great public virtue. We do more or less honestly try, but keeping all the laws of the community and of nature and of God is a task well beyond our powers. A spirit of lawlessness leads us astray just when we talk the loudest about keeping the law.

We really mean to live in love with other people. It is not too hard to know what this means but, it sure is hard to do, even when we try our best. Other people just don't respond to our effort as we think they should and we become irritated. We find ourselves striking out at those about us in ways contrary to love.

We know that we should not be selfish and self-indulgent. We promise ourselves every day we will try to be thoughtful of others and put service above self. But we also know that we do not do a very good job of it. We are so centered in ourselves until it is impossible to leave self behind. We try to take comfort in comparing ourselves with others but it doesn't help much since we know ourselves too well. We drive ourselves trying to do better, trying to still the inner voice that refuses to be fooled by our efforts. We wear ourselves out doing good or trying to pay for not being good.

Sooner or later we cry with Paul, "Who shall deliver me from the body of this death." He found the answer when he found you cannot be good by your own efforts. The miracle of God's grace lies in the gift of Christ who lives in those who accept Him, and are willing by faith to live in Him. He forgives our sorry failure. He takes our frail efforts to be good and to be loving and He helps us grow in our ability to succeed in these efforts. Best of all, when God looks at us in our weakness and sin, He acts towards us as though we were good and loving because Christ lives in us.

Living by this faith is not easy, but it is far easier than trying to live without it.

MAY 6　　**AND we urge you brothers help the weak...always try to be kind to each other?**

I Thessalonians 5:14,15 (NIV)

FAITH TAKES CARE OF THOSE IN NEED

We do a lot of talking about religion and the influence of our Christian faith. In our community there is a group of people who put faith into action in an inspiring way. I know of nothing like it in our area. I would pay tribute to it on its anniversary and it cannot be better done than by using quotations from a brochure written by Dr. William Huck, the first executive director of the Atlanta Union Mission.

"The Atlanta Union Mission was born on May 22 in the year 1942. This was the result of many months of prayer. The large number of alcoholics, drug addicts, those just released from jails and penitentiaries, the transients passing through the city, older people with physical disabilities, all of whom lost their families, their jobs, their friends, were resulting in wasted manhood."

"We had to operate entirely by faith. Not a single pledge was made to work. There were 32,706 beds provided to homeless men and 23,663 meals were served during the first year. Many a time during the early years the 'cupboard was bare' and hungry men were waiting for something to eat. Never once when the bell rang for meals were we without food. Invariably someone, or some company, would send us sufficient food for that day."

"This last sentence describes the story for its twenty years. It covers the paying of indebtedness on the old location on Crew Street. It covers the providing of more than $225,000 for buying, remodeling and furnishing of the present quarters on Ellis Street. Such faith has provided in the first 20 years 1,198,836 meals for the hungry and clothing is furnished when needed. Medical care is available. Support comes in response to faith. "We do not ask, nor do we receive, any support from the Community Fund. We operate entirely by faith and prayer. We do not make any citywide appeal for funds. Yet God has supplied our minimum needs." So writes Dr. Huck. So it has been.

Again in this brochure: "The heart of our work is religious. We have two religious services every day. Every night since the Mission was organized we have held a service in which men are invited to participate. It is good to put a new suit on a man. It is much better to put a new man in a suit."

MAY 7   IT is one thing to go through a crisis grandly, but another thing to go through every day glorifying God, when there is no witness, no limelight, no one paying the remotest attention to us.

Oswald Chambers

GOD WILL LET YOU MASTER PRESSURE

Where are you going in such a hurry? What's the rush? For a few minutes sit quietly and try to give some answers to these questions.

The effort will help you get control of your life. Life for many is a mad tumble from one demand to another. Pressure is heavy upon us and we are rushing around because so many things have to be done - the business must be attended to or the children must be driven here and there or the civic and social obligations must be met. A flood we cannot control carries us along and the sum total of it all leaves us worn out. It also leaves many with a feeling of utter futility.

As everything gets bigger and faster and more complicated, we get more and more lost in so far as our feeling of personal worth is concerned.

There must be an answer. The answer will not come from a lessening of the pressure. This pressure is a part of our revolutionary day. The answer can come only as each of us finds it in our own lives.

We were created by God to be masters of the pressures of life instead of their slaves. As obedient children of God, Adam and Eve were given dominion but they became slaves when they lost God. The answer to the pressures of life lies in the direction of the rediscovery of our proper relationship to God.

The answer is really found in opening our hearts to God, who loves us and seeks us in our lost state. God is in Christ seeking the lost. In Christ, God becomes so real that we become again the obedient children of God. As we seek to do His will and serve His glory, the pressures of life are eased. The manifold duties of life take on meaning as God touches them with divine purpose. Still having to lead busy lives, we are free men and women under God and not slaves of circumstance.

All this many sound impractical as a solution to your frustrated life, but it is not as impractical as you may think. Spend time each day obeying God as He says: "Be still and know that I am God." See the Bible as the record of His pursuing love. Dwell on His promises of forgiveness and of personal concern for you. In these moments think through your day in terms of His will for your life. Believe that by His spirit He will guide you if you are willing to do His will.

Walking in these directions, the burden of your pressures will fall away. You may be as busy as ever but into your life will come a deep conviction of divine purpose. Confidence in yourself will grow as your confidence in God grows.

MAY 8   BUT I trust in your unfailing love; my heart
             rejoices in your salvation. I will sing to the
             Lord, for He has been good to me.

                                     Psalm 13:5,6 (NIV)

SOME PEOPLE ARE FRIGHTENED WHEN THEIR PROBLEMS RUN OUT

Two people in the last week have presented an unusual problem: that of the person who is getting along well. These people are disturbed by their good fortune. One said he had lost no loved ones and had no real financial difficulties, and his family's health was good. He feels guilty being fortunate in the face of so much misfortune. A young married woman said: "What is coming? All goes so smoothly. We have relatively so few problems compared to those of other people. She and her husband are happy, they have not had all the "adjustments" they were warned about, but strange to say, it worries them a bit.

The problem presented by these two people is not unusual. Many things contribute to such feelings. Human nature is complicated. One of its darker threads is what seems to be a tendency to resist getting along well. Some people seem to do things to themselves to destroy their well being. These feelings are encouraged by the way we do things today. We approach everything as a problem - problem-solvers are a dime a dozen in every area of life. If you do not have a problem you are regarded as a little strange, so the person who is getting along well feels he has a problem.

Certain suggestions may help you if you are getting along all right.

1. Since the goal of problem-solvers is to help people get rid of their problems, you can at least regard yourself as normal.

2.   The secret of any help you will get is in the proper relation of your life to God. This is as true of the person doing well as of the person in trouble. The person doing well is tempted to feel himself responsible for his good fortune. Pride and arrogance come easily to some who are free of difficulties. If we gratefully realize that all things come from God and humbly accept them as undeserved gifts, we will be led toward peace. This will save you from any feeling of false superiority.

3.   A real surrender of ourselves and our circumstances to God for His use is a further step along the road. This is as true of our good fortune as of our tragedies. God uses people in their misfortune. He also waits to do great things through people to whom He has given the privileges of health and material advantages.

4.   We all need to accept the forgiveness of God that our guilt may be taken away. A general feeling of guilt oppresses everyone. We know we do not deserve our good things. Then there is guilt for our specific mis-doings. God will take all this away if we will trust Him. This is the heart of the Christian Gospel in which Christ takes our sin upon Himself.

5.   It will help wonderfully to live with our family, our friends and our community in gratitude to them for all they mean as instruments of the good that is ours. In service to them, we find channels for useful and happy living.

MAY 9   **but a woman that feareth the Lord, she shall be praised.**

Proverbs 31:30 (KJ)

WHY THEY RISE AND CALL HER BLESSED

A short time ago I was shown a Bible used by a godly woman over a period of some years. In front and back she had noted the dates when she had read through it. She had the habit of selecting one verse of the Bible as her guide for a certain period, and there was a long list of verses and the dates of their use. The Bible was the authority for this woman's life. She knew where to go for assurance, for guidance, for comfort, for strength. Thousands of children and adults whom she taught the things of God remember her with gratitude. She accepted life's sorrows with grace and bore a long illness with uncomplaining cheerfulness. At every point in her life she was constructive. She was firm in her convictions and charitable in her judgements. Her life can be explained only by the work of God's spirit in response to her faithfulness to God's word.

In these troubled times, the Bible is still a sure foundation on which to build a life. The spirit of God will mold any life that takes God's word as the center of authority.

The average person is confused today by all the things that are happening. Revolution is everywhere. The Bible gives the assurance of God's presence in and through all that is happening. This assurance is grounded in the creation account in the first chapter of Genesis and runs as a golden thread to the very end of Revelation.

The Bible is a sure authority for our conduct. It will give you guidance for your daily living. The Ten Commandments, the Sermon on the Mount, the prophets - all the Bible - will be a true light on your path if you will let it. The rebellion today against authority is not new and is no more destructive than it has been in the past. Obedience to God's Word still produces the good life and rebellion still produces death.

To those who trust the authority of God's word there is given strength and comfort for the day, whatever it brings. We all join the common caravan of needy, suffering humanity. The difference lies in the resource we have to meet what comes. Fidelity to the Bible makes the difference.

IT is written, man shall not live by bread alone, but by every word of God.

Luke 4:4 (KJ)

THE BIBLE AND US

A few years ago there was a release from the American Bible Society which noted that Anatoly Rudenko was the Director of the newly formed Bible Society of the Soviet Union. At one time, because of his faith in Christ, he served time in a KGB psychiatric clinic "to bring him in conformity with the rest of society."

Recently, he was invited to present Bibles to the police of Moscow's Center of Criminal Administration. There were 500 present and Rudenko was explaining how the Bibles would be distributed and he asked them to sit calmly while he explained. The Deputy Director spoke out: "How can I sit calmly and wait for the Bible. I will come up right now and get a copy from you. We must show mercy to our brethren. Give me some Bibles we can share now, please." In the Soviet Union the churches are open and Bibles are in demand.

How is it with people in our land, especially with Christians? Are we reading the Bible? A college student became interested in referring to the Bible. Although from a Christian home, he did not have one at school and he could not find one among 75 young men in his fraternity house. How general is this? Does this matter or is the Bible an option? Or is it a necessary power source for the foundation upon which a life must be built? Is the Bible only something to learn about or is it the channel of the power of God? As we remember the beginnings of our nation, it is only dimly recalled how the early communities gathered around the church and the school as their center and the family Bible was the center of the home and formed much of the material of schoolroom text books. All this laid foundations upon which our nation was built and which supported the brave people who pressed ever westward.

If you are at loose ends in your life, if you are morally adrift and seek a better way, if you have lost the sense of the meaning of your life and of your society...if you are lost and know it, give God a chance through the Bible. Read it as you read any book with the honest prayer: "God if you have something to say to me, speak to my spirit by your Spirit." Try this an hour a day for two months. For encouragement in doing so, read Isaiah 55:6-13 and Hebrews 4:12. It is likely that you will not want to stop as you experience the changes that take place within you.

In all the shaking and turmoil of our day, God is working His will and His purpose. It may be time to get to know Him better.

MAY 11 **AND so I am giving a new commandment to you now -- love each other just as much as I love you. Your love for each other will prove to the world that you are my disciples.**

John 13:34 (TLB)

LIFE'S ONLY REAL NEED IS LOVE: LOVE OF SELF,
OF GOD, AND OF OUR NEIGHBOR

Jesus put His hand upon the "Pulse of Life"as He dealt with a man who came to ask Him, "What is the first commandment of all?" He put His hand upon the center of life when he began to talk about love. In your life and mine there is only one thing we really need, and that is love. Life shrivels and dies when love is absent. The strange thing is that despite the fact that it is the only thing we really need, there is so much hatred and viciousness in the world, especially when we think of other people who are not like us. Even in the family, where God has so planned it that love may have full sway, there is so much bitterness, so many barriers and so much unhappiness.

Jesus said that the first commandment had to do with love and there are three parties to it: God, yourself and your neighbor. "Thou shalt love God with every part of your life, heart, soul, mind and strength." It means simply bringing to God the life that we live, the achievements of our mind, the achievements of our heart, the strength of our lives and just offering them to His glory and living for Him.

The second commandment is that thou shalt love thy neighbor as thyself. We forget that at the heart of that commandment is ourself. It is as difficult to love ourself as it is to love our neighbor. It is not easy to like ourselves because we know ourselves so well. We know that every apparently noble act has a black thumbprint on it; that every apparently beautiful flower that grows out of our lives has a crushed petal. Yet we cannot love God or our neighbor until we love ourself. So Christ said, "Love your neighbor as yourself." He did not say to love your neighbor at the expense of yourself. He said to give to your neighbor the same consideration you give to yourself.

Then He talks about your neighbor. In the Christian faith and in your life, your neighbor is everybody, particularly those who are unfortunate, particularly those who are in need: of every race, of every class, of every kind -the rich and the poor. In the circle of your life, He invites you to love others as you love yourself. I am quite sure that some of the things that are said by people who feel themselves to be Christian could not be said if they honestly faced the implications of Christian love. We are invited to love - to love God with all our hearts and to love our neighbor and ourselves. Now, how are you going to do it? In your own right you cannot do it. The only way that love can ever be born in the human heart is to have that human heart really stand before the Cross of Christ until we come to understand what God is doing here as He gives Himself in love to us.

IF any of you lacks wisdom, he should ask God, who gives generously to all without finding fault, and it will be given to him. But when he asks, he must believe...

James 1:5,6, (NIV)

THE WISEST OF US KNOW VERY LITTLE

It is an humbling experience to walk into a library. Will Rogers once noted that we are all ignorant and differ only in that we are ignorant about different things. It was recently said that in certain branches of science, knowledge about them gained 10 years ago is now a handicap rather than a help.

A commencement speaker once made the point rather vividly to a class of graduates of a professional school. He said there certainly was a measurable difference between what they knew and what a moron knew. He pointed out, however, that there is not too much difference between what they did not know and what a moron did not know.

With all that we know, we really are not as smart as we pretend to be. When you get through all that is written about our social problems, one discovers areas of vast ignorance. Delinquency, crime, alcoholism, mental illness, immorality, war - these are all personal and social problems in which our ignorance far out-runs our knowledge.

At a different level, we live out our days, not knowing what is going to happen to us the next second or minute or hour or day. Whether we know it or not, all of us live dangerously all the time.

It is hard for me to understand how a person can be conceited. We do need help along the way. In the kind of world in which we live, we need help to provide the simplest necessities of life. We do not know how. We are dependent on others for nearly all we use. It should make us humble and grateful.

With all our self-assurance and supposed knowledge, we are still dependent on people about us for affection and love. We cannot provide these things for ourselves. We do not know enough, nor shall we ever, to supply the deep things that the affection of friends and loved ones supplies. We can only humbly and gratefully receive.

Surely most people feel a need for God. Here our ignorance is at its greatest height. The knowledge of man finds it hard to scale the walls of the knowledge of God. We do know only in part and we do see through a glass darkly. We are dependent on what God sees fit to reveal of Himself. As He gives us light to walk through His word and the Holy Spirit, we can only be humbly grateful.

In this day of supposed knowledge and of pride in man's work, we do well to face the fact that we know very little. We need people and God. We can have them only as they give themselves. Let us receive them in humility and in gratitude.

MAY 13   **FOR since the creation of the world God's invisible qualities - his eternal power and divine nature - have been clearly seen...**

Romans 1:20 (NIV)

HOW DO YOU LOOK AT HISTORY? IS MAN OR GOD AT THE CENTER?

It makes a difference what we think about history, about events as they have occurred and as they are occurring all about us. As you read through the Bible you find part of human history at every point. It has been hammered out of the blood and tears and sacrifice of men and women who have lived as citizens of their communities down through the ages.

You can decide one of two things about history. The first choice you have is that history is simply the record of man on his own, that man is the center of life and that everything flows out of him and revolves around him. It seems that most of our lives are determined today by this kind of an idea of history. It is not only in Russia that men believe that events have taken place because of these human centered principles. Much of America's belief is in the same vein.

There is a second view: the Christian interpretation of history. The Christian interpretation says very simply that at the heart of all that happens is a sovereign God, that the events of life and the events of history have at their center not man, but God.

The Bible takes for granted from the beginning to the end that no man and no nation can live in rebellion against God and the Bible takes for granted that all of history: Egypt, Assyria, Babylon, Persia, Greece, Rome, the Holy Roman Empire, Germany, Russia and here in America, all of it has only one purpose, and only one meaning: that it is the story of man's rebellion and of God's determination to save man and that everything that happens has its meaning within that drama.

Accepting the Christian view of history will do certain specific things for you. It will enable you to read the newspapers without panic because you can believe that whatever is there and however it may appear, however wild evil suddenly seems to become and however deep tragedy seems to have fallen, you can believe that underneath it and around it and in it is a sovereign God, who has so loved the world that He gave Himself for it and that somehow, somewhere, these things will work out for good. It enables meaning and purpose to come into life.

So it is that in this day, when everything seems shaken loose from its moorings, perhaps we need most the same message that God sent to Judah by the Prophet Isaiah, when God said, "Go and say unto the cities of Judah, 'Behold! Your God!'" And so God would say to us today: Behold your God!

192

MAY 14 WHERE there is hatred - let me sow love.
Where there is injury - pardon.
Where there is doubt - faith.
Where there us darkness - light.
Where there is despair - hope.
Where there is sadness - joy.

St. Francis of Assisi

EVERYONE CAN DO SOMETHING TO HELP

"What can I do to help?" This is a question asked by those who are concerned about the many problems that trouble us. There are more of us talking about the problems than there are pointing out ways they can be solved. "Viewing with alarm" is easier than suggesting definite ways to help.

There are some things anyone can do to help:

1. We need to realize that no one of us can do something about everything. You and I cannot save the world. Each one of us has a limited area in which we can work.

2. We need to realize that there are people who want to be helpful in every area of life. We are not alone in our desire to be useful. We can trust others to be as dedicated in their area of life as we are in ours.

3. Hence, each of us needs to limit his energies and devotion to those areas in which he finds himself.

4. We need to believe that one person can be valuable. Problems finally break down into individuals in trouble. One person helping those around him sets going influences that spread in ever-widening circles.

5. At the heart of any confidence we may have, there must be a faith

in God who is the source of our desire to be useful. It is God who is first interested in seeking and saving the lost, in comforting those in sorrow, in feeding the hungry and in strengthening the weak, in healing the sick and in releasing the oppressed. In every desire and in every effort of our lives, we follow in His footsteps.

6.   This being true, we can do what we can in the confidence that God will, by His Spirit, take our efforts and unite them to those of others and give them success according to His will.

7.   Our usefulness really centers in the way we live. Our concern for public problems will be useless unless it is based on honest efforts to do what we can where we are. Our first attack on juvenile delinquency is in training our own children by example and precept. Are we what we want our children to become? Our first attack on the immorality of our day is at the point of our conduct: the books we read, the movies we support, the language we use, the people we count as our friends. Our first attack on the godlessness of our day is in our faithfulness to God's Word and God's Church.

8.   Beginning at places such as these, we will be open to wider areas of usefulness and greater fruitfulness in our life. Your own answer to the question 'What can I do?' will become evident.

MAY 15   SUBMIT to God and be at peace with Him; in this way prosperity will come to you.

Job 22:21 (NIV)

EARTHBOUND RICHES ARE A DELUSION

Jesus called attention to the fact that it is hard for them that trust in riches to enter the Kingdom of God. Riches upon which we are tempted to depend, come in many forms. In the first place, in this prosperous land of ours we are all so surrounded by material things that they threaten to choke us. It is hard to think of anything we really need. Yet we continue to spend our money for more things that we are led to believe will add to our happiness. What they add is the crowded condition of our homes and offices. The closets are crowded, the rooms are full, the driveways are congested, yet we are no nearer the Kingdom than before we bought our last gadget.

Surrounded by a multitude of material possessions, we are easily tempted to believe that God is optional. We are led to depend on material things to bring us satisfaction. The necessity for God becomes a dim unrest somewhere in our souls. We cannot quite escape God but we don't trust Him either. We rather feel God to be optional, to be taken or left.

There are also the riches of culture and good will. We find ourselves depending on these things to make a good world. We are tempted to trust ourselves and thus to act nicely and to do the right thing. This is true in the family, the neighborhood, the nation and the world. God is not taken very seriously. He is considered by many to be an option which we can take or leave without affecting the results one way or another.

Truly it is hard for those that trust in riches of any kind to enter into the Kingdom of God. It is hard because this is not the road to the Kingdom. By the very fact and nature of our creation, God stands at the very center of all of life. He is not an option. He is a necessity for all who would live richly. Knowledge, goodness and material things are created and given by God to be used for His glory and according to His will. Only as we put our trust in Him to provide fullness of life is such a life possible. Trusting riches is a snare and delusion.

We shall continue to flounder until we learn to take God seriously in worship and in obedience.

BUT if you seek the Lord your God, you will find Him if you look for Him with all your heart and with all your soul.

Deuteronomy 4:29 (NIV)

DO YOU REALLY BELIEVE IN GOD?

A man recently told me of a sermon preached by the Roman Catholic Archbishop in Atlanta. It impressed him greatly. The sermon had to do with the question, "Do you really believe in God?"

The sermon set my friend to thinking and our conversation set me to thinking. This matter of faith in God is a starting point of religion. If you believe that God is involved in your personal daily life, it will affect every part of your existence. If you do not believe that God is dealing with you and with your affairs, then you will find all that is said and written about religion to be of small interest.

As you move about among people you find a strange mixture of concern about God and an indifference to Him. You get the feeling that they would welcome Him if He were to come charging into the situation in some dramatic way, yet nothing much is expected. People even pray for His presence and then, hearing no answer, go on their way alone.

However, we do not go our way with any real confidence. We are constantly looking over our shoulder to see if God is looking or maybe following us. Such a mixture of belief and unbelief gives life a strange uneasiness. It keeps us apologizing for the kind of people we are and the kind of lives we lead.

One by one, each of us is aware that we have dealings with God. It is hard to get away from this inner voice. God does not leave Himself without a witness. Off by ourselves, we know far better than we admit how we ought to act. We know that our failures have to do with something more than our own mind or the demands of society.

We know what David meant when he said to God: "Against Thee and Thee only have we sinned."

We deal with God but we also deal with our own ambitions and with the demands of the world of which we are a part. These ambitions and demands require us to do things contrary to our inner conviction of what we ought to do. We yield to these pressures and we act as though God did not really exist for us. We pattern our lives by the idols of our ambitions and of the world's standards.

You can see this in the thoughts of your own heart, in the conversation of your friends, in the conduct of all of us in our homes, businesses, in politics, and in social parties. You can see it in the carelessness of the majority in the matters of the public worship of God, in family worship, in private devotions, in our keeping of Sunday.

The place to start any change in ourselves and in our unhappy world is with an honest answer to the question: "Do I believe in God as the central fact of my life?"

MAY 17   **I am sorry for the men who do not read the Bible every day. I wonder why they deprive themselves of the strength and of the pleasure.**

Woodrow Wilson

HOW SHOULD YOU READ THE BIBLE? THINK OVER THESE 5 SUGGESTIONS

When we feel the need for help and support not found in the things of this world, the Bible will be of interest. Coleridge said of the Bible: "It finds me." Each of us is somewhere in its pages and it speaks to our need. It leads to forgiveness for sin, comfort for sorrow, strength in weakness, guidance in confusion. It leads to God.

"How to read the Bible?" seems to present a problem to many.

Here are some suggestions I hope will be helpful.

1. Any profitable reading of the Bible takes decision. You won't find much help if you read it only when you feel like it. No one does anything worthwhile if he acts only from his feelings. The housewife, the businessman, the student, the athlete would all fail if guided only by feelings. This is true of this important matter of bringing your life into contact with God by reading your Bible. Decide to read it regularly and then do it.

2. Read your Bible with a fair open mind. Let it speak for itself. Put aside your doubts and your intellectual difficulties. The fact that the Bible is God's Word for you will be proved to you only as God's Spirit speaks to you as you read it. Arguments about the Bible convince few people. The proof is in what happens to you as you read it.

3. Read the Bible expecting something to happen. All around you are people who have found in the Bible the help you seek. You are following the footsteps of untold millions who bear witness to the truth of the promise, "Seek and ye shall find." When you plug in your radio you expect something to happen. When you connect your life to God's presence in the Bible, you can reasonably expect something to happen.

4. Read your Bible with a willingness to follow where it leads. As you read, you will be reminded of things you ought to do and of things you ought not to do. Obey these readings as they become clear to you. For each person these things will be different. As you obey in the definite leadings of God's Spirit, His presence will become more real.

5. Read your Bible intelligently. If you receive a six-page letter from a friend, you don't read a line here or there over a period of a month, yet we try to read the Bible this way too often. We read a short story or an article from beginning to end. Try reading your Bible in the same way. Read one of the Gospels straight through. Mark passages that appeal to you. Do the same with Paul's letters. Do the same with the Old Testament narratives and prophets and poems.

As you read, one day the printed page will flow with the living, personal presence of God as the Holy Spirit whispers in your heart:

MAY 18   THE earth is the Lord's and everything in it: live in it; for he founded it upon the seas and established it upon the waters.

Psalm 24:1,2 (NIV)

GOD IS THE ANSWER TO OUR CONFUSION

What is going to result from all of our disorder and tension? How is it going to work out: the racial strife, the growing confusion among the executive, legislative, and judicial branches of our government, the moral decline among our people, the growing conflict between interest groups, the rising tide of revolution in our world? Where is the end to the increasing speed and pressure felt by the individuals as they seek to make a living and to make a home?

Do we not know what we want personally and as a group? Are we just victims of great impersonal forces over which we have no control? Are we just lifeless logs being carried end over end downstream? Is there no power anywhere working in it all, curbing the evil, supporting the good, moving toward an end and a goal that will make it all make sense?

If the answer to this last question is "no," we are of all men most miserable. About the best we can do is to study our problems, use big words to describe them, pit our puny solutions and strength against the insolvable problems and pass our failures down to the next generation. The problems of war, revolution, big business, big government and moral delinquency of children and adults are too big for the vocabulary and the human efforts of science, psychology, sociology, economics, politics or welfare. There is a fatal flaw in human nature that makes it impossible for man to save himself.

The Christian faith affirms that God is involved in our world and in the life of each individual.   No person need ever be at the mercy of impersonal forces. No group or nation is left to work its will

199

outside the will of God. The ability of evil to destroy and to win was forever broken by the death of Christ on the cross. He moves in resurrected power to lead humanity to its final goal, which is the Kingdom of God, where all do His will in love.

Such faith gives to every person a goal and a purpose for living to all who accept the goal. It gives a confidence that never dies to those who live in faith. It gives a meaning to life that makes every experience of suffering, sorrow and even death bearable, because God is in it and will use it by His grace.

Such faith gives to all who seek to solve our problems the assurance that they are not alone, but are the servants of God who moves in and through them to work His good pleasure.

MAY 19   IF you want to pray better, pray more

Mother Teresa

PRAYER IS THE STARTING POINT FOR SOLVING ALL OUR PROBLEMS

There is no shortage of problems. There is also no shortage of people working to solve our problems. There are people of good will giving themselves to make life better. There is scarcely a problem of physical weakness, of moral breakdown, of economic need, of social disorder, of mental illness or of political disorder that does not have people striving intelligently and sacrificially to meet it. In spite of all these efforts, our problems seem to grow faster than our solutions.

I want to suggest that part of the reason for our seeming failure to meet the needs of our day lies at the door of us who are members of the Christian community. We have failed our day because we have failed to pray as we should. It is hard to understand why there has not arisen in the Christian Community a great tide of prayer. You can get fewer people to an announced meeting for prayer than for any other kind of religious gathering.

In a letter to his friend Timothy, Paul wrote: "I exhort therefore that first of all supplications, prayer, intercessions, and giving of thanks be made for all men: for kings and for all that are in authority that we may lead a quiet and peaceable life in all godliness and honesty."

Paul made it clear that prayer is the starting point in solving our problems. He calls on the Christian community to begin with prayer because of what it believes. We believe, or claim to believe, that there is one God of all who has personally involved Himself in our world. He is present, working His will in the affairs of men. This is the message of our Bible from start to finish. The Bible also makes it clear that the prayers of men are a vital part in the affairs of men.

As a Christian community, we also believe that God works in the affairs of men to redeem man. There is one mediator between God and men, the man Christ Jesus, who wants all men to be saved. Wherever men of good will work to serve the needs of men, God is there to give power to their efforts. God moves always to save the lost, to heal the sick, to bring order out of confusion. Again, our Bible makes it clear that the prayers of men are a vital factor in God's work of saving men and of solving their problems.

Man's problems cannot be solved without God working in and through our efforts. All through our Bible it is made clear that God does His saving work as men saturate their efforts with prayer.

Who will surround our troubled world with prayer if we do not? Our greatest service in this day can be our prayer that the Christian community may be given the spirit of prayer. Otherwise our problems will continue to grow faster than our solutions.

Robert Lowery, Hymn

IF YOU FEEL THE NEED OF GOD, YOU'RE ON WAY THE TO FINDING HIM

Faith in God is offered as the way by which we can have a personal experience of God's presence to save us and to help us. It is not easy to keep God's face in focus. We get so involved in the details of daily living. It is increasingly hard just to do things that have to be done each day. They tire us out mentally and physically. We find it hard to think about God in all the rush.

We are constant victims of propaganda from all directions. Promoters are busy drumming up support for all kinds of causes. They keep us depressed by their sad tales of need; exhausted by their ideal solutions and guilty because we don't want to do what they make us think ought to be done. Driven by all the man-made schemes of salvation, God seems to dim out on us.

Conflicting loyalties make it hard to keep God's presence in the center. Social and business pressures make us do things we really do not approve. It is hard for me to believe that everyone is comfortable with the degree to which drinking has become a necessary part of business and social life. It is even harder for me to believe that we want this situation for our children, yet we follow the crowd and include our children in it. All this builds guilt and guilt causes us to hide from God. Thus His presence fades.

These things which make it hard to know God personally also make us need Him so badly and if you really feel the need for God, you are at the start of the way along which you can find Him. Your sense of need is the sure sign He is walking by your side, although you do not recognize Him. He always comes to those in trouble, seeking to be recognized and received so that He may help.

God comes personally to help as we make ourselves familiar with Him as He is revealed in Jesus Christ. Jesus said, "He that hath seen me, hath seen the Father." If your need sends you to learn of Him in the Bible and in church, you are on your way to an experience of His presence. As you walk where He walks, one day you will feel His presence and find grace to help in your time of need. Although you stumble, He will keep you from falling. From weariness, He gives you rest; in responsibility, He gives you strength; from sin; He is your refuge and your forgiveness.

The light of His presence will make bearable the complexity of life and will make you stronger to withstand the pressures along the way. Your sense of need will be met by His voice deep within you, "Lo I am with you always, even to the end of the way."

MAY 21   GIVING: The best thing to give to your enemy is forgiveness; an opponent, tolerance; a friend, your heart; your child, a good example; yourself, respect; all men, charity.

F. M. Balfour

SELF-GIVING LEADS TO A FULL LIFE

The Gospel of Christ is a revolutionary thing, yet it is at home in a revolutionary world. It never is very much at home in a world of comfort and convenience. It finds its way best in a day of upset. Jesus came to bring men to birth in a bright, new world; a bright, new world that lives in the midst of an old worn, tired world. There was no world more worn out and tired than was the Roman world into which that dream was born.

He came to bring men to glory; He came to restore to men the glory for which they were created, a glory that had been forfeited as man sought his own welfare. The Gospel came to put at the center of man's life the things of the spiritual world, rather than the things of this world. That, in itself, is revolution. Jesus came that men might devote themselves to self-giving rather than self-seeking. That, in our day, is revolution.

It is a hard road that has a Cross at its heart. The Cross is the pattern for all worthwhile living. Jesus said it is like a seed. You can take a seed of corn and you can do one of two things with it. You can keep it or you can plant it. You can keep a seed of corn, I suppose, indefinitely, but at the end of your keeping of it there is still one seed. It "abideth alone," He said, "but if it dies, it bringeth forth much fruit." If you plant it, it will disintegrate. The stalk of corn, or the stalk of wheat, comes up with countless grains. Now, He said, if you are going to live in this world, and if you are going to live in the world to come, which is really the important thing, there is really only one road to Glory, and that is the road to self-giving. That is the road of the Cross. It becomes a Cross-marked road because of the kind of world we live in.

In the way of the Cross - in self-giving - there is only one deep-seated motivation that will see you through, and that is the committal of it to the Glory of God, believing that He will take it and do whatever He wants to do with it, making it most valuable.

So, Christ went His way to the Cross and followed it by the Resurrection. Through His death and resurrection, Jesus proved forever that the pattern of life, which is always the one of value, is that which gives of itself.

**MAY 22   WHATEVER is to make us better and happy,
God has placed either openly before us or
close to us.**

Seneca

GOD HELPS MAN TO BE WORTHWHILE

The cruelest thing you can do to a person is to belittle him. Like a man caught in a swift current fights for his life, so in our kind of world each of us fights for our self-respect. We must somehow feel that our lives are worthwhile. Most of our conduct can be explained by our struggle for a sense of personal value. So often we are critical of others out of our desire to feel important. Usually such criticism is directed at people who threaten our own sense of being worthwhile.

The effort to achieve status or position is but an expression of our inner need to stand out from the crowd. Our interest in money is based on our belief that it can be used to make us feel more worthwhile. Many become interested in occupations and professions that serve people, seeking to satisfy their need. They feel that if they can be a social worker or physician or minister or schoolteacher, they will feel worthwhile.

Where is the answer to our need to feel worthwhile? It cannot lie in "getting ahead" or in status. There are two reasons for this. First, very few people ever make the grade. Most of us never really get very far ahead of the crowd. Second, it is true that those who do get ahead too often lose their sense of being personally valuable in the process.

Exactly the same thing is true of money as a means of feeling worthwhile. Not many make enough for their purpose and those who do find that it takes more than money to achieve a sense of personal value.

Also, our job is not the answer. There seem to be about as many unhappy people in service jobs and professions as anywhere else. If you do not feel worthwhile in your present job, the chances are you won't improve matters by changing jobs.

The answer to the need must be one possible for everyone, high and low, rich and poor, sick and well. The common people heard Jesus gladly because he gave them the answer to their need. The answer lies in a person's relationship to God, "But as many as receive Him, to them gave He power to become the sons of God."

Paul wrote to slaves and led them to a sense of personal value by teaching them to do their work as unto the Lord. By doing so, they found the answer - even in slavery.What matters is not what you do but who you are and why you do it. As a child of God, doing your job as unto the Lord, you find the Spirit witnessing to your spirit, assuring you that you are valuable for time and eternity.

This is the one satisfying answer to the need for status that drives us all.

BUT Moses told the people, "Don't be afraid. **Just stand where you are and watch, and you will see the wonderful way the Lord will rescue today."**

Exodus 14:13 (LB)

ADVENTURE OF FAITH WILL HELP YOU OUT OF LIFE'S BLIND ALLEYS

Someone has said that change is the only permanent thing. It is true that we never can stay where and as we are. We are always being forced out of our present situation into something different. We have to move into the future whether we want to or not. This is true of groups of people. It is true of each of us as individuals. As old ways of life break up, our desire for security must find an answer.

The ancient account of the Hebrews crossing the Red Sea can be helpful. They had left the security of Egypt. Their life there had been hard but it had provided food and shelter and clothes. Ahead of them there seemed nothing but a blind alley. The Red Sea blocked their path. Many of the people longed for the past because the future seemed so uncertain, but they could not go back. Like the Hebrews, we can never go back however dark the future looks, because the past is gone.

These Hebrews could not stay where they were because the Egyptian army was closing in on them. As difficult as the future looked, they had to do something or be destroyed. Often it is a temptation for us to try to avoid the threat of the future by hiding in the present situation. Life won't let us do it. Always we are moved ahead whether we like it or not.

The solution lies in the adventure of faith:

1. God had led these people into their situation by a pillar of cloud by day and a pillar of fire by night. In your situation, whatever it is, there is help in daring to believe that a sovereign God is working in it and through it. Life is different for those who

believe that we are guided and are not the helpless victims of circumstances.

2. God spoke through Moses: "Stand still and see the salvation of God. The Lord will fight for you." God promises us that if we will stand still and quit milling about in panic that He will go before us to build our future. He will work out what seems a hopeless situation for good. We are invited to believe that tomorrow belongs to God.

3. Then God spoke again: "Speak unto the people that they go forward." Going forward meant moving toward what seemed an impossible barrier - the Red Sea, yet they were told to take the next step and start moving. God opens the future only as we start walking toward it. All He asks is that we have faith enough to start.

4. So the Hebrews found God faithful and they were delivered. This same faithfulness is witnessed to by generations of those who have trusted Him. You will find an adventure in faith helpful to you in your blind alley.

MAY 24   **I long to accomplish great and noble tasks, but it is my chief duty and joy to accomplish humble tasks as though they were great and noble.**

Helen Keller

SIMPLICITY IS THE KEY TO HAPPY LIVING

Every one of us wants to get satisfaction out of living. We want to do things that give us a contented feeling. This is a desire that is common to all people. Too many people seem to have the idea that you must do something big and important, but if this were true, not many would qualify.

The truth of the matter is that most of life's satisfaction comes from simple things available to each of us. I would like to suggest some of them.

1. There is satisfaction in doing well whatever you do. If you sweep a floor, or wash dishes, or drive a car, or sell an order or run a business, feeling good about it depends on doing it as well as you can. If you skimp or just get by, you rob yourself of some of the pleasure of living. Paul once wrote: "Whatever you do, do all to the glory of God." If what you do is between God and you, you will be led to try to do a good job.

2. It is a source of pleasure in living to be loyal to love of the home. If you are one of a family there are those who depend on you for affection, support and approval. You are dependent on your family for these things. Given and received, these things can bring music to the heart. Too many people are busy about many things and neglect the things of affection in the home. They do not mean to do it. They just put it off to a more convenient season. Much of the satisfaction in living is thus lost and they never know the reason.

3. You can add to the satisfaction of living by being helpful where you have a chance. It doesn't have to be something big, just lend a helping hand. You don't have to look for opportunities. Keep your eyes and heart open and they will come to you.

4. Satisfaction comes from those things we do which we know to be right, yet are hard to do. Many of us rob ourselves of much of the joy of living by giving in too easily to some attractive temptation. We are so made that this always dulls the pleasure of living.

5. The foundation for satisfaction in living is regular worship of God. God made us that way. We need to open the windows of our souls and let the refreshing breezes of Heaven blow through. This is as important for our spirits as food is for our bodies. In worship, we find the answer to our need for forgiveness, for comfort, for strength. It gives a lift to life we cannot do without.

MAY 25   IF you are tired of the load of your sin, let Jesus come into your heart; If you desire a new life to begin, let Jesus come into your heart.

Lelia N. Morris, Hymn

OUR PROBLEMS ARE SYMPTOMS OF OUR BROKEN KINSHIP TO GOD

As you read the Bible you discover that the people of Biblical days had about the same problems that plague our modern world. They had a hard time making a living and they knew sickness and personal tragedy. From the days of Abraham on, they knew war and its horrible results. The Israelites took the Promised Land by the sword. They built their nation by conquest. For hundreds of years, their country was invaded by the major powers of Babylon, Assyria, Persia, Greece, and Rome.

The people of the Bible knew all the problems of weather and poverty. Alcohol was a continuing threat, as it is today. Pagan religions spread among them until, at times, they even practiced human sacrifice. The fertility cults often made immorality a religious exercise. The Bible gives the full picture and in the picture you can find yourself and you can find resemblances to our so-called modern day.

Where the Bible differs radically from our day is that it treats all these problems as symptoms and results of a deeper problem - the problem of man's relationship to God. This is true of nations and individuals. So the Bible has one theme: the reconciling of man to God. It does not ignore the troubles men have nor our efforts to help ourselves. It just addresses itself to the primary problem of man's separation from God and presents the solution of this problem. Without the solution, all our economic, political, social and personal problems will still be with us regardless of what we do.

All this is summed up in God's word to Solomon as he prayed for his people: "If my people, which are called by my name, shall humble themselves and pray, and seek my face and turn from their wicked ways, then will I hear from heaven and will forgive their sins and will heal their land."

The prophets unite with one voice in calling people to God as the first attack on their problems. The New Testament is the record of what God has done to reconcile us to Himself by the death of Christ and thus to give us abundant life here and hereafter.

Our problems of the common market and trade, of the gold drain, of Russia, of crime, of human need, demand the best efforts of us all. But they are symptoms of the more serious problem of our broken relationship to God which also demands our best efforts.

In the midst of all our efforts to work out our difficulties, there must be the steady call of the Bible: "We beseech you on behalf of Christ, be ye reconciled to God."

MAY 26   **We can do no great things, only small things with great love.**

Mother Teresa

GOD OF COMPASSION IS ALWAYS WITH US

We read in the New Testament that Jesus looked out on the multitude and had compassion on them for they were as sheep having no shepherd. These words ran through my mind as I read the newspaper recently. Reduce all these accounts to people who are really just people like you and me and you can begin to feel something of the agony of our world: "Charred Body of a Man Found Under Mysterious Circumstances" – "Three Killed As Truck Rams Rest Home" – "U.N. Hands Ultimatum" – "Cabinet Quits After Riots" – "800 Go on Strike" – "Man Shot: Neighbor is Held."

Add to these stories those about the millions who are without food. Think on such a statement as this: "There isn't one nation, large or small, captive or free, that isn't today engaged in a desperate struggle with economic distress." Economic distress means people. It means people losing jobs, people with families they can't support. It means people who are hurt and who do not know where to find help; people who are as sheep having no shepherd.

As this kind of world is presented to us day by day, I am more and more grateful for the revelation of God in Jesus Christ. This revelation means that God's arms of compassion are around our world. It means that we are not dependent finally on the good will of men or the programs of government for the answer to our needs. It means that God cares and that God has personally involved Himself at every point of man's suffering. It means that God has set Himself against the evil that men do.

This does not answer the question of why evil is here or why men suffer so much at the hands of evil men. Christ Himself had to be the victim of evil before He could be the Victor. This revelation of God does mean, however, that the events of our world are set in the frame of God's compassion and of God's guarantee in the resurrection that evil shall be defeated.

It is the mystery of the faith that those who trust Him find that, even at the place of their suffering, there is the experience of His compassion and of His saving grace. Faith in the revelation of God in Christ does enable us to labor for God and for the good with confidence and hope. It means that every act of compassion, of kindness, of integrity, of courage against evil and of purity is the work of Him who looked on the multitude and had compassion on them and gave Himself for them.

FORBEARING one another, and forgiving one another, if any man have a quarrel against any...

Colossians 3:13 (KJ)

PEOPLE IN TROUBLE KNOW FAITH BEST

For some men whose world was falling apart, Jesus used a withered fig tree as a signpost to security. The disciples were facing experiences that would try their souls. They were to be denied the things they wanted. One they loved was to be taken from them in death. Their future would, for a time, seem to offer nothing but desolation. Everything they had hoped for and worked for appeared to be lost. Everyone shares this experience at one time or another. At such times it can be helpful to remember the things Jesus told his disciples.

First He said, "Have faith in God." He pointed to the fig tree as an example of how all things are subject to the power of God. It had been withered by a word. He said that with faith, a mountain could be moved. He said that if we come praying, believing that we will receive, the answer to our prayers is sure.

There is mystery here but it is a fact of experience that faith grows stronger when one's world is falling apart. People who are in the midst of misfortune understand what it means to have faith in God better than those who are free of serious trouble do. Even as they lose that which seems necessary, there comes a confidence that they are in God's hands and that God will work for good out of the misfortune that has come. To keep a strong hold on your faith in God will not answer all your questions and will not banish your sorrow; however, it will answer your deeper need for security and for hope and for confidence. As time goes on you will join those who witness to the fact that mountains have been moved.

The second thing Jesus said to these scared disciples was, "When you stand praying, forgive if ye have aught against any man, that your

Father which is in heaven may forgive you." This points to the only way we can keep the channel open by which God's help comes to us. We can expect God to answer our prayers only as our sins are forgiven by Him. He can receive us as forgiven sinners only as we forgive any who have injured us. There is no way to escape this condition. If you have not forgiven any person any injury that person has done you, the way to God and from God is blocked.

Jesus gives a prescription for stability and security in the face of life's storms. First, hold fast to your faith in God and second, hold nothing unforgiven against any man. There is nothing easy about this advice of Jesus, but if your world is falling apart you will find that it will remove mountains. You will discover that your loss is surrounded by God's presence and that along your difficult way is the assurance of his never failing love.

MAY 28   SWEET hour of prayer, sweet hour of prayer, that calls me from a world of care...

William B. Bradberry, Hymn

LET'S NOT FORGET THE POWER OF PRAYER

At one time or another, prayer concerns all of us. People of all religions and of no religion pray, in one way or another. This is especially true in the crises of our lives. We don't need to argue about prayer. We do need from time to time to remind ourselves of its power. We need to be reassured that our prayers are a part of the divine order. The necessity we feel to pray is the work of God who welcomes our prayers.

The Christian faith gives to us a God who is personal. He has revealed Himself in human form; therefore, we do not pray to some vague outline. We pray to God like we pray to Jesus. When we think of God, we think of Jesus and take heart.

In Jesus we see that God is chiefly interested in people in trouble -

all kinds of trouble. So often people hesitate to pray when they are in trouble because they have not prayed much before trouble struck. The God of Jesus would have you know that it is to people in trouble that He most gladly comes to help.

In Jesus we see God interested in helping the sick, the crippled, the mentally ill, the sorrowing. He comes to those with lives ruined by evil and makes them whole again. He extends His hand to help those threatened by storms. He even helps some fishermen find a catch. He feeds the hungry and gives water to the thirsty. When His friends are tired, He takes them aside to rest. He shares the concern of parents for their children. He takes people whose lives are in blind alleys and sets them on the open road to worthwhile living. He answers our fears that arise out of the physical necessities of food and clothes and shelter.

As you come to pray, you are invited to come boldly unto the throne of Grace to find help in time of need. It matters not what your need may be, God is interested and He wants your prayers as the channel for His help. He invites you to come in the name of Jesus. It matters not how stumbling the prayer, God is present to hear and help.

It helps to remember that there are at least three answers to prayer: yes, no and wait. We won't always get what we want but we will get an answer. There are many questions that prayer raises but most of these questions find an answer when earnestly and sincerely we pray to God revealed in Jesus.

MAY 29   ...IN everything, by prayer and petition, with thanksgiving, present your request to God.

Philemon 4:6 (NIV)

DON'T GIVE UP ON YOUR PRAYERS

We need assurances that when we pray, God answers our prayers. In Jesus Christ we have word from God about this matter. Jesus said men ought always to pray and not faint or give up. Perhaps the main reason we receive so little results from our praying is that we fail to keep on praying until the answer comes.

We get confused by the talk we hear that this is an orderly world, run by natural laws, and that it is not reasonable to suppose God will interfere with the way things are run just because we ask him for something we want. Then the poor results of our prayers discourage us. We pray for one thing and another thing happens or nothing seems to happen.

Jesus told these stories about prayer, and both speak to these difficulties we have in our prayers. He told of a man who needed bread at midnight to set before an unexpected guest. He went next door and woke up a neighbor who refused to get out of bed. The man kept hammering on the door until the neighbor got up and gave him the bread in self-defense. The second story is about a poor widow who had been unjustly treated and who could get no justice from a heartless judge. She followed him around, making life miserable for him until he disposed of her case to get rid of her. Jesus said that if you can get your needs met by a neighbor who doesn't care and by a judge who is not interested, them how much more can you get in answer from God who loves you and who desires to give you every good thing.

Jesus says we are not to be discouraged. Keep on praying. The orderliness of so-called natural law is God working in His own faithfulness, and the delays in answering are only a part of the divine mystery of His love.

Why God works this way, Jesus doesn't say. However, God's demand that we persevere in prayer makes sense in many ways. It proves we are in earnest; it indicates we are willing to work for the results we seek and it shows that we have faith in God to answer. As we persevere, we are led to the place where our selfishness is dissolved and we are able to say, and mean it, "Thy will be done." So prayer is answered.

MAY 30   AND Jesus said unto them...for verily I say unto you, if ye have faith as a grain of mustard seed, ye shall say unto this mountain, remove hence to yonder place; and it shall remove...

Matthew 17:20 (KJ)

IF YOU DON'T PRAY THEN YOU LACK FAITH

We are rich in many things today. Perhaps we are richest in problems that worry us and in solutions that don't work. Our prosperity is plagued with its product of unhappy people; our politics are confused by human selfishness; divorce chases marriage; our cities are growing crime centers; education seems incapable of developing the character it talks about and religion appears to be standing on the sidelines.

We like to think of ourselves as a Christian people, as believers in God. Yet the means of contacting God for His help are sadly neglected. The Bible is one long story of God's dealing with men. It records God communicating with men, and men communicating with God. It is the account of what happens when men believe in God and pray - and when they do not.

The Bible leads us to believe that if we pray, God moves to answer prayer. He moves through individuals and nations in their personal and public lives and prayer determines how he moves. Yet we don't pray. You can get your smallest crowd in a church by announcing a prayer meeting. The political, economic and social life of Christians is carried on without much thought of what prayer can do to make such efforts channels of God's power. We don't really count on prayer to be the means of solving our personal difficulties.

Our failure to pray is an indication of our lack of faith in God despite our confessions of faith. We believe more in natural law than in God's direct action. We trust our own skills and that of others, and leave out any real confidence that God wants to work in and through

216

us and our skills with His power in answer to our prayers.

We go only part way toward solving our problems when we use all available human knowledge and skill. In love, God waits to flow through this knowledge and skill if we will only pray in faith. He promises we can move mountains if we will add faith to our works and prayer to our efforts.

This promise covers everything that concerns us personally and in our private, business, political and social life.

Those who believe in God can best serve themselves and their lost day by taking seriously the disciples' petition: "Lord, teach us to pray."

Until churches again become houses of prayer; until homes have as their center an altar of prayer; until men who work, who seek to erect sound political structures, who seek to serve men in their need, seek first God in prayer, it is not likely that our efforts and our solutions will do other than complicate our problems.

Prayer that changes things could begin with you.

MAY 31 **YE shall not go after other gods...lest the anger of the Lord thy God be kindled against thee, and destroy thee from off the face of the earth**

Deuteronomy 6:14,15 (KJ)

SODOM'S FALL AND DESTRUCTION STILL HAS MEANING FOR US

The name "Sodom" has been inscribed in the memory of man as a symbol of human wickedness and of the judgment of God. It is remembered because of its connection with Lot through whom God sought to deal with Sodom in mercy instead of judgment. Lot was a farmer who decided to move into the city to live. He had done well in

217

the country. Then he decided he wanted to enjoy the comforts and pleasures of a modern, prosperous urban community. It didn't work out well.

In the first place, he could not enjoy the city. Sodom was known for its wide-open evil. It had all the vices of "prosperous ease." The record says that it laid out its immorality for all to see. All this weighed on the conscience of Lot who was a good man at heart.

Then he was captured in an enemy raid on Sodom. He was rescued, but the experience certainly shook him up.

Finally, God warned him that Sodom was to be destroyed for its wickedness. Lot was told to warn his fellow citizens of the coming judgment of God. He did, and we read that he seemed to them as one that mocked. They thought he was unbalanced. The idea that God would really judge men for their sins, especially in a wonderful place like Sodom, seemed silly.

Then the blow fell as fire and brimstone destroyed Sodom in a volcanic eruption. There are some things in this story that bear thinking about today.

Are the evils of our day - crime, immorality, delinquency, civil violence, war - the result of bad environment and poor heredity? Or, on the other hand, are they sins against God? Are these things problems to be solved or are they sins to be repented of?

What about the exclusion of God as a vital interest in our public and private lives and institutions? Is this maturity and progress or is it a denial of the very foundations upon which human life rests?

What about war? Is it the result of man's fine nature going out to slay dragons or is it the judgment of God for our sins?

What about the calamities of nature? Are they just the misfortunes of natural law or, in some mysterious way, are they linked to God's judgment for our sins?

These questions and answers run all through Scripture. Jesus said a strange thing that bears thinking about. He said that it would be more tolerable in the judgment for Sodom than for those who refuse His message and His messengers.

JUNE

JUNE 1 **'MID all the traffic of the ways, turmoils without, within, make my heart a quiet place, and come and dwell within.**

John Oxenham, Hymn

WORSHIP ON BOARD A SHIP WAS STIMULATING

On a ship bound for Europe there are people of all nations and of all races. There are people from Africa, Asia, Europe, Australia, and America. They represent a wide variety of religions. As the days move along you note the different backgrounds, different cultures and different interests. Some drink as a normal way of life; some do not. Some play the shipboard horse races, some go to the movie and some dance and play.

The largest crowd of any ship gathering came together for divine worship conducted according to the Book of Common Prayer of the Church of England. Admittance to the service had nothing to do with race or color. It had nothing to do with nationality. It had nothing to do with whether one drank or did not drink, or whether one danced or did not dance. It had to do only with a desire to worship the God and Father of our Lord Jesus Christ. Here in the main lounge there was gathered the church of one faith, one Lord, one baptism.

As the hymns were sung and the Bible read and the prayers said there was the evident answer to the Lord's prayer "that they all may be one." The faces all had the same expression of those moving out of themselves to find One greater than themselves. There was the feeling that we were united across our barriers. From the staff captain who conducted the service to the cabin boys who participated, there was a common bond.

We confessed together our sins: "We have left undone those things we ought to have done; and we have done those things which we ought not to have done...Restore Thou them that are penitent according to the promise declared unto mankind in Christ Jesus, our Lord."

Chapter 18 of Jeremiah was read and the account in Luke 4. There was particular meaning in the Old Hundredth Psalm: "Be sure that the Lord, He is God, it is He that hath made us and not we ourselves; we are His people and the sheep of His pasture." It was deeply encouraging to recite with this group the Creed and to know the faith is shared across the world.

The service ended with the singing of "The Church's One Foundation is Jesus Christ Her Lord." This foundation is laid among all people. Christ is worshipped and in the worship, the Holy Spirit is creating His church. With all our struggle to cross the barriers that divide us, it is true that God is moving across our world making all men one in Christ.

Here in worship is the one uniting influence on board. So it is in our community. So will the church grow until every knee bows and every tongue confesses Jesus Christ as Lord.

JUNE 2   FAITH of our fathers! living still In spite of dungeon, fire and sword...

Henri F. Henry, Hymn

AN ANCIENT CHAPEL BOLSTERS FAITH

LONDON - The Tower of London is an astonishing thing to see. It is fort, castle, prison, a little 13-acre world of its own. The central part was built around 1080 A.D. For nearly 900 years it has stood guard over the city. The blood of executed men and women literally stains the pages of its history.

At the heart of the White Tower is the St. John's Chapel, built by William the Conqueror in 1080. It stands almost exactly as it was when he looked on it and worshipped in it. It was small but perfect in its Norman architecture. It is a kind of miniature monument to the beginnings of modern England.

After visiting the chapel, I was discussing it with a young woman just graduated from an American college. She was thrilled by her visit to this chapel and I was interested in what it meant to her. She said that when she was alone, she often got to thinking about what she believed about God, about the reality that lies behind faith. It is not easy for a young person, or for anyone, to hold on to faith in our kind of world. For the most part, it seems that the world rushes by, paying little attention to the things of the spirit. It seems important to be a part of the rushing parade in its search for money and pleasure.

The young lady said that as she looked at a place of worship that had been built so long ago, she found support for the faith within her. As she looked, she could see the long line of men and women who, through the centuries, had found something of reality in their faith in such a place as this ancient chapel. All this encouraged her in her confidence that something deeply real is there in answer to her faith.

It is a source of strength to know we are not alone. In our religious faith we are not individuals groping our way. We are one of a great company that stretches across the centuries. Buildings dedicated to God mark the centuries, evidences of the faith we share.

To most of us come those times when we find doubts creeping across our souls. We face difficulties that threaten to defeat us or misfortunes that we feel helpless to meet with courage. We wonder deep within us if God is there to answer the probing of our faith.

When these times come, it does help to catch step with the centuries' long procession of those in like circumstances who have followed and who have left evidence of their faith along the way. It will help to walk about where you live and look at the houses where men worship. You will discover you are not alone. In the fellowship of believers, there is strength for the soul.

AND he told them, "You are to go into all the world and preach the Good News to everyone everywhere."

Mark 16:15 (LB)

AT OLD ST. GILES A VISITOR WONDERS

EDINBURGH - Since 850 A.D. there has been a church where Edinburgh's St. Giles Cathedral now stands. Around 1150 one was built whose massive pillars still serve the building. The cathedral took its present form from 1450 to 1500. Someone has written that St. Giles is the very heart of Scotland. Its influences have gone out to mold much of our own history through the scores of thousands who came to our shores as Scots and Scotch-Irish colonists.

Today the Church of Scotland is Reformed or Presbyterian, while the Church of England is Anglican. When the Queen is in residence in Edinburgh, she attends St. Giles. All this and more passes through the mind as one worships in this church. It is still an active parish in the city.

One wonders if it is still the heart of Scotland, or of Edinburgh. One wonders if that for which it stands still is capable of stirring men and nations to care enough for the worship of God to give their lives gladly for conscience's sake. One wonders if the fire burns brightly enough to send men and women across the seas to light the fires of freedom and faith in new lands.

There is little evidence to be seen that our land alone is marked by excess materialism and that countries like England and Scotland are truer to the spiritual values of life.

For three weeks I have been reading English and Scottish newspapers and magazines. I have talked to a good many people. There is almost total absorption in the subject of the Common Market. There is almost total emphasis upon the material advantages or disadvantages.

All kinds of groups are striking or talking about striking. Everyone is interested in money. I am convinced that there is less interest in and devotion to the spiritual and moral values here than in our own country.

It seems that the whole world is embarking on the adventure of seeking first material things and letting the Kingdom of God take care of itself. This is true with us, but certainly no less true here.

Church attendance is low. Probably only about 10 percent of the population goes to the church at all. In the chief theological faculty of the Church of Scotland they have only about 60 students. So many of the churches in England and Scotland give you the impression of being monuments rather than centers of radiation for the Gospel.

With all the faults and problems in our American Christianity, it may well be that the major part in the maintenance and spread of the Light of the Gospel is given by us in this generation. Ours is more nearly the church of the people. It was thus in Scotland when St. Giles was the heart of Scotland. Even as they were greatly used, so may we be.

JUNE 4   **REVIVE us again, fill each heart with thy love; may each soul be kindled with fire from above.**

John J. Husband, Hymn

IN EUROPE, AS AT HOME, MEN RUSH AROUND BUT FIND NOTHING

Having been a visitor on foreign shores for nearly a month it is interesting to try to sort out the impressions gained. One big impression is that everyone is in a hurry to get wherever they are going. We Americans are often accused of rushing around more than others. Those who feel this to be true haven't spent much time in London's five o'clock rush, or on Edinburgh's busy streets or in the midst of Paris traffic. Where everyone is going at such speed, either at home or abroad, is hard to define.

Then there is the impression of the vast complication of our world with its many nations and groups and the differing interests that clamor for their place in the sun. It seems almost a miracle that there are not more disagreements than there are. People are different and nations are different. These differences get mighty close together in our world with communications being what they are.

On the other hand, people are very much alike. Regardless of nation or of group or of color, there is a basic similarity of nature. Family life is about the same - a mother tending her child is about like any other mother watching over her child at play. Men go to work to make a living in one place about like any other place.

The language of handholding and the way of a man with a maid seem about the same whatever the nation or group. There are the same desires everywhere for peace and happiness and health and meaning and purpose.

Today everyone seems to be seeking these things in about the same way. Material prosperity seems to be accepted generally as the answer to man's needs. This is as true in Britain and Europe as in our country - maybe more so.

It can easily be a superficial impression that man's relationship to God is not generally a major concern. One never knows what goes on in the hearts of men. However, it is hard to get any other impression from the public evidences one meets.Man's need for God, common to all, appears neglected.Man's fragility before the awful complication of our modern world seems to be unrecognized. Man's sin as the cause of our unending troubles seems almost completely ignored.

Material things have never served man or a nation as a sound foundation upon which to build a life. The whole teaching of the Bible points to the fact that the things of God must come first.

This all leads up to an impression of concern for the future. At home and abroad, men seek first the things of this world. Perhaps the men and women who care may serve our day best by constant prayer that there may come in our time a revival of religion - a revival that will once again give men a burning concern over their relationship to God.

...ALWAYS remember that you, too, have a master in heaven who is closely watching you.

Colossians 4:1 (LB)

CHRIST AS MASTER OFFERS A SAFE HARBOR

Riding the Queen Elizabeth across the Atlantic brought to mind a ship story that happened some years ago. The regular captain of the ship had to remain at home because of a death in the family. A substitute had been placed in command at the last moment. At the first port of call the ship was slightly damaged by dragging over a submerged mud bank. Hasty repairs were made and the trip was resumed according to schedule.

As the ship moved across the ocean, I was sitting in a barber's chair. The barber had been sailing on passenger ships for some 30 years. He was typical of the men who follow the sea as a life work.

I asked him if he could tell the difference in the ship when the regular captain was not in command. "Oh yes," he said, "you can always tell the difference when the master is on the bridge." Here was a man having little to do with the operation of the vessel, hidden away in the depths of its vast bulk, conscious of a sense of insecurity because the right master was not on the bridge.

This is a parable for our lives. It does make a difference to each of us if the right master is on the bridge of our life. Each of us has at the center of our lives a control center. From this center the chief direction of our lives is determined. Not only is the general direction determined but the details of our daily lives are directed in such a way as to move our lives in the direction we have decided to go. The crew members on a ship do a thousand different jobs but all are done to serve the man on the bridge. In him and by him, they are centered to move the ship toward the chosen destination.

We in our interests do a thousand different things. We work and play. We are related to those we live with and play with and work with in different ways. Yet all of us and all we do move in a chosen direction. All is coordinated and used by the Master on the bridge of our lives.

If the wrong master is on the bridge, our personal lives and our every contact are invaded with a sense of insecurity. There are mud banks ahead where our lives are damaged, sooner or later, beyond repair.

We have a choice in matters. Either we direct our own lives, serving as our own master, or we invite God in Christ to take charge. We are not able to handle our lives. We are the wrong master for the voyage of life. Christ, as our Master, offers sure guidance through all the experiences of life and a safe harbor at last.

JUNE 6   OH, the difference between nearly right and exactly right.

Horace J. Brown

CHARACTER IS VITAL -- BUT WHAT KIND?

Character building is a popular idea. Many organizations promote themselves as being worthy of support because they build character. All parents give at least lip service to trying to build character in their children. Today, you are hearing a good deal about our need to return to moral integrity. Our sex mania and our scandals in business and politics are finally causing concern over our popular morals.

If we really do take seriously, either as a parent or a citizen, this matter of character building, we will discover that there is a lot of loose talk about it.

In the first place the word "character," taken by itself, is a blank word. It means nothing without an adjective. When you hear someone talk about building character, it is necessary to ask, "What kind of character?"

What kind of morals do you want your child or your country to have? America was thoroughly founded on the Christian religion and its idea of character and morality. It is a shock to realize that this standard is no longer accepted without question. The Christian faith is being eased out of our public life and treated indifferently in our private lives. The result is that Christian character is breaking down. You can't have Christian character without a commitment to the Christian faith.

Character grows out of that which we worship. Many idols, many religions seek your loyalty today. Each produces its own kind of character. There is the idol of self, the idol of the state, the idol of pleasure. You will be the kind of person your idols or your religion make you.

All the effort to build character is following false roads unless there is prior commitment to God. If you want Christian character for your child or your land you must surround that child and that land with the Christian faith.

Christian character is formed as a child or an adult is taught the facts of the faith and is constantly in contact with those who live the faith they teach. Character is the result of teaching by an association with those who have the kind of character we desire.

The molding hand of God forms the character in child and adult as God's word is taught and lived. There can be only further breakdowns in our moral standards as long as our first loyalties are to the idols of self, of state, of money, of position, of pleasure.

If there is to be any revival of moral integrity there must come first a revival of religion in the home and in the churches. There must also be a revival in our public loyalty to the things of God.

The kind of character most of us recognize as good is the result of the indwelling spirit of God given to those who belong to God by faith.

JUNE 7 THE great thing in the world is not so much where we stand, as in what direction we are moving

Holmes

DISCONTENT CAN BE A BLESSING - COMPLACENCY KILLS USEFULNESS

Facing, as we must, the ever-changing problems in life, it is easy to try to take our stand on the rigid ground of the past or, on the other hand, to adapt our lives to the shifting sands of the present opinion. One side would have us adopt stubborn adherence to all things of the past, while the others would have us still our consciences and adopt the views of the impermanent present.

Either way is followed at our peril since each leads to an unhappy and barren life. In our individual lives and in our life as a nation, we will find both complacency and conformity fatal to useful living. If we are to live boldly and with confidence, as God would have us do, our character must find a place for divine discontent. We are not meant to be satisfied either with the past or with the present.

We can never be quite content with what we have made of our lives. Always we should be striving for nobler living, seeking to mold ourselves in the likeness of Him whose word instructs us: "And be not conformed to this world, but be ye transformed by the renewing of your mind that ye may prove what the will of God is that is good and acceptable and perfect."

It is for us to accept with dedication the role we are called upon to play in life, but we should never be wholly content with the manner in which we have played that role.

In every walk of life, on the playing field, in the office, in the factory, on the farm and above all, in the home, we should always strive to do a better job. A divine discontent should ever drive us to do a better job under God.

We will find that blessings flow from our discontent. We will grow in inner stature and in the strength and help we bring to others. The efforts we expend as a result of our discontent will, in the long stretch of life, bring greater happiness and greater satisfaction to ourselves and to those we touch.

We human beings are capable of great and high things. The discontent that drives us is the urging of God as He seeks to move us ever upward toward the fulfilling of our proper destiny.

This is what Paul had in mind for himself and for us as he wrote: "Brethren, I count not myself to have apprehended it. But this one thing I do, forgetting those things which are behind, and reaching forth unto those things which are before, I press toward the mark for the prize of the high calling of God in Christ Jesus."

JUNE 8   **... WHOEVER wants to be first must be slave of all. For the Son of Man did not come to be served, but to serve.**

Mark 10: 44,45 (NIV)

JUST TRY GIVING INSTEAD OF SEEKING

There are some things that you can do on this day to help lift the burdens of others and make your own heart glad in the doing. Too often we retire into our own shell because we feel the darkness of the world is too great for us to do anything about it. When we do this, we fail those about us and we fail ourselves. If there is to be a better day tomorrow, it will be because people like you and me do what we can.

You can pray for that about which you are concerned, whether it be the problem of war, or race, or of your own family circle. Take your concern by the hand and lead it into the presence of God. He loved our world enough to give His Son to die for its evil. You will find God will receive your prayer. In your own heart, put your

229

concern in an eternal frame.

You can offer yourself in surrender day by day, to be used in whatever circumstances may arise. If you are open to be used, you will be surprised at the chances to be helpful which come along. If we can turn ourselves into the direction of self-giving rather than self-seeking we will find that door is open to us into the hearts of those who need our help. Making it a sales gadget has cheapened the idea of service, but the idea remains the source of our usefulness to others.

You can do your best to make sure your heart does not reflect the hatreds and divisions that are all around us. The atmosphere is poisoned by ill will. Individuals separate themselves from one another because they clothe their differences with hatred. Wide chasms of hatred divide groups who differ. You can determine that you will live in love and charity with all men. You can resolve to think of all men with love and charity. Nothing but the love of God in your heart will make it possible. However, unless we learn to love our enemies and bless them that curse us and pray for those who despitefully use us, we will be destroyed by our hatreds.

You can do your best to face life with faith instead of pessimism. Things are bad but those who are to help make them better will be those who believe that God is not defeated. The good and the true and the merciful are girded by the promise and presence of God. It is helpful to look evil in the face and dare to believe that it cannot win because God stands in its way.

You can remember that over our world there are countless people who pray daily for our world, who seek to live in love with all men and who face life with faith in God. As you take your place with this company you will find strength - and you will be a source of strength for others.

JUNE 9   PRAYING is no easy matter. It demands a relationship in which you allow someone other than yourselves to enter the very center of your being, and to see there what you would rather leave in darkness, and to touch there what you would rather leave untouched.

Henri Jim Nouwen

WHY DO WE PRAY IF WE'VE NO FAITH?

One of the most active battlegrounds in the hearts of all of us is that of prayer. We pray because we cannot help praying. Yet in the very act of praying, we are confused by our own inability to fully believe that we shall be answered.

We are confused by things people say about prayer that seem to contradict one another. We are confused by our failure to secure answers to prayer that seem to be right. We are confused by the frequent victory of evil over good, disease over health, war over peace.

We pray and our praying is a continuing struggle between our necessity to reach out after God and all the things that seem to push God farther away. It is illustrated by the small child who prayed each night, "God, make me a good little girl." One night, after saying the usual line, she looked up in utter frustration: "Mother, why doesn't God make me a good little girl?"

But we keep on praying and because we do, answers come not only to our prayers but also to our confusion. Victory on the battlefield of prayer is not won only by the arguments of the mind or by the accumulation of facts about prayer. Prayer is the conversation between persons who are intimately related to one another

You do not argue yourself into love or into friendship. You can know a thousand people who witness to love and who testify to friendship, yet such knowledge does not give you love or friendship. These come only as you keep close contact with another person.

Love and friendship grow out of a personal relationship.

Prayer is the result of a personal relationship. Once this is understood, we will begin to win some victories on the battlefield of prayer. We will understand that the only way to answer our problems of prayer is to pray. This means that we will keep in close contact with God. As we do, we find a response to our praying and an inner assurance that, in this personal relationship, God is hearing and answering us. As we continue to pray, we develop our own convictions about prayer based on our experience with it. We become less anxious to debate prayer and more willing to witness: "I know whom I have believed."

When crisis comes we cry out for help. Those who have neglected the things of God usually seek God in some way if perchance there may be a divine hand to help. Surely our world, its leaders and its people, need the prayers of all of us.

JUNE 10   AND as He was praying, the heavens opened....

Luke 4:21 (LB)

TURNING TOWARD GOD LEADS TO PRAYER

In days of crisis, men turn their thoughts to God. Some turn in faith, some in fear, some in unbelief, some in doubt, some in rebellion, some in questioning, and some in despair. In the hearts of many, all these thoughts race through the mind and heart in confusion.

This turning toward God in whatever way is at least the anteroom to prayer. Prayer is opening your heart toward God. It is seeking an answer to the questions and to the needs of the human heart in the middle of the experiences of life. Prayer extends all the way from the agonized cry. "Why?" to the confidence of the psalmist: "Thou art my hiding place and my shield. I hope in Thy word."

232

There are certain paths along which prayer moves to bring help to the one who prays. No two experiences are exactly alike. But the experience of many people over many centuries indicates that God becomes real as we include certain things in our prayers.

One of these is adoration or worship. In the midst of our concern over our world, it is helpful to remind ourselves that "In the beginning God created the heaven and the earth. We need to remember that God is greater than our world and to bow our hearts in worship before so great a God.

As we are concerned over the hatreds and divisions and fightings that plague our world, it will be a strong support to remember that God so loved the world that He gave His only begotten Son to save it. "God was in Christ reconciling the world unto Himself." God is more concerned with our sin-cursed world today than we are. As we come to pray, it will help to pause in the beginning and let our hearts go out in worship to so loving a God.

In our need to pray we can find the way to God more easily if we pause to worship God, who cares for each of us in our particular circumstance. That is the message of the 23rd Psalm. Jesus made clear in all His ministry: "But the very hairs on your head are all numbered."

As you come to pray, begin with some definite effort to see God, high and lifted up, concerned for your world and for you. Repeat to yourself words of adoration: "Great is the Lord and greatly to be praised." "Bless the Lord, O my soul, and all that is within me, bless His Holy Name." "The Lord reigneth; He is clothed with majesty." The Doxology or Gloria or any other similar words familiar to you, will open the door that leads to reality in your praying. God comes to meet those who worship in spirit and truth.

JUNE 11   ALL to Jesus I surrender, humbly at His feet I bow...

Winfield S. Weeden, Hymn

SURRENDER IS THE PATH TO CORRECT PRAYER

In the days of crisis, prayer moves more nearly into the center of our lives. It is important that we understand the paths along which we can move and find reality in our praying. We need to know that God loves us and, in that knowledge, bring Him our adoration and praise.

We then must come to Him in the surrender of ourselves. If we are going to receive the things of God, He requires first that we humble ourselves before Him. We come because we are not strong enough or wise enough to take care of ourselves. We come to receive that which we need. It is not too much to ask that we be willing to receive our answers on God's terms.

We need to surrender our sin to God. We are not able to prevent the results of our sin. We must come thanking Him that He receives us just as we are, forgiving our sins and removing their blight from our lives if in repentance we surrender them to Him.

We are not strong enough in mind or body to work out our problems. God promises that His strength is made perfect in weakness that is surrendered to Him.

We are not wise enough to foresee the future. We cannot predict what the results of our actions will be. We cannot be sure that what we think we want is what we ought to have. Therefore, we need to surrender our ignorance to Him.

Unconditional surrender is a pathway to power in prayer. Probably nothing is harder for us. Anyone who sincerely seeks to pray knows what it means to have fightings and fears within the heart. This inner warfare is a lonely battle, hidden often from those who are closest to us. Our pride makes us rebel against surrender

234

even to God. Our nature leads us to cling to a trust in ourselves. Our sins entice us and part of us does not want to give them up. Our guilt makes us afraid to open our hearts completely to God. These things and more make the battle of surrender more serious and more important than wars between nations.

As you come to pray, make a definite act of surrender to God. Offer yourself by specific words. Surrender your plans for the day. Place your life in God's hands, offering to accept what He sends. Believe that God knows the way you should go and will guide you in it.

Whatever concerns burden your heart, begin by seeking to surrender them absolutely to God. Cast all your care on Him because He careth for you.

This is not all of prayer, but it is a pathway along which God comes to meet you. He can come only as you open the way by surrender.

JUNE 12   **O loving and kind God, have mercy. Have pity upon me and take away the awful stain of my transgression.**

Psalm 51:1 (NIV)

REPENTANCE IS A VITAL STEP ALONG THE PATHWAYS OF PRAYER

There are definite paths along which people find reality in prayer. A necessary path to follow is that of repentance. When we come to pray, we are asking God to hear us and to do something for us. This is true whether we are asking for some material thing or whether we are seeking comfort or strength or wisdom or closeness of fellowship with Him.

It is not unreasonable to think that when you ask a favor you should be willing to receive that favor on the terms of the giver.

Especially is this true if you are helpless and dependant on the favor for your very existence. It is even more true where you believe the giver to be wise and strong and loving. Your chances of receiving what you ask are better if you are willing to give up your way of doing things and to accept the suggestions of the one to whom you come for help.

We come to God in prayer believing He is able to help us and that He loves us enough to do so. We believe He is wise in all things. We come conscious of our need, which we cannot meet in our own strength and wisdom. Turning from our own ways with a willingness to walk in obedience to His will is repentance. Repentance is a change of direction. Unless we are willing to live His way instead of our way, God finds it hard to help us, however much He loves us.

We forget this too often. At the height of the Cuban crisis there was a good deal written about prayer. Certainly, many prayed. Yet there was no word I could find anywhere about repentance. We seem to want to be delivered from danger, but to go on living as we are living and to go on doing what we are doing. The break in the crisis came on Sunday afternoon. A church that usually has a large crowd on Sunday nights reports that the Sunday morning crowd looked like Easter. The Sunday night crowd was the smallest in 15 years. I have read of no groups called to meet to give thanks for the easing of the tension.

One wonders if we have come to the place in our pride where we believe that God owes us a living. God does not deal with us because we think we are better than someone else. He deals with us on the basis of our relationship to Him. The beginning of this relationship is our willingness to walk in His ways. The first step is repentance.

As we come to pray, we will do well to heed the Word of the Lord spoken to Solomon long, long, ago. "If my people, which are called by my name, shall humble themselves, and pray, and seek my face, and turn from their wicked ways, then I hear from heaven, and I will forgive their sin, and I will heal their land."

O praise the Lord, all ye nations: praise him all ye people.

Psalm 117:1 (KJ)

LET'S NOT SLAM THE DOOR ON RELIGION

Whatever our forefathers may have meant by the doctrine of the separation of church and state, they did not mean to separate religion from the political and educational and business life of the country. It does make a difference what a man believes and if he believes wrongly he will act in a wrong way. A man who believes the wrong things won't try to do right.

In America we pride ourselves on our regard for human beings. The value of every individual is a part of the American heritage. Where does it come from? It comes from those who believed in a God who loved man enough to give His Son to die for him. Men found that if God so loved them they ought to love one another. In early America men learned this in their churches and built their schoolhouses to teach it to their children. However, selfishness is so powerful that the individual is always threatened with tyranny except where the Christian doctrine of God's sacrificial love is made a part of education and of politics.

We have a tradition of personal integrity and honor in this land. The Puritan tradition of moral conduct placed its stamp on our land. The Christian code of morality was accepted as our standard. It still receives lip service, but that is about all. It can be no other way when we have severed the tree from its roots. Faith in a God who has revealed Himself in Christ and who judges men and their institutions by their obedience to His way of life is the only source or safeguard of moral conduct. Educating men to be good without religious commitment is as useless as trying to keep alive a tree that has been cut from its roots.

Our defense lies not in armaments. It lies alone in men and women and children whose politics and business and social life begin to flow again from their faith in God who loved them and gave Himself for them.

JUNE 14   **HOW sweet on a clear Sabbath morning, To list to the clear ringing bell; Its tones so sweetly are calling, Oh, come to the church in the vale.**

Dr. Wm. S. Pitts, Hymn

NOTE TO CHRISTIANS WHO SKIP CHURCH

This is just a note to the Christians who were at the auto races on a recent Sunday. Also, it may be read by those who were out on the highways going places for pleasure or waiting around the clubhouse for the rain to stop so your favorite amusement could get under way. It is also addressed to those who bear the tag "Christian" who stay away from worship to pursue pleasure. We missed you at church. Of course, it did rain hard, but from all reports the race was well attended.

It isn't that there is anything wrong with auto racing or with many other forms of amusement if you are a Christian. In this note I am not arguing with adherents of other religions or of no religion - just those who say they are Christians. It worries me that so many of us do not find it necessary to worship regularly.

Of course, Sunday is a fine day for crowds. People can't take time off from business. But is it safe to take time off from God? You may lose more by neglecting God than by neglecting your business.

It may help your conscience that you are against communism. But by your actions you may be against God - or you may bring God against you. I am sure you are for democracy and good education and decent conduct. You are probably for honesty and justice and kindness, but if you neglected worship to spend the day in pleasure, you cast your vote against all these things.

238

Thank God the churches were all open. Services went on and there were those who came. They kept fires burning you would let go out. They bore witness to the great Christian truths: Christ's control of history and of His certain victory and of our value as individuals because we are created by God in His own image and redeemed by His sacrificial love, of the power of God's Spirit to lead us into Christian living. By their worship, the faithful were used to strengthen the things you say you believe in. They themselves were made stronger to live as Christ would have them live.

The ability you have to do as you please, the confidence you have in your own importance, your form of government, your code of morals - all these are direct results of the church at worship Sunday by Sunday.

Without the rigid discipline of worship, Bible study, and prayer, Christian profession and usefulness develop a mighty hollow sound.

JUNE 15   AND Jesus said "...Love your enemies, do good to those who hate you..."

Matthew 6:27 (NIV)

WILLINGNESS TO FORGIVE FOES IS THE RIGHT WAY TO WIN THEM

She had been badly treated by one she had considered her friend. She sat in the chair and said: "I'll get even if it is the last thing on earth I ever do." Jesus hung on the cross and said: "Father, forgive them for they know not what they do." Here you have the heart of the challenge that the Christian faith makes in our dealings with one another. Believer and unbeliever will hear much of the events in the life of Christ which center in his death and resurrection. These events have as their meaning God's forgiveness of us and our forgiveness of one another. They speak of God's love for us and of the love we ought to show to one another.

If we take this seriously it makes us uncomfortable. Of course if you just accept God's forgiveness without taking seriously its demand that we maintain an attitude of forgiveness to others, it can be very comforting - and, also, it can be very false - rather like taking a narcotic to cure a fatal illness. All we get is a little relief from pain and no cure for our trouble.

The purpose of God's forgiveness, of His Gift of Christ, is to win those who are His enemies. He invites us to accept His forgiveness but makes it a condition that we be willing to win our enemies by our attitudes and actions. Because we are forgiven, we must be willing to forgive.

This sounds strange. Today it seems that we want to destroy our enemies by words in our neighborhoods, by guns among our nations. We seem to want to hate both the sin and the sinner, but this is a long way from being Christian. Christ gave His life in battle to destroy sin and to save the sinner. The Christian lives under the divine command: "Be ye kind to one another, tender-hearted, forgiving one another as God for Christ's sake hath forgiven you."

There is the ready answer: "It won't work with those who are your enemy." Is anyone prepared to say our present attitudes and actions are working?

The world is being driven to bankruptcy making bombs. We are having trouble winning and keeping friends, much less enemies. Mental illness is a national problem; crime is flourishing. The world is an armed camp. The majority of the peoples of the world live in police states.

Most of these problems go back to people who live with unforgiving spirits. Hate and hostility poison our best efforts. You can't solve the world's problems but you can begin their solution yourself. God offers you forgiveness for your sin against Him.

You have trespassed against Him far more than anyone has against you. Therefore, you must forgive those who have trespassed against you.

240

Proverbs 19:22 (TLB)

JUST TRY SAYING SOMETHING KIND

You often hear someone described as a person who says what he thinks. Almost always it means he says unpleasant things. I wonder why this is true. It is a strange quirk of human beings that we find it easier to express our ill will than our good will. We do think unpleasant things, but we also have pleasant thoughts about people. Why shouldn't it be our "trade-mark" that we express these when we "say what we think."

I attended a meeting of the Atlanta Rotary Club, which was observing a club birthday. It was a sentimental occasion. There were present four of the original group.

The appreciation for these men was evident. They had started a good work that has borne good fruit. Gratitude and honor were unashamedly expressed. Memory brought to mind fathers and friends who had made their contribution through the years. There were tears here and there in the eyes of strong men. It was a good occasion because the rush of life and the heat of business were stopped a bit that men might remember.

I sometimes wonder why we are embarrassed by sentiment. There are few people whose lives are not longing for it. I dare to believe that most people long to express it. Have you ever felt like saying: "You are a wonderful person" or "I think the world of you" or "I appreciate what you are doing" or "You are doing a wonderful job" or "Your courage is an inspiration" or "Thank you for being you."

Have you ever felt like saying things like this and then failed to do it because it might sound sentimental? Try doing it. It is sentimental and also it is the stuff out of which happiness is made.

We talk so much of the tensions of life and of solutions. Within the reach of each of us is a solution that can dissolve most of the barriers that separate us. Try saying the kind, affectionate things that you think.

More problems are solved by the heart than by the mind. This is part of what is meant by the proverb, "Keep thy heart with all diligence for out of it are the issues of life."

JUNE 17   **BUT the fruit of the spirit is love, joy, peace, patience, kindness, goodness, faithfulness, gentleness, and self-control.**

Galatians 5:22,23 (NIV)

CHRISTIANITY MOLDS PERSONALITY TRAITS

People ask: "What is the Christian faith doing?" Part of the answer is that it is producing the kind of people who can successfully live in this world and in the world to come. Jesus said: "By their fruits, ye shall know them." It creates in a person definite personality traits that mark that person as a Christian. Paul summarizes these in his Galatians letter.

The first trait is that of love in the midst of hate. Unless we have men and women who genuinely seek the good of all men, we are doomed.

Then there is the trait of joy. This is the ability to live with optimism in a pessimistic world. The Christian has confidence in God and can meet his days with enthusiasm and hope.

Peace is there, the harmony of the inner man. Nothing can give peace to the heart until you have found peace with God and guilt is removed. We get crossed up in ourselves, and we are crossed up in ourselves because we are crossed up with God.

Patience in a world of quick tempers is a Christian fruit. Caring

242

enough to see another's viewpoint, we come to understand the person better and patience is born.

Kindness is a mark of the Christian. Kindness is in short supply. We act kindly toward those who are kind to us...but when a person is on the "other side," kindness comes hard.

Goodness is found in a Christian, goodness judged by divine standards. The goodness is never perfect, but the Christian will be found trying to do the right thing.

The Christian develops dependability. You find among them people whose word is as good as their bond.

Humility is a Christian virtue. It is not popular today, but necessary nevertheless.

The Christian exercises self-control. The appetites, passions, and ambitions are kept in balance by the will surrendered in faith.

JUNE 18   HONOR Christ by submitting to each other.

Ephesians 5:21 (LB)

COMMON RELIGION BONDS MARRIAGE

Only one country in the world that keeps statistics on the matter has more divorces in proportion to its population than the United States. Many things make marriage difficult today and divorce more prevalent. Some of these are:

1. In the minds of a growing number of people, marriage is not associated with a primary relationship to God but is considered chiefly as a contract between people to be kept as long as it is mutually satisfactory.

2. The role of the woman in marriage and, hence, the role of the man, have greatly changed in our modern day. There is no general agreement as to what these roles are. This brings confusion to many marriages.

3. The place of children in the home is also confused and this is often a cause for difficulty in the marriage.

4. Working wives and mothers add to the difficulties of many marriages.

5. The necessity for men to be away from home complicates the marriage relationship.

Yet I believe the joys of a happy marriage are possible in spite of all the difficulties. A Christian marriage, properly understood and entered into, will lead to mutual happiness.

A Christian marriage is centered in God and not in man. It is a commitment of husband and wife to God in a relationship breakable only by death. They are made one flesh by the act of God. A new unity is created in which one plus one equals one. There is no way this unity can be broken without serious consequences to the people concerned and to society.

In Ephesians, the fifth chapter, the relation of the man and woman in marriage is compared to that of Christ and His church. Thus Christians are admonished to marry Christians that through their mutual faith, the love of God can keep refreshed the love that binds them through the years. The percentage of divorces among people of like faith is about one-third that of marriages without this common factor.

In looking toward marriage, it is important to associate yourself with those who share your basic religious beliefs. There are the difficulties that all marriages face in common. It is not possible for a couple to foresee all of them.

It is possible for each couple to keep themselves so open to God by commitment and by worship that His love and care can give the wisdom and strength necessary for a lasting partnership.

FOR a husband is in charge of his wife in the same way Christ is in charge of His body the church (He gave His very life to take care of it and be its Savior !)

Ephesians 5:23 (LB)

THE MAN'S ROLE IN THE FAMILY

It is hard to describe the proper relationship between husband and wife. All personal relationships defy capture by words. They have to be experienced and then can only be described in a general way.

In a home that is Christian, the husband and father is the symbol of authority exercised in love. In our day of debunking authority, the image of the father has suffered. There is lots of talk about the rights of women and children and less about their duties.

Dagwood is good comedy, but it makes a poor example for living. Today we have equal rights and poor homes. A home cannot be run by a committee. In every group there must be finally a center of authority. In the Christian home, this center is the husband and father. This has nothing to do with the equality of husband and wife in value. It does mean they are not the same in function or authority.

A good deal of modern sociology has scared the man out of his place in the home. The place of the woman in society and in the home is thoroughly confused in the teachings of our day.

We are so afraid of damaging the personalities of children by authority and we are ruining many of them by refusing to exercise the very authority they cry out for. In our society, the average man is afraid of his child.

In a Christian marriage each plays his and her part in love and unity. Each has a specific place and function. Each is indispensable. But if the home is to be balanced, the man must be its guiding center.

Paul says that in marriage the man is head of the woman as Christ is head of the church. The man is to love the wife and give himself to and for her as Christ did the church. Where there is this kind of love on the part of the husband, a love that completely gives, the way is open for the wife to give in return.

Christian marriage is different in its beginning, in its nature and in its relationships. It does result in good and happy homes. It results in happy husbands and happy wives and in homes that give children security and love.

JUNE 20   **THIS is my commandment, that ye love one another, as I have loved you.**

John 15:12 (KJ)

MODERN MARRIAGES OFTEN FORGET IMPORTANCE OF FATHER'S AUTHORITY

God's word has a good deal to say about marriage. It is not the favorite textbook on marriage today, and neither is marriage our most successful institution. In Ephesians we read that marriage is a great mystery. The richer your marriage, the better you understand this statement. The Christian teachings about the home differ from the popular ideas about it in many important respects. The relation between husband and wife is different when both are Christian.

In the home that abides, the husband is the symbol of authority in love. This has been true in all generations. It is still true. We like to debunk authority today. It is presented as degrading to be under authority. We hear today of the rights instead of duties.

God paid to the man in the home His greatest compliment when He said God is to be called "Father." Somewhere in every group there must be at some point a final authority. This is true of the home.

We hear today of the 50-50 homes. The very idea has no meaning.

246

Men and woman are different and cannot be equated in marriage on any percentage basis. Their functions are different and marriage requires that they each give 100 per cent.

Man has been scared out of his position in the home in part by the modern emphasis on the rights of children. "Rights" are today generally interpreted to mean getting what you want. Everyone has to be "pals." I am grateful that my father did not want to share all my play as I grew up. He would have gotten hurt. Deep down, children don't want a pal for a father. They want a loving center of authority to which they can anchor their lives.

This does not mean that the woman or children are of lesser importance or value. The function of each member of the family is of equal value - but the functions differ. In a Christian home these functions do not come into competition.

Where the man exercises authority in love, he loves his wife as Christ loved the church and gave Himself for it. Where such love is, there is no question of who is boss. If this question arises, something has already gone wrong. Such love is so great it allows itself to be refused. But it cannot be refused without fatal damage to the home.

The Christian home does produce both authority in love and loving acceptance to it.

JUNE 21   **TO love and to be loved is the greatest happiness of existence.**

Sydney   Smith

CHRISTIAN WAY OFFERS HAPPY MARRIAGE BUT NO ESCAPE HATCH

Egypt is the only country that has more divorces in proportion to its population than the United States. This indicates that marriage is a difficult relationship to maintain. The shifting roles of men and women in society contribute to the difficulty. Children are demanding a new place in the home. Working wives sometimes make marriage more difficult.

The mobility of people does not make home building easier. Then there are too many outside interests. Husbands and wives often give attention to everything but one another.

With all this, I do not believe that marriage is as complicated as we today are led to believe. If it were, only the experts could be happily married, and the experts do not do any better at it than the average person.

I doubt that reading all the books on marriage which outline its problems help those very much who are entering into marriage.

Marriage can be more wonderful as the years unfold, and it is far simpler than we are making it sound with our problem solving. You can have a happy marriage if you make a Christian home.

This means you center your home in God and not in one another. In the Christian faith marriage is the commitment of one life to another, breakable only by death. Marriage is not just a human contract where two persons decide to live together as long as they think it is working to suit them. There is no escape hatch in Christian marriage. This is not a popular idea today but neither is marriage working very well. Marriage was the first institution created by God. He made man and woman one. Every marriage is a miracle of God. Two lives are fused together, never to be separated.

This is why the church has always resisted divorce. There are few exceptions, but they are few and far between. If men and women married "in the Lord" and knew it to be permanent, most divorces would be avoided.

Paul compares the relation of man and woman in marriage to that of Christ and His church.

JUNE 22   **SHE that is married careth for the things of the world, how may she please her husband.**

Corinthians 7:34 (KJ)

WOMAN'S HAPPINESS IN MARRIAGE LIES IN CONFORMING TO HUSBAND

Marriage has changed radically in the last two generations. It is no longer the kind of career for the woman that it was. The women's rights movements, the wide education and training of women and the fact that great numbers of married women work are some of the factors that have swept man out of the center of the home. I doubt that either man or woman is happier with the changes. Man is still in the front line of work. Earning a living for the family is filled with pressures never before known.

Home is the place to have the hurts of the competitive jungle healed. God gave woman the gift of making the home a place of refuge, and too many women fail to make it so.

There are three roles the woman in the house can play.

The first is that of the old-fashioned wife, dedicated to her husband, her children and her home. She finds here the center of her life and the heart of life's meaning as a wife. Modern propaganda has made this appear inadequate.

The second choice is that of a companion-wife. She bowls and golfs and keeps herself perpetually young. She is always planning things to do and places to go. She is a delightful partner at parties and outings. She is a wonderful companion, even if the home is neglected and the children cared for by people employed for the job.

The third choice is that of the 50-50 wife. She is the equal-partner type. She decides how much time she is going to give her husband, her children and her clubs. She decides how much help her husband is going to give in the home. She has as much right to decide how the home is run as her husband, and she exercises it.

The truth is a woman needs to be a little of all three. She desperately needs a standard by which to choose. The Christian home has a definite pattern and requires a definite choice. God created woman to be a "helpmate" for the husband. As Christ is head of the church, so man is head of the woman; therefore, woman is to find her true place in marriage as she conforms herself to her husband.

This is the ideal. Unless the husband "loves the wife as Christ loved the church," the woman cannot so conform herself. Hence, if you are to have a Christian marriage, the admonition to "marry in the Lord" must be taken seriously. If marriage partners do not share a common faith, their chances of happiness together are not good.

Where faith is shared, you have each giving self completely in love. Where this is true, each gives to the other all the completeness for which God ordained marriage. I have never seen a really unhappy home where the relationships were founded on a Christian commitment to one another.

JUNE 23   **LIFE is short, and we never have too much time for gladdening the hearts of those who are traveling the dark journey with us. Oh, be swift to love, make haste to be kind.**

Henri Frederic Amiel

KEEP THE HOME A CHRISTIAN ONE

The popularity of the sociological studies has made it difficult to rear children in this day. It is made to appear that it is necessary to know the answers to a long series of problems in order to be a good parent. We are told that unless we have read the latest book or secured the latest flash from the experts, our chances are not good to have good children.

Most of us might as well give up if having a good home depends on this sort of thing. We are overburdened with studies and with experts in this and in most other areas of our lives.

There is a way of life that makes a good home and which produces good, stable children. Where both parents are committed to the Christian faith and seek to rear their children in this faith, the results are uniformly good. There are exceptions but they are rare.

Such a home will have its difficult times, but most of the time the home will stand and will produce well-adjusted people. The chances for a good home are not good without a foundation of faith, however much the parents may know about the learned solutions of domestic problems.

A Christian home is one where a man and woman are united in oneness by the miraculous touch of the Spirit of God. In that home Christ is the Center of the circle and the father is the symbol of authority in love. In such a home, children are a gift of God and are a sacred trust. There is permanence in such a home, which is a basic need of children.

The Christian home provides an environment of love and is constantly renewed from God, the source of love. There is integrity where each can depend on the other. There is authority and there is also forgiveness. There may be little money and few luxuries, but there will be a kind of security on which life can be built.

In such a home the child will be taught to worship God by precept and example. This will be done in the home and in the church. There is no influence as powerful in the life of a small child as that of seeing his or her parents at prayer and sitting with them in church.

In a home where these things abide, the authority of the family is accepted by the child as normal. It is an authority based on the authority of God. The children accept it because they see their parents accepting it.

THE BEST COMES OUT AT GRADUATIONS

Once when the disciples of Jesus had been very busy he said to them: "Come away by yourselves to a lonely place and rest awhile." After a period of useful activity it is well to take time out to break the pace and to take stock of things.

Going to several graduation ceremonies, I was reminded of this need. The pace of life is fast. Our young people are caught in this pace. They are being rushed from one stage of life to another with too little time to take stock of what has taken place in their lives.

In the slight pause that comes between graduation and the next step, it is good to come apart and rest a bit. At the rest time, we do well to remind ourselves of some of these things that graduation represents.

1. Graduation is a time when we recognize a job well done. However much lies ahead, something that has real meaning has been done. We need a time to take the spotlight off the necessities of the future and to enjoy the feeling of having reached a worthy goal.

2. Graduation is a time when the finer things of life show through. As one grandmother expressed it, "This has been a family project." Family love, family sacrifice and family solidarity shine through the whole event. Watch the graduates as they come in. Each shyly looks over the crowd until the loved ones are spotted. The face breaks into a smile and then relaxes. They are there. For the family, there isn't but one graduate. For many it has meant real sacrifice, but in the moment of mutual recognition, it all becomes worthwhile.

3. Graduation is a time when there is little room for the cynic. Unashamedly, we express our faith in the virtues that abide. All the pettiness of life, its immoralities and its dishonesties, are seen for what they are. For the moment, at least, life that is reverent, pure, noble, sacrificial and useful, is seen as the true way of existence.

4. Graduation is a time when we almost instinctively turn to God. Where else can you bring the ambitions for the unknown future? Where else can you bring your high ideals for strength to make them real in your life?

Graduation is a time for love and gratitude and for recognition and pride in its best sense. It is a time for God. Given these, the next step is easier.

JUNE 25   FOR in Him we live, and move, and have our being...

Acts 17:28 (NIV)

DIVINE ASSISTANCE NECESSARY IN MEETING LIFE'S CHALLENGES

There is so much for each of us to do today. We have the daily routine to carry out; we have character to form, homes to make, a city to build and a world to save. There is so much to do and so little time to do it and often we wonder if it is worth the effort. Too many are bogged down by the burden of it. More and more of us are going to bog down unless we find the correct answer to the question of how to do the things that face us.

Do you, by your own strength and resources and by the collective efforts of people, live your life, form your character, make your home, build your city and save your world? Or after we have done our best, does success or failure depend on whether we have started with a proper relation to God? The story of Moses speaks to the question. He was born of Hebrew slave parents. He was taken and reared as a member of the royal family of Egypt. For 40 years he lived as a child of his time. He lived by his own ability and cleverness. He was remarkably successful. Inwardly, he was torn with tension as he enjoyed his luxury while his people were slaves. One day he exploded as he saw one of his people mistreated by an Egyptian. He killed the man and had to flee from the country as a murderer.

For 40 years he sought to make amends by his own efforts. He lived a model life, but at the end of it he was still finding no answer but to tend a flock of sheep in the desert; his life was in a blind alley. Then one day God spoke to him by name and asked him to surrender, offered him forgiveness and gave him a promise of usefulness.

There is help for us in this story as we face our frustration.

Here is the warning that we cannot make our own lives by human resources alone. There always comes a desert experience of failure. It does not always result in outward collapse, but many a person whose life gives the outward appearance of stability knows he is living in a desert. However, there is the assurance that God is present in our desert experiences.

The divine love seeks the lost. If you are in a blind alley and plagued by feelings of inferiority and failure, God is speaking to you by name, offering you forgiveness - on condition that you surrender.

JUNE 26   "... I know the plans I have for you," declares the Lord, "plans to prosper you and not to harm you, plans to give you hope and a future."

Jeremiah 29:11 (NIV)

HOLD TO YOUR DREAMS, YOUNG GRADUATES!

It is graduation time again. Graduation represents a task completed. It is a milestone on the road of life. It is the symbol of something accomplished. To graduates everywhere, from all kinds of schools, I would say, "Congratulations." We need to pause a while and enjoy these moments between yesterday and tomorrow.

Hold on to your dreams. Criers of doom are on every hand. The contents of the daily news furnish encouragement for pessimism. These are only part of the story. You can hold on to your dreams and believe in them because this is God's world. He loves it. He gave His Son to die for it. He raised His Son from the dead and He lives to make dreams come true.

The forces of God are stronger than the forces of evil. In this confidence you can take your next step. Happiness lies in following your dreams in faith, perseverance and integrity. There may be painful delays. At times it will seem that surely all dreams die and that evil always wins. But hold on to your dreams.

No one asked me for this little homily to graduates; however, this season always gives me a lift as I catch again the idealism that lies at the heart of youth. The cynicism and sham of so much of our lives are pushed aside. At graduation, dreams of the future are in the air.

Anyway, I hope that our young people today will enjoy their graduation time. I trust they will keep true to their dreams. Tomorrow offers more than any future ever has. Problems are only battles to win.

The future is in God's hands and He has in faith promised the victory to those who dream great dreams.

JUNE 27   **IN Him was life, and in that life was the light of man. The light shines in the darkness, but the darkness has not understood it.**

John 1:4,5 (NIV)

THE REVOLT AGAINST GOD

Recently, I was reading through Paul's letter to the Romans. The first verses of Chapter 13 read as follows: "Every Christian ought to obey the civil authorities, for all legitimate authority is derived from God's authority, and the existing authority is appointed under God. To oppose authority then is to oppose God and such opposition is bound to be punished."

The ideas expressed here have been the foundation of American life for more than 175 years. A respect for law has been based on our confidence that law reflects the will of God for our lives.

The Bible has been used in legislative halls and in courts as the final source of man's authority. God has been appealed to as the ultimate witness to our sincerity.

Some of us have dared to believe that the unique character of our land has been the result of our open acknowledgement of God in public and in private. Now we are witnessing a revolt against the acknowledgement of God everywhere.

The majority of American homes have long since made their revolt against God, and the majority of Americans abstain from active church participation, even though membership statistics are impressive.

With God gone, what proper approach can be made to the

immorality, to our growing disregard of law and order, to the divorce rate that is the highest in the civilized world? Upon what does the court base its authority if not in God? Why is one group's right any better than another's if there is no final divine sanction? What do you mean by "good" and "bad"? If God's love is no longer relevant, what do you mean by love?

The present controversy about God goes far deeper than a question of the separation of church and state. It goes to the question of the foundations upon which we rest.

If we are not to be united to one another by a common loyalty to God, what other common tie can you suggest?

JUNE 28   COMMIT your way to the Lord; trust him and he will do this: He will make your righteousness shine like the dawn, the justice of your cause like the noonday sun.

Psalm 37:5,6 (NIV)

THE RIGHT WORDS ARE NOT ENOUGH

Like a coin, religion has two sides. You cannot separate the two sides either of a coin or of your religion and have what you started with. The Christian religion is made up of faith and works. Christian religion without Christian conduct is dead. Jesus said, "By their fruits, ye shall know them."

Believing the right things is necessary, but unless we work with our wills and our energies to do the right things, our believing will not save us or help others.

Paul is the great apostle of faith, but in every letter that he wrote, he went into detail about how Christians must act.

The Christian is called on to believe as though it all depended on God, and to work as though it depended on him.

257

The church is failing to exert its proper influence today, largely because too many of us feel that God receives us if only we believe the right things. This leaves us free to live in a world, pagan by religious standards. Our conduct is that of the world. Like the world, we act in generosity and love only towards those "on our side."

All too many people hide their ill will toward others under pious language. Others are careless in their personal and public conduct, feeling that because they believe the proper things, it is all right.

Writing to the Ephesians, Paul calls on Christians to walk worthy of their faith, to walk not as the non-Christians walk. Paul mentions specifically some areas of conduct where Christians must be on their guard to be different:

"Put away lying, speaking every man truth with his neighbor, for we are members one of another.

"If you are angry, be sure it is not out of wounded pride or bad temper. Never go to bed angry.

"The thief must give up stealing and instead work hard and honestly with his own hands that he may have something to share with the needy.

"No bad language must pass your lips, but only what is good and helpful to the occasion so that it brings a blessing to those who hear it.

"Be generous to one another, tender-hearted, forgiving one another as God in Christ forgave you."

The only way people will be influenced by us who claim to be Christian is that we act like Christians.

...BE ye kind to each other, tender-hearted, forgiving one another, just as God has forgiven you because you belong to Christ.

Ephesians 4:32 (LB)

HOW TO GET ALONG WITH OTHER PEOPLE

Christ is concerned with and about people. He is concerned about them personally and about how they get along with one another. The secret of happiness lies in our relationships with other people. We do not live unto ourselves. We belong to other people. No material or physical resources can make us happy if we are crossed up with those with whom we live.

If you would draw people to you in affection and in friendship, Christ offers the way. He makes a negative suggestion and a positive one.

First, negatively, he says: "Don't be critical of other people." He gives two reasons. First, he says that we will be judged by our judgment of others and will be measured by the measure by which we measure others.

The law of life is that what we say of other people will be said about us. What we think of other people will be thought about us. What we do to others will be done to us. Every unkind word or deed will sooner or later come back to us. If we fail in a duty to another, someone, sometime will fail in duty to us. We reap exactly as we sow.

Second, we are not to be critical because it does no good. Our critical spirit is like a log in the eye of one trying to remove a speck of sawdust from the eye of another. We do not help people by condemning them.

Positively, Christ says: "Do unto others as you would have them do unto you." If you want to have affection of people and if you want to help them, do for them what you want done for yourself.

Surely each of us wants consideration, kindness, understanding, sympathy. We need forgiveness and love. We want a chance to make amends. How do you conquer your critical spirit and do to others as you want them to do you? Only by the grace of God!

We are by nature critical and selfish. We seek by nature to tear down in order to protect ourselves. Only God can change us. Only as we come to God with empty hands and ask and seek and knock can we receive from God the power to live with others as we should.

God offers His love to us as we accept Christ by faith. Only the gift of this divine love can enable us to love others as ourselves.

All our plans for efforts toward civic, political and social betterment will be confused towers of Babel unless we begin with faith that changes us from critics to lovers of men. "By grace are you saved through faith" is true, not only of our relationship to God, but also to one another.

JUNE 30   **SEE if there be some wicked way in me; cleanse me from every sin and set me free.**

Edwin Orr, Hymn

FOR THE SINS OF THE WORLD

The Christian faith is for all people, of all time, of all kinds and in all places. The Christian faith is for the saving of all people from their sins, calling them to repent and to believe the Gospel.

The heart of the Gospel is that God has come into this world in Jesus Christ to die for the sins of the world and to be raised from the dead for their life in this world and in the world to come.

Surely there is in our whole world today every evidence that people need saving from their sins and from the results of these sins. Stories in the media are evidence that the world is in the control of destructive forces.

Surely it must be dawning on people that we cannot depend on training and money to answer our problems. Surely in the face of the evils that are everywhere we cannot continue to believe that man is naturally good and will produce good of himself. The breakdown of communism is making the word "democracy" a catchword for the future, but the growing picture is one of confusion. Jesus looked on the multitudes and was moved with compassion for them because they fainted and were scattered abroad as sheep having no shepherd. He still does.

He looks on mankind and takes their sins on Himself, giving His life in death on the cross for the forgiveness of sin and for reconciliation to God that mankind can find the answers for lostness and for the results of sins. Christ's call "Repent and believe the Gospel" is the beginning of any answer to our evils, whether they be greed, immorality, crime and drugs and whether we find any foundation for our catch words "democracy" and "freedom." John the Baptist looked at Jesus and said, "Behold the Lamb of God which taketh away the sin of the world."

We here cannot do it all, but we can do what we can and God will use it. We can repent and believe the Gospel and we can use our personal witness and our money to send that witness out into the world. We have His promise: "For whatsoever is born of God overcometh the world and this is the victory that overcometh the world, even our faith. Who is he that overcometh the world but he that believeth that Jesus is the Son of God." (I John 5:4,5)

JULY

OFFER pardon and peace to all, wonderful words of life...

Philip B. Bliss, Hymn

READ THE BIBLE TO FIND SECURITY

In the midst of the changes of our day there is a constant search for security. We seek some solid ground on which to stand as the storms blow about us. It is finally becoming clear that we are living in a day of revolution. The foundations are being shaken and the results are being felt in every household and in every heart.

The outward form of our lives has not been greatly altered. Day by day, we follow our regular routine of work and play and of meeting family, business and social responsibilities, yet a threat hangs over all of it. This routine does not provide the security it once did. Men, women and children are beginning to search their hearts for some answer to unsatisfied inner longings.

The increased pace of living, the mad rush for pleasure, the growing use of alcohol and tranquilizers, the vast social unrest all are one great sign reading: "Help Wanted."

For any who are really seeking help, I would like to suggest the reading of the Bible. Start at the first and read it through as you would read any other book. Some people treat the Bible as a book of magic. They feel that if they read a few verses, they have somehow protected themselves against evil spirits for the day.

The Bible is the record of what some have called "the mighty acts of God." In reading the Bible as a record of God's work through men and nations, you will begin to sense His work in your life and in your day. God will accompany your reading with His Spirit if you will ask Him to interpret your reading for you.

262

Let me assure you that you will understand most of it. As it speaks of God's dealing with men and nations you will understand it well enough to be troubled by your own sins. As you follow the unfolding of His purpose to save mankind by His working in history, you will take hope in our day.

As you discover the greatness of God's love in the New Testament you will find rest for your soul. Here in Christ, all history finds its center and its meaning. In reading, faith will grow as you come to know God as revealed in the Bible. As faith grows, you will find the security you seek in our day of revolution.

Security is possible only by a vital faith in God. This faith is impossible without knowledge of God. This knowledge is in the Bible. God's Spirit and your needs invite you to read it. If you accept the invitation, I believe you will be surprised at the results.

JULY 2   **THE secret of my success? It is simple. It is found in the Bible, "In all Thy ways acknowledge Him and He shall direct thy paths."**

George Washington Carver

THE MYSTERY OF LIFE HAS A SOLUTION

Behind all the events of our daily lives, behind all the events that make up the happy and unhappy news of our day, is the vast world of the spirit. The world is a world of mystery where we walk by faith whether we want to or not.

No one understands the things that make up our lives beneath the external happenings. There is the mystery of life itself, of love that binds lives together. There is the mystery of physical and mental healing which men never understand. There is mystery hidden in man's hate of himself and of others which leads him to destroy what

263

he wants most to protect. No one knows why one man chooses the law or why one falls victim to evil and another does not.

The orderliness of the physical world makes science possible. It is accepted, but the mystery of it knows no human solution. The course of our lives is directed so often by circumstance beyond our control. As the years go by, the mystery of Providence deepens.

In history, man has been conscious of the mystery that is human existence and has expressed it in his religion. In bowing in reverence before God, man has found his only satisfying response to the mystery of life. The unlettered so-called savage bowing before an idol may be nearer the truth than the modern intellectual who scorns to humble himself before God.

Man's worship of God does not answer the mystery. It does make him one with God who is the Creator and Ruler of the mysteries. In Christ, God revealed Himself as a God who loves this world and its people. By our faith we become the children of God.

By faith the creation is known to be the servant of man, the mystery of healing and God's way of ministering to each of us. Love is a gift of God's heart to keep us close to Him and to one another.

Much of the mystery, we shall never understand. The evil that is so strong, the tragedies that are so frequent, all are beyond us to explain. There is confidence for life born, however, in the faith that in all things God has involved Himself. He took them all upon Himself on the Cross. He assures us all of final victory over them by His Resurrection from the dead.

Life will always become too much for you unless you commit your way to God in regular worship and trust Him to carry you through the mysterious world that He made. We were created to be dependent, our spirits upon His Spirit. This is the supreme mystery, which is the solution of all other mysteries.

KNOW therefore that the Lord your God is God; He is the faithful God, keeping His covenant of love to a thousand generations of those who love Him and keep His commands.

Deuteronomy 7:9 (NIV)

WHAT DO WE HAVE TO OFFER IN THE PLACE OF COMMUNISM?

A group was sitting around after discussing the state of the world. Communism was one of the topics of conversation. The question was asked: "What do we have to offer instead of communism?" We as a nation are against communism. What is it we are against? Can you clearly state it? What is it you are for in its place? What is it that is so fine that we must take it to South America and Cuba and Africa and expect it to be more attractive than communism?

I am under the impression the communist knows what he has to offer and is willing to sacrifice to get his message across. I am also under the impression that the average one of us is not very clear about what we mean by our American way of life.

The hallmark of our American dream is freedom, yet freedom is so easily misused. Freedom is not the right of each to do as he pleases. That is anarchy. Freedom cannot mean the right to express oneself without restraint. Our jails witness to that.

Freedom is possible only where there is inner surrender to that which is true. Freedom is possible only in slavery to a compelling commitment to truth.

This is what William Penn had in mind when he said that if God did not rule men they would be ruled by tyrants. A man who is free of moral restraints imposed by God will not long be free. A society that allows freedom to men to defy the divinely moral obligation to obey God will find that freedom soon disappears.

The Ten Commandments and the Sermon on the Mount are God's Word as to how men must live. We are free only as we walk in these ways. They are God's ways revealed to men supremely in Jesus Christ. He said, "I am the Truth, the Way and the life." In slavery to Him is freedom.

I believe it can be demonstrated that our American dream of freedom was born out of men's worship and obedience to God.

As we face communism we do well to come to a clear understanding of what we are for. Our standard of living is not enough, nor is our devotion to sports and movies. The moral level of our entertainment world and the world of art and literature will add very little to our stature.

Our one strength is that of a people who worship and obey God and who, walking in the liberty of the children of God, invite others to join them.

This may sound impossibly religious to you. What do you offer in it place?

JULY 4   GOD without man is still God.   Man without God is nothing.

From "Apples of Gold" quoted by Jo Petty

FOUNDING FATHERS BASED OUR NATION ON FAITH IN GOD

As we think about our country in this Fourth of July period, it can be helpful to remind ourselves of some of the things said by our founding fathers, such as: "Of all the dispositions and habits, which lead to political prosperity, Religion and Morality are indispensable supports. In vain would that man claim the tribute of Patriotism, who should labor to subvert these great pillars of human happiness."

"Tis substantially true, that virtue or morality is a necessary spring of popular government," said George Washington.

"Statesmen may plan and speculate for liberty, but it is religion and morality alone which can establish the principles upon which freedom can securely stand. A patriot must be a religious man," said John Adams.

"Can the liberties of a nation be thought secure when we have removed their only firm basis, a conviction in the minds of the people that these liberties are the gift of God? Indeed I tremble for my country when I reflect that God is just; that His justice cannot sleep forever," said Thomas Jefferson.

Benjamin Franklin said, "I have lived, sir, a long time, and the longer I live, the more convincing proofs I see of this truth - that God governs in the affairs of men. And if a sparrow cannot fall to the ground without His notice, is it probable that an empire can rise without His aid ? We have been assured, sir, in the sacred writings, that 'except the Lord build the house they labor in vain that build it.' I firmly believe that without His concurring aid we shall succeed in this political building no better than the builders of Babel. Our little partial local interests shall divide us; our projects will be confounded, and we ourselves shall become a reproach and by-word to future ages. And what is worse, mankind may hereafter from this unfortunate instance, despair of establishing governments by human wisdom and leave it to chance, war and conquest."

The Supreme Court's decision on prayer in the school will not be in vain if it serves to awaken our people to face the questions: What are the real foundations of our nation? What do we consider to be necessary to preserve them?

JULY 5   DO good with what thou hast, or it will do no good.

Penn

THE CENTRAL DEMAND OF RELIGION IS TO TRY TO DO WHAT IS RIGHT

Behind all our problems of jobs, race and political turmoil is a deeper and more difficult problem. It is the problem of getting people to do what is right. Our failure to do the right thing is not usually caused by ignorance. It is caused by our love of self. All our beautiful plans to meet our problems are wrecked because people dodge this primary problem of doing what is right as God gives them to see it.

Jesus Christ was crucified because he did perfectly the right thing - at all times. He was true to His prayer: "not my will but thine be done." He told His disciples that following this course would cause Him to suffer many things; to be rejected by the power structures of His day and, finally to be killed.

He also said that anyone who wanted to be His disciple would have to understand that it means following Him in doing the right thing as God guides one to see it. He said that living as a Christian means denying yourself as the measure of your conduct and accepting obedience to the will of God. This means that you will show your religion to men by seeking to deal with all people all the time in the right way.

Jesus said plainly that in the kind of world we live in, if you take your religion this seriously, it will mean a cross. It will mean you will suffer many things. You will find rejection by the power structures of our day. It will cost you money at times. It will prove costly in terms of social ambitions. It can easily bring you into conflict with political and government forces. These things are happening all over the world and in our own country every day.

Jesus tells us that if you will follow Him in faithful obedience,

268

you will save your soul. This means that you will keep the integrity of your conscience before God. Jesus reminds us that this is the most priceless possession any person has. He tells us that if we gain all our heart's desires in money, power and position, we are poor indeed if we have compromised our inner integrity. Once lost, no money can buy it back.

In calling men to repentance for our sins and to faith that leads to obedience to the will of God at every point in our lives, the church lays the only secure foundation upon which any person or any society can rest.

"Seek ye first the Kingdom of God and His righteousness" is still the best advice ever given to us as we seek to live together.

JULY 6 WONDERFUL grace of Jesus, greater than all my sin;

Haldor Lillenas, Hymn

THE GRACE OF GOD IS NECESSARY

Once you get away from religion, you get away from the solution of your problems. If you refuse the grace of God, you refuse the only resource capable of dealing with the forces of evil, which threaten always to destroy us.

We give assent to good things, but in our own strength we are not able to produce them. This is the fact that divides the believer from the unbeliever. If you believe you can make a good life or a good home or a good community apart from the grace of God, you live in a different world from one who believes you cannot. There is almost no common ground where problems can be discussed.

We can argue that there is a wide chasm between what we are and what we ought to be. Few would argue that we are not even what we pretend to be. In this area between what we are and what we ought to

269

be, lie all our problems. The question is: Can a man or a group of men close this gap by their own efforts or is it necessary to have the supernatural grace of God?

The Christian faith teaches that the grace of God is necessary. We are sinners. This means that, left to ourselves, we will choose the evil and not the good. It means that everything we touch becomes tainted by our self-interest and that no man can make a good life unaided by the grace of God. No society can be made good by human ideals or efforts. Education serves its purposes, but it has no power to make men good. Programs and crusades based on high ideals finally fail without the grace of God.

The grace of God comes to those who are conscious of the chasm between what they are and what they ought to be. The grace of God comes to those who repent and who determine to turn from dependence on themselves to faith in God, as Jesus Christ reveals Him.

In the grace of God the believer received two gifts. He received forgiveness of sins, forgiveness for the chasm between what he is and what he ought to be. He received also the gift of God's Spirit. Faith opens the life to the direct, supernatural working of God to do His will. Therefore, we become more nearly what we ought to be and we become channels of God's grace to others.

All problems are finally problems of God's divine grace and of man's relation to it. "The fear of the Lord is the beginning of wisdom." Those who find answers to today's problems will be able to say with Paul: "By the grace of God I am what I am."

JULY 7 O Lord, be gracious to us; we long for you. Be our strength every morning, our salvation in time of distress.

Isaiah 33:2 (NIV)

WHY ATTEND CHURCH REGULARLY? IT PROVIDES CONTACT WITH GOD

Why is it necessary to go to church regularly? Of course you won't think it necessary if you consider yourself only a superior type animal. If you seek only a comfortable nest or den, if you find the answer to your needs by competing for your food, playing with your kind, preening yourself for the admiration of your fellows, laying up a little for a rainy day, then you will see no use disturbing yourself by going to church. The church speaks in a rather critical way of these things as goals for human beings. When one is so busy building a nest and having fun, such criticism makes one find reasons not to attend services.

But you are not just a superior type animal. You are a wonderful, complex creation of God in His own image. God made us for Himself. He put us in this world to work in it for Him. He gave to man dominion over all creation.

From the very beginning, God walked and talked with men. God never intended for man to go it alone. He knew and knows that we are neither strong enough nor wise enough to meet the evil in our world or to handle its problems and responsibilities by ourselves. From the beginning God purposed to lead men through this life and at the end receive them to Himself in Heaven.

So God gave us His Word through prophets and apostles and finally in His Son. In order that this Word might have access in all ages and to all men, God gave man the church. The church is the body of believers bound by their faith into a living fellowship of God and men. This fellowship is the channel God has chosen to give men His grace, compassion, wisdom and power.

271

In worship as a part of this believing fellowship you discover your true identity as a child of God. You find your true purpose in service to God and in your service to others. In worship, you open your heart and life to the true source of all good.

A light burns only as long as it remains in contact with the source of power. A human life remains what God meant for it to be only as contact with God is faithfully maintained. Neglect it and you will soon get lost in your nest building and your playing.

It is necessary to go to church because of who God is, because of what you are and because God has given Christ to be the Head of the Church, which is His body, the fullness of Him that filleth all in all.

JULY 8 **BE still, and know that I am God; I will be exalted among nations, I will be exalted in the earth.**

Psalm 46:10 (NIV)

SUPREME COURT'S BIBLE RULING: WHAT DOES IT REALLY MEAN?

The Supreme Court's decision on prayer and the Bible reading in public schools has created much confusion. There is a wide difference of opinion as to what it really means. This is not limited to ministers, but also includes judges, lawyers, school administrators, teachers, businessmen and housewives. The decision itself shows signs of confusion as to its scope. What it really means will not be known until its workings are tested in our schools.

The very fact that the decision was made disturbs a host of people, among whom I count myself. Whatever it means or does not mean, it calls into question the open, public appeal to God for His help in the most vital area of our public life, namely, the education of our young.

No one has suggested that it is the function of our public schools to teach religion. This was not involved in the test case, as I understand it. The issue at stake is the acknowledgement of God who is the Creator and Giver of all things to all men. Our concern is based on the conviction that man is unable to do or to maintain any good thing without God's presence and help, that our best efforts in all our endeavors must fail unless they are kept open before God in worship.

This is what the writer of Proverbs 3:5-6 had in mind when he wrote: "Trust in the Lord with all thine heart and lean not upon thine own understanding. In all thy ways acknowledge him and he shall direct thy paths."

For years, it has been one of the surest marks of the American way of life that it has kept its private and public life open before God. I dare to believe that this is the source of the blessings that have crowned our nation. I find it hard to believe that this has been a mistaken interpretation of our courts, our Congress, our legislatures, even our business conventions.

It will be strange indeed when a class or a whole school cannot be quieted for a period to acknowledge God in gratitude and in petition under the leadership of those chosen by the community to prepare their children for life through education.

Those who lead this effort to remove the acknowledgement of God from the schools already are moving into other areas of public life. We are told that the home and church are the places to teach religion. This is true and the more effectively they do the job the more positively people resist efforts to remove God from our public institutions.

God is Lord of all of life. To the believer, this is a matter, not of opinion, but of fact. Thus to acknowledge God in all our ways becomes a necessity, and not a choice, for our well being.

JULY 9   YOU may have to fight a battle more than once
to win it.

Margaret Thatcher

OFFICIAL OPPOSITION CAN MAKE PEOPLE HAVE STRONGER FAITH

I read an article by a worker in the Christian Church in East Germany. He said that the church there may be serving the future of the faith in greater ways than we in the West suspect. In East Germany the church works in a society and among people who are openly atheistic. They do not believe in God. The public institutions have no reference to God except to deny any faith in Him.

In the West, there is still lip service to God, but in conduct there is practical atheism. Our way of life, he said, is the result not of faith we profess but of the demands of our secular society. The writer indicated that it might be easier for the church to make clear witness of its faith in an openly hostile society than in one whose profession is still largely Christian but whose actions show little evidence of this faith.

Without entering into argument at this point as to the desirability of any one of these things, no one can contend that our Western and American emphasis upon money, comfort, pleasure and armaments is the evidence of a people living in obedience to God.

Our scandals, our crime, our strife, our lack of any concern over immoral conduct, our growing use of alcohol and pills - all these things are symptoms of practical atheism.

Mixed in with all these things is a strong outward show of religion at least in our own country. Yet it is hard to get a real hearing for a clear-cut witness for God as He has revealed Himself in Jesus Christ. We find general acceptance of our country as a pluralistic society. This means that we take for granted that there are many gods, all of which must be equally respected.

274

This idea is found to have widespread acceptance among non-believers and among believers. This idea was behind the Supreme Court decision on prayer and Bible reading in the schools - and the approval of it by church groups.

The writer on East Germany said that sooner or later the pious mask would be removed from our practical atheism. Then the church would be freed of its compromise with an atheistic society that no longer pretended to honor God. The history of Christian witness in East Germany will be helpful since it has been forced to make itself felt in a hostile environment.

The Supreme Court decision has had the result of causing the church to think more seriously about its message and its mission. This is good. If the present drift away from God, in public and private, continues, our writer will be right when he says that we can learn a great deal from a church that has maintained its witness in an unfriendly society and often under direct pressure.

JULY 10   **MAN is unjust, but God is just; and finally justice triumphs.**

Henry W. Longfellow

WIDESPREAD EVIL IS NOT THE TRUE PICTURE

It has become popular to emphasize the things that are wrong. Literature depends today on picturing people who make a mess of their lives. The evil that men do is presented as the normal expression of human nature.

People applaud stories that describe the break-up of character under stress. Delinquency in young people is presented as to appear the trademark of youth. Religion is almost lightly dismissed as not being relevant to our day.

Of course, there is much that is wrong with people. Too many do break down morally under temptation. Lots of young people are delinquents. God and religion are irrelevant to many who wish to cut loose from all restraint, human or divine.

But there is much that is right in our world. There are multitudes of people, young and old, who are moral and sober. There are millions for whom religion is not only relevant but is the support of their lives and the inspiration of their service to others.In the midst of the most difficult future any generation of young people has been called to face, a great majority of them are trying hard to find the right paths and to build decent, useful lives. Percentage-wise, I would guess more young people are finding support in their religion than any other age group.

Every community is filled with people of middle age, carrying heavy burdens with courage and good success.

The writers of our day who constantly magnify the evil do no one a service. There is evil present everywhere. The best of men know the heavy pull of evil. But the grace of God is greater than our sin and the power of God is greater than our evil. We need to remind ourselves over and over again that Christ died and was raised from the dead to guarantee that evil cannot win.

JULY 11   COMMIT your way to the Lord; trust Him and He will do this: He will make your righteousness shine like the dawn, the justice of your cause like the noonday sun.

Psalm 37:5,6 (NIV)

GOING THE WRONG WAY ON A ONE-WAY STREET

Truth and goodness are a part of the real and permanent order of things. They are the expression of the nature of God in whose world we live and move and have our being. To live apart from truth and goodness is like driving the wrong way on a one-way street. There is no future in going the wrong way. In the long run, God always wins. Truth and goodness survive every attack and rise again after every defeat.

You have the power to chose which way you will go on this one-way street. If you choose to go the wrong way you can be sure of trouble. It never works out for you or me. It always brings trouble to others as we collide with them.

The old saying "You can't beat the game" needs to be hammered into our heads again. God is not mocked, and what we sow, we reap.

Purity and honesty and loyalty and patience and forgiveness and love seem to have gone out of fashion. They are sneered at as weakness. Greed and cruelty and force and immorality and dishonesty appear to be accepted as the way of life. We need to face what is happening to us.

Speakers at all kinds of functions speak of the confusion of people going the wrong way on a one-way street. The confusion is made plain by two news items about a large manufacturing concern. One told of their record profits. Another told how the Federal Trade Commission ruled that they were a party to using "camera trickery" to fake television commercials about auto window glass...the picture supposedly taken through plate glass was filmed through an open window, the commissioner said.

We are confused because we give lip service to the fixed things of God and actual worship to the things of selfishness and greed and immorality. One can only hope that we will get so confused that we will be turned again to the simple virtues God taught in the Bible. Life then won't be so confused. We will be going the way of the main traffic of God's creation.

This will begin with you and with me in our own circle of influence. There is no use bewailing the sins of others until your own life is running in the right direction.

This will involve a turning from the worship of self to the worship of God. Only those who depend on God for forgiveness or for strength can move in the ways of God.

JULY 12   **WHEN God gives any man wealth and possessions and enables him to enjoy them, to accept his lot and be happy in his work...this is a gift of God.**

Ecclesiastes 5:19 (NIV)

CONTENTMENT DOES NOT COME FROM A HIGH STANDARD OF LIVING

The story is told that someone asked Maurice Chevalier, the French actor, how it felt to be 72 years old. He is said to have replied, "When I consider the alternative, it feels wonderful." A friend who has had a serious operation related this incident to me. He is restored to full-time activity but is under some handicap and is restricted to a limited diet.

Four of us were at lunch and my friend was enjoying himself. One of us asked him how he got along on so limited a diet. He repeated the above story in answer.

The apostle Paul said that he had learned in whatever state he found himself therein to be content.

I know there are those upon whom misfortune has come who have a right to be disturbed. However, most of the complaining comes from people that are not suffering from major misfortune.

Why is everyone discontented today? Not many people are enjoying their lives day by day, minute by minute. There is a strange sickness that has taken hold of us. Whatever we have, we feel we must have something else or more of what we have. Wherever we are, we want to be somewhere else.

If you stop and honestly face yourself, you probably have everything you need for contentment. You have enough food for the day and a roof over your head. You very likely have those whom you love and who love you. You have, or can have, something useful to do. Of course, no one can assure you these things will always be there - but you have them today.

We don't need to raise our standard of living to produce more contentment. It would probably help if something would happen to break our cycle of increasing material prosperity.

Contentment will come when each of us is brought to realize how fortunate we are where we are, just as we are. Enjoy your food. Many people are hungry. Thank God for shelter. Many are homeless. Live today in love with your family. Tomorrow they may be gone. Not only count your blessings, but enjoy them.

First of all, seek until you find your proper relationship with God. He made us for Himself and Augustine said we are restless until we rest in Him.

JULY 13   PRAISE God from whom all blessings flow...

Doxology

GIVE 'THANK YOU,' GET CONTENTMENT

A key is a very small answer to a big problem. If you have the key, you can open the door with ease. If you do not have the key, you are in trouble. One of our chief problems today is the matter of contentment. So few people are satisfied where they are with what they have. We have lost the key to contented living.

Material goods and good health do not seem to bring contentment. In fact, the people who have these blessings often are the most dissatisfied with life in general. With all our abundance, we are a generation of complainers.

I want to suggest a key to contented living. If you will give it honest use, it can change your life. The key is in two words: "Thank you." These words represent something that is in short supply. We

279

use them casually, but very little effort or time is given to expressing gratitude. Jesus healed ten lepers one day. Only one returned to say: "Thank you." This is one in ten and it may be a high percentage.

1. Spend a little while each day saying "Thank you" to God. He made our world so that it supplies every need you have. He sustains it in its regular order by the word of His power. He has revealed Himself in human form that we may know Him and be reconciled to Him.

2. Day by day, take time to remember how much you depend on people and make the effort to say: "Thank you." You can't live at all without the help of those about you. How long has it been since you really said and meant "Thank you" to your loved ones, your friends, your fellow-workers, your neighbors, your postman, the bus driver, the teacher of your children?

If you will try this, you will be amazed at what a rare thing you are doing and how much joy you bring to others. Everyone hungers for appreciation and gets very little. You will make life easier for those about you as you help them to know that what they do is appreciated.

Their response will bring joy to you. Contentment will grow in your own heart as you understand that it is more blessed to give than to receive. You will come to enjoy what you have where you are. You will complain less about what you do not have.

God promises His peace to those who make their needs known with thanksgiving. If you will try using this key, it will do so much to unlock the door of happiness to you and to all with whom you have contact.

JULY 14   **THAT he may know how to refuse the evil, and choose the good.**

Isaiah 7:15 (KJ)

WE HAVE FREEDOM TO CHOOSE, BUT THE CHOICES ARE BUILDING

I have an idea that people are unhappy today because they use their "rights" in the wrong way. It is all very well to fight for your rights. It is more important to use those you have in the right way. The truth is that you can keep the rights you have, only as you use them as they should be used. Jesus was stating a fact of life when he said that to them that have shall be given, and that which they have will be taken away from those who do not have the wisdom to use it wisely.

Freedom is one of our basic rights. At the same time, it is our most dangerous possession. Freedom is the right we have to choose that to which we will give ourselves. If we make the mistake of making freedom the right to do as we please, we will find our freedom taken away. If we give ourselves to the wrong thing, we will become a slave and not a free person.

We are free to choose, but we must abide by the demands of the choice we make. A young person is free to choose a career. Once the choice is made, he is bound by the demands of that career. If he fails to obey the discipline of the career, he loses his freedom to choose it.

Couples are free to choose whether they will marry and make a home. Once the step is taken, they are no longer free. They are bound to obey the rules of life that make a good home possible. If they use their freedom to break rather than keep these rules, they will lose the blessings of the home.

You and I are free to choose whether we will give ourselves to God as His faithful servants, or whether we will follow the desires of our own natures.

Our choice will determine the kind of life we live, the relationship we have with other people and our eternal destiny. If we choose to respond to God's invitation of love to serve Him, we will find our freedom a growing joy. If we seek to serve ourselves, freedom will be lost as we become slaves of our lower nature, of our appetites and of our sins.

In these days when every one is seeking his "rights," it is high time we began to be equally interested in how we are using the rights we have. The more rights a person has, the more necessary it becomes that he know how to use them. We are made or ruined by how we use what we have.

JULY 15   **AND the second is like unto it, thou shalt love thy neighbor as thyself.**

Matthew 22:39 (KJ)

LOVE CAN CROSS ALL THE BARRIERS

There are lots of people in this world. There are many differences that are easily seen. There are differences in races of which we are quite conscious today. There are differences in nationality which modern travel brings home to nearly everyone. There are wide differences in culture, education, and ability. There is the difference between men and women. People look different and have different likes and dislikes. In truth, each individual is different from all others. To mix it all up, each individual, each race, each nation, each cultural and economic group has a human determination to advance the interests of his own group.

How do you suggest we overcome all these differences so that people can live together in peace?

These questions thrust themselves upon you as you travel about. You see and feel all these differences. You read the newspapers that represent many of these differences. If you are honest, there is very little that seems to be drawing people together, other than physically.

Jesus looked out on his world of people and had compassion on them because they were as sheep having no shepherd. There is little reason to think the situation has changed.

There is one thing all people have in common - the need for love and for appreciation. Here each individual is exactly like all others. It is at this point that we can find common ground where the differences that divide us can be bridged.

This is the point at which the revelation of God in Jesus Christ meets all people whatever be their sex or condition. Here is the Good News that God loves each individual just as he or she is. He would have each accept that love and find that because God loves him, he can love others. This love, accepted and lived, does make people one. In this love there is a leveling of barriers of race, sex, class and nation.

Human pride and animal selfishness will defeat every grand plan of man where God's love is left out. He came in human form so that we could understand this.

Nothing is as relevant to our troubled day as the fact that God seeks us to be His own in love and to live in love with one another.

JULY 16   PRAISE the Lord, O my soul.   Praise the Lord.

Psalm 104:35 (NIV)

WHAT ABOUT GOD IN GOOD TIMES?

God is our refuge and strength. Nearly everyone seeks this refuge and strength in time of trouble. There are not many people who do not ask God for help when in some emergency all human supports give way. We know what it means to come to God in our weakness, in our sorrow, in our disappointment.

Yet, too many of us forget that God seeks us in our strength to serve Him. How many of us there are who have promised God such great things if He would grant us reprieve from disaster. Our prayer answered, we have refused to fulfill our promise.

If you are young and strong, God would enlist you in the day of your strength as His servant. In a day when men deny the very presence of God, He calls you to witness to His reality.

If in your mature years you have influence and money, God stands at your door asking you to use the things of your strength for Him.

The apostle Paul came to Christ in the full flower of his youthful vigor saying: "Lord, what woulds't thou have me to do?"

It is hard for a person who is fortunate in person and possessions to surrender himself or herself to God for His service. Such surrender may or may not involve change in place or occupation. It does involve the idea of letting God determine how life shall be lived and possessions used. Jesus said that this was as hard as it is for a camel to go through the eye of a needle. It requires a miracle, which Jesus promised to any who would volunteer.

These are days that require the best that is in us. God would bring rebellious men into His family of love. He would bring peace and harmony and affection where hate and division rule. He would put honesty into business and true service into politics and purity into our relations one with another.

If the Kingdom of God is to move with power in this day, we must lift up our eyes to see the need, put our shoulders to the wheel and give our strength to the task. There is a part of this task close at hand for anyone who will commit himself. If you seek the place where you can serve, you will surely find it. It will require the best you are and have. God seeks you and your gifts - for your sake and for the service of others.

JULY 17 TROUBLE and distress shall come upon me, but your commands are my delight. Your statutes are forever right; give me understanding that I might live.

Psalm 119: 143,144 (NIV)

PRAYER FOR A TIME OF DEEP SORROW

As this is being written, I am returning from standing by with a family where a 27-year-old son was shot to death near his home in Washington. He was walking his dog around the block late in the evening when he was attacked and killed. The young man was the last of his generation to bear the family name. He had already added luster to it. I have not known a finer person. Educated at excellent universities at home and in England, he had taken his place on the faculty of a large college. He had every promise of dedicated, useful service to God and to men.

His brutal death brought grief to and raised indignation in a large segment of our capital city. At his funeral in the chapel of St. Albans School, a prayer was offered which I pass on as one of the most helpful that has come into my experience. In this prayer there is tribute concurred in by all who knew the young man. There is affection felt by all who were privileged to be his friend.

The prayer opens the way for God's comfort to all who loved him. It challenges the devotion of all who seek a better world. It surrenders the mystery of evil to Jesus Christ, who took the evil that killed Him and used it as a channel of redemption.

This prayer was offered by Canon Charles Martin, head of St. Albans School, close friend of the young man and of his family through many years:

"Almighty God, in whose hands are the living and the dead, we give Thee humble and hearty thanks for this Thy servant, Newell, and for the qualities of mind and heart that made him loved and

285

respected among us. And especially: For his quiet goodness and his generous concern for others.

"For his integrity and his earnest good will.

"For his considerate helpfulness and his utter dependability.

"For his complete loyalty to family and friends and school and all He held good.

"And we give thanks for his life in the hurt of his death. Grant that both through his life and his death, we may be made more sensitive to the problems of our times, and may dedicate ourselves with new wisdom and strong resolve to the building of a better community and a better world, where the senseless and the brutal may give way to the ordered and true and beautiful.

"All of which we ask in the name of a young man, a teacher, whose life, before it seemed fulfilled, was broken by the evil of his time.

"Yet who lives among us, as among men ever since, as our Hope and our Savior, Jesus Christ our Lord."

JULY 18   ALL I have seen teaches me to trust the Creator for all I have not seen.

Ralph Waldo Emerson

FAITH OVERCOMES FEAR OF THE FUTURE

Fear of the future is common. Nearly everything that is written seems to try to make us afraid of something. There are certain facts about the future that, by their very nature, tend to make us fearful. The future is inescapable, it is unknown and, finally, it is beyond our control.

As you face your future, you have two choices. You can be a child of Adam and try to handle your own future. You can depend on your own wisdom and strength. You can gather the resources and tools of this material world which include education, money, culture, friends and family. You can gather the best of the world, and then do the best you can. The end will be for you about what it was for Adam: disorder, pain, defeat and death.

Or you can be a child of Abraham and live by faith in God. You will still deal with all the things of this world, but you will not depend on them to secure your future. You will depend absolutely on God to see you through. Abraham was saved by his faith, and God, who raised Jesus Christ from the dead, has covenanted to save all who follow the example He set.

This saving faith includes several things. Those who live by faith, live by the conviction that God calls us by name, one by one. We are not lost in the crowd. Not only that, but we are led by faith to the conviction that God guides us in the experiences of life by His plan for us.

Living by faith involves believing God will supply our needs. Abraham found this to be true as he went out not knowing whither he went. God will clothe, feed and shelter us. God promised Abraham that He would make him a blessing to others. He died with no proof but the word of God. Yet Christ was born of his seed and nations today call him blessed.

God promised Abraham that he would end his journey in heaven. So in all his life, he sought a city that has foundations, whose builder and maker is God. So as we live by faith, we live in the certainty that at the end, Christ will come and receive us unto Himself, that where He is, we will be also.

JULY 19   O, How I love Jesus, Because He first loved me!

Frederick Whitfield, Hymn

MORALITY REQUIRES GOD AT LIFE'S HEART

We are as a nation shaking ourselves loose from our religious foundations. Whatever the technical explanation of the decisions of the Supreme Court concerning prayer and Bible reading may be, they have called in to question the fact we are one nation under God. When you remove God from the center of your life, you no longer have an absolute standard of morality. You also remove the only motivation for morality in the Christian meaning of the word.

Loving and fearing God because He first loved us is the only standard and motive for morality as we have understood it. Remove these and there is no argument or defense against those who claim the privilege of living as they please and of gaining profit from the weaknesses of our nature.

It allows men and women to follow art for art's sake with no accepted guidelines. It allows men in public life to speak fair words and promote worthy programs with little obligation to make their lives conform to that for which they publicly stand. It allows men and women who defy Christian standards of morality to receive public support and material gain.

When the love and fear of God goes, then we are the victims of whatever power structure there happens to be in business, in politics and in the entertainment field. The only hope we have for any change in the moral climate of our country is a religious revival that will put God in the center of your life and mine, of your neighbor's life and that of the people you know and do not know. Until that happens, all our efforts will be play-acting. Without it, the word "character" has only the meaning any person wants it to mean. Only a person who loves and fears God can be led into right paths or be trusted to lead others.

It is not popular in this day to inquire into a person's relationship with God. We are vitally interested in his health, in his ability, in his observable conduct - in everything but his religious commitment. If he is clever and smart and educated and talented, if he is a money maker, we are satisfied. As long as this attitude prevails, our troubles will increase.

In selecting a person to marry, or to work with, or to hire, or to serve in a public office, or to follow as a popular figure, the one question that matters above all else is, what is his relation to God? Before you dismiss this as too narrow, look into your own heart and see if it is not true of your own life.

JULY 20   **"I see Jesus in every human being. I say to myself, this is hungry Jesus, I must feed him. This is sick Jesus. This one has leprosy or gangrene; I must wash him and tend to him. I serve them because I love Jesus."**

Mother Teresa

DO WE TRULY SEE THE PEOPLE WE MEET?

Do you see the people you meet each day as real human beings or as cogs in a machine? You hear it so often said that we are losing the individual in the organization and rush of our day. You can help overcome this by remembering that each one you meet has the same ambitions, longings, needs and hurts that you have. This was brought home to me in a parking lot not long ago. The same man has been parking my car whenever I go downtown. The exchanges between us have been pleasant but nothing more. On this particular day, I stepped into the little shack that serves this lot as an office. On the table was an array of oil paints. There was one picture finished and standing on the floor against the far wall. He was in the midst of painting another one.

I thought to myself that you never know what goes on in the heart of another. Here in this man of little culture, as some count these things, was evident a sense of beauty. He earned his living parking cars, but he was involved in a rich area of life where few would suspect it.

I was with a friend who said as we walked away: "You never can afford to write off anyone." And yet we do. More and more we live in a "faceless" society. The name plates people wear bear witness to this fact. In a sense they are the badges of our secular day. Whenever a society stops taking God seriously, people no longer regard one another with affectionate concern.

Without the influence of God's love, we lose interest in other people, except insofar as they can serve us. We don't want to get involved in their problems or their dreams. Their personal affairs are their own, and too often we want them to stay that way. This attitude is in neighborhoods and in business. Often it is in families. All the time the person you run across or work with or live with is longing for your recognition of him as a person of value. There are dreams he would like to share, there is sympathy he needs or appreciation he has earned and no one has given.

The common man heard Jesus gladly because the lowliest found in Jesus One who treated him as a person of great value, of eternal value. Jesus saw each person He met as one whom God loves.

JULY 21   **LET the wise listen and add to their learning and let the discerning get guidance. The fear of the Lord is the beginning of knowledge...**

Proverbs I:5,7 (NIV)

RELIGION IS REQUIRED FOR A MORAL LIFE

I once read an article entitled "Character and National Health" by Paul S. Campbell. In that article, he gives some interesting information. He defines national health as the social energy or power that enables us to solve our problems and to advance in art, politics, and science and in personal, national and international relationships.

He calls attention to the fact that this social energy is the direct product of character. He quotes a Dr. Unwin of Cambridge University as saying that there is a direct relationship between the moral purity of a society and the ability of that society to meet its problems and to advance in culture. Chastity before marriage and strict monogamy after are a necessity for a society's progress. These conclusions are the result of the study of 80 civilizations that extended over 4,000 years.

Character as we have understood it here in America is the result of the Christian faith. Here men and women and children have found the answer to the questions of right and wrong and to the power whereby character is formed. Here the standards of moral purity were learned and accepted. Out of a narrowness in personal faith and conduct flowed energies that made us great.

Today there is a steady attack on chastity and monogamy. Support for what has been known as immoral conduct comes from all sides, even from churchmen. Many forms of entertainment present promiscuity and illicit forms of sex as normal. Publicity is given on all sides to those who defy the Christian code of conduct.

At the same time there is a movement away from founding our personal lives and public institutions on the acknowledgment of the God of Jesus Christ. The Bible is no longer regarded as having divine authority. The statement, "Thus saith the Lord" is scarcely understood.

These two things - the denial of faith and the breakdown of moral purity, go together. The result is the poverty of personal and social life. The result is finally death to all that enables a person or a society to survive.

The cause of our troubles is sin and the answer begins in divine forgiveness and the giving of our lives in obedience to the will of God. Here character grows. Moral purity becomes a fact, and the social energies flow toward solution of problems and toward advance in the finer things of life.

JULY 22   **SHOW me your ways, O Lord, teach me your paths; guide me in your truth...my hope is in you all day long.**

Psalm 25: 4,5 (NIV)

CHANGING WORLD, STEADY GUIDELINES

Life is so modern and new things meet us on every hand. However, there are some old things that are as modern as tomorrow. It can well be that if we neglect these old things, the new ones will destroy us. The old things have to do with how to live steadily in our changing world. These things have not changed with the changing times. Faith and character and conduct have the same guidelines yesterday and today and forever.

Some of these guidelines are set forth in the ancient story of Joseph. You will find this story interesting reading. It begins in the 37th chapter of Genesis. Joseph passed through experiences that would shatter the lives of most people. He was betrayed by members of his own family, sold into slavery, robbed of his reputation, jailed as a criminal. Yet he came through all these misfortunes with victory. Few will have exactly this kind of life, but everyone faces experiences that threaten the stability of their lives and which can destroy them unless there are deep inner resources of spirit.

There were three things in Joseph's life that enabled him to win:

1. Joseph had a deep conviction that God had a plan for the world and that there was a place for him in this plan. He believed that God would carry out that plan in his life, regardless of all that evil could do against him. He had plenty of opportunity to test that faith. He found God was faithful to carry him through. When you think of events today, it makes a difference whether you believe they are a meaningless jumble or whether, behind them, God is working out His eternal purpose.

2. Joseph chose to maintain his obedience to God in the realm of his

personal integrity. This was hard for him. It is hard today. This means the hard choice of doing what we believe to be right in the daily decisions that face us.

3. Joseph did the best he could to be useful to others in every circumstance. It will help us to live with victory, if we will do the best we can in whatever situation we find ourselves.

These are ways to successful living that are as old as the hills and as new as tomorrow.

JULY 23　　　**...WHOEVER humbles himself like this child is the greatest in the kingdom of heaven.**

Matthew 18:4 (NIV)

A CHILD'S FAITH HAS MUCH TRUTH IN IT

These are days when the old ways are changing. There is no hiding place from changes that force themselves upon us. Not only are things changing, but also they seem to get more complicated. Nothing seems easy any more. Pressures build up. Our days are filled with rushing around to meet demands that leave us frustrated. For more than a long time, we need to remind ourselves that there is One that has not changed. Christ revealed God who is the same yesterday, today and forever.

In Hebrews, there are words that can help us. "Yet once more I shake not the earth only, but also heaven. And this word, yet once more, signified the removing of those things that are shaken, as of things that He made that those things that cannot be shaken may remain. Wherefore, we, receiving a kingdom which cannot be moved, let us have grace whereby we may serve God acceptably with reverence and godly fear."

Perhaps God is making things so complicated to drive us back to the faith of a little child. It can be that He is shaking our man-made creations to draw us back to simple trust in Him. It may not be so unsophisticated after all to believe that God loves us and to trust that love as a small child trusts the love of a good parent.

Religion and theology can get very complicated, but at heart it is a matter of trusting God with your life and believing He cares for you and will take care of you now and forever. It is believing that no matter how bad you are God seeks to forgive and receive you. It is believing that no matter how hurt or afraid you are, He waits to heal your hurt and give you courage. Christian faith is trusting God's love for you and then loving others because He loves you. It is helping to heal the hurt of others because your hurt has been healed. It is having a forgiving spirit because you have found forgiveness in the Divine Heart.

Security in our insecure day is found in reaching out for the hand of God as a little child and trusting Him to see us through.

JULY 24   **"...I will refine them like silver and test them like gold. They will call on my name and I will answer them; I will say, They are my people and they will say, 'The Lord God is our God.'"**

Zachariah 13:9 (NIV)

TRAGEDY MAY BEAR SOME GOOD FRUIT

We have become accustomed to having the things that are wrong with us and our nation and our religion drummed into our ears and eyes. Critics and debunkers of the good and of the things that are right have been having a field day. We have begun to lose confidence in ourselves, our nation and our religion.

In the days that followed President Kennedy's death something happened to Americans that I believe will have lasting influence. For a little more than three days, we were stopped in our tracks and forced to take stock of ourselves.

1. Millions of our people found themselves going back to God in their own hearts to ask some deep questions about life and death. In public places and in private, people turned to God. It will be more difficult now for those who seek to divorce our institutions from acknowledging God. The eternal things of God were felt almost instinctively to be our help in ages past, our hope for years to come.

2. There came almost suddenly a new pride in our country. The apostles of hate and division had shaken the faith of many in our nation. As crisis struck, our representative form of government stood without a tremor. The torch was passed to other hands with no other thought than that all was well with our national structure. There is a new thrill for untold millions as the national anthem is played and as "America" is sung.

3. Then there was born out of this tragic circumstance a new confidence in one another as Americans. There are differences that divide us one from another. Many of these will remain. Some will continue to cause pain. However, bridges of understanding have been built and communication is made easier, even where agreement cannot be reached. No one expects that we will be alike or think alike. However, it is necessary that we deal with one another in mutual respect.

In those days, the storm bared the foundations of this land. They were revealed as standing firm. These foundations are faith in God, in representative government and in one another.

JULY 25 **EVERY good tree bears good fruit, but a bad tree bears bad fruit. A good tree cannot bear bad fruit, and a bad tree cannot bear good fruit. Thus, by their fruit you will know them.**

Matthew 7:17, 18, 20 (NIV)

WHICH ONE'S FIRST: APPLE OR THE TREE?

If you are a farmer, you will understand that you cannot produce fruit without trees. You will also take it for granted you will get peaches from a peach tree and apples from an apple tree. Even those of us reared in the city understand these things.

When it comes to the things of moral conduct, both personally and in society as a whole, we talk and act as though fruit could be produced on any kind of tree.

It is as though a farmer decided that all he was interested in was the fruit from his apple orchard. He let the apple trees wither from blight and be infested with worms. He cared not when friends planted some peach trees and some oak trees here and there. All he did was count the trees and expect apples to grow on all of them regardless of the kind of tree or of its health.

This is the attitude of many social reformers of our day. They decided what kind of conduct there ought to be between people and nations and races. It really never occurs to them that conduct is the fruit of the tree of life. The kind of tree of life you grow bears the fruit of your conduct. The kind of tree of life you grow depends on what you believe about God. Social actions are the fruit of what individuals believe and there is no short cut.

There are those who have taken their social goals from the tree of the Christian faith. Love of your neighbor as yourself grows only when you love God with all your heart, mind, soul and strength. However, many proceed as though this fruit of brotherly love can be produced from any tree or from none. Such liberal reformers are impatient with any insistence that you must begin and stay with the cultivation of the right trees if you are to produce the right fruits.

What I am getting at is the need for what is called evangelism. It has almost disappeared today. Social crusading has displaced evangelistic fervor and the very fruits we seek are drying up. Social crusading without Christian commitment leaves all the problems of immorality, hatred, personal disintegration, inconsistency, cruelty, and war.

JULY 26   **WHEREVER a man turns he can find someone who needs him. Even if it is a little thing - do something for which there is no pay - but the privilege of just doing it. Remember, you don't live in the world all on your own.**

Albert Schweitzer

HOW DO YOU LIVE LIFE HAPPILY, USEFULLY?

We all share the same desire. We want to live abundantly. We want to break out of our restrictions and monotony and enjoy life. Nearly every advertisement is directed to our ambition to live it up. The most pressing question anyone faces is: How can I live happily and usefully? There are two ways open to you - the way of the world and the way of the Christian faith.

The way of the world may be fairly summed up as seeking to satisfy our physical desires, our desires for material things and the approval and rewards of people. Jesus points out that this is the road most people take.

It seems so logical to think that if we use our heads and use the resources so richly present in our world, we can make our own happiness. Surely a man will really live who satisfies his physical needs in a legitimate way, accumulates sufficient material things and makes good by getting ahead of others.

The other road is that marked out by Christ. He notes that this road has a narrow gate and is traveled by comparatively few people. One enters this road by finding in Christ the forgiveness of sins and accepting Him as the absolute guide for life.

The man walking the Christian way decides his actions by asking: What would Christ have me do? He approaches his life's work, his marriage, his business and social decisions in the light of God's will for his life. His own ideas and the pressure of the world are pushed aside as he honestly seeks divine guidance at every point.

Most people who try to satisfy themselves by giving their energies to meeting their physical needs, by accumulating material things and by getting ahead in the world, fail in their effort and are left unhappy. Those who succeed find that these things fail to produce abundant life. The more they succeed, the more problems they seem to have.

Those who walk the Christian way make some amazing discoveries. They find eternal life as Jesus promises. Eternal life is life that has found peace with God and with self and with other people.

JULY 27   I have hidden your word in my heart that I might not sin against you.

Psalm 119:11 (RSV)

PEOPLE ALSO NEED A REFERENCE POINT

An engineer was asked how a building is put together so that the floors come out level and how they meet exactly other floors that they join at the same level. The answer was that all are measured from either an arbitrarily fixed point or from sea level.

In other words, the harmony and usefulness of the whole building are made possible by having each part rightly related to one chosen fixed point from which everything is measured. This is just as true in building people as in erecting office buildings.

It is putting it mildly to say people are confused today as to what is right and what is wrong. Politicians and preachers join in urging moral reform. Honesty in government and business, decency in entertainment, moderation or abstinence in drinking alcohol, modesty in dress, fair play in race relations, are all subjects of widespread conversation and action. Everyone seems to want to improve things, but the efforts being made only make the confusion worse.

If an architect and a contractor found their building with floors slanting and walls crooked, with floors failing to meet where they should, they would suspect that the drawings and the construction were carried out with no reference to a fixed point agreed on by all concerned.

Our efforts to improve our moral climate will continue to breed confusion unless we find a fixed point of judgment from which to measure our desires and our conduct. If you and I can do as we please, only chaos can result. Law is no fixed point because it changes with changing ideas of people.

In building a life or a community, the only fixed point is the word and will of God. God has not left Himself without witness. The Bible is in your hands. It is given in a way you can understand. God finally came in human form so that no one could miss the way. The will of God is given in a person to person message. Here is a fixed point from which all conduct that is harmonious and useful is measured and which judges it.

Unless this will of God is taken seriously again by individuals and by all groupings of individuals there will be no answer to our present moral confusion. Only judgment will remain.

JULY 28   I WRITE these things to you who believe in the name of the Son of God so that you may know that you have eternal life.

I John 5:13 (NIV)

WHAT FOUNDATION WITHOUT FAITH?

It is popular today to say that religion is not relevant to our modern day. We are told that we have outgrown our need for faith in God. Evil is now to be overcome by doing away with poverty, by civil rights, by social adjustment where we are taught to understand one another, by education, by strong armed forces.

We are told that since it is hard to know God and since there are so many different ideas about God and about how to worship Him, it is better just to leave Him out. So, this is what we are doing. We are leaving Him out of our personal lives, our homes, our business life, our clubs, our courts, and our government.

But suppose for a moment that God really exists. Suppose the Apostles Creed is the truth about God and man. Suppose the Bible is the Word of God. How do you leave God out of anything and expect it to survive. Suppose God is the source of our lives and the source of our every good. How do you expect to live the good life without the Bible and without prayer whatever you do, private or public?

If God is not relevant in your life, how do you decide what is right for you to do? What is the basis of your conduct? If you do not feel accountable to God, what finally do you judge yourself by? Another question: why do you criticize your neighbor if he takes advantage of you or treats you badly? If there is no God, he has as much right to his ideas of conduct as you do.

If you have outgrown God, where do you go with a broken life to find forgiveness and a new start? Where do you go with a broken heart and find comfort? Where do you go with a broken body and find strength?

If God is not the God of our nation, where do you go in her emergencies? How do you turn to God who has been banished, with faith that there will come grace to help in our time of need. Faith in God is the foundation upon which every strong man and every strong nation has been built. An ancient Psalmist asked a question that is relevant today: "If the foundations be destroyed, what can the righteous do?"

WALK in all the way that the Lord your God has commanded you, so that you may live and prosper and prolong your days in the land that you possess.

Deuteronomy 5:33 (NIV)

OBEDIENCE TO THE LAW IS ROOTED IN GOD

It is high time we became alarmed over the spread of lawlessness. Almost everyone agrees with such a statement. Not many seem to agree as to how we are to meet the problem. Law is the expression of the will of the people. It can be enforced only so long as people are willing to have it enforced. Large groups differ as to which laws are to be obeyed. The result borders on legal chaos.

Lawlessness is contagious and it spreads to include all manner of evil. Where do you begin to overcome lawlessness? There is only one place to begin, and that is with our relationship to God. If our human law is not the reflection of God's eternal nature, it has no other foundation than the changing demands of the group in power at any given moment.

At a period in the Roman history, Paul listed the evidences of lawlessness present for all to see. It is an ancient list, yet as modern as today's newspaper - illicit sex, unrighteousness, immorality, wickedness, covetousness, maliciousness, envy, murder, strife, deceit, malignity, backbiting, hating of God, insolence, haughtiness, boasting, inventing evil things, disobedience to parents, lack of understanding, covenant breaking, lack of natural affections, unmercifulness.

God's word says that these things resulted "because that, when they knew God, they glorified him not as God, neither were they thankful, but became vain in their reasoning and their foolish heart was darkened. Professing themselves to be wise, they became fools."

Until we begin again with God in every part of our lives, public and private, we are not likely to begin solving our problem. Repentance, faith and obedience to God are the only foundations upon which life can be built. This is as true for a nation as it is for an individual. It begins with you and me.

Only as we seek to make those laws that conform to the will of God can they have binding effect on the consciences of men. Only as the consciences of men are made aware that in obedience to law, they are dealing not with man but with God, will law find respect and obedience. Only as we surrender ourselves to God as His creatures will the power of God work in us and through us to establish peace.

An ancient promise of God is still valid: "If my people, which are called by my name, shall humble themselves and pray, and seek my face and turn from their wicked ways; then will I hear them from heaven and will forgive their sin and heal their land."

JULY 30   **DO NOT store up for yourselves treasures on earth, where moth and rust destroy... But store up for yourselves treasures in heaven for where your treasure is, there will your heart be also.**

Matthew 6: 19-21 (NIV)

QUEST FOR MONEY BETRAYS VALUES

Are you ever worried about money? If you are, your faith probably is at fault, not your economics. We deal with money out of necessity. The important thing is not how much money or how little we have. The important thing is that we believe the truth about money. Most people won't admit that Christianity has anything to do with economics because they don't want to believe what Christ taught about money.

Most school courses that teach about money deal with it as though it were neutral, something that is in itself neither good nor bad and that if a man is smart and deals with it in a clever way, money will produce the good life.

Christ taught that money has within itself the power to destroy the good. Paul said truly that the love of money is the root of all evil. Jesus said if you take laying up treasure on earth as your goal, it will cost you the good things of life and finally your soul.

The love of money breeds pride, greed, envy, hatred, anxiety and finally, death. It produces split personalities, split homes, divided communities and nations at war. Men and women sacrifice their dearest personal relationships on the altar of money.

Christ says these are false values. He says the more money, the greater the unhappiness, if money is your chief interest. This is true for one man or for a nation. You can lose your soul in building bigger cities. Jesus says the only way to find the good life is to lay up treasure in heaven, to seek first the kingdom of God. We seek the kingdom of God and lay up treasures in Heaven by a way of life.

1. The door is faith in Jesus Christ by which we are reconciled to God.

2. As God reveals His way to us, we find the good life by obeying His will.

3. There is release from anxiety as we trust God to provide the necessities of food, shelter and clothing. He promises to do it.

4. We build our faith, obedience and trust through regular worship.

5. We find meaning for our job, whatever it is, by working for the glory of God, seeking to serve Him in everything we do.

6. We break the grip of greed by giving away our money generously for the support of the church and for helping those who are in need.

IF MY people, which are called by my name, shall humble themselves, and pray, and seek my face, and turn from their wicked ways; then will I forgive their sins, and will heal their land.

II Chronicles 7:14 (KJ)

GOD'S PROMISE TO HEAL THE LAND

We are a troubled people. The concern we feel is made worse by our bewilderment over what we can do about the spirit of lawlessness that obsesses so much of our country. Here is sound advice for God's people: "If my people who are called by my name humble themselves and pray and seek my face, and turn from their wicked ways, then I will hear from heaven and will forgive their sin and heal their land."

This is God's Word in answer to Solomon's prayer for his people. In the midst of our own land there is a large body of God's people. It is to them that this promise is also addressed. It is to you if you count yourself among them.

The promise sets certain clear conditions. First, we are to humble ourselves and pray and seek the help of God. We are witnessing the judgment of God on a people grown proud in their presumed wisdom and strength. The answer to our troubles cannot lie in more of the same pride.

The second condition is that we turn from our wicked ways. Here again it refers first to the people of God. We come confessing our sins, not someone else's. Before we bring the sins of society to God in condemnation, we must bring our own. The people of God can then confess the sins of us all because we are all members of one another.

There is God's promise that forgiveness and healing will come. Streams of new life will flow through channels of government and business and social life. In judgment we will find God remembers mercy. This will begin with you and me if it begins at all. There are things you can do, and as one of God's people, must do, if you are to be a channel of God's mercy.

God calls us to come to daily prayer in humility. In this prayer, we confess our sins and promise to seek daily to do God's will in every relationship. I believe God calls his people to go to church where God's people gathers. In public worship, private faith is nurtured and given dynamic expression.

In short, any light in our darkness will await a revival of religion that will bring God's people to wait on Him in repentance and faith.

AUGUST

AUGUST 1 THE ANGEL fetched Peter out of prison, but it was prayer that fetched the angel.

Thomas Watson

ONE THING YOU CAN DO IS PRAY

One does not have to be clever to draw a word picture of the disturbed condition of our world or of our nation. There are problems galore and the news media gives daily, dramatic descriptions of them. Our main problem is that we are in danger of feeling hopeless in the face of our difficulties. Most of us feel unable to do much about the various things that are wrong. If you are Christian there is something you can do that will be relevant and helpful. There is something the Christian community can do without which all other efforts will fail.

The Christian and the Christian community can pray. Paul wrote to Timothy: "I urge first of all that supplication, prayers, intercessions, thanksgivings be made for all men: for kings and for all in authority."

It is important that the church takes its place in trying to solve the social problems of our day. However, the primary contribution the

Christian community can make is to pray for all men and for all situations. This is the one thing that will not be done unless the church and its members do it. Prayer is to be made for those involved in our social disorders and for all in authority.

We are to pray first of all because of what we believe about God. There is one God who wants all to be saved. God is Lord of all men and of all situations. He has the one purpose to save men and to bring them to the knowledge of the truth. He has given His Son to be the mediator between God and men.

In his providence, He has ordained that the prayers of His people shall be used by Him in His saving work. His saving work waits the prayer of His people. It may be that our growing tensions and our increasing moral breakdown may be due to the fact we have not taken prayer seriously. There is no shortage of knowledge or effort in our attack on the problems we face. There is a shortage of prayer. Churches are known today for their activity. They are a part of every good movement, yet there are few of them that are known for their efforts in prayer.

AUGUST 2   DEAR Lord and Father of mankind, Forgive our foolish ways.

John C.Whitter, Hymn

THE GOSPELS ARE AS RELEVANT AS EVER

We are being told today that the Christian faith must be made more relevant. This means that it must be applied more directly to our modern problems. Preachers and laymen are saying we need to modernize the vocabulary of the gospel. Some say the church must no longer be concerned with the local congregation but to think in the larger terms of the whole community.

All this leaves me confused. The articles and the advice usually end up advocating the involvement of the church in some special project of the writer, whether it be a sociology project or a recreation project.

I wonder if there is as much new in the needs of our world as we like to think. It may be that our problems are about the same as those of past generations and past centuries. I have an idea that the vocabulary of the gospel is fairly well understood. The problem lies in a modern unwillingness to accept what it says, which is very old indeed.

The gospel is well aware of social responsibility for the ills people suffer, but it points to each individual and says: "You are responsible for your sins." People don't like that.

The gospel says that you can't have a better home or community or nation unless you have better people. This focuses attention on each individual, and people don't like that. To escape the discomfort of personal change, they call for better programs.

The gospel says clearly that the only way to make better people is to bring them in touch with God by telling them about what God has done in the life, death and resurrection of Jesus Christ. Our modern day doesn't like that and tries to pretend it doesn't understand the vocabulary.

It is useless to try to change a person or a nation unless you offer something that speaks to the basic needs of the human heart. These needs are the same in every human being of whatever color or race or nation. They are the same for every century. These needs are in terms of sin, of pride, of loneliness, of sorrow, of suffering, of greed, of hate. Only God's program that meets these needs at the heart of individuals can be relevant to our day or to any day.

AUGUST 3   **LORD, show me where love and hope and faith are needed and use me to bring them to those places.**

Alan Paton

A CHURCH SERVICE THAT WAS HELPFUL

One Sunday recently I went to a service of worship that was helpful. It was in a resort community. The pretty church was well filled. As the congregation sang "Holy, Holy, Holy" the participation gave you the feeling you were in the presence of God. The mood lasted throughout the service. There were the customary prayers and Scripture readings, choral music and offering. There was a sermon that made contact with the hearers and blended in with the total atmosphere of worship. When it was over, one had the impression that a majority of those present felt it had been good to have been there.

The minister who presided and preached was retired and was filling in for the regular pastor. For nearly 50 years, he had served churches in his denomination. His sermon was a heart to heart talk of an older man. It was filled with experiences of his past, but it was framed in the needs of our present day. All in all, it was the personal testimony of a man who had found the Lord faithful during a long lifetime and it was a plea to his hearers to let God dwell in their hearts that they might know this same faithfulness of God.

He left the distinct impression that in this heart-religion lies the secret of those who carry life's burdens with courage and of those who add wisdom to the problems that are ours as a nation. He made it clear that as a people, we need preachers and laymen who have found that by turning to God in surrender, God turns to them in grace and peace and power.

What gave the service and the sermon their power of divine communication was the preacher. He was informal. There was no appeal to order of discourse or to cleverness of language or to

308

scholarship. There was the simple and profound appeal of a man whose face and bearing bore witness to the reality of his faith.

Maybe this is what we need most from the church today -the assurances of faith. Whatever our age or our task, we need the word of God assuring our hearts that God is present with us to guide, to strengthen, to comfort. We need to be told over and over again of His forgiveness and of the value of our lives as they are lived for Him.

AUGUST 4 **THRO' days of toil when heart doth fail, God will take care of you; When dangers fierce your paths assail, God will take care of you.**

C.D. Martin, Hymn

IT'S EASY TO FRET, BUT DOES IT PAY?

If the people who are getting along all right would quit complaining, things generally would be a lot better. To put it another way, in my experience, the people who are in trouble usually complain less than those who are free of it. You can hear more conversation about how bad things are from well-heeled, secure people than from the people for whom things are bad. Or, to put it another way, you hear very little emphasis upon thanksgiving in any circle.

Paul said in his letter to the Philippian Christians: "Don't be filled with anxiety; but in everything by prayer and supplication with thanksgiving, let your requests be made known to God."

We are not slow to let our requests be known to God and to man. We are terribly slow to salt them down with thanksgiving. I recently spent a few days in a home where there were children age 8 and 13. I stood amazed at the ceaseless flow of their requests to do and to have. They worked on the principle that if you ask for a lot of things, you are bound to get some of them. These young people are typical of most of us.

Look at your own life just as it is. How are you getting along? What do you really need that you do not have? Sure, each of us has desires that are not satisfied. But most of us have the materials out of which to make a reasonably happy life if we will use what we have and stop complaining about what we lack.

If you are not affected by the disorders of our day, be grateful. If you are able to enjoy the gift of the new day with its beauty, if you can see the beauty of a rose and hear the songs of the birds, be grateful. If you are blessed with means and opportunity whereby you can be helpful to others, gratefully use them.

There is much that is wrong in our world and in our community and in each life. But there is a good deal more that is right. We are the most blessed of all the people on earth. Our blessings are given to us by God to be used for His glory and in service to others. If we will accept them gratefully and use them faithfully, we will find God's peace that is true happiness.

AUGUST 5 WHAT time I am afraid, I will trust in Thee.

Psalm 56:3 (KJ)

FIGHT FEAR THROUGH CONTACT WITH GOD

It is possible to break the grip of fear and anxiety that colors all our life. We are made afraid because we give our attention to those things that threaten us. We fail to give attention and time to that which can relieve our minds and hearts of the feeling of impending doom.

Most writing and speaking today concerns the dark side of life. Day by day we are bombarded by scare propaganda; the evils of life have the center of the stage. The imperfections and failings of men are emphasized and each presents the other as a threat to our security!

There are two things you and I can do to meet this constant "brainwashing."

First, we can set aside a part of each day to maintain contact with God. We are so created that we must keep our hearts open to eternal things if they are not to be victims of earthly fears. Only as we obey God's injunction: "Be still and know that I am God" can we be found by God. This is a matter of decision. You have time if you will take time. We take time to read and hear about the violence and confusion about us. Unless you are willing to take time to draw aside for a period of quietness with God, you can be sure your fears will stay with you.

Second, in your quiet time, fix your mind on the things that are good. "Whatsoever things are true, honest, just, pure, lovely, of good report, think on these things." This is Paul's counsel to the Philippian Christians. Let your mind and heart dwell on the beauty seen in nature and in the lives of those close to you. Think about the goodness that has touched your life by your friends and by the love of those who sustain you. Be grateful for the love of God that has been patient with you. See afresh this love poured out in Christ who forgives you and makes each day a fresh beginning. Remember the host of men and women who are fine and true. Be grateful for all who unselfishly give themselves in service in all walks of life. Share through your Bible the eternal assurance that God has defeated evil and that the good must finally win.

You will find yourself strengthened with might by God's Spirit in the inner person. Faith will grow where fear dwelt and you will go forth able to face life's disorders with new power. You will find a new confidence in God as the Ruler of the affairs of men. You will discover virtues in your fellowmen to praise rather than faults to condemn. You will find the secret of peace in your heart.

ALL A man's ways seem right to him, but the Lord weighs the heart. To do what is right and just is more acceptable to God than sacrifice.

Proverbs 21:2,3 (NIV)

GOD BELONGS IN ALL AREAS OF OUR LIVES

Some things are hard for me to understand. The relationship between our nation and God as interpreted by the Supreme Court is one of them. This interpretation is spelled out in the decision concerning prayer and Bible reading in the public schools.

Church bodies and newspaper editors insist that those of us who object to the decision do not understand what was said, yet the net result is a wedge being driven between the acknowledgment of God and the instruction of our children. School administrators have found it legally necessary to forbid prayer and Bible reading in our classrooms.

It is, of course, legal, we are told, to study about God and religion in an objective way. As if this were possible. The idea of human beings being objective about anything is an illusion. There is no way to deal with facts without taking a stand about their meaning. You cannot make sense out of any fact unless you know the meaning behind the fact. Newspapers try to be factual, but because we are human, every line is of necessity slanted by what the writer believes. Above all things, you can't teach religion objectively. Nor should you.

This nation was founded on a faith in God. This faith is the source of her standards of morality. Respect for law is imbedded in respect for God and His law. As individuals, we are the creatures of God's hand. Within us there is a spirit that reaches out for the divine Spirit. It is not possible for anyone to be objective about God.

Our schools are a part of our lives. In them our children have their characters formed. Our schools are the extension of our homes. No one expects them to teach religion, but many of us expect them to put what they teach in a framework of humble acknowledgment of the God in whom we live and move and have our being.

Our schools are not instruments of the state. They are arrangements made by the people for the training of their children. No government would look with favor on our schools dealing objectively with patriotism. In God there is a higher and more pressing loyalty than any state. Remove God from our public life, and it will not be long before the very ones who demand it will lose their freedom to demand it.

Removing the acknowledgment of God from public institutions seems to me exactly like disconnecting your reading light from the electric outlet. Only darkness can result.

AUGUST 7   **MANY waters cannot quench love, neither can the floods drown it...**

Song of Solomon 8:7 (LB)

WE NEED LOVE TO LEAN ON

She was 12 years old. Misfortune had deprived her of her family. She was being temporarily cared for by a state institution. The kindly head of the institution was trying to comfort her. The young girl kept crying: "I want to go home. I know I don't have a home, but I want to go home." One wonders sometimes if we realize how important home is.

Every divorce is the failure of a home and all too often the failure of the lives involved. In so many homes where there is no divorce, the family is taken for granted. In others there is less kindness and courtesy than in business and social contacts. Yet by our homes we rise or fall. We are insecure creatures. We can't make it alone. We need love to lean on.

God in His goodness gave us love to bind us together. Love is earth's deepest mystery and its most precious reality. The simplest and most profound thing that can be said about love is that it is the gift of God. Many profound reasons are given for the breakdown of our homes. However, it has been my experience that in most homes where love has died there has been a breakdown in communication with God before there came a breakdown in communication among members of the family.

There is a way to have a home to which you can always return and find a resting-place where love abides. Insofar as I know, it is the only way. It is the way of worship where the hearts of the home are kept open to the daily-renewed gift of God's love.

The way begins in accepting God's love at the point where He has fully revealed it in Jesus Christ. When a couple meets at this point secure foundations are laid. The way involves taking time regularly to read the Bible and to pray together. It involves worshipping together in the church.

The result will be a home to which you can always go back and find love. Even when the years have passed and the home has been broken by departures to far points of earth and heaven, you can go back down memory's lane and warm your lonely heart at the still glowing coals of love.

AUGUST 8   IN ALL these things we are conquerors through Him that loved us.

Romans 8:37 (KJ)

NEW TREATMENT: CURE, NOT AILMENT

The New Testament makes worthwhile reading for people today. Every paragraph has a positive ring. Instead of endless discussions of problems, it offers solutions. The New Testament is filled with optimism for the good. It offers a way by which bad men can be changed, while making it clear that their future is not encouraging if their evil way is continued.

Each writer in the New Testament is full of confidence. This is remarkable, since neither the condition of the writers nor of the times in which they lived offered much to support their confidence. The men who wrote the New Testament had no worldly wealth or position. They were often in trouble with the power structures of their day, both civil and religious.

The times in which they lived and wrote were full of problems. They could have written volumes about the social, economic and political cruelties and injustices of their day. Certainly they had no reason to believe they could do anything about them by their own efforts. Yet they wrote as men who had found the answer and who were given to change things by witnessing to the answer which they had found.

These men had been captured by Christ. They had confidence in Him as the channel through which all men would share this victory. They went out to bear witness to what God had done for them and to what He was willing to do for all who would accept their message.

The New Testament is a record of how the problems of men gave way before this message of hope. Evil is attacked with the positive message of God's love in Christ. They had no time for endless discussions of problems or for dissertations on how bad evil was.

Most people are aware of the evils of our day. What men seek is a positive answer, not a continuing negative attack on the things that are wrong. The Christian has a great opportunity today to lift a voice of confidence to our fear-ridden day. It is easy to point out the dangers we face. It takes great faith to declare with confidence that the evil of the world is already defeated and cannot win the victory. The Christian affirmation that God has involved Himself in our affairs by the incarnation in Jesus Christ is the positive message that offers hope to our day.

IS THE CHURCH IRRELEVANT? EXAMINE YOURSELF!

I have an idea that most of those who find the church and the Bible irrelevant today find them so because they want it that way. The church and the Bible speak with authority about God and what duty God requires of man. Many people want neither authority nor God. They would rather hire some experts to study problems that are already clearly solved in the Bible.

They would rather talk about juvenile delinquency as a "complex product of many factors: social, psychological, and economic" - and leave out rebellion against God, neglect of worship, failure of the family altar, failure of the parents to see to it that their children are given Christian training in church and home.

People today would rather think in terms of making good people by education, luxury living and physiological adjustment than by reconciliation to God by faith in Christ, which is the only way bad people can be made good.

Over most of our efforts today to solve our problems is the statement of Christ to the rich young ruler: "One thing thou lackest." He was inviting this man to cease depending on material things and come and follow Him in complete surrender.

Unless you are willing to begin your efforts to make a good life at the point of surrender, then you will think God and the church and the Bible are irrelevant. Unless you are willing to pursue your education, your business, your politics, your home, your science, your social life in the framework of faith, the things of religion will be irrelevant to you.

However, they won't be irrelevant for you. You will be judged by refusal. You will find your personal life without meaning, your home without love, your efforts to serve to be futile and your society in the mess it's presently in.

If you are finding that the things of God have no use for your life, you had better be sure you are not running from your conscience. Instead, seek honestly and you will find the things of God spoken in the Bible through the church to be the answer you have been seeking.

AUGUST 10   HOLY Bible, book divine, precious treasure thou are mine;

William B. Bradbury, Hymn

A FIXED POINT FOR OUR LIVING

The person who is at home in the Bible has a great advantage over a person who is not familiar with it. Almost without exception, those who come to know the Bible find that they regard it as the revelation of God. Believing that the Bible is the word of God gives a person a fixed point of reference for the very difficult task of living in this world.

The Bible is a record of how God acts under every kind of event that can happen to a person or to a nation. It reveals to anyone who will study it what God is like and what his relationship is to all of us. The Bible shows God as the creator of all things and as the ruler of all things. It is full of case histories of men and women, of races and empires. It clearly shows how God deals with His creatures. In the Bible we see God controlling nature and natural events for His purposes.

In the Bible, we come to know God in a very personal way as He took upon himself the form of a man and so entered into our human experience of joy and sorrow, finally taking upon himself our sins in the common experience of death. The Bible has as its final theme the victory of life over death, of love over hate, of virtue over sin. This victory is centered in the resurrection and final return of the Christ.

The person who believes the Bible has a real advantage in reading the newspaper and listening to the radio and TV news. Bombs in China and changes in Russia and scandals in the United States are not as disturbing as these things are to those who have no Bible. The Bible makes God real as a point of reference for all these things. They are in His hands. Behind all the movement, there is a divine hand at the controls.

God deals finally with men and nations on the basis of obedience to His will. We do our part as we seek to live by faith and to serve faithfully in our appointed places.

The person who lives by faith in the Bible finds support and strength for the hard places of life. God bears our grief and carries our sorrows. He sets lights in the dark.

AUGUST 11 **IF WE confess our sins, he is faithful and forgives us our sins and purifies us from all unrighteousness.**

I John 1:9 (NIV)

EACH IS RESPONSIBLE FOR OUR MORAL CLIMATE

The matter of morals is widely discussed today. The truth of the matter is that it always has been. However much attention we give to material progress, there is the negative intuition that our welfare finally depends on our conduct. There are some important questions that need answering before progress can be made in improving the morals of people. There is the question of who is to blame when there is a decline in the character of society or of an individual.

It is popular today to blame someone else. Social conditions such as slums and poverty receive the most attention today. No one can deny the evil influences of bad environment, but moral conditions will not improve until each person faces honestly his and her own responsibility.

Many reasons can be given for the "dropouts" and for delinquency of all kinds. However, the individual involved always bears responsibility and, in his conscience, he knows it.

Then there is the question of an accepted standard of morality. Does each person decide what is right in his own eyes or is there an absolute standard toward which all strive? Today, people have rebelled against accepted standards and the very meaning of the word character has become foggy. It can only create confusion to talk about the good life if you have no model that is accepted.

There is a further question of how you produce character. This question is usually dodged today. We like to think it is produced by education and psychological adjustment within the framework of economic comfort and good health. Despite almost limitless efforts and money expended in these directions, problems seem to increase.

The Christian faith has specific answers to these questions. The Christian accepts responsibility for his sins and freely confesses his wrongdoings. However unfortunate his environment or his inheritance, he knows himself to be responsible before God. He looks to God for forgiveness by faith in Christ instead of looking for someone to blame.

The Christian accepts Jesus Christ as an absolute standard of conduct and strives to live in obedience to Him. He fails often, but at least he knows what kind of person he is trying to become.

AUGUST 12   THE GAME of life is a game of
boomerangs: our thoughts, deeds and
words return to us sooner or later, with
astounding accuracy.

Florence Scouel Shinn

WE REAP THE ETHICS WE HAVE SOWN

Sowing what you reap is the basis of farming. An intelligent farmer expects it. The same law holds good in human relations, but apparently we don't like to believe it. It seems that we have a warped idea we can beat the game and reap good results from shoddy efforts. This is evident in the rather sudden concerns for ethics in business and politics and sports.

It looks like we are beginning to reap the fruits of some seed we have been sowing, and we don't like the harvest. The daily newspaper is full of such indications. Ethics bills are being offered in the Legislature and called for in the city, but there is the prior question of what you use as a standard of ethics.

Marriage mills must be shut down, we are told. Often we are told that shoddy work seems to be the hallmark of much of our manufacturing and of the services people give.

In sports, ethics are a problem. Who is going to make the rules and why should they be kept if they don't suit you? What is the binding standard of ethics? Why not go where the money is?

In the entertainment world, people wreck many of the standards of ethics that once were thought to be binding. These people become the idols of youth. How do you talk to youth about ethics?

You cannot talk about the authority _of_ ethics unless you accept an authority _for_ ethics. In bowing God out as the final authority for conduct, you open the door to what we have today. The Christian faith gave form and substance to the Western world because it taught that each individual is responsible to God for his conduct and will be held responsible in Judgment. This applies to your and my conduct toward ourselves, toward our family and toward our neighbor and it means that we run for office and do our daily work as unto the Lord. It means that business and sports and entertainment must reflect the fact that those participating in them are guided by a desire to seek God's will and obey it.

It means that an expert, in any field of human effort, needs to have knowledge of God's word and to experience divine worship of Him wherever God's will is known and taught.

AUGUST 13   I WILL love thee, O Lord, my strength.

Psalm 18:1 (KJ)

WHAT KIND OF GOD DO YOU WORSHIP CLOSE?

"Thou shalt have no other gods before me." This is the first commandment and it is not first by accident. It is first in order because it is first in fact. In the building of your life, you begin with God or you begin wrong. God exists. We are His creatures. Worship of and obedience to God are the primary requirements of life.

In this worship and in this obedience, we find the proper direction for our lives. In His will we find the proper conduct for our actions. The worship of false gods leads to wrong actions.

Every man and every woman has a god that is worshipped and obeyed and depended on to produce what is wanted. Daily sacrifices are offered to whatever god is worshipped.

Many of us worship self. Those who do refer everything to self as the center and object of everything and everybody. We do what we think best for ourselves. We use everyone we can for our own advancement.

Others worship money. We do what will bring money to us. We sacrifice health and family and friends in order to have money. Some worship pleasure. The end of life is to have fun. Business, home and friends are servants of this god.

The state is a favorite object of worship. All tyranny demands that people sacrifice everything for the state. Nazi Germany made the state the idol god. Communism follows its lead.

Various religions offer various gods. Each god produces people of its own making. The conduct of a person is made by the god he worships. It makes a difference what god you worship.

The Christian is sure that the God revered in the Old Testament and New Testament is the one true God. Truth of belief and truth and beauty of life center in Him.

God is a jealous God and will have no other gods before Him. He demands our first loyalty because only as we give this loyalty can we be what we ought to be. Only by this loyalty can we resist the temptations to worship false gods.

If you want to know a person, find out what that person worships.

AUGUST 14   A FRIEND loves at all times...

Proverbs 17:17 (NIV)

SHARING IS VITAL IN JOY AND SORROW

Every now and then one has an experience that makes it clear how wonderful it is to have family and friends. I have married my daughter to a fine young man. It was a happy occasion. It was made a happy occasion by the family and friends who stood by and did the hundreds of things that needed to be done.

Often in the midst of it all, I thought how barren it would have been without those who cared enough to stand by in affection. The young couple was happy in their love, but there would have been a dark cloud over their joy if there had been no friends and no family to support and share in their happiness. Truly we are members one of another.

I have seen over and over again the part played by those who care in times of joy and sorrow. God works miracles through people who give themselves to others in the high moments of their lives. Out of such experiences comes a deep sense of gratitude to God and to people.

Such an experience leads to certain thoughts. Often we allow the "busy-ness" of the day to cause us to neglect those nearest us. So often we lose our friends and alienate members of our family by careless or unkind conduct.

We need to be reminded how dependent we are on those close to us and how barren life is without their support and affection. There is nothing that takes their place in our times of stress. We can do nothing as important as those things we do to keep strong our ties to family and friends.

Another thought comes concerning this. In many instances, others depend upon us to support them in their joys or sorrows. It is a serious thing to let them down. It is easy to be too busy to indicate our interest. We can persuade ourselves that we will not be missed.

We generally know where we are needed. We usually know what we ought to do. It would add much to human happiness if we would determine to let nothing we can control keep us from standing by those who need us.

Most of all, each of us can help life along by being grateful to God for our friends and for our family and by showing that gratitude in our lives.

AUGUST 15
IF THERE be some weaker one, give me strength to help him on; If a blinder soul there be, let me guide him nearer Thee...

Whittier

FIND ETERNAL LIFE IN SERVING OTHERS

Jesus spoke often of abundant life. He had in mind life that is satisfying in this world and acceptable to God in the world to come. He spoke of this as eternal life. A man asked Him one day how a person could be sure of this kind of life. Jesus asked him what he thought about it. The man replied with a quotation from the Bible: "Thou shalt love the Lord thy God with all thy heart and soul and strength and mind, and thy neighbor as thyself." Jesus approved the answer, saying: "This do and thou shalt live."

The key to abundant living is loving God and your neighbor. The man was troubled because he knew that he usually included in his thinking only his own narrow group as neighbors. So he asked a second question: "Who is my neighbor?"

In answer, Jesus told of the Good Samaritan. In this story Jesus answered the first question and in doing so, he answered the second. You can measure what your religion has done for you by this story. It is important to believe the right things, but unless our faith produces compassion, it will not produce eternal life. The priest and the Levite who refused to help gave evidence that their religion had done them little good.

Jesus also makes it clear that the spirit of compassion knows none of the barriers that are present in our society. The Samaritan and the Jews were enemies. They had no dealings with one another. We often excuse our lack of love by our feeling that the one in need is not one of us. We label people and dismiss them. Under popular pressure people who call themselves Christian do strange and cruel things to people who are not of their color or their social or political or economic group.

324

The heart of the story speaks to the question of whether you are a neighbor. If you are, then everyone you can help is your neighbor.

The spirit of compassion is a gift of God. You cannot love God and man by your own effort. God gave Christ to be for us the Great Samaritan, loving us and redeeming us from our sin and hardness of heart. "We love because He first loved us."

By Christian love we find life and in loving we give life. This is the law of life.

AUGUST 16 **YOU know the grace of our Lord Jesus Christ, that though he was rich, yet for your sakes he became poor, so that you through his poverty might become rich.**

II Corinthians 8:9 (NIV)

RICH TOWARD GOD VS. RICH IN GOODS

Material things have a way of getting the upper hand over us. If we are not careful, they will run us to death. We start out to supply our needs for food, clothes and shelter for ourselves and our families. Material things are necessary to meet those needs of our bodies, and it is good that we seek them to the best of our ability, but we have other more important needs of the spirit. We need the love and companionship of other people. We need inner strength to meet the fear, insecurity and anxiety that attack all of us. We need comfort in our sorrows. We need a sense of purpose for our lives. We need to be useful to others as we go along. We need some answer to the guilt we feel because of our failure to measure up to the demands our spirit makes on us.

It is a sad fact of human nature that we believe we can satisfy the needs of the spirit with the things that satisfy the needs of the body. Jesus told a story to illustrate how foolish this is. A certain man found himself unexpectedly prosperous. He had worked hard and honestly to provide for his physical needs. So he secured them for the future and congratulated himself on having enough for many years. He then sat down to eat, drink and be merry. The only trouble was, it didn't work out. He died without having ever really lived. Jesus said that this is the way it always works out when a person is not rich toward God.

The needs of our spirits and our personalities are met only as we are rich toward God. If we are not rich toward God, more goods will only increase our poverty.

We become rich toward God by recognizing that these strange personalities of ours were made by God for Himself and that they find their needs met only as they relate themselves to Him. No human wisdom or effort can satisfy the soul of a man.

Being rich toward God means to have your will so surrendered to God that every decision is made seeking His will. Being rich toward God requires an act of faith in God as revealed in Christ, an act of faith that turns from a foolish confidence in material things to a deep trust in God to supply all your needs.

AUGUST 17 THOUGH I walk in the midst of trouble, you preserve my life...

Psalm 138:7 (NIV)

REMEMBER THESE IN BAD TIMES

Sooner or later, each of us has the experience of having the rug jerked out from under us. So often it happens just at the moment we think everything is going our way. So many unhappy things can happen to us. We are such dependent creatures. We are dependent on the proper functioning of a very complicated human body. We are dependent on our friends, business associates and the social group to which we belong.

In all these areas things can go terribly wrong and at some time, in some of them, something always does. Certain things have proved helpful to me and to others. I pass them on with the prayer that they may be helpful to someone else in a moment of agony.

1. It helps to admit frankly that there is no satisfying answer to the question. One thing is sure: God has not hurled some angry thunderbolt at you because you have been unusually bad. "He hath not dealt with us after our sins, nor rewarded us according to our transgressions."

2. It helps to remember that in our pain and sorrow we are at home with all other people. It happens to everyone. It would be strange indeed if it did not happen to you. Such things are part of human life as it is.

3. It helps on the positive side to admit the question cannot be answered and to ask a second question: "What would God have me do with my pain?" The simple prayer: "Thy will be done in and through it" will start you on the road up again.

4. It will help to surrender yourself and your pain to God. Surrender is the open door through which God comes. In surrendering, you dare to believe that God will take care of you and use your loss for some constructive purpose.

5. Then just ask God to show you what to do next and keep on doing what appears as the next thing to do.

Some of the answers we will never know until we see God face to face. However, we can find that the answers do not matter as much as we at first thought. And we will find strength for the day, His strength made perfect in our weakness.

AUGUST 18   "...wait for me." declares the Lord...

Zephaniah 3:8 (NIV)

HERE ARE GUIDES TO FRUITFUL PRAYER

People who are experts on how to live successfully in our world are a dime a dozen. Most of the expert advice has about the same effect as trying to teach a person without arms to row a boat. We aren't able to follow it. Life's problems are too difficult, its temptations too strong and our own will, wisdom and strength are too small.

As the world must have the sun, so our hearts and lives must have God to forgive us, to empower us and to guide us. God comes as we open our hearts to Him in obedient prayer. Most of us need help in praying..

I was asked to speak to a group about prayer. A member of our church staff, Mrs. Clyde McCrary, gave me a guide to prayer she had worked out. It has helped me, and believing it can be helpful to others, I am passing it on.

"Be alone, relaxed, in a comfortable position. By a definite act of will, put out of mind all thoughts of the day's duties and problems. Be still, mentally. Repeat the Twenty-third Psalm.

"Ask God to make you aware of His presence. Then wait, quietly, before you proceed. Think of His creativeness, His goodness, and His mercy. Ask that all fear, tension, worry, be taken from you.

"Pray that every known sin be removed from your heart and forgiven. Be specific. Call by name your unconquered weakness: pride, jealousy, resentment, laziness, self-will, impatience. Ask God to complete the surrender of your will to His.

"Ask Him if He has any special task for you this day. Do not be disappointed if no specific direction comes at once. When God wants

328

you, He will let you know. Pray confidently for your family, friends, church, God's Kingdom, all men and special persons, by name.

"Request increased faith and greater sensitiveness to His response to your prayer. 'Whatsoever things ye desire, when ye pray, BELIEVE that ye receive them, and ye shall have them.'"

AUGUST 19   JESUS loves me, this I know.

Sunday School Hymn

ESTABLISHING ORDER IN A BROKEN WORLD

Revolution and change stalk our world. Our way of life may be compared to a house that has been blown to pieces. The pieces are still flying through the air. They will sooner or later come down and be formed into a new structure, but of today's change what the form of it will be no one knows. The present result is growing violence, increasing insecurity and bitter divisions, which infect almost all relationships.

What can you do to give your children a solid foundation on which to stand? What can you do to face your days with confidence and hope?

You will find the answer in the basic things of religious faith. It can well be that God is shaking our world "removing the things that are shaken, as things that are made, that those things which cannot be shaken remain."

God has revealed Himself in Jesus Christ as one who loves each one of us. This fact is imbedded in history and cannot be shaken. He loves you and me as we are, in all our weakness and rebellion. He loves all people just as He loves us.

He knows we can't live as we should nor treat others as we ought, so He offers forgiveness and the indwelling power of His Spirit to do in us, for us and through us, what we cannot do for ourselves.

Only by faith can we become people who find an answer to insecurity, to fear and to divisions that plague us. Faith is the gift of God to those who seek Him. It can come only as you take this search seriously. This seeking will mean opening the channels of your mind, your home and your time to the things of God. It will take decisions on your part. You won't drift into faith, but these things are possible for anyone:

1. Spending some time reading the Bible. Try reading through the New Testament - one of the newer translations may be helpful.

2. Gathering your family for a period of worship each day. The old-fashioned family altar can work new miracles for your home.

3. Worshiping God regularly with your family in church.

4. Following the spiritual insight that comes to you as you go about your business and social life.

The results of seeking faithfulness will amaze you as you begin to perceive the presence of a loving God in the midst of your disordered day. The insecurity and fear and divisions of life will begin to find answers in your children and in you.

AUGUST 20   FOR NOW we live, if ye stand fast in the Lord.

I Thessalonians 3:8 (KJ)

EDUCATION AND MONEY ARE NOT ENOUGH

No one questions the need for education. It is certainly a good thing to meet the needs of those who are blocked out from opportunity because they are poor, yet there are some questions that require an answer if our attacks on ignorance and poverty are not to lead to worse problems. Do you believe that adequate educations and economic security will lead to happy living for an individual and an ordered society for all people?

Let us suppose that everyone is finally educated and made secure financially. Would this produce the utopia of the social planners?

Any idea that it would makes fine reading. It even gives a warm glow of idealism to those who believe in these things as the solution for our problems, but any such idea ignores the basic fact of human nature. You and I will misuse our education and our money unless there is a commitment to a noble goal or purpose.

It is because education has become general that we have the massive production of low literature. People everywhere are concerned over the moral tone of much that is offered to the American public. The good that we have done becomes a tool of those who profit by our weakness. Any solution must go beyond education. It must find a way to give man a noble goal and a way to lead man to choose that goal. This is a matter of religion, which has been neglected by our educational process at its peril.

In itself, the possession of money has never given relief to social and moral problems. It develops selfishness. It provides the means for the growing threat of gambling and alcoholism. It breeds the dishonesties that plague our society.

Education and money without a noble goal can only produce tragedy on a grander scale. These things are tools to be used according to what you believe about God, your neighbor and yourself.

Without God, we will misuse these tools of life in an effort to serve ourselves, individually and as a nation. We are sinners by nature and we do not have the ability to rightly use education and money. Only as we are changed by the grace of God, only as we confess our sin and seek God's forgiveness and God's help, can we find God's gifts a blessing and not a curse.

OUR FATHER which art in heaven, hallowed be thy name. Thy Kingdom come. Thy will be done, as in heaven, so in earth. Give us day by day our daily bread. And forgive us our sins, for we also forgive every one that is indebted to us. And lead us not into temptation; but deliver us from evil.

Luke 11:1-4 (KJ)

HOW TO PRAY? JESUS TAUGHT IT

Prayer of one kind or another is almost instinctive. When we get into a close place we can't handle, we look for help from a power outside of us. In spite of all the talk you hear about independence, we are dependent creatures by nature. We are not able to stand straight by ourselves. We must have someone or something to lean on. Prayer is the natural expression of this fact of human nature.

Yet it is hard to pray. We often get confused when we pray. We find it hard to reconcile our praying with the results of our efforts in this direction. Maybe we are confused most of all by the different ideas about prayer we hear.

When the disciples came to Jesus with their request: "Lord teach us to pray," they were voicing a deep need of each of us today. We need contact with a power greater than ourselves. The pace and growing complexity of our lives are demanding more than we have to give. We need to find an answer to the unsatisfied yearning within us for a higher purpose than the search for material things.

The most familiar prayer to us is what is known as The Lord's Prayer. This prayer was given by Christ in answer to the request of his disciples. If you are having trouble with prayer, if you are confused by the advice of conflicting voices, if you are unsettled by having prayed without receiving the help you have sought, I commend to you this prayer taught by Jesus. You will find it in Matthew 6 and Luke 11.

This prayer is the truth about God and about prayer. It is the very word of God about Himself. If you will take some time to make this prayer your own, word by word, you will find help in your time of need. Making a habit of doing this day by day will build a sure foundation for added confidence in praying.

AUGUST 22 **THE FEAR of the Lord is clear, enduring forever: The judgements of the Lord are true and righteous altogether.**

Psalm 19:9 (KJ)

IGNORE JUDGMENT AT YOUR PERIL

Somebody today needs to say a word about judgment. Our smooth-talking generation has chosen to erase the idea of divine judgement from our thinking. It makes no difference that flabby thinking and irresponsible living follow such an omission. This is part of the judgment that is ignored. We assume we can escape judgment because we decide it might be unpleasant or might interfere with our own control of the situation.

Yet judgment is on each of us. It is working all about us. We do well to be aware of its working lest it destroy us while we are calling it something else. There are moral and spiritual laws, as rigid as physical laws. We violate them and judgment is on us. God is not mocked. We reap as we sow.

Children know the fact of judgment. They expect to be judged and punished for doing wrong. Children are done a grave injustice by those who would deprive them of judgment by which their guilt is purged. Children grow up warped and delinquent when indulgent parents allow them to believe they can escape judgment.

Actually, we never really grow away from our fear of judgment. Nor should we. We are sinners by whatever name and we know we are guilty. No one does us a service by saying it doesn't matter. It does and we know it. We have to deal with judgment in some way. If we escape it at one place, we bring it on ourselves at another, often deliberately.

We recognize judgment in our community as we support our police, law courts and jails. Judgment rides all about us in our friends who have tried to live by false values and who have followed the ways of self-indulgence. You don't need a prophet to point out the marks of judgment on them.

Judgment is beginning to appear in our land. We in America are part of two or three world generations that have been the bloodiest and most savage in history. Once again we are living by the sword. If we continue, we will die by it.

No body of experts or technicians can hold judgments back once its time has come in God's timetable. Only God can stop judgment by His mercy, but finally penitence alone is the key to His continued mercy.

AUGUST 23   **"...AND WHATSOEVER thou shalt bind on earth shall be bound in heaven..."**

Matthew 16:19 (KJ)

CHURCH ATTENDANCE IS AN ENCOURAGING SIGN

The many things that disturb us get the majority of the publicity; however, there is much to encourage. One of the things that gives me confidence for tomorrow is the fidelity of men and women and children to the worship of God. After the critics have called attention to the failings and its friends have bemoaned its weakness, the church is still there. Everywhere you go men, women and children gather to worship God. Criticize the comparative fewness if you will, yet there they are holding on to and witnessing to the eternal things.

I was on an air corps base and went to church on Sunday. There was a good crowd. It was an interesting group. I counted three races represented. There were airmen, non-commissioned and commissioned officers. The men who took the offering were divided among these groups. The commanding general is a regular attendant. I sat on a row next to the wife and daughter of this officer, with a second lieutenant, two airmen and a non-commissioned officer and their wives filling out the row.

As this congregation sang the old hymns familiar to the communion service, as they listened to the Bible read and preached by the chaplain, as they partook together of the Lord's Supper, all were equal. No man or woman could rise up and demand privilege because of earthly position. No one needed to feel inferior because of the lack of it.

After the service each went his or her own way. The duties and positions were different but no one could go away without some conviction of our unity in Christ. Because this group had come to worship, their witness permeated the whole base. The very fact that the service had been held made Sunday different even for those who chose to pass it by.

In every armed forces base, in every village and town and city of our land, people gather regularly to worship God. There is lots to criticize about the church, but don't forget that it is there. As long as men and women gather to open their lives to the things of God, God will work in and through them to save his people. In our dark day, the words of Jesus to His followers are still true: "Ye are the light of the world."

MY HOPE is built on nothing less than Jesus' blood and righteousness...

Edward Mote, Hymn

IN JERUSALEM AND ELSEWHERE, OLD WAYS AND OLD PROBLEMS

Jerusalem, Jordan - Looking out a hotel window at Jerusalem on its hill across the Kidron Valley I think of Jesus Christ who came to save the world. He walked these hills where much of the life goes on as it did when he was here. The grain is cut by hand, hauled to the stone threshing floor by camel or donkey, beaten by the tramping of animals and winnowed by throwing it in the air and letting the wind blow the chaff away. Also the world of men has not changed very much here or around the world. There is the ferment and unrest wherever you go and in whatever you read.

In South America, in Africa, in the Middle East, there are tensions and divisions. Men and nations with new freedoms are trying to learn what to do with them. The leaders of nations in the Afro-Asian areas are constantly moving about, meeting with one another and seeking to resolve differences and to find help for their problems. Widely varying religious and cultural backgrounds give great difficulty in efforts toward unity. No one of the stronger nations is able to exercise any sustained leadership, politically or morally. Truly the multitudes are sheep without a shepherd. In this very city where Christ died for the sins of men, there is a dividing line which is hard to cross. Here, too, are a wall and closed gates.

The gospel of Christ, of God's love which he gave and which He would have men share with one another, is a long way from wining the world. Traveling in African countries where religion is hard to define and in Moslem countries where it is clearly defined, impresses one with the challenge that faces Christians, but there are some things that clearly stand out. It makes a difference in a man's life what he believes about God. It makes a difference in a society what its people believe about God. Christian values are the fruit of Christian faith and where Christ has been preached and believed, you can mark the difference in character and in hope and in social conditions. One religion is not as good as another and I am more convinced than ever that there is no other name than Christ's whereby we must be saved.

Conferences by political leaders about the problems that plague our world will go on. In the long run their success or failure will be determined by the faithfulness with which Christians follow Christ and make Him known all over the world.

AUGUST 25 THOUGH the eye of sinful man Thy glory may not see...Holy, holy, holy....only Thou art holy...

Reginald Heber, Hymn

COMMERCIALISM AND RIVALRIES MAR THE IMPACT OF HOLY LAND VISIT

HONG KONG - In traveling around the world my interest has largely been trying to discover the place and influence of religion in the various countries. Religion plays a more strategic part in what happens in most places than people in our country realize. The gods men worship usually make them what they are. Different religious loyalties produce different kinds of people.

There is no place in my experience where religion is more confused than in what we know as the Holy Land. I am sure it will injure the sensibilities of some when I say that it takes a vivid imagination to keep the sacred meaning of the Holy Land in focus.

You can manage to do it if you disassociate yourself from the specific sites that are set aside as places where this or that happened in the life of Christ. If you can keep in mind that this is the land where God became incarnate in Christ, where he walked and taught and lived and died, something of the old thrill returns.

However, when you are pulled hither and yon by those who want to show you the holy places for a price, when you see them with the curious Christian groups competing for space - and when you know how unlikely it is that these are the real places - it does something to you. Or it does to me.

The Church of the Holy Sepulchre is one of the suggested places for the crucifixion and burial. Peace is kept by keeping the Moslems in check. You no longer can travel to Bethlehem by the old direct road of five miles. It is necessary to travel 20 miles in order to skirt territory that belongs to Israel. Bethlehem is a thrill as a place and somewhere in the hills outside, the angels sang to the shepherds; however, the edge is taken off by the barrage of sellers of various items and by guides who steer you to stores and by the variety of altars.

Back in Jerusalem, you walk along the wall separating Jordan and Israel with armed guards patrolling the two sides of land that is a buffer area. On the maps that you buy in Jordan, Israel's name does not appear. Their country is designated "Occupied Territory."

The land where Christ was born is today a living parable of how much remains to be done all around the world before His kingdom of love and peace approaches anything like reality.

AUGUST 26   GO, TELL it on the mountain, over the hills and everywhere...

John W. Work, II, Hymn

THOSE CITING THE CHURCH'S FAILURES OUGHT TO TAKE ANOTHER LOOK

It is popular today to speak and write about failures of the church. Even churchmen are heard to declaim the fact that we are in a post-Christian era. There is going about in learned church circles a lively debate about the role of the local congregation. No one can deny that the church is failing to do much that it ought to do; however, when the critic has had his last word, the fact remains that the church is going about its business in a remarkably successful way. The local congregation is the main channel through which this business is carried on.

The New Testament Christians show no concern over the fact that they are a pitiful minority. The reason for this is that their business was not to outnumber the pagans. It was to bear witness to something God had done. They went about telling the story of the life and death and resurrection of Jesus. They believed that the story carried on its power. They planted seed that would bring an inevitable harvest.

They believed that man is warped so that he will not do the good he knows and that he could not if he would. They believed that the good news they were spreading was the only way any man could overcome his warped nature and be saved. Being saved meant - and means - being in a relation of love with God, yourself and your neighbor. This business of witnessing to a story with its built-in power is what the church is doing today. Even as it was true in the first century, it is doing its business with remarkable success.

If you want to experience the church at work, mediating the power of God with success, really look at your church. If you do not go to church, take a month or six weeks and visit around. Watch small children respond to the story as faithful parents bring them to Sunday school. Watch it give to young people security and challenge. Look, as it cements families in love. Attend a worship service where all ages are fused together in oneness.

Then move out into the community and check on the men and women who carry the burden of unselfish service. The great majority were formed in character in the church. Go into the schools and mark those passing on something besides facts. They will be church people largely.

Go to Brazil or the Congo or to any of a score of nations on the move. Examine the progress in education, welfare and in character. You will find the church in the lead.

The church is God's instrument for making, by His Holy Spirit, the men and women who are making the world. There is no other source of such men and women. It is the church or nothing.

AUGUST 27 "...I AM the way, the truth, and the life: no man cometh unto the father, but by me."

John 14:6 (KJ)

IT'S DIFFICULT TO SURRENDER TO GOD, BUT IT'S THE ONLY WAY TO LIVE

The Christian faith speaks to us of our inability to make life work out by our own wisdom and by our own resources. If you are trying to make it on your own, sooner or later you will find yourself with Moses on the back side of the desert. Life will turn out to be a blind alley. Moses found that forgiveness is often presented too glibly. It is hard to give up our dependence on ourselves.

But there are deeper reasons why we cannot surrender our lives to God.

First, we join Moses in his fear of himself. God called Moses to a new life and he replied: "Who am I?" For him, so he thought, life was over. He ruined his life by his sin and he could not imagine there being anything worthwhile for him to do. Most of us know that we are responsible for our own failures, and we find it hard to believe that God will give us another chance.

God replied to Moses and he says to us also, "Certainly, I will be with you." As you try again, you will not be working in your own strength alone.

Second, Moses was unsure about God. He had a guilty conscience because of his sin and failure. He could not imagine one such as he receiving God's blessing.

We share this fear that God will fail to sustain us if we do surrender to Him. Our fear of ourselves makes us afraid to trust God. We don't deserve His goodness and His forgiveness and His help. We ask God with Moses, "Who are you?" In the Christian faith we have God's answer to that question. Look at Jesus Christ. God is like that. It is folks like us that God loves. It is to the weak and to the failure and to the guilty that He comes offering Himself in strength and in forgiveness.

Third, Moses was afraid of what people would say if he came to them talking about God. He was afraid they would remember what he had been and would say: "The Lord hath not appeared unto Thee."

We find it hard to surrender because we fear what people will say. God gave Moses certain assurances that He would honor Moses' surrender with evidences of his power that would convince people that God was with him. He promises you "My strength shall be made perfect in weakness."

God offers us forgiveness and usefulness if we will surrender. He understands our feelings of inferiority, our fear of God and our fear of people. He offers an open road into the future and out of our blind alley. It is not an easy way, but it is actually the only way. You and I can't make it alone.

AUGUST 28   O LORD my God, in thee do I put my trust...

Psalm 7:1 (KJ)

BIGNESS IS NO THREAT TO THE DIGNITY OF THOSE WHO HAVE FAITH

Our struggle today is for the dignity of man. Automation is basically not as much a threat to your job as it is to your dignity as a human being. It is no joke to find a machine can do your job better than you can. Nor is it primarily an economic problem. Big business is here to stay, as is big government. They will produce little men as pawns of their big business. Space science enlarges our physical world and brings doubt as to man's place.

We make a mistake, however, if we consider the problem of little people in a big world a new one. Men have always felt inadequate before the forces of nature and the inventions of men. In the days of primitive men and in older days, man was wiser that we are. He had sense enough to seek his answer in religion, which is the only place it can be found. We are trying to maintain human dignity by money and by knowledge and by government decree.

The Eighth Psalm speaks to this age-old problem. It contains the wisdom of the ages. Man's dignity and value lie in his relationship to God. Leave that out and money, knowledge and government will make a slave out of man.

The writer begins by his affirmation of faith in God as one ruling in all the earth with the glory above the world. The truth understood and proclaimed by a little child is wiser than the pronouncements of the learned.

The writer is impressed by the bigness of everything: space, the planets, the moon. He faces honestly the question: "What is man?" He finds the answer in the fact that God created man only as a little lower than Himself. God has crowned man, you and me, with glory and honor. You and I as human beings are made in the image of God. On the humblest of us and on the worst of us, there is the stamp of eternity.

We are made to have dominion, rule and control over all the creation of God. All things are, by creation, under man's authority. Our efforts only make possible what God has already given in creation. All other creatures - beasts, fowl, sea creatures - are subjects to man's lordship as the agent of God. The universes are man's to explore and control because God made it so.

It is a matter of fact that the men and women and children who maintain their dignity as human beings are those who maintain the reality of God in their lives. In the midst of life's bigness, the man for whom God is real can still say with gratitude: "O Lord, our Lord, how excellent is thy name in all the earth."

FOR GOD sent not his Son into the world to condemn the world; but that the world through him might be saved.

John 3:17 (KJ)

MAN CAN'T ESCAPE JUDGMENT, BUT GOD FORGIVES THE REPENTANT

Judgment is not a popular subject in discussions of life and of religion, yet is a central fact in both. In the modern approach to the problems people have, attention is properly given to circumstances in which these problems arose. However, the central fact is seldom mentioned, that in most of his problems, man is also under judgment for his own wrong choices. Few are innocent victims of circumstances. You and I usually know that deep within us that, to some extent, we bring our troubles on ourselves. We are under judgment.

Religion has at its heart the experiences of the judgment of God for our sin of rebellion. Rebellion without repentance leads to sure destruction. Religion is fundamentally a call to man to repent and to turn to God and, in turning, to be saved from wrath. Only when this call has been heeded is there an experience of the saving grace of God. Any diagnosis of your problem that leaves these things out is superficial and can lead only to poverty of results. No man is made better by education or by improvements in his living conditions or by understanding himself unless he has come to terms with himself before God.

All problems involve guilt, and the guilty person does not buy the solution that finds the only reasons for his troubles in some external cause or in society. Deep within us, we echo David's words, "Against thee and thee only have I sinned and done this evil in thy sight."

Alcoholism turns into a disease but it begins in a waking choice. The alcoholic carries with him or her a deep sense of guilt that no medicine can cure. He knows he faces a moral problem.

The juvenile delinquent and those who seek to help him find some comfort in the explanation that his or her background or society is to blame. Buried somewhere in the heart, however, is the conviction of personal responsibility.

Each of us is under judgment and held responsible by God for obedience to His will. No effort of man can relieve another of this responsibility. No program of man can relieve you or me of the sure result of personal rebellion and sin.

This can be done only by God. This is the secret of the good news of the gospel. God sent Christ to take our rebellion and sin on himself that we could be forgiven and freed from the results of our rebellion. The acceptance by faith of what God has done is the only sure foundation upon which our human effort can build better lives and a better society.

AUGUST 30 HELP me to walk aright, more by faith, less by sight.

Mansell Ramsey, Hymn

ANSWERS TO OUR PROBLEMS CAN'T BE FOUND IN OURSELVES ALONE.

There is a good deal more spiritual poverty than there is material poverty. There are not just pockets of spiritual poverty; it is present in mass proportions. Spiritual poverty is evident in the dissatisfaction and unrest of so many people. People are unhappy with one another. The central cause of our spiritual poverty is the self-centeredness of each of us. The Christian faith begins with the conviction that you and I cannot cure our own self-centeredness. Hence, we cannot find in ourselves the answer to our spiritual weakness and general unhappiness. We cannot find peace within us or with others by any purely human adjustments.

We are so made that we must have the presence of God working in us and through us. It is not popular today, nor is it regarded as scientific, to believe in a supernatural power available for our lives. But it happens to be as true as it is necessary.

God has made His presence and power available to each of us by faith. Faith is the human response to the divine offer. This can be partly illustrated on the physical level. Bodily strength is needed and is offered to us by the presence of food. Food is all around us, but it requires certain acts on our part to receive it. When we receive food can it work by the processes of the body. In like manner, we receive God's power by the act of faith.

Faith, however, is a more difficult act than partaking of it. Faith itself is a gift of God, and our receiving it depends on our willingness to put ourselves where it is available.

There are three suggestions for those who truly seek faith as a way to spiritual strength.

1. A regular, systematic reading of the Bible is necessary. Here is the knowledge of God one must have. God has come to those who do this in too many instances to doubt it as a channel of God's power.

2. Regular worship with God's people is another must. There are miracles present where people gather to worship.

3. Sacrificial giving of your money to the work of God will open the doors of your spirit to the inflow of faith and power. Money blocks spiritual growth for more people than anything else.

If you honestly want to break out of your prison of self with all its unhappy consequences, these are some things to do. If you are faithful in them, somewhere along the way, at one time or another, God will become real to you. This won't solve all your problems but it will give divine help and divine guidance.

WHEN the record of all lives is truthfully revealed, it will probably be seen that not those who astonished the world with their own powers, but those who quietly, through prayer, used God's powers, were the ones who made the world move forward.

E.P. Roe

PEOPLE CHOOSE THE WRONG WAYS TO ESTABLISH THEIR 'EQUALITY'

It is proverbial around the world that Americans do not make good servants. On foreign ships and planes, the traveling public finds a kind of service that is usually more pleasing. There is a general complaint about the standard of service in our retail establishments. Office managers tell a tale of woe over the response of many office workers to their jobs. It would seem that the average American resents being a servant. No matter what the job, there appears to be the necessity to prove "I'm as good as you are." Instead of proving it by superior performance, the effort is made to prove it by demanding to be treated as an equal.

Among our people there is a mania to be free and equal. To be a servant is regarded as being neither free nor equal; hence, people in lowly jobs and in high places go about with chips on their shoulders seeking to make sure their position is respected.

The trouble is that it is not possible in this world to be either free or equal. No man is free except to choose a master. We are free only to commit ourselves to someone or to something. We are not equal as the world measures such things. Men differ in ability, in opportunity, in training and in character. Except in God's sight, men are not equal, and no society that pretends that they are can endure.

How do you achieve and maintain dignity and self-respect in a world where you are neither free nor equal? I know only one answer

346

in which the humblest man is a child of God and is a servant for Jesus' sake. A man who has come to know that God loves him and has given himself in Christ, for he is freed from the slavery of comparing himself with other men. Out of gratitude, he seeks to serve God in the only way he can serve God - by serving those who are his associates.

Human relations begin with a relation to God. The Christian faith is relevant to business and to everything else that has to do with people. With it, the lowliest and the highest positions become places where one can serve others, not for their sakes, but for Christ's sake.

Before you dismiss this as too idealistic, read the New Testament and see it lift a generation of slaves into men and women who changed the world and whose spiritual descendants are still changing it.

SEPTEMBER

SEPTEMBER 1   **LEAD us, O Father in the paths of right; Blindly we stumble when we walk alone...**

William H. Burleigh, Hymn

WHAT GOOD WILL 'STATEMENTS' DO?

Stands and statements aren't as easy to come by as some people think. Ministers aren't always any wiser in finding God's specific word for a situation than some who aren't ministers. Sometimes stands and statements obscure the real issues involved. The church takes a stand and the minister makes a statement and those who agree feel their position is supported by God and those who disagree wonder how the devil got into the church and the ministers in order to mislead them.

Of course we who are Christian are against sin. There are many things that most Christians agree are wrong. Mobs beating up everyone in sight troubles the conscience of people. The ground gets a little shaky when the resistance to law is labeled as sin. Law is obeyed until it violates conscience under God. It is then to be disobeyed and the consequences taken.

It isn't always easy to make a statement but perhaps there is one statement that has some meaning for all sides of the question. A Christian is one who follows Jesus Christ in obedience. Many a person who professes to be a Christian would be greatly troubled in his own heart if asked to face honestly the question "What would Christ have me to think and do?" Is this evasion? I don't think so. There is a lot of difference in talking about Christian principles and in facing a Christian decision in your own situation.

Frankly, until there is a revival of genuine Christian commitment that is strong enough to override our pride, our greed and our fears, stands and statements aren't going to do much good. This generally applies to the people who profess to follow Christ. They are the church.

The stands and statements which are going to count are those which are lived by men and women who are in places of leadership and who are just ordinary citizens.

Jesus said you could tell His disciples by their fruits. This is still true. This is true in our racial concerns and also in other problems where there is a demand for someone to take a stand or to say something.

PRAYER IN A DAY LIKE THIS

It is not easy to pray in a day like this. Things appear to be out of our control. The Word of God can guide our efforts but only if we know and believe what it says. Its message is a revolution in itself.

The outline of that message is this. God by Jesus created the world and all that is in it. He rules it and all that is a part of it. He created people after His own image. Both nature and people were created to find their true life in fellowship and obedience to Him in accordance with certain requirements.

The Bible is the authority which governs how we are supposed to live to honor and to serve God. These requirements are fully revealed in the life and teachings of Christ. When people choose to live by their own wills and desires in rebellion against God, which is our basic sin, they reap the results of their rebellion in nature, in themselves and in the social order. You can check the media for evidence of how this is working out today.

Out of His love for His creation in nature and in people, God moved to rescue both nature and people by coming to earth in human form to teach and then to die on the cross. Here He took upon Himself the sins of the world, restoring to a right relation to God all who accept for themselves His forgiveness of sin or rebellion and who seek to obey Him. By the body of believers we call the church, God moves by His Spirit to win the whole world to Himself in Christ. From the church, the earthly body of Christ, comes whatever order we can know in this world, personally or in society.

In prayer for ourselves and for others we begin with a faith in the God to whom we are praying. We pray first for faith in Christ, our God, to be born in those for whom we pray. Above all we pray for a revival of faith among all people. Evil and rebellion are too strong for anyone but God to handle. The Gospel of Christ is a rescue operation from judgment and the Bible says there is no other name whereby we must be saved.

SEPTEMBER 3   **TAKE my will and make it Thine! It shall be no longer mine.**

Francis R. Havergal, Hymn

ONLY ONE ROAD LEADS TO VICTORY

What is this thing of living all about? This is an urgent, personal question for each one of us. It cannot be answered too glibly. It must be answered by each one of us in the framework of our ambitions, our desires, our struggles, our victories, our defeats, our sorrows, our joys.

It must be answered in terms of the lives of the people we live among - our families, our friends, our fellow-workers, the people we know well and those we know casually and those we only pass on the street or just read about. What is the life of each of these all about? The question must be answered in terms of what is happening in our world: the mad rush toward self destruction on the one hand and, on the other hand, the frantic efforts to save ourselves.

On the surface, the question of what life is all about seems to get lost in the noise and confusion of daily living. Men scurry about the canyons of our cities and across the furrows of our farms seeking to make a living and to get ahead. They herd together in work and play, each looking to the other for some gleam of an answer to the question of meaning that throbs under the surface.

We are the string to tie together all the different parts of life, a string that will give life meaning and beauty. A bunch of beads is of no real value until they have been strung by someone who understands their meaning and can string them in their proper order.

So it is with life - everyone must find his answer for himself.

350

Where can the answer be but in faith in God who ties all our experiences together in the string of His love and providence? The dark beads of sorrow, the light beads of joy, the shimmering beads of mystery - all find their place under His master hand.

We find our sense of purpose and meaning in seeking His answer in obedience to His will. Often we do not get our answer in the detail we desire. We do get the inner assurances that we are in the hands of One who knows the answer and who places all the beads of our lives on a string that will hold our lives together and give them meaning.

This is the victory that overcomes the world.

SEPTEMBER 4   **BE MY law and I shall be, firmly bound forever free.**

Samuel Longfellow, Hymn

HOW TO BE FREE INSTEAD OF A TOOL

The individual is getting more and more lost in the fast moving events of our day. Add this to his difficulty in finding his place in the bigness all around us and it gets harder all the time to believe in the importance of one person.

This is a personal matter with each of us. "What is man," the Psalmist asked God, "that thou art mindful of him?" This is the most important question you can ask yourself.

Some answer that a person is a tool for the purpose of making money. As long as he can produce, he is valuable. When he no longer is able to show a profit, he becomes useless. Others hold that a person is a tool for the purpose of making the nation or the party strong. He has value only as he serves the interests of the state. In one of these views, man gets his value from the successful business; in the other he gets the value from the successful state.

Most people today do not seem to really know what man is. You can talk about the value of the individual and you can feel that you are valuable as a person, but unless you know why, you fall easy prey to those who want to use you as a tool. Only those who are sure of who they are will stand up and fight those who try to make tools and slaves out of them.

It needs to be said over and over again that freedom is the result of the actions of free men. Free men are those who know themselves to be the children of God, created in His image and redeemed by His love. They are men who have come to know that God calls each by his name and orders the life of each by His loving will.

A man's religion determines what he thinks about himself. If you turn your back on God, if you deny or neglect your proper relationship to God, you will become a tool to be used by someone or by some group.

To those who live close to God comes the conviction that God loves them. They find their sins forgiven and their guilt removed. This is the heart of the Christian Gospel. They discover that one person is of more value than all the physical world. Christ came to individuals living in a world of slavery and tyranny. By His life, death and resurrection, He gave them power to live as free men.

SEPTEMBER 5   **UPON thy bended knees, thank you God for work; work - once man's penance, now his high reward! For work to do and strength to do the work, we thank Thee, Lord!**

John Oxenham

FAITH IN GOD CAN PROVIDE A SENSE OF MEANING FOR WORK

It has always been true that things change. When change becomes rapid, we call it revolution. We are living in a day of revolution. Among the areas of our lives most seriously affected is that of employment. There are few people who have not felt the results of the threat to their job in these days of revolution. Automation, mergers, changing needs and changing methods move into every level of employment, upsetting the old order of things. The economic revolution has at least made more evident a feeling of discontent among people who have jobs.

Few people seem to enjoy their work. There is not much talk today of this dignity and value of work. People seem to feel work is an unpleasant necessity. The pursuit of pleasure and recreation and the growing use of alcohol and pills are evidence of our failure to find our work satisfying. Yet, we were created to find the eternal meaning of our life in work. God put us into the world to take care of it. Unless we can find purpose and meaning in our jobs, we will find it nowhere else in our lives.

At the end of the Sermon on the Mount, Jesus said that those who heard his words and obeyed them would be like a wise man who built his house on a rock. The storms beat against that house and it was not destroyed. This promise of Jesus applies to all areas of life. It promises stability to any person who hears and obeys the words of Jesus. It offers an answer to those caught in fears concerning their job or in a sense of meaninglessness in their work.

Jesus invites you to live by faith.

1. He invites you to live by faith that God deals with you by name as a Person to a person. It is the genius of the Christian faith that it brings a man to believe he is known and loved by God and that God cares for all that concerns him.

2. Christ invites you to live by faith so that, in your job, you work for God. This will give guidance in selecting a job. It will give a conviction of value and meaning to what you do.

3. You are invited to live by the faith that God will make all things work together for good in your affairs if you will trust Him. This means that even the changes will be guided by God for good.

4. Christ invites you to believe that the power of God will work in you and through you as you do your job. You need not be the

victim of cold economic law. God works in you to do His good pleasure. Supernatural power can be yours.

SEPTEMBER 6   THE SLEEP of a laboring man is sweet.

Ecclesiastes 5:12 (KJ)

NO JOB IS 'MENIAL' IF IT'S WELL DONE

Two of the most pressing problems concern unemployment and racial tensions. Even if we did not have the problem of race, jobs would be an increasing problem in our day. The growing use of machines is seeing to that. However, the two problems overlap and complicate one another. There is a growing resentment toward "menial" jobs. Everyone seems to want an "important" job.

Money and prestige are held up as goals for all people. The menial jobs seem to be those that do not provide these things. People are trying to escape being servants of others who have money and prestige.

This kind of thing can only bring unhappiness to the great majority of people. Most people do work for someone above them. The great majority of jobs are jobs where we serve the wishes of someone else. When we honestly face it, a vast number of people will always work in what can be called menial jobs, jobs that offer very little prospect of money or human prestige.

The answer to our attitude toward our job lies not in economics, but in religion. The early Christian Church faced this problem among the slaves who became Christians. Their faith changed their attitudes and their attitudes finally changed the system:

"Slaves obey your master sincerely with a proper sense of respect and responsibility, as service rendered to Christ himself; not with the idea of currying favor with men, but as the servants of Christ, conscientiously doing what you believe to be the will of God for you.

You may be sure that God will reward a man for good work, irrespectively of whether the man be slave or free." (Ephesians 6:5-8)

Here is motivation that can change a menial job into a divine opportunity to serve God by being useful to people. The job is no longer menial. It is one that, done with good will as unto the Lord, is rewarded by the Lord.

I have seen many men and women in humble positions wield great influence because of their dedication to the Lord. They have found happiness in their jobs because they used them in His service. So many people with money fail miserably in life because they forget they are also servants.

SEPTEMBER 7   THE BLESSEDNESS of life depends more upon its interests than upon its comforts.

MacDonald

MATERIALISM'S TIDE MAY BE EBBING

The tides of the sea ebb and flow. There comes a point where the high tide begins to ebb or the low tide begins to flow. If you are watching it is hard to know the exact minute this happens. However, if you continue to watch, you see small signs of the change.

It is the same in many human affairs. There are small indications that the tide is beginning to turn in our worship of the material. We are beginning to question money as the measure of a man's success.

Our country was built upon a foundation of moral integrity, based on a simple faith in God to whom each one was responsible in time and in eternity. This kind of faith and its moral fruits were once accepted as the standard among our people. Then we became rich as a nation - and smart. Education, which was nurtured in the bosom of the church, gradually divorced itself from its source.

The piety and morality of our fathers was debunked. Science and psychology became the high priests of a new day. God as Creator and Ruler and Judge was taken from the center of life and man's wisdom was made the measure of all things.

Today we are reaping the results. Our nation is torn by dissention with no rallying point in sight. Crime, alcoholism, and sex are running riot and there are no tools in man's wisdom to combat them successfully. When God is mentioned, we are told we live in a pluralistic society where all gods must be acknowledged lest any be offended.

But there are small evidences that the tide is turning. Voices are calling in question our worship of a standard of living as a measure of success. Men of wealth and influence are, here and there, being judged by what they are rather than by what they have. Our churches have more young couples worshipping together with their children than in a long time. Social gatherings find the conversation sometimes drifting to things religious.

There is a growing feeling that making money and having fun are not enough to give meaning to life. There is evidence that people want more for their children than tools by which they can make a living and be socially acceptable. There is a growing conviction that tolerance is good, but it becomes a vice when it denies conviction about the things of truth.

God's revelation of Himself in Jesus Christ assures us He waits in love for the prodigal's return. This return begins with each of us - and with all of us - praying for a revival of true religion. Only as we are right with God, can we be right with one another.

THAT we are alive today is proof positive that God has something for us to do today.

Lindsay

ONE PLACE WHERE AN INDIVIDUAL HAS INFLUENCE IS IN HIS OWN LIFE

Our attention is too much fixed on the physical universe. We are too concerned with the vast problems of economics and society. We are too little concerned with the universe within each of us. It is from within yourself that your future and your destiny will come. Jesus said: "The Kingdom of Heaven is within you." Your present and future are the results of how you live within yourself.

It is well to be concerned about the breakdown of moral law. We need people who will stand for right, even though it costs something. You and I need to obey what seems right, regardless of what others do or do not do.

Our real problem today is not communism. It is an inner decay of moral integrity. It reflects itself in regular disclosure of businessmen's putting profit above integrity; in political scandals that place position above honesty and in social life that puts acceptance above conscience. It reflects itself in the amount of time and money that is wasted in the idle pursuit of pleasure. You see it in the demand of material security as the hallmark of our day.

No reform movement will save us. We must have again some men and women who, under God, are rugged individuals who live within the kingdom of their own souls as members of the Kingdom of God. We wait for those who prefer to live by the approval of the inner voice, rather than by the favor of others.

You say you have little influence and can do little good. Yet, you are your first responsibility. You have here all the influence. By your choices, you determine your own life. Unless you are committed to doing right, as God gives you to see it, nothing on the outside can help you. Therefore, you have more influence than you think. A candle light is small, but it is a light that makes a real difference when there is darkness around you. Try following your convictions in the face of the habits and customs and demands of those you love, work and play with. You will find you make more difference than you think. Some of the difference will probably be costly to you.

We need fewer of us worrying about the big problems and more of us making sure we are rightly related to God who made us to be His obedient children. We need more of us trying honestly to live as we know He would have us live.

SEPTEMBER 9   **BE KIND and compassionate to one another, forgiving each other, just as in Christ God forgave you.**

Ephesians 4:32 (NIV)

MARRIAGE MUST BE NOURISHED BY LOVE

The most gracious social institution of God's creation is the home. In the very beginning, God made man and woman to be one in marriage. Marriage is not only the first in time but it is first in importance to the earthly happiness of a man and a woman. Few, if any, find happiness anywhere in life if, being married, they fail to find it in one another.

We need one another so desperately. We are dependent creatures. Independence is a figment of the imagination. Nowhere is this need as great as the need for support of a wife by her husband or a husband by his wife.

A multitude of men and women would be happier and more useful if they could remember this. With the single exception of one's obligation to God, the first duty of a married man is to support his wife in love, and the primary duty of a married woman is to surround her husband with the support of affection.

Within the marriage bond we are more open to compliment or to criticism than anywhere else. Yet it is a tragic fact that criticism too often displaces compliments. There are not many people who need to be "taken down" at home. The world will take care of that. For every person, there needs to be someone with whom he or she is first.

Failing to find in one another the comforting security of love can bring only hurt and disappointment. Pride masks the hurt by indifference and by unkindness. Sharp words and sly cuts, discourtesy and unkindness begin to mark the relationship. The fruitless search for the happiness only marriage can bring begins in "busyness" with work or play or "doing good." It too often ends in seeking the elusive happiness in someone else, with all the tragedy that involves.

Many marriages can be made to glow again with satisfaction if we can stop to realize how much we need one another. If a husband and wife will take as his and her first duty, the privilege of giving the other the strong support of affection, miracles will take place. If honest effort is made to treat one another with kindness, courtesy and consideration, marriage will become what God, in His love, created it to be.

SEPTEMBER 10   **IF any of you lacks wisdom, he should ask God, who gives generously without finding fault, and it will be given.**

James 1:5 (NIV)

A REVISED LITANY FOR MATERIALISTS

We are being told on every hand that we are in danger of trusting too much in material things. No one denies the necessity of these things, but to make them the chief interest of our lives is fatal to the higher and better things of life. The things of the spirit do not thrive well on a purely material diet.

Recently the following "litany" came to me. In a dramatic way, it gathers together the dangerous drift of our day. I believe it will impress you as it did me. It appeared in the church bulletin of Trinity Episcopal Church, Swarthmore, Pennsylvania. I do not know the author:

A MODERN LITANY OF GENERALIZED SUPPLICATION

O Scientific Accident,
source of heaven and earth,
Have mercy upon us,

O Material Power and
Prestige, redeeming
satisfaction of this world,
Have mercy upon us.

O Blessed Money,
sustainer of our status,
Have mercy upon us.

O Science, Technology
Industry, Banking and Politics,
Have mercy upon us.

From bear markets, lower
price supports and loss of government contracts,
Good Lord deliver us.

From all competition, from
shortened coffee-breaks
and hard desk chairs,
Good Lord deliver us.

From all physical toil and adventure,
Good Lord deliver us.

From that open individual
integrity called non-conformity,
Good Lord deliver us.

From unpopularity or

sacrifice for any reason,
Good Lord deliver us.

From any challenge that
calls for lonely witness,
Good Lord deliver us.

From all silence and spare time,
Good Lord deliver us.

From all controversy and
change of any kind,
Good Lord deliver us.

O Social Life, occupy us.

O Television Tube, anesthetize us.

O Dow-Jones, be favorable unto us.

O God, leave us alone.

Amen

SEPTEMBER 11   **I WILL bless the Lord who councils me;
He gives me wisdom in the night. He
tells me what to do.**

Psalm 16:7 (LB)

HOW TO REPLENISH THE SOUL'S FUEL

We would not think a man very wise who had the engine of his
car overhauled when the trouble was that he had run out of gas. Yet
much of the frustration that people feel is due to the fact they have
run out of power. Just as a car has a certain fuel by which it runs, so
does a person.

A young person can get behind in his schoolwork, get crossed up with his family, and lose out with his girl and his friends, all because he has lost touch with the proper source of inner strength. This is equally true of an older person.

Different people run out of power at different ages and under different circumstances. But all who neglect the sources of power run down sooner or later and problems of business or marriage or friends or health or alcohol may overwhelm them. There is nothing permanent that can be done unless the person is willing to put himself or herself where the power is.

In the experience of years, men have found power to live by in two places: the Bible and the Church. It may not seem important for you to read your Bible and to go to Church, but the witness and weight of the centuries are against you. If you are defeated by life, if you are frustrated, if it does not seem worthwhile to try, if purpose and meaning have gone out of your life, try spending a while each day reading your Bible. Then worship each week in the Church of your choice.

Somewhere along the line you will find the clouds lifting from your life. Your frustrations will begin to disappear. God will become more real and your relation to Him more important. There will still be problems, but there will also be answers that often surprise.

If you are having trouble with yourself and in your relation with others, it may well be you are experiencing the normal result of having cut yourself off from the Source of Power.

Your chances of being helped are not good unless you begin at this point. If you are willing to give God a chance through the Bible and the Church, you will find grace to help in your time of need.

SEPTEMBER 12   **...I BOW my knees unto the Father of our Lord Jesus Christ, of whom the whole family of heaven and earth is named.**

Ephesians 3:14,15 (NIV)

WORDS OF THE PROPHETS RANG WITH TRUTH

I have been reading the words of some of the Old Testament prophets. These men were preachers who sought to bring their hearers to the place where they would take God seriously. The common idea about prophets is that they were chiefly predictors of future events. They were predictors, but their ability to see the coming events was only a part of their overall purpose, which was to preach the word of God.

They presented to their day a word that was God's word. "Thus saith the Lord" was the theme of their preaching. History records the truth of their preaching. In the providence of God, their preaching has been preserved because on it still remains the divine seal: "Thus saith the Lord."

The prophets talked about the people of God and the nations of the world. They spoke of the practical matters and there was very little that could not be understood. There is very little in our modern day that was not present in their day. Total war was the experience of many. The weapons were different; the results, the same. The same pride, ambition, greed and cruelty were in their day and they are in ours. Cruel, godless nations threatened and ran over godly nations. Immorality was so general until, in places, it held the stature of a religion. Liquor was a central problem. Things haven't changes much.

Preparedness against the military aggression of evil men was a main theme of the prophets, but as you read these prophets, you are impressed with one startling fact: the affairs of nations and of the people of God are ordered by God on the basis of their obedience to

Him. No amount of military might can save a nation that lives outside this obedience and no amount of military weakness can destroy a nation or a people who obey Him. Holiness, morality, kindness, worship, obedience to God's will are all more important than military might. The theme of the prophets is "not by might, nor by power but by my Spirit, saith the Lord."

We will do well to take God far more seriously than is true generally. Our scandals in business, in labor, in sports; our concentration on sex and alcohol; our obsession with material success and secular pleasure; our gambling and greed and our neglect of God's Word and God's day and God's church - all these things are more dangerous than threats from other nations.

The Book of the prophets makes required reading for our day. Beneath all the efforts of men and nations is the work of God. He guides the decisions of heads of nations and advisers toward His purposes. These purposes have to do with bringing men and nations into obedience to Him.

Over it all is the word of the prophet: "Thus saith the Lord."

SEPTEMBER 13   CAST me not away from thy presence...

Psalm 51:11 (KJ)

'HEAR THE RUSTLE OF ANGELS' WINGS'

God is always with us, nearer then breathing, closer than hands and feet. Whatever we are doing, good or bad, God is present. So much of the time, we are not aware of His Presence. We get so busy, so wrapped up in ourselves until we do not feel His hand on our shoulders nor hear His voice in our hearts.

There are times, however, when we do "hear the rustle of angels' wings" and feel the divine presence. These high moments are our God-given opportunities to know Him and to respond to Him in gratitude, love and surrender. He does not leave Himself without witness in any heart.

1. There come those moments when we desire to seek Him. We feel we would like to know and serve Him better; this means He is seeking us and has drawn near. Follow the promptings of your heart.

2. There are those moments in life when the love of another person is very precious. The gracious experience of shared love opens doors to an experience of the Divine. Even the most irreligious person feels the tug of God on his heart. In such a moment God talks to you of His love. Pause to listen.

3. The birth of a baby opens doors of vast mystery. It must have more than human meaning. The hardest heart is softened as a new life is given and the eyes instinctively look up to God for help. Many have found God, led by the grasp of tiny fingers.

4. Strange as it may seem, the angel of death leads the heart straight to God. There are few who do not somewhere in the valley of the shadow reach out to touch His hand. Here all the mystery and the defeat of human life meet and only God has an answer. The answer is really the gift of Himself. There is light along the path of those who follow where He leads.

5. Everyone is moved at some time to do a kindly deed to help someone lift a load that is too heavy. Did you ever wonder whence comes the warm feeling of inner approval? It is the voice of the Master saying: "Inasmuch as ye have done it unto one of the least of these my brethren, ye have done it unto Me."

6. When we do wrong there is within us an inner voice that condemns. Do what we may, we cannot escape it nor can we easily rid ourselves of it. No human solution is able to wash it out. In this voice, God is proving that He would not have a single soul perish but that He would have each of us to be saved. It is His voice calling us to turn from our sin and to become His own as we accept by faith His forgiveness through Christ.

We do well to heed His voice. At some point in your life God is breaking through to say to you: "Seek ye the Lord while He may be found, call ye upon Him while He is near."

IF WE confess our sins, He is faithful and just to forgive us our sins, and to cleanse us from all unrighteousness.

I John 1:9 (NIV)

POWERFUL ENEMIES ARE WITHIN THE GATES

"While the danger is the greatest the world has ever seen, it is not primarily because of communism that we face the struggle for survival. It is not the uncommitted nations, or an atomic intercontinental ballistic missile war, or international economic competition - serious and decisive as these are.

"Underlying their danger is a greater danger - the decline of the religious conviction, moral strength, national purpose and personally responsible brotherhood and citizenship. To the extent that we possess or lack these qualities, we will win or lose our struggle for survival."

These are not the words of some preacher who "does not understand practical problems." They are the words of Mr. George Romney, president of American Motors Corporation, as recently quoted in a newspaper article.

I sometimes wonder if we are so obsessed with our material playthings and so determined to have a good time until we no longer know the truth when we see it. Voices are being raised all around us saying what Mr. Romney is saying and most people just smile and take another drink.

It comes down to the question of who the people are that are threats to our free society. The Communists to be sure - but if we are the right kind of people, their attacks can never win. One of the real dangers lies in the people who break down our religious and moral standards.

Few people start out to be a danger to society. They just end up that way without ever meaning to. The first step toward being a danger to society is the drift from religious conviction. One gets too busy to go to church or read the Bible or to pray seriously. Or maybe one skips it all because he had to do too much of it as a child. One excuse is as good as another. Anyway, the things of God and of sin and of human dependence on Divine Help fade out. In their place come comfortable living, busy schedules, good parties, good clothes, and fine cars.

There follows a loss of moral conviction, as night follows day. Right and wrong get blurred. The old moral laws seem narrow and old-fashioned. Live and let live is the motto. Any protests over loose living are laughed at. Conduct is determined by what the crowd is doing. Shady living, shady parties, shady stories, all under the guise of good fellowship, are the order of the day.

Now the way is open for these who trade on man's weakness and our books and our magazines and movies break through the old moral barriers in the name of the new freedom. Scandals in business and in politics no longer stir more than momentary interest and generate almost no moral reaction.

So we get ready for the attack of the enemy. It is time we begin to recognize the enemies within our gates before it is too late.

SEPTEMBER 15   **FOR I am with thee to save thee and to deliver thee, saith the Lord.**

Jeremiah 15:20 (KJ)

IT TAKES COURAGE TO BELIEVE FIRMLY

Life can get into a blind alley. Sometimes the future seems impossible. This sort of thing happens to everyone, even those that have always believed in God. In such times you have to decide whether you will take God at His word and go forward even if there seems nowhere to go, or whether you are going to turn and run. It takes real courage to believe in God when the future seems

367

impossible.

The Hebrews faced such an experience at Kadesh Barnea.. They stood on the edge of the Promised Land under command of God to go in and possess it. Behind them was a year of continuing proofs of God's ability to provide all their needs. Delivered from Egypt by a miracle, they had been preserved by His Presence. Led by a cloud by day and night, fed by His miracle, they had come to the port of entry of the Promised Land, Kadesh Barnea.

All they had to do was to trust God and go in and possess the land. At this moment they lost their courage to believe in God. They heard how big and strong the people of the land were and how high the walls of their cities were. They decided that the difficulties were too great for God to remove them, in spite of what He had done in the past.

The story is true of human nature. We find ourselves in it. In spite of His past favor, we often fail to trust Him as we face some difficult situation. Today our future is uncertain. The whole world is upset. One of the main assertions of faith is that God is the Ruler of the affairs of men. It takes courage to hold fast to this faith in the face of conditions as they are. Yet only as we believe it, can we face life and the future unafraid.

The heart of our faith is its confidence that God cares for each of us, that each is the object of His love. In view of what is happening to people everywhere, it takes courage to believe this. Many who read this will be facing personal difficulties which make it hard for them to believe that God cares for each of us and that each is the object of His love. Many who read this will be facing difficulties which make it hard for them to believe that God can provide a future that is good. For many, there are giants moving against them. Sickness, failure, the grip of some evil, poverty, a load too heavy to bear, sorrow, loneliness - these and other things can put a real strain on faith.

When we face a future that seems impossible, God bids us to remember His faithfulness in the past. You have been cared for up to the present time. In the life of each, there is witness to His care in the past. God who has been faithful will see you through your present difficulties and into a good future if you will trust Him and go forward in courage.

SEPTEMBER 16 BECAUSE of the Lord's great love we are not consumed, for his compassions never fail.

Lamentations 3:22 (NIV)

THERE IS RELIEF FOR WEARINESS

Most people have burdens and carry heavy loads. It would take a great deal of optimism to predict that our burdens are going to get lighter. They may well get heavier. The burdens that come through misfortune will continue to fall on us. Then the work of the world will press heavily on those who carry responsibility in labor and business, in politics and in the various professions!

We must find some relief from the strain of it all. We just can't go on getting tighter and tighter and running faster and faster. The mental and moral breakdowns of our day are due to the strain of daily living.

I stood not long ago beside a large river and watched the heavy traffic being carried by its ample waters. The river carried all the traffic required of it and never grew too shallow to do its job. Here is a parable for our lives. The river could carry its heavy load because it was constantly receiving water from sources outside itself. It would soon run dry and leave its burdens mired in the mud if it refused to accept fresh water day by day from outside itself. The rain from above was the main source of its great strength. Yet most of the rain from above it was received from springs and creeks and other rivers which flowed into it.

Most of us are like the river. We are meant to carry loads. At any moment, the strength seems to be our own. It is our body and our minds and our spirits that do the work. Yet, we did not create our own strength nor is it really our own strength from above. At any one moment our strength is a strange combination of our own, of that of others and, above all, of God, the "giver of all strength."

369

Even as the river can't carry its burdens if it ceases to receive, neither can we. Part of our weariness and breakdowns are caused by our failure to receive daily from God and man. The great commandment that calls us to love God with all our heart, soul, mind and strength and our neighbor as ourselves, speaks to this point.

If your burdens are too heavy, check and see if you are living in love with God and with your friends and family and associates. If you are cut off by your neglect or by your selfishness, you will fall under your burdens. Only as God's strength can come to you as you open your heart in response to His love and to that of your fellows, can your spirit and body be constantly refreshed for the tasks of the day.

SEPTEMBER 17   **WITHOUT ceasing I make mention of you always in my prayers.**

Romans 1:9 (KJ)

HERE IS A WAY FOR YOU TO HELP

It is beginning to get through to lots of people that things in our world are at the place where everyone had better lend a hand if the ship is not to sink. Around lunch tables, at cocktail parties, in business conferences, people are asking, "What can I do?" Some are old and feel there is nothing they can do. Others have been useless so long until they have no idea where to begin. Nearly all are confused.

There is something each one can do, young or old, sick or well, working or retired. You and I can pray. This can be the thing that must first be done before anything else can be of very much help. The useless life can well find in prayer the key to a life of positive value. However, there are some things that need to be said about prayer. Unless you take it seriously, there isn't much use praying. Truly to pray involves a definite attitude towards God and towards life.

If you come to pray, you must come willing to seek the will of God and to do it as you find it. If you pray for peace so that you can continue to be undisturbed in your comfortable, self-centered life, you might as well skip it. If you pray for anything without committing to use the answer to God's glory and in His service, your praying will fall short.

Prayer will lead you to know certain things you should and shouldn't do. These you will have to take seriously. If while you pray you know you are not living as you should, you had better start with yourself. If you are spending more money on clubs and parties than you are on your church, your prayers are of dubious value. If you are too busy working and playing to worship and serve in your church, don't crowd your schedule with prayer. If you are divided from family or friends by quarrels that you have not tried to reconcile, your prayer won't help you very much. True praying probably begins with the prayer of the publican: "God have mercy on me, a sinner."

Prayer is something that demands surrender and it demands obedience. It will revolutionize any life that takes it seriously. If you want to do something to help in our day, take prayer seriously; pray for yourself and for all men everywhere. Here is the beginning of usefulness. Other doors will open then.

SEPTEMBER 18   I NEED Thee every hour...

Annie S. Hawks, Hymn

A BATTLE IS WAGED IN THE SOUL OF MAN

The soul of a man is a vast arena where the battle of life is fought to a decision. Here the issues of life and death are fought out. On this battleground gather all the forces of our past, a past of countless generations. Here gather the influences of our homes, our own experiences, past and present. Here gather for the fight our hopes and our dreams.

On the battleground of the soul, the ugly army of Satan marshals its forces "for we wrestle not against flesh and blood but against -

spiritual wickedness in high places." There gather also the forces of the Lord and His angels. The really important struggles in our world are not in the halls of public debate or even on fields of armed conflict. They are in the souls of men and women. Out of these struggles of the souls of men come the outward battles among men.

In the heart is the battlefield where virtue is won or lost, where the red badge of courage is put on or trampled in the mire of cowardice, where purity is maintained or forever stained. Here is won or lost the battle between love and hate, pride and humility, hope and despair. Here are born the Christian virtues of love, joy, peace, long suffering, gentleness, goodness, faith, meekness and temperance or the evil traits of immorality, idolatry, wrath, strife, envy, murder, drunkenness and such.

This struggle within you is one in which eternal powers are contenders for your soul. Jesus told Peter once: "Satan hath desired to have thee." This is true of each of us. Everyone is conscious of the inner struggle. The person who tries to be good feels it most intensely of all. Such a one finds that, like Paul, the good he would do, he fails to do and the evil he would not do, he does.

The struggle is no mock battle. It is not one we can postpone until a more convenient season. It is won or lost every day. It cannot be won with our human strength or by our human cleverness and wisdom. Where victory is won men and women who humbly look to God win it. In his victory, Paul thanked God through Jesus Christ.

Our victory lies in daily putting on the armor of God: truth, righteousness, peace, faith and salvation. Victory comes to those armed with the sword of the Spirit which is the Bible, and it comes to those who surround themselves with prayer.

We are troubled about many things. We need to heed the sacred words: "Keep thy heart with all diligence for out of it are the issues of life." In the arena of our own heart, we are making our chief contribution to a better world or a worse one. If we are concerned about things, we do well to begin with ourselves.

SEPTEMBER 19   **I WRITE unto you little children, because your sins are forgiven you for His name's sake.**

I John 2:12 (NIV)

THERE'S A BIG NEED FOR EVANGELISM

I am not sure why evangelism is so dead today. In the face of the terrific need, you would think that we Christians would be hurrying about to bring the unchurched into the church and to Christ. We seem almost dead on our feet in comparison with some religions who seem to have a passion for their mission and their message. Unless the church is continually reaching out to bring others in - it will die. BRINGING THEM IN is evangelism!

In the old days, the church was intolerant enough to insist that men could not be saved without Christ. Today we are tolerant; but we are the victims of a false tolerance. We are inclined to feel badly if we try to change the convictions which are wrong. Until we get over this misplaced sense of guilt about witnessing to the truth, evangelism will not do well.

We need evangelism for the church itself. We need it to revive our own faith and our own spirits. Unless there is this revival in the near future, the church is going to continue to be an ineffective element in our society.

People outside the church need evangelism. I do not know where people can take their sin and find forgiveness except to Jesus Christ and His church. All of the solutions of our day that leave out the redeeming grace of Christ are too often just wind and fury.

I do not know where the heart that has been broken can take itself to be healed - if not to Christ and His church. I do not know where the confused mind and heart of a man can be taken to find peace - outside the church and its Christ.

People need what we have. And I do not know where our lost day will find salvation, unless there is a return of evangelism. We need organization through which God can work, but we must stop looking to organization itself to accomplish what only God can accomplish.

We must really believe that Christ and His church are necessary for the people around us. We say we believe that but the average church member does not really believe it. If he did, he would do something about it. We must ask for this faith - and then simply wait until the answer comes.

We need to pray for a real concern for the people about us. You don't have to argue with them. All you really have to do is to witness to what you have and simply invite them to come and see Jesus and His church. It should be simple and natural. It is time we stopped being against things and gave evidence that we are for what we say we are for.

SEPTEMBER 20   JUST pray for a tough hide and a tender heart.

Ruth Graham

HERE ARE GOALS WORTHY OF PRAYER

I have written before about the necessity for prayer and mentioned some of its conditions. A friend suggested that I write about some of the things for which we should pray. The best answer is to pray for whatever is on your heart. In prayer, there is nothing too small or too great because you are dealing with God who made and rules everything from the outskirts of space to the sparrow's fall. In Jesus, God revealed that He is concerned with anything you are concerned with.

You are certainly concerned with yourself, your health, your ambitions, your loved ones, your problems, your sins, your sorrows, your joys, your defeats, your successes. Talk to God about them. Talk to God about your relationship to Him.

There are those in the circle of your contacts in the home, in your work, in your social group, among those you meet casually, for whom you develop concern for one reason or another. Pray for them.

Surely in this day, you are concerned about the conditions in our nation and in our world. Nearly everyone is conscious of something that is wrong or bad in the neighborhood or in the community. Whatever your particular concern is, pray to God about it. It may help more to talk to God about some evil than to go out talking to everyone you meet about it.

We all are concerned about the bad international situation. Prayer can put you in touch at the very center of every conference table. Prayer can bring you into contact with every leader about whom you read. God can change hearts. After we have prayed David's prayer for ourselves: "Create in me a clean heart, O God, and renew a right spirit within me," we can pray it for those we feel to be evil men.

In our world there are many leaders and people who are trying to live as God would have them live and are seeking to do His will. Pray for them. All the lights have not gone out. Your prayers can make them shine more brightly. Pray for God's will to be done on earth.

God has brought a revival of faith through His church by the touch of His spirit in many a past generation. You can hasten the day of revival by your prayers. These are just signposts along the way. If you pray, willing to obey the guidance you receive and willing that all your answers shall be used to the glory of God and in the service of others, you will be led to pray for the proper things. Your prayers will also lead you to do what you can where you are.

Out of such praying and living, God builds His tomorrow.

GOD HAS A PLACE IN OUR SCHOOLS

There is concerted effort in our land to exclude any worship or even any mention of God in places supported by public funds. Certain atheistic societies and non-Christian groups have attacked the use of the Bible in our schools. The pageantry of Christmas and Easter are being prohibited here and there in public schools. The Supreme Court ruled long ago that it was unconstitutional for the federal government or any state to require "a belief in the existence of God" as a qualification for public office.

It is well to protect the rights of minorities, but to allow them to override the convictions of the majority is asking too much. We talk very glibly about atheistic communism. We do well not to follow in their footsteps in excluding God from our public life and from our public education.

For years we have claimed to be opposed to communism and vow that we must fight it with all our might. But how do you fight its basic evil of godlessness if you bring your children through a process of education that leaves God out? How can you educate without God in this world if you expect to produce men and women able to stand against materialistic Communism?

How do you educate people as to the sacredness of personality, as to human rights and liberties, without telling them of their relation to God? How do you educate a person to be moral and to have respect for others without educating them in the things of God? The problem is a difficult one, but an increasing number of people are beginning to be unhappy with the idea of education without God.

It is not enough of an answer to say that this is the job of the church and the home. The people in the churches and in the homes, by and large, are the people who provide the schools. The great majority believes in God and wants their children to believe in Him. They have a right to have God acknowledged in the public institutions that their money provides.

Education without God is like giving a carpenter a bag of tools without giving him any training in the use of them. Only in the knowledge of and obedience to God do we have direction as to what is moral and what is good. To talk about building character without teaching about God is to try to build a house without building materials.

This is what George Washington had in mind when he wrote, "And let us with caution indulge in the supposition that national morality can prevail in exclusion of religious principle." However difficult the solution of this problem may be, the proper answer can mean life or death to all we hold dear.

SEPTEMBER 22   **THE LORD's curse is on the house of the wicked but he blesses the home of the righteous.**

Proverbs 3:33 (NIV)

AN OPEN LETTER TO PARENTS

Dear Friends: Your children are growing up in a world of wars and rumors of wars. Stability and confidence and serenity of spirit are rare. Your child will need these qualities. They have their roots in these younger years of your children. Adults who have these qualities bless parents who were faithful in the things that really mattered. This is an appeal to you to take seriously the things that matter most in the training of your child or children. For many, it is too late. It can be too late for you sooner than you think.

One of the things that matters most is teaching your children the things of God. A young child responds to God as a flower turns to the sun. Foundations are laid in character that time and temptation can never shake as, night by night, you kneel with your child and pray. The stories of the Bible become steel girders of the soul as they are taught by parents' lips. Are you taking your child to Sunday school and church where the Holy Spirit molds the young life in the likeness of Christ?

You are very careful to do all that is necessary to make your child physically strong. Yet if that child is not spiritually strong, he or she will only have more energy to put into wrong channels. You are careful to train your child to avoid physical dangers. Are you as careful to warn your child of the perils of loving self rather than God? The social graces can be important, but when temptation comes, as it surely will, only the grace of God will keep your child safe and your heart from being broken.

It is also very important how YOU are living. You say you want your child to be good, unselfish and useful. It would help some parents to honestly face the question of whether they are living as they want their children to live. It is not easy in this day of endless business and social demands to live as you know you should, but it is necessary if you are to lead your children in the right paths. You can't stay on the party circuit and leave the children at home with the admonition to be good and expect them to be.

Juvenile delinquency is too often a matter of parents reaping as they have sown. The tragedy of young lives ruined and of parents' broken hearts is too often the earlier tragedy of parents who ignored the things that matter most.

Give God a chance with His precious gift of children. Give your children the chance God meant for them to have. By your training and your example, lead them in the things that matter most. When they are older they will not depart from them. You will give to life strong men and women who will rise up and call you blessed.

SEPTEMBER 23   HOW can a young man keep his way pure? By living according to your word. I have hidden your word in my heart that I might not sin against you.

Psalm 119: 9,11 (NIV)

HELP IS AVAILABLE IN YOUR SEARCH

All of us need help in making our Christian faith meaningful in our daily living. We are so caught in the demands made on us by the routine of living that there hardly seems to be a time or place for much thought or effort about God. When some crisis comes we frantically search about for spiritual help but even here, we often fail to make connection between God and our need.

For some time in the past we have had the idea that religion was something to help us along our own way. We have been centering our attention on ourselves. We have been willing to believe in a God who would help us be healthy, wealthy and wise as individuals and strong and safe as a nation. We have insisted on living our lives for our comfort and pleasure. If God could help us, fine. If not, then we have pretty well decided to go it on our own.

This has not worked very well. At least dimly we are beginning to see that God demands to be the center of our lives if we are to be His children. We are beginning to hear Jesus as He says that if any man wishes to be His disciple he must leave self behind and take His cross and come with Him. We are just a little nearer to understanding what Jesus meant when he said that if a man seeks to save his life, he shall lose it. We are beginning to understand that our relationship to God must be one of obedience. Only then will our faith have a central place in everything that concerns us. It makes it necessary to know God's will as he has revealed it in his Word and in Jesus Christ. It makes it necessary to seek this will in every situation that concerns us.

SEPTEMBER 24   **I WILL lie down and sleep in peace for you alone, O Lord, make me dwell in safety.**

Psalm 4:8 (NIV)

COURAGE IS BORN BY KEEPING FAITH

No one needs to be told that these are bad times. What we do need to know is that there is something we can do to live with hope in the face of the storm. Courage and hope are qualities of the spirit and do not depend on outward circumstances. We learn to live worthily by tending our spirits and not by changing outside conditions.

If you have ever lived through a hurricane you have watched trees bend to the wind and still stand through the storm. The trees that fall usually prove to have had faulty roots or were rotting within. The same thing is true of us human beings. Let it be said that it is no easy task for a man or woman to keep the roots of life healthy or to keep the inner life from being rotted out by evil. One of the reasons so many of us have trouble meeting our confused day with courage and hope is that we just haven't worked at it. We have given our time and our energies to the things of this world and then have been surprised when they failed us in our times of crises.

Worldly things were never meant to support our spirits. God made us for Himself and our spirits can find strength only as we keep ourselves in touch with Him. We must work at keeping our roots firmly fixed in their native soil of God's presence. This means setting apart some time each day to talk to God and to listen to Him. He speaks through His Word and the daily use of it will bring Him near. From the divine depths there will flow into your life faith, strength, comfort, forgiveness and guidance for the day. It means also regular worship in the church where you have contact with others who are on the same quest.

As you proceed faithfully to keep in touch with God you are led to believe that behind - and even in - the turmoil of life, He lives and rules. You begin to rest in this confidence and courage is born.

Then, too, you come to the place where you believe that history is the story of God working out His own plan. He sent His Son to reveal that plan as one of redeeming love. In such confidence, hope is born. We dare to believe that the end will be good because already He has made it clear that evil cannot win, and that the final victory belongs to God.

SEPTEMBER 25   BE STILL and know that I am God...

Psalm 46:10 (KJ)

IT IS NECESSARY TO KEEP THE SABBATH

"Remember the Sabbath Day - to keep it holy." It is the fourth commandment of our Lord. We don't worry today about the "one day in seven." Many Christians even feel that ministers have more important things to discuss. There are so many problems and difficulties.

But what we fail to realize is that our problems are simply symptoms of the deadly problem at the very root of life. And with this basic problem, the observance of the Sabbath is very much involved.

Those opposed to keeping the Sabbath are very boastful. They have spread the feeling that any attempt to keep one day holy unto the Lord is simply an effort of certain "religious folk" to narrow the path of their lives. We are put in the position of taking the joy out of life - by trying to force on non-religious people the necessity of doing what we Christians and Jews think ought to be done. That simply is not true. The man who cares nothing for God has as much at stake in keeping one day in seven as the most devout Christian. Without it, civilization cannot exist. The world is just made that way.

The law of the Sabbath was here long before Moses. The Code of Hammurabi - 600 years before Moses and 2,000 years before Christ -

has as its very heart the keeping of one day in seven holy unto their God. The matter of keeping one day in seven goes back to Creation. There are no people today smart enough to outsmart Creation. On the seventh day God rested. He hallowed it, and it has been one of the great cornerstones of life since that day.

Jeremiah was a prophet in the days when his nation was destroyed. He told his countrymen simply: "If we will stop and properly keep holy unto the Lord one day in seven, the Babylonian Army can't capture us." Remember this - the most powerful nation in the world could not capture the weakest nation, if the weakest nation kept one day in seven!

Voltaire - who was never a friend of Christianity - said that any man who would destroy Christianity would first have to destroy the Christian Sabbath. Emerson called the Christian Sabbath the core of civilization. Disraeli - a great English statesman and a Jew - said, "The Christian Sabbath is the cornerstone of civilization." If the statements of prophets like Jeremiah are all false - then eat, drink, be merry, and forget it! But if they are true, then we are in real trouble because practically nobody today takes the Sabbath seriously.

Jesus said the Sabbath was made for man. It is made for man as he is today and for man in all his eternity. The Sabbath was made and given to man as a channel of grace - as a channel of the power of God. You do not just pluck God out of the air. You put yourself where He is. Keeping one day in seven holy unto the Lord is one place where God is and always has been. This is a door through which God comes - Keeping the Sabbath is not an option. It is a necessity if the church is to last. And if the Christian church does not last, then society is through.

SEPTEMBER 26 WE DO not lose heart. Though outwardly we are wasting away, yet inwardly we are being renewed day by day. For our slight and momentary troubles are achieving for us an eternal glory that far outweighs them all. So we fix our eyes not on what is seen, but on what is unseen. For what is seen is temporary, but what is unseen is eternal.

II Corinthians 4:16-18 (NIV)

WITH FAITH, YOU NEED NOT FEAR

These are some thoughts that have come to me as I have listened and talked to people of all ages who are worried about our present threatened day. Some of this may seem childish to people who are looking for some big thing to do to ease their fears. However, child-like faith may be our answer.

It is a good time for people who have no faith in God to be afraid. If all we have to trust is the unaided wisdom and goodness of men, then we do well to be afraid because there isn't much of either. However, I do not understand the near panic of people who have a faith rooted in God. Faith is at home in bad conditions. The great assurances of the Bible come in almost every instance from times as bad or worse than ours. Isaiah called a nation to faith in God in the face of almost certain disaster from Assyria, history's cruelest nation. Jeremiah left a heritage of faith that came out of his experience of God in the face of the destruction of his nation by Babylon. Jesus lived a life of faith in the face of every tragedy that could befall a person. He won His victory not by evading tragedy, but by accepting it head-on. There is no character in the Bible favorably reported who did not maintain faith in the face of what often seemed to be disaster.

We believe this is God's world. He created it and rules it. He loved it enough to give His Son to die for it. Surely we can trust Him.

Christ looked the evil of the world in the face and said, "Fear not, I have overcome the world."

There is not a thing most of us can do in any direct way to remedy the situation. It looks to me that the simplest thing is to trust each day to God and then go about the duties and pleasures of the day with the prayer that He will use your efforts to His glory in the service of this generation. The simplest task or pleasure can be committed to Him in this way if we are seeking to do His Will.

What are you afraid of? Maybe it is conscience reminding us we are not living as we should. If so, these may be days that will bring good.

Actually, faith is most at home when the conditions of the world are at their worst. Try leaving the big things to God and just concentrate on doing the best you can to enjoy each day as it comes, seeking to do God's will in it. This will do wonders for your faith.

SEPTEMBER 27   **WHEN a person is at his wits end it is not a cowardly thing to pray. It is the only way to get in touch with Reality.**

Oswald Chambers

TURN TO PRAYER INSTEAD OF FEAR

We have all been reading about hurricanes. I was reared in hurricane country and have experienced a number of them. When you live in a well-built house above the water line, you go through a hurricane without any real degree of fear. The odds are against anything serious happening to you. Hurricanes do their chief damage to those houses located in low places or to poorly built houses located in high places.

Life is like that. We are living in a cross current of storms. It is just beginning to occur to us that the storms may not stop and that they may get worse. We have always thought we were the favorites of the universe; but we are now beginning to believe that something very bad can happen to us. Something close to panic, the panic of those living in lowlands in hurricane country, is beginning to grip our lives. And if the storm blows too hard, we now suspect that the whole structure of our lives may well collapse.

We have put great stock in science. We have been led to believe that we could depend on the laws of nature, yet now a great many outstanding scientists are telling us that nature may not be rational or reasonable. They say that all you can do is build on "theory." The sure foundations of science are getting shaky.

We have put stock in philosophy. This is the science of the mind that attempts to fit together different parts of life, giving life a meaning. But philosophy now tells us that there may probably be no single unifying principle which ties all of life together. Apparently it is every man for himself. So philosophy is proving to be a kind of blind guide to the blind.

Those who built this country put great faith in morals. Today, it is almost taken for granted - even in this Christian era - that there are no absolute standards. The idea is that nothing is right for everybody, everywhere, all the time.

These are days when the foundations of life seem to be shaking. Ours is not, however, the only day in which this has been true. The tragedy of our time is that we fail to realize that history is like an old Hollywood movie. In many respects it is played over and over and over. Santayana, the late great philosopher, said: "Those who do not know history are condemned to re-live it."

The crisis of our time is the same crisis faced by every nation in history that tries to live without God. We are primarily excited about aggressive countries and their bombs and other weapons of mass destruction. We should be excited about God. Instead of recoiling in fear, we should kneel in prayer. We should remember that God is still on the throne - and that no combination of dictators or nations or missiles is going to brush Him off.

In any storm we face - individually or nationally - the high ground and the strong building represent our faith in Christ. In this faith we can have total confidence in God's power to hold us and to use us, however strong the storm may be.

SEPTEMBER 28   LIFE must be measured by thought and action, not by time.

Lubbock

FINAL ACCOUNTING AWAITS EVERYONE

"It is given unto every man once to die; but after this, the Judgment." All of us are familiar with television plays and skits - and the importance of their background music. Background music is generally used to give us the meaning of what is going on.

Paul tells us - in Romans 14 - that "every one of us shall give account of himself to God." We have the same thing in Hebrews 9:27: "It is given unto every man once to die; but after this, the Judgment." These words are the great background music of the play of life. Behind all the actions of all men there is this throbbing music that tells of a rendezvous with God.

We have an engagement with destiny - with the Lord Almighty. One day we are going to account to God for everything we have said, done or felt. This is true of me; it is true of you; it is true of all people. This is the recurring theme of the Holy Bible. It is one theme we can't escape. Jesus says there is nothing that is hidden that will not be known. Even for every idle word that we speak, we will have to give account on the Day of Judgment.

This background music of judgment is also deep in the heart of every person. Whenever we are completely honest with ourselves, we know - deep down within us - that we cannot ignore it however hard we try. And everybody feels this same sense of responsibility. Even a child has it - not only toward God, but also toward all authority. A child expects to give account - and so does an adult. We don't think much about the Day of Judgment, but there it is in our intuition and in our Scripture.

Christ will be the Judge. Our actions will be the basis of the

Judgment. There will be a separation between the sheep and the goats. "Come unto Me and inherit that prepared for you from the foundation of the world," the King of Kings will say to some. "Depart from Me, for I do not know you," He will say to others. On that day, there will emerge for all to see, both Heaven and Hell. All separation will cease.

The fact that life has a final accounting is the only thing that makes life make sense. It is the only thing that gives to our days a common destination. It alone ties together Russia, Japan and America - giving them a unity, because they are all moving toward a common point in destiny. They will all meet the same Master - the same Judge - at the same place.

Therefore life has meaning. It is tied together. It is going somewhere. It makes a difference where you are going. And obviously it makes a difference what you think is at the end of it all.

SEPTEMBER 29   **THIS is the day the Lord has made. Let us rejoice and be glad in it.**

Psalm 118:24 (NIV)

SERIOUS OBSERVANCE OF THE SABBATH CAN LEAD TO A FRUITFUL ADVENTURE

I want to say more on keeping holy to God one day in seven because of a deep conviction that it is necessary if we are to find inner strength. It is necessary if we are to realize our divine potential. How are we to keep the Sabbath holy unto the Lord? You will have to work the details out for yourself. God will guide you. The principal thing is that you commit yourself to doing it!

People argue about what is right on the Sabbath to keep from doing what they know to be right. Forget the arguments; do the best you can. Do not worry too much about what the other person thinks you ought to do. Some people get more messages from the Lord for other people than they get for themselves.

What you must do must include at least four features:

1. Worship. There are no people who are Christians in any creative sense who avoid the regular worship of God. That needs to be said today. If you are able to worship - and you are able to worship - yet you do not worship - you lose touch with God. The Holy Spirit of God is given to individuals in company with Christians. This is consistently shown in the New Testament. You cannot go to church to worship and then leave without having been changed somewhat by having been there. The change has to do with what happens between you and God.

2. Rest. The Sabbath must have something of rest in it. The hardest thing you and I have to do today is to do nothing. It is necessary to regularly turn aside from our work and let our bodies and minds relax. God has appointed one day in seven to give us a chance to rest.

3. Time for the family. Family life cannot live or prosper unless some time is given to it. The family is held together by love. Love needs to be cultivated. This can be done only as the family worships together and then spends time together in congenial activities. One day in seven kept holy to God gives opportunity for these things. Those of us who came up in a home where the Sabbath was taken seriously can witness to the value of it. It puts something into life that nothing can take away.

4. Deeds of love and mercy. People don't have the time today to show kindness. We are just as kind as we ever were, but we don't have time to get around. One reason is that we have filled every day with the things that concern us.

Jesus said, "As much as ye have done it unto the least of these my brethren, ye have done it unto me." The Sabbath gives time for us to serve God by serving others.

You will find it a fruitful adventure to take seriously the observing of one day in seven as holy unto the Lord.

DO NOT be overcome by evil, but overcome evil with good.

Romans 12:21 (NIV)

THE WORLD'S PROBLEMS ARE IN YOU, TOO

This is written in the midst of three days of meetings. The great problems of men have been bandied about in great style. Wonderful vocabulary has framed the problems and the solutions - such things as: "What new cultural factors need our careful consideration?"

Everyone has problems - even Peanuts of the comic strip is trying to get consideration of world problems. A speaker begins: "Our world is not a very happy place." This is true in a sense, but actually a world cannot be happy or unhappy. Only people are happy and unhappy. Whether your world is happy or unhappy depends on you and not on unhappy statistics which some expert works out. Jesus spoke to the point when He said, "the Kingdom of Heaven is within you." So is the Kingdom of Hell.

What I am trying to say is that about all we can do about world problems lies within ourselves. Within you, the word lives and moves and has its being. Heavy documents and multitudinous meetings cannot solve any more problems than the people involved can solve within themselves.

You will help solve the problem of fear only by finding some way to quit being afraid. You won't be much help in working out race relationships until you have found some answer in yourself. You will increase the happiness of the world best by finding happiness within your own heart. Fighting in our world will be eased to the extent you and I quit fighting ourselves and others.

Education is a good thing, but it is no answer if the educated person is not the right kind of person. Meetings can confuse more than they solve if they become tools of selfish people or causes. Time spent discussing problems is wasted if it gives us an idea that we have thereby done something about them. The person who has found solutions for his own problems and who has found happiness will learn what needs learning. He will have sense enough and grace enough to do what needs doing.

The early Christians had problems but the word is not mentioned in the New Testament. They faced every problem we face. They met suffering and struggle and were "filled with joy." They believed God could be depended on. They went about their daily lives trusting Him to show them what to do and to give them power to do it. They had a way of letting the future alone without imagining, as experts do, what problems it would bring.

They solved the problems of their own hearts and God used them to change the world. The real solutions to our problems will come through such people today more than through uncounted hosts of experts who only project problems and call meetings to solve them.

OCTOBER

OCTOBER 1   **THE CHRISTIAN ideal has not been tried and found wanting. It has been found difficult and left untried.**

Chesterton

SACRIFICES ARE NECESSARY IF A PERSON IS USEFUL

Nearly everyone wants to be useful in this world. We read and hear of people who have served their fellows well and we are a bit envious. Those of us who bear the name of Christ know we ought to follow Him in His ministry to men, yet at the same time we want to be comfortable. We think in terms of health, wealth and happiness as the goals of life. The trouble is these two things don't fit together.

The New Testament gives little comfort to those who would first seek their own comfort before the welfare of others. Jesus said that the person who seeks his own safety is lost. He invited everyone to follow Him but clearly pointed out that a cross is involved. We shy away from crosses which involve the loss of our personal advantages.

It is a fact of life that most of those who have done much to lift life to higher levels have given up their worldly advantages. It is hard to be comfortable without growing lazy, or prosperous without becoming selfish.

The Christian religion gives little place to self-love. Jesus said any follower of His must leave self behind. He had no home, no money, and no friends at the end. He was constantly badgered by the secret police of His nation. His family suspected him of insanity.

Paul turned his back on earthly success and chose a life of privation, loneliness and suffering. The early Christians won their way as witnesses of Christ from crosses and arenas of death and in suffering the loss of possessions and position. We read the Bible today in our own language because men and women were willing to die to give us this privilege.

History's brightest pages have been written by men and women who came to America, who went to Asia and Africa and South America and to the islands of the sea, to tell the story of Christ. They gave up everything to minister in His name to the bodies and minds and souls of men.

Today our children are educated largely by those who have given up hope of gain so that they might serve. In the circle of your own family and friends, the chances are that those who mean most are those who have sacrificed most.

All this indicates that in the kind of world we live in, the road to service and to usefulness is one of self-giving and of sacrifice. So difficult is the road that only those walk it who have walked with God in the sacrificial love which He has given us. We love because He first loved us. We give because He has given.

Exodus 40:4 (NIV)

TOO BUSY TO PUT FIRST THINGS FIRST?

Most of us seem to have too much to do. There are too many obligations. We belong to so many groups that require our time and energy. All these things can be good and yet become poison to us as they pile up on us. We are members of a family group; we have a job to do. We have friends and acquaintances. We are active in this and that social circle, in a trade or professional organization or in one of many community service groups. We belong to a church and may be active in its busy life.

The result is we get confused as to what matters the most to us in the long run. It becomes easy to fill our time and to drain our energies with things that may be good but which rob us of a chance to cultivate those things that matter most. The good can become the enemy of the best.

We too often take for granted that if we are busy, all is well. We realize that our way of life has cost us more than we intended to pay. Our most precious possessions are crowded out beyond recall before we are aware of what is happening.

The only way out is to face honestly the question as to what is really important to you and then having the courage to give the important things first place in the use of your time and energy. Once you start, it will be easier than you think.

There are two areas of life which, if put first, will support you all the way. They will give meaning and direction to all else you do. Neglect these two areas and sooner or later all else will become drudgery. These areas are your church and your family. Putting your church first will maintain your relationship to God, without which any person is less than human. Here the eternal springs of forgiveness, of mercy and of daily strength will feed your soul. Here will come wisdom for your decisions and divine help for your daily tasks.

Putting first your responsibility to those who love you and whom you love will keep fresh the springs of human affection without which we also are less than human. Whenever our busy lives violate these two areas we lose something and life becomes barren.

Our two most precious possessions are God's love in Christ and human love in those who care. Put them first in your time and in the spending of your energy. You will be happier and, strangely enough, you will be more useful.

OCTOBER 3   **LET ALL things be done decently and in order.**

I Corinthians 14:40 (NIV)

CHRISTIANITY IS A CLEAR LIGHT IN A WORLD OF CONFUSION

Little motto cards are popular today. One says, "If you're not confused, you don't know the facts." The word "confusion" is descriptive of our times and ourselves. We are intellectually confused. We are stressing education and yet today we are not quite sure what to do with what we know. The idea begins to creep in that unless you can find some reason to know things, it is not necessarily important that you know them.

We are morally confused. We have no moral standards that everybody agrees upon. Many years ago there was a movie actor, the most popular comedian in this country. He was involved in a scandal involving events of a few hours one night. His career was ruined because our people had a standard they were not willing to see lightly defied.

But today if you're a public figure in the entertainment world, it seems that the worse the scandal, the more popular the person becomes. There has been a complete upheaval. However much lip service we give to any particular code of conduct, we are not particularly concerned that it is observed.

We are religiously confused. We hardly know what we mean by the word God. It has no clearly defined features. We are wondering whether the Hindu God, the Moslem God and the Christian God are not all just part of a picture. Or maybe there is no face in the picture at all and God is just a great unknown.

In the midst of our confusion, our world is running away. One thing is certain: confusion is not the answer. It may be difficult to find the answer, but our present confusion isn't it.

The voice of the Gospel still is clear. What is it that is "Good News?" It doesn't mean that our problems are solved, but do we really want all our problems solved? In my opinion, that isn't what we want. We want to be challenged. We want something always beyond us. The Christian faith makes no pretense of solving our problems.

The central message of the Christian faith is: "God was in Christ reconciling the world to Himself." You cannot hide under the pretext that you cannot find out what God is like. God has broken the silence. Suppose it were announced - and everybody knew it to be true - that God would reveal Himself tonight at 9 p.m. on every radio and TV station in the world. Even the most godless man would keep his radio or TV on for God to come through.

In Christ, God has already spoken long before there was any radio or TV. He is still speaking. But only those who are listening hear Him, and in these comparatively few lives, there are still problems, but not confusion. For those who listen, there is a purpose for education in doing His will and as a moral guide as we walk in His footsteps.

OCTOBER 4   HE THAT abideth in me, and I in him, the same bringeth forth much fruit...

John 15:5 (KJ)

RELIGION IS THE WAY TO BETTER LIVING

It may be that you face difficulties and problems that offer no visible solutions. Many people do. The world we live in is full of situations that offer no ready answers. To persons in trouble and to a world in difficulty, the Bible comes with its message of hope and of miracles. Real religion is always offering to change things that need changing. It is never bound to the limitations of man's mind or man's physical strength. It brings to bear upon the humblest person the supernatural power of God who created us to be his own.

Christ came bringing God to men and men to God. The process still goes on. It always changes men and the situations in which men live. As the men and women of the Bible came into contact with God, strange and wonderful things happened. Slaves were changed into free men even though they remained outwardly slaves. These men finally made slavery impossible. Poor illiterate peasants were changed into men with a purpose upon whom the Lord built His Church.

Lives that were broken by sin and by evil habits were cleansed and made to live again in purity. People, sick with all manner of diseases, were made well. Disturbed minds were touched by His presence and sanity was restored. Selfish men were made generous. Those who were so defeated by life that hope was dead, found joy in living. The blind received their sight, the deaf heard again. Weak men were made strong. Man's final enemy - death - was overcome by victory.

The power of God is still with us. This is the meaning of the Christmas season that will soon be here again. The miracle of God's presence is ours by faith for, with God, nothing shall be impossible. By the touch of His hand, slaves are still made free, the sick are healed, order is brought to disturbed minds, lives broken by sin are made whole and the grip of evil habit is overcome. The poor and the dispossessed are made builders of His Kingdom. Selfish people are made loving and generous. Tyrants and cruel men still are made to destroy themselves by their own cruelty. Failure and defeat are made pathways to success. Strength is made perfect in weakness.

God's world of the Spirit waits for our acceptance by faith. The great discoveries of tomorrow must be in the realm of the wonderful things that happen when a person is touched by God. This can begin with you and me. It requires time and effort spent in the study of the Bible and, in worship, guidance will come as to what God would have us do. Obedience to His leadership is the pathway to His power. Thus, you can experience miracles of His grace and by your witness, you can bring them to others.

This is the victory that overcomes the world.

OCTOBER 5   **SO GIVE yourself humbly to God. Resist the devil and he will flee from you...draw close to God and God will draw close to you.**

James 4:7,8 (TLB)

WE TRY TO RUN FROM OUR SIN

Lots of us are on the run lest our sins and mistakes catch up with us. We are like people running from law. We are anxious about everyone we meet lest they be "on our trail."

We worry about the stranger who sends word he wants to see us, lest he comes to confront us with some neglected duty. We run from one thing to another lest in standing still we get caught by our failures. We often go to parties, not to have fun, but to escape the pain of our own company. Drinking is attractive to some because it releases them from the nagging pain of conscience. We are restless and uneasy; we fly to our own defense at the least criticism. We enclose ourselves in a protective armor. We never relax with a person unless we are sure he is "on our side."

We are unhappy within ourselves and we stay busy in order to ease the pain. John the Baptist asked his hearers why they were fleeing the wrath to come. He put his hand on one of our main troubles: we are running from God. We know we are not able to face God as we are, so we do all we can to evade Him. Deep within us, our running away from ourselves is a running away from God.

John came, calling men to stop running and to face God in the only way we can face Him - with repentance for our sins. He pointed out that repentance is a matter not only of making up our minds to turn from our sins but also doing something about it. Faith without works is dead and repentance without works is useless.

John gave three areas where we demonstrate our repentance:

1. In our concern for those who have need. Most of us build up guilt by our failure to meet the needs of others who look to us. We must make up our minds to do what we can for our families, our friends and the people we meet in our daily lives.

2. Our repentance must show itself in our willingness to take only what is rightfully ours. Too many people can't resist taking advantage of the opportunity to "make a killing."

3. Repentance must show itself in our careful use of power. Everyone has power over someone. There is always the temptation to use our power to advance our own selfish interests at the expense of others just because we can.

If we are willing to stop running from God and face Him squarely, repenting of our sins by word and deed, He promises to come to us through the door of our repentance. In Christ, He comes with forgiveness and with peace.

If you will come to God in repentance, you will find you no longer have to be always on the run. Much of the tension in your life will be relieved.

OCTOBER 6   TAKE care of the world, lest it unawares steals away your heart.

Susanna Wesley

WHY ALL THIS MADDENING RACE FOR LIFE'S MATERIAL COMFORTS?

I wonder if it is not time that we faced some questions about our way of life. Why is it that everything must be the biggest or the best or the fastest or the most? Why does business have to get bigger year ever year? Why does everyone have to be working towards a promotion? I heard recently about a man who was fired because he was not "going anywhere." Why is it necessary for us to be working toward a higher standard of living, which usually means a larger house, better furniture, fancier car and better labels on our clothes? Why all the mad rush toward bigness?

Why are we in the rat race for material things - a race that often takes seven days a week? Why does a man have to "make good" in the frantic climb up the ladder of promotion? Why is it necessary to keep American families constantly uprooted in the checkers game of job changes?

Where are the people who were satisfied with a comfortable living, a steady job and a warm easy chair in a house made home by the joys and sorrows of years of living? Where are the people who spent their days learning to live rather than being constantly driven to make a living?

This sounds like a desire to turn the clock back. It is - but try to face some of these questions before you dismiss them too easily. There are no easy answers but it can help just to raise the questions.

There is a friend who has been in the same job for many years. He has taken time to develop his soul under God and his mind and heart by attention to people and causes that needed him. When he speaks,

398

people listen because he has something to say. He has had troubles but he has also had peace. It has never seemed to bother him that the "march of progress" has passed him by. He is a rare kind of person, but he may be on the right road. Jesus said that the gate to life is narrow and that there are few that find it.

We are very concerned today about our way of life. There is a sincere desire to make it better and to defend it against its enemy. While we are busy working on problems, we need to remember that the best things in life come from certain roots. These roots lie in the words of Jesus: "Seek ye first the kingdom of God and His righteousness, and all these things shall be added unto you."

OCTOBER 7   **Is any one of you in trouble? He should pray. Let him sing songs of praise.**

James 5:13 (NIV)

THROUGH PRAYER, WE FIND SERENITY

These are great days in which to be alive. The question is "How can a person find love and serenity?" The answer is prayer. Prayer keeps the human soul together and gives meaning to our existence. Prayer is difficult, but because we do not practice it very much, there is a kind of poverty in our lives.

We are too busy. Martin Luther was so busy he had to pray three hours a day. That sounds fantastic to us but God's word warns us we have not because we ask not. Prayer will take time and effort but the results will amaze you if you will try it.

1. Prayer will bring you into God's presence where His glory will fall across your life. We were made to live in contact with God. When we meet Him in the silence of prayer, something of the Eternal Glory seeps into our souls. You find yourself able to live more securely in an insecure world when God touches your life.

2. Prayer gives you opportunity to express gratitude and to find a blessing in offering thanks. We do not thank God enough for His goodness to us. All we have are gifts from the divine hand. It takes a bold man indeed to claim he deserves the blessings he receives. The common things we take for granted - food, shelter, loved ones, friends, health, work - are miracles of God's love. The fact that God constantly pursues us in His love is something we could never deserve. In prayer we bring our sacrifices of thanksgiving and we find a strange joy in so doing.

3. Prayer gives us a chance to confess our sins and to be relieved of our guilt. It is a relief to invite God into our hearts and to share our sins with Him. In Christ, He comes to take them on Himself and He leaves us His forgiveness. Only in prayer can we find peace for our souls, which so easily become burdened by our failure to be what we ought to be.

4. Prayer allows us to take our needs to One who hears in private and answers in public. You can cast your care on Him, knowing that He cares for you.

Grateful people in every generation have witnessed to the fact that as they have come to Him in their weariness, He has given them rest.

These are not easy days and they are harder for some than others. Those who will take the time to pray will find themselves walking on their knees toward confidence, courage and serenity. These qualities of life cannot be produced by the efforts of our own hands. They are gifts of God that He Himself gives to those who come to Him in prayer.

OCTOBER 8   ONE can live in the shadow of an idea without grasping it.

Elizabeth Bowen

YOUNG PEOPLE HUNT FOR IDENTITY IN THIS TOUGH, MIXED UP WORLD

In the past months, several college students from different schools have indicated that they are concerned with the question, "Who am I?" Whether it is coincidence or whether it is the result of discussions common on many campuses, I do not know. Certainly, it should not be thought strange that young people are asking the question in this mixed up world. It is a question that all of us do well to ask. By asking it over and over, it might serve to hold back the pressure on us to give up our faith in ourselves.

The value of one individual is a cornerstone in all that is best in our American tradition. Still paying lip service to this sentiment, the influences that play on us seem to seek to destroy the sense of value.

It is not easy for a young person to know who he is because he is often pressed into the mold of conformity. He finds that his value is in terms of his ability to fit into the routines of a college course, or into the already established demands of a job he gets. It is hard to keep dreams alive in a routine that never seems to change. A young person sees the mature people rushing around heading nowhere -and are getting there. This prospect does not seem attractive so he rebels and begins to wonder, "Who am I anyway?"

He gets very little help from society about him, which deals mostly in large numbers of people. Efforts for the betterment of living conditions or racial understanding or economic improvement deal in programs rather than people. More and more, life seems to consist of keeping in step with the long line of people going your way.

Where do you find an answer to the question, "Who am I?" - one that will satisfy the hunger of the heart for recognition as a person of real value? You will get it from the Christian faith. You will find your sense of value in discovering that you are valuable to God. As a child of God, redeemed by His act of love in Christ, you are an individual of supreme value. Because God so loves you, you are not a mere cog in a machine.

No tyranny has ever been able to stand before the calm assurance of men and women who knew themselves to be children of God. Sooner or later the shackles of political and economic slavery are broken on the rock of faith.

He who has found that God loves him has found the answer to the question, "Who am I?" The answer is "A child of the King."

OCTOBER 9　　　**FOR the Lord sees not as man sees; man looks on the outward appearance, but the Lord looks at the heart.**

I Samuel 16:7 (RSV)

IT'S REWARDING AND DISTURBING TO LOOK WITHIN YOURSELF

One of the good results of the present popularity of the mental health movement is that it makes us look at ourselves. Definitions of mental illness are hard to find. Like so many other things, it is easier to use the words than to know what we are talking about. Actually, the person who is mentally ill is just like other people, only more so.

One of the most rewarding and disturbing things you can do is to spend some time looking within yourself. Most of us take a brief look and, not liking what we see, we quickly run away. We get busy with other things or we worry about the world or we criticize others for what we see within ourselves. We could not recognize faults in others if we had not first seen them in ourselves.

If we will look deeply within ourselves, we will find there some of the same turmoil we read about in the headlines of our newspapers. Jesus made this clear when He said, "It is what comes out of a man that defiles him. For from inside, out of a man's heart, come evil thoughts, acts of fornication, of theft, murder, adultery, ruthless greed and malice, fraud, indecency, envy, slander, arrogance and folly; these evil things all come from inside, and they defile the man."

Paul has given a classic description of your heart and mine in the seventh chapter of Romans. Its theme is: "For the good that I would I do not, but the evil which I would not, that I do."

If we are going to solve the problems that face us, we must first solve the problem of our own hearts. However important science and education and social reform may be, they leave the real problem of the human heart untouched. You and I need more than scientific tools; we need the kind of heart that will use them for good and not for destruction.

We need education but we need the kind of heart that will use education for good and not for selfish ends. We need social reform but in it must be the kind of heart that will use it to build men instead of building a society of dependent and dishonest people.

External adjustments will not make good people. The Christian faith addresses itself to the problem of making new people out of old, of creating new hearts and right spirits.

Paul asked the right question: "What shall deliver me from the body of this death?" He gave the right answer: "I thank God, through Jesus Christ, our Lord."

OCTOBER 10 TEACH me your way, O Lord; Lead me in a straight path.

Psalm 27:11 (NIV)

TO CHANGE THE WORLD, WE MUST CHANGE OURSELVES

We often hear the statement: "Our world needs a spiritual awakening." General MacArthur said it at the surrender of Japan. Even scientists are saying it. Most of us agree. It does not take much intelligence to realize many things need changing; however, there is something deeper which does not always command the same agreement: each of us needs changing.

Before things about us can be changed, we need to let God change us. Only changed people can change things. Social reform will always break on the rocks of unreformed people. Greed often destroys the best-laid plans for helping others.

The problem of changing a greedy man into a generous one, or an immoral person into a moral one or a selfish person into an unselfish one, is not an easy one. It does not yield itself to education nor does it allow itself to be solved by good intentions. It requires the touch of the divine hand in what really is a miracle. You and I were created by God to need God and no amount of human pride will change it. It is popular today to trust ourselves to lift ourselves by our bootstraps. It is a false trust. We will continue to see every human effort, however well intentioned, end in defeat until we take God seriously.

The world will not be changed as a group or as a whole; change is an individual matter. You and I as individuals have the fate of the world in our hands. You can ignore the necessity of your own change but if you do, you remain a part of the problem.

Change begins by our repentance. This is a religious word, but it is a necessary one. Repentance is a sincere desire to be changed. If you don't want to be changed, you won't be - except for the worse. It is a turning of our hearts, minds and wills toward God and away from our selfish ways. It is the desire of the heart for righteousness and a longing to be different from what we are now.

The second necessary step toward change is to believe that God forgives the past of those who truly repent and trust Him. He has made possible this forgiveness by the death of Christ on the cross.

Repentance and faith are the conditions of change. The change in us is worked by the grace of God in the hearts and lives of those who meet these conditions. It is an act of God and can only be accepted. In the change, lies our spiritual awakening. In those so awakened lies the hope of any awakening in our community and in our world. One person is still the key to the solution.

OCTOBER 11   CHILDREN learn best from example; the trouble is they don't know a good example from a bad one.

Unknown

LET'S HELP OUR YOUTH TO KNOW AND LOVE GOD

Not long ago the mail brought to me the poem that follows. It may be that it is neither the best possible poetry nor the most polished English. It is, however, a witness to the best possible method of building people. Statistics tell us there are millions of children and young people in our country who do not receive religious training. Some of these have no one who cares enough to give them guidance.

However, most of them must have parents who care for them, but not enough to lead them to God. It is hard for me to understand how parents can profess love for their children and fail to give them a chance to know God and to pray to God to make Himself real to them.

The best possible education and the most careful schooling in the things of culture are only tools our children will use. How they are used will depend on the relationship of your children to God. Few have been saved from the pitfalls of life who did not hold in memory the prayers of a good mother or of some woman who stood in a mother's place.

I pass this on in tribute and in encouragement to every mother who prays for her children and as a reminder to all who do not:

"Do we care if our children are treading the downward way?
Do we care enough in our rush through life to fall on knees and pray?
Or do we keep on going in our striving for worldly things?
Not stopping to consider what these worldly things may bring?
Do we tell them about Jesus or things that lure the mind?
Into doing the wrong, which are many, and never hard to find?
If they smoke, gamble, steal or drink and stay out late at night
Do we tell them to follow Jesus?
Then they will know these things are not right.
Do we show them that we love them in every way we can?
And when we see them stumble, do we take them by the hand –
And lead them back into the light that always shines
To guide our footsteps all the way unto the end of time?
God help our Fathers and Mothers to wake up before it's too late.
Live a life for Jesus, set the example for them to take.
Then when our life on earth is done and we go home to glory,
We can leave this world rejoicing that we told them the wonderful story.

OCTOBER 12   BEWARE of the barrenness of a busy life.

Socrates

RICH OR POOR - WE ALL HAVE 24 HOURS EVERY DAY

We are so busy until time gets by without our having the pleasure of spending it on the things we really value. Not everyone has the same amount of ability or money, but we all have exactly the same amount of time each day. The poverty of our lives is caused more by failure to spend time wisely than by lack of money. If we are so busy we don't have time, then we are too busy. We even get so busy that we rush along doing nothing. One of the Roman Catholic retreats has a slogan that says, "If you don't have time to make a retreat, you need one."

The time we have or don't have is a matter of our attitude and not of the clock. We have all the time in the world. The less you rush, the more you have. Just for a day, try to be master of your time. When you start to rush ahead of another car, don't. When you hurry to get through the door before another person, slow up and look at the person with interest as he goes ahead of you. When you find yourself in a store rushing from counter to counter, stop where you are and try to enjoy yourself. Slow down the turmoil inside you. When you feel like rushing by someone you really want to talk to, stop and do it. When there is someone you should call, but are too busy, stop and make the call.

In our rush, we so often brush aside those who mean the most to us and we speak with haste. Try taking time to be patient, tolerant, understanding. Take time to listen, to give and, best of all, to receive. In our rush, we do many things that are not necessary and we fail to do those things that we should do and really want to do. Try taking the time to cultivate your ties with your family and your friends. You will discover that you do have time and the results will please you.

Most people fancy themselves too busy to take time to pray and to worship. Try taking some time each day in meditation and in prayer. You will be surprised how much time these moments will give you to do other things that are good and needful and desirable. The key to our rush may be that we do not "take time to be holy," as the old hymn says.

If you will take time by the forelock and become its master, you will find it becomes a slave that will make you rich in the things that make life worth living.

OCTOBER 13   GOD made you as you are in order to use you as He planned.

S.C. McAuley

IF LIFE BOGS DOWN, THE FAULT IS IN YOU

Many people are frustrated and lots of people are just bored with living. They get no pleasure out of what they are doing. Others are always complaining about their lot in life, about how people treat them and about how unappreciated they are. Others take it out in dissipation. They try to deaden the pain of their lostness by alcohol consumption and by a steady trot from amusement to amusement.

The result of frustration is shoddy living: we cease trying to do our best. So much work today is not well done and, in fact, it is surprising when you find someone who has real pride in his work. So much of family life is shoddy because we seek to find satisfaction outside the home. We get more concerned about meeting our obligations to outsiders than to those in our family circle.

If you are frustrated where you are, there is no use trying to change your place and circumstance. You will be the same person somewhere else, and you will remain just as unhappy as you are now. If you do not like your job, the chances are you won't like the next one. If you are bored in your home, you will be bored if you change it a dozen times. The truth is that life is lived to its fullest at the level of the commonplace and at the level of the rut and the routine.

Jesus is the most useful and influential person who ever lived. He was born in a peasant home. He knew poverty. He worked from boyhood as a carpenter. At an early age he had to support His mother and family. For three years He was an itinerant preacher. He had no home. The only possessions He owned were the clothes on His back. His friends were fisherfolk and social outcasts. Finally, He was executed as a common criminal. Out of this common life was made to shine the very glory of God. In His contacts with the poor, the sick, the dispossessed, the discouraged, the dying, we see God more clearly than anywhere else.

If life has bogged down on you the fault is in you, not in your place in life. Christ found His answer in taking all life brought Him as an opportunity to do God's will. His work was work for God. We will find our answer by doing what needs to be done each day "as unto God."

He takes the rut of your life and casts around it the light of eternity. It is a venture of faith to believe that in all we do we work for the Lord, yet it makes a vast difference in our living.

OCTOBER 14   I HAVE hidden your word in my heart that I might not sin against you.

Psalm 119:11 (NIV)

PEOPLE APEND NATIONS CRUMBLE FROM WITHIN, NOT FROM OUTSIDE

After an egg has hit the floor and broken it is hard to do anything about it except mop it up. It is much safer not to drop the egg. After an individual has wrecked his life, something can be done, but it is hard to do. The Christian faith rebuilds wrecks but it also is dedicated to the task of preventing the wrecks from happening. After moral decline grips a nation, it is hard to stop. It is safer and more fruitful to work at those things which prevent the decline in the first place.

Religious convictions and moral commitments prevent breakdown in personal lives and in national character. Religious convictions undergird all personal and group life. What you believe about God and how you worship Him matters supremely. Certain basic convictions are necessary for successful living. Above all other needs, we need to be reconciled to God. Christ is the agent of this reconciliation; He is the mediator between God and man.

These convictions grow only in certain soil: worship, Bile study and prayer. Some think they are too busy for these things. Others feel that they are too smart to need them and others are just careless. Whatever the reason, if you neglect them, religious conviction withers and dies. When this happens, life loses the only foundation which can withstand the storms that beat upon it.

This is true because the way you act will always directly reflect what you believe. Your moral commitment is the result of your religious convictions. What you believe about God will determine how you think you ought to act. The kind of God you worship will determine the kind of conduct you show. Only when we keep alive our spiritual convictions will we be able to live in such a way as to defeat those who attack us and our way of life.

If you are concerned about your lack of strength to meet the demands and temptations that face you or if you are concerned about the moral breakdown of our land, begin with a search for the right religious convictions. From this will flow strength of character and rightness of conduct. Talking against communism and secularism is of little value unless you are the right kind of person. Even knowing all about them won't help unless your own faith and conduct are right.

The real battles today are going on in the hearts of people like you and me. Here, the war for all that we count dear will be won or lost. People and nations fall from within, not because of outward enemies.

OCTOBER 15   **AND NOW, brethren I commend you to God and to the word of His grace, which is able to build you up, and to give you an inheritance among all them which are sanctified.**
                                          Acts 20:32 (KJ)

DENY FOOD TO THE SPIRIT AND DISASTER RESULTS

Jesus said, "Man does not live by bread alone but by every word that preceedeth out of the mouth of God." This is a true saying and worth believing by everyone. Nobody doubts that we need material things. Nobody doubts that we live in a space age. Although there are problems connected with earning a living and of adapting to a space age, there is a greater problem: How do you pursue material things without ruining your life?

The spirit of man - the person - the personality - the thing you mean when you say "I" - how do you feed it to make it strong and brave and wise and loving and good? We all know that if we stop eating food, the body will become weak and unable to meet the demands of the day. We also understand that the wrong kind of food will finally ruin the body and make it weak. We will die unless we are fed properly.

Exactly the same thing is true of the spirit. Fail to feed it or feed it the wrong kind of food and soon the demands and temptations of the day will destroy you. This is what worship is all about. Worship feeds the soul because it brings man into surrendered contact with the Spirit of God who is the source of strength for the soul.

Jesus said, "I am the bread of Life." This is the word of God. The word of God is the true food for the spirit of man. In worship, this Word is given to those who receive it by faith.

Without worship, the spirit grows lean and hungry. The individual finds earning a living unsatisfactory. Marriage loses its glow. Play is not much fun. Loves dies and our relationships become marred by jealousy and hate. We become lost.

If you are a man or a woman trying to make a life or a couple trying to make a home, decide now to open your lives in worship to God by faith in Christ. God's Spirit will then feed your spirits and the fruits will be love, peace, joy, patience, gentleness, goodness, faith, meekness and temperance.

Love your enemies, and do good...and your reward shall be great...

Luke 6:35 (LB)

LIVING BY THE SERMON ON THE MOUNT CAN LOOK LIKE AN IMPOSSIBLE TASK

People often try to escape the Christian faith by saying that they try to treat their neighbor right and live by the Sermon on the Mount. They don't realize what an impossible burden they take on themselves. If you have ever seriously studied the Sermon on the Mount, I doubt you will be willing to risk your eternal destiny on your effort to live by it. It begins with the Beatitudes. These are Christ's recipes for happiness.

We think of happiness in terms of knowledge, material security and freedom from sorrow and suffering. The Sermon on the Mount locates happiness somewhere else entirely. It bids us to find our happiness in being poor in spirit, finding our security not in ourselves but only in God. It locates happiness in the midst of sorrow and not in escaping sorrow. If you are going to follow Christ you will find your happiness in purity of heart and not in the shady stories and amusements of our day. In the Beatitudes we find the happy man to be one persecuted for the sake of righteousness, not as one escaping suffering.

In this Sermon, murder is brought uncomfortably close. Jesus said if any man hates his brother without a cause, or if he says unto his brother, "Thou fool," he is in the same class as one who killed his brother.

Then there is the matter of adultery. "Thou shalt not commit adultery. But I say unto thee, if any man looketh upon a woman to lust after her, he hath already committed adultery in his heart." Few can plead "Not guilty."

Anywhere you touch the Sermon on the Mount, you will find that

412

your effort to be a good fellow by following it leads to despair. You are in trouble if you try to follow Christ only as a teacher.

Again, "Love your enemies, bless them that curse you, do good to them that hate you, pray for them that despitefully use you." Few can say, "I do."

Actually, the Sermon on the Mount cannot be followed well enough to commend you to God. Paul says the law was given as a straight edge to show us how crooked we are. These teachings are to lead us to see how badly we need God's grace and forgiveness.

It is the good news of faith that by the life and death of Christ, our inability to do what we ought to do is compensated for. By His grace we are accepted by God as righteous because of Him in whom we believe and trust. As children of God we no longer have to earn His love by our acts.

We then try to obey out of gratitude for what Christ has done for us.

OCTOBER 17   ...the will of the Lord be done.

Act 21:14 (LB)

ONLY THE DEDICATION OF GOD'S WILL CAN DO AWAY WITH OUR UNREST

Underneath much of the unrest in our lives is the lack of purpose. We do all the things people are supposed to do and end up wondering why we are doing it. Let's illustrate it by a fine young couple who get married and begin their life together. The young man has a job that is interesting and which pays enough to support the family. They are deeply in love and of fine character, so they marry and begin to live as such couples do. They go about their work, they get together with their friends, they attend church and they take part in some worthwhile activity in the community, either together or separately.

Let us suppose that the young man does well in the job and begins moving up the ladder. The marriage proves happier as the months unfold; then a baby comes and new happiness unfolds.

Yet, in spite of all the natural happiness, there begins to come a feeling that something is lacking. There stirs the question: Why are we doing all we are doing? What is the purpose and goal of it? What are we really doing that has value? What contribution are we making in these upset times? Have we really found our place in life?

The answer to this often unspoken questioning lies in remembering that man's chief end is to glorify God and to enjoy Him forever. A sense of purpose and value comes into the lives of the couple as they dedicate their marriage to God and to do His will. Here they connect their home to the eternal purpose of God and as the couple seeks God's will to do His will, a new dimension comes into their lives.

They feel the conviction that their jobs are the place where God would have them to be. Where they work becomes their place of service in His plan; changes in life become a part of His plan for them. They find that they have a guide for their conduct in His will as He reveals it through the Bible, through worship and through His Voice in their hearts. As mistakes are made, there is forgiveness from God and from one another. In weakness there is strength and in sorrow there is comfort.

In seeking to find happy usefulness for your home and for yourself, the secret lies in the words, "I come to do Thy will, O Lord."

414

OCTOBER 18   ...SPEAK, Lord, for your servant is listening.

I Samuel 3:9 (NIV)

SILENCE USHERS IN THE REALITY OF GOD

Our hearts and minds are like the waves of the sea: restless, rolling back and forth, never still. It is hard to fix our attention on anything for long. Television and radio are reflections of the lack of concentration in our lives -a bit of music or dialogue, then a switch to an announcer, then a commercial, first sung, then spoken, and a bit of music. We rush from one thing to another all day long and into the night. In sleep, our dreams chase one another through the hours.

The Psalmist bids us, "Be still and know that I am God." Did you ever feel a hush as you suddenly came upon a scene of beauty: a vista across mountaintops, or a sunrise that broke open the night, or a flaming sunset that put the world to rest? Beyond words, it seemed that God was there.

Have you ever tried getting alone with God for 15 minutes? Go into a room alone. Close the door. Better still, go into some church that is open for prayer. Set for yourself the challenge to sit there 15 minutes, just opening your mind and heart to God.

You perhaps won't be there but a moment or two before your mind will tell you that it is time to go. A dozen reasons may occur to you why you must be winging away. You may be tempted to feel that such a period can only be useless. Just sit still and hold on to your effort to open your heart and mind to God. A verse of Scripture will help - or just the word "God" repeated over and over again. Then the mind will begin tumbling over and over with a rapid-fire succession of things "on your mind." It won't be quieted if it can help it.

Don't give up. Gradually you will feel somewhat relaxed as the mind begins to give up the struggle. As you sit it out, God becomes more real and your need to leave a little bit less pressing. You begin to wonder what may happen as you seek to concentrate on God alone and on your contact with Him.

Finally the time is up. Nothing stupendous may have happened. But you will go out with a sense of your burden lifted a bit, the next step clearer in the mind, with your body refreshed and your spirit strangely lifted. You will understand better what Jesus meant when He said, "Come unto Me all ye that labor and are heavy laden and I will give you rest."

In so doing, you will grow in grace and in power to live with courage and victory.

I believe you will want to try such moments of silence often as you find God by whom and for whom you were made.

OCTOBER 19   IT IS the Lord you must follow and him you must revere.

Deuteronomy 13:4 (NIV)

TOO MANY GET WORD FROM GOD FOR OTHERS INSTEAD OF THEMSELVES

We are well educated in the fact that certain basic instincts or drives of our human nature demand some expression. If they are not satisfied normally they often break out in abnormal behavior. The horror movies and the various presentations of sex are popular because they give expression, directly or indirectly, to certain kinds of traits. Perhaps the most compelling drive we have is often neglected - the necessity to do what is right.

Like other instincts or drives, if we do not do what is right, it causes us to behave abnormally. We are forced to call what we do "good" by explaining it or excusing it. Few dare say, "I am bad and I am proud of it," yet when we behave badly, we know it.

You and I maintain our self-respect as we honestly face the demand to do right. You are your own assignment. You cannot escape your responsibility for yourself by getting interested in what is right for someone else. The outspoken critic of others is usually disturbed about his own conduct. Too many people get messages from God for other people rather than for themselves. If you ever take seriously the demand that you do the right thing, you will find you have a full-time job with yourself.

Certain things will help you do what is right:

1. You must come to know the Christian ethic. In Christ we are shown how men and women are supposed to live. You cannot even try to do right until you know what it is. People who do not read their Bible place themselves beyond help. The convictions that you ought to do right won't help unless you have the proper knowledge.

2. You must trust your faith that God is at hand to help us if we will but ask. Prayer is the door to wisdom.

3. Be sure your action seeks the welfare of others. We are our brothers' keeper. "Thou shalt love thy neighbor as thyself."

4. Test your action by the divine imperative: "Whether ye eat or drink, whatever you do, do all to the Glory of God." Ask, "How does it look to God?" Can you offer your action to God and say, "This I do for God's glory?"

5. We must know what to do with our failures. We so often compromise or deliberately choose the wrong. We make mistakes. We need to accept by faith His forgiveness offered to us in Christ by His sacrifice. He takes our sins, removes our guilt and sends us out forgiven and ready to try again.

The adventure of life is made or broken as we succeed or fail in doing right. No one escapes this hard test.

TAKE time to be holy, speak oft with thy Lord; abide in Him always, and feed on His Word.

W.D. Longstaff, Hymn

THE FOUNDATION OF LIFE IS FAITH IN GOD

As a nation we are being tested as to whether a democratic way of life can govern itself. We are giving more and more of our freedom to centralized government and to centralized business. No one knows how it will work out. The result will not depend on documents. Not even our Constitution or Bill of Rights can guarantee freedom.

The result will depend on what citizens believe and what they are for. A fine document can easily be set aside when men no longer believe in its statements. When people lose their balance under pressure they often forsake freedom for the security of outside control.

The only thing that will enable a person to maintain his balance midst the pressures of our day is a great faith in a great God. Such a God is the God and Father of our Lord Jesus Christ. God has revealed Himself. The foundation of this revelation is that God is the Creator of heaven and earth. Genesis opens: "In the beginning God created the heaven and earth." John begins his Gospel of Jesus Christ: "In the beginning was the Word - all things were created by Him and without Him was not anything made that was made."

God's creative power is put first so that we shall know that all we have and are is the work of God's hand. Here is God who is greater than our universe and more powerful than our problems.

Such a faith in such a God does certain things for us.

It gives a first cause to life. It is the necessary foundation of all our thinking. It makes us know that all life is interdependent and that it all hangs together. This is an orderly world with each part dependent on every other part. The flight of Col. Glenn was the result of coordination of all the powers of nature and of man - physical, mental, moral and spiritual. God made them all and in Him rests their harmony. This faith in God as Creator makes us take seriously the oneness of man. Beneath differences of color and culture, we are all alike. There are the same desires, dreams and longings in all of us. You can tell the story of God and His love and men everywhere will respond.

Whenever men have prayed to God in confidence they have rested their faith on God as Creator, on the God of the Psalmist: "Before the mountains were brought forth or ever thou hast formed the earth and world, even from everlasting to everlasting, thou art God."

OCTOBER 21   PRESERVE me, O God: for in Thee do I put my trust.

Psalm 16:1 (KJ)

TROUBLED ONES CAN TRUST A GOD WHO LOVES THE WORLD AND PROVES IT

Faith in God as Creator gives us a first cause for all of life. It teaches us that all parts of life are interdependent. Faith in God as Creator is the basis of the oneness of mankind, whatever the race or nation. God the Creator has revealed Himself in Christ. "Christ is the Word which was in the beginning and without Him was not anything made that was made." So John tells us in the beginning of His Gospel.

When you get fearful and disturbed about our world, remember that at the center of it all is God the Creator who loved it so much He gave His Son to die for us. The God who made the world and who governs it is a God of love. You can trust a God like that. It is His world and He is greater than the people who seek to destroy it. You can sleep at night without worrying too much about what is going to happen.

You can pray to a God like that. You can pray in confidence to the God of our Lord Jesus Christ who made it all and who is so loving that He redeems it all. He is a God who cares for the works of His hand. He cares for each of us. The hand that keeps the stars spinning is the hand that holds your hand. Whatever may be your difficulty, God the Creator is able and anxious to help you.

You can work for a God like that. You can work without fear. Everything in the Universe, in the mind and in the heart of man, is yours to investigate and to discover. He challenges each of us to work in whatever may be our daily task in the assurance that He will use us and our work by His power and for His own purpose. If we keep our hand in His, work can become the adventure of sharing His creative power.

In a day when the world about us seems to be shaking on its very foundations, our stability depends on what we think about God. We can keep our balance and find peace and usefulness as we commit ourselves to a great faith in a great God.

If the anchor of our faith holds here, no storm can drive the ship of our lives on the rocks. To all who trust Him, He says: "Fear thou not; for I am with thee: be not dismayed: for I am thy God: I will strengthen thee: yea, I will help thee; yea, I will uphold thee with the right hand of my righteousness." (Isaiah 41:10)

OCTOBER 22   ...WHEN I see the blood, I will pass over you...

Exodus 12:13 (LB)

THE LORD'S SUPPER IS THE CORE OF FAITH

The heartbeat of the Christian faith is the Lord's Supper. Here the death of Christ as the Lamb of God sacrificed for the sins of the world is remembered. This memorial supper has its roots in the Jewish Passover where the lamb is sacrificed in memory of the deliverance of the children of Israel from Egypt.

The Lord's Supper is not only a memorial. It is a channel of the power and the grace of God to those who take part in it by faith. The Cross of Christ is set at the very crossroads of human life. It does certain things without which human life would be hopeless.

The Cross of Christ where He took upon Himself the sins of the world is our assurance that evil will be defeated. Cruelty and selfishness and moral degradation are everywhere. Call the roll of nations and you list the places of the earth where men and women suffer under the weight of these things. Men without God see little hope for the things of peace and goodness and truth. Only those who believe that God was in Christ, reconciling the world to Himself, can be sure that God did so love the world and that Christ defeated evil - evil which rises only to fall on its own sword.

Each one of us is an empire within himself. In you and in me, all the forces of evil swirl and contend for our souls. Selfishness and greed and immorality are strong within us, too strong for us in our own power. Guilt builds up and the older we get the more hopeless seems the fight. The Cross of Christ where he bore our sins in His own body is our only hope of victory over our sins and the guilt they pile on us. We find the power of God working in us by faith, which keeps us from being destroyed by our sin and which relieves us of our burden of guilt.

A third assurance of the Cross comes to those who seek to do the will of God and to do good to men. Serving people often seems to be a fruitless job. Honestly trying to do what we believe God would have us do can bring us into hard places. Christ found it brought Him to the Cross. His death and resurrection are our assurance that victory and success come even through the outward failure of our efforts. If He had not suffered and died in the line of divine duty we never would be able to follow through in our efforts to do His will.

Whenever the Lord's Supper is observed, the hearts of men are made strong by these three assurances of the presence of the power of God through the death of His Son.

TAKE time to be holy, Be calm in thy soul; each thought and each motive beneath His control.

William D. Longstaff, Hymn

BUILD INNER CONFIDENCE TO KEEP A STEADY LIFE

An ancient proverb says, "As a man thinketh in his heart, so is he." Another reads, "Keep thy heart with all diligence for out of it are the issues of life." These proverbs are saying in plain words that our thoughts and emotions are far more important than what happens to us. They are also saying that it is possible to direct out thoughts and emotions and to control our response to outward circumstances, directing the course of our lives in the midst of them.

In a very real sense we create the kind of world in which we live by our thoughts. Sooner or later they come out in action.

Too many of us are always fighting the outside world. We are busy resenting what people do to us and getting even with them. We try to make enough money to keep us from being afraid of poverty.

We build a social life to keep us from being lonely. We watch our diet to keep from getting sick. We let our pride make us pretend to be the kind of persons we really aren't in order to build what we think is prestige.

We are so busy fighting the world that we are like a steamship captain who is so busy sweeping the deck and oiling the machinery and painting the hull and mixing the drinks that he forgets to stay in the quietness of the bridge and guide the ship.

At the center of every life is the control room. In this control room is the secret of an ordered life. "Be still and know that I am God" is the wisest advice man ever received. Stop. Withdraw within yourself. Look at yourself. Listen. Be aware of God. Think about God as the keeper of the heart. He will take care of your security. He will correct your mistakes. Paul went through stormy seas all his life with confidence and peace. His secret: "I live, yet not I but Christ liveth in me."

Each day, every day, all day keep Him on the bridge of your life. Stop often and be sure He is there. "In quietness and confidence shall be your strength." (Isaiah 30:15)

OCTOBER 24   **Breathe on me, breath of God, fill me with life anew, until my heart is pure, until my will is one with Thine...**

Edwin Hatch, Hymn

CHRISTIANS' MOTIVES ARE OFTEN UN-CHRISTIAN

The relationship between religion and conduct is not clear in our private and public lives. Every Christian - at one time or another - has promised to make obedience to Christ the guide of his or her conduct. Where this promise is carried out, it is bound to show itself in one's public and social conduct.

In our community the majority of people bear the name "Christian." The churches are well supported in money and in attendance. Yet it is evident on every hand that the search based on the question: "What would Jesus have me do?" is a question not prominent in enough in our private and public decisions. We are being more and more directed by other standards.

Financial profit is a powerful motive. Social acceptance is providing a more powerful force in molding our lives than Christian conviction. Judging ourselves by the conduct of the crowd, we conform to what the crowd is doing although our conscience points in another direction. It is a lonely business to live by Christian convictions in our world.

Personal satisfaction is the only standard many accept for their conduct. Marriage is often entered into as a human contract to be kept as long as it suits both parties. Christian marriage as a divine merging of two people into a permanent unity is considered too old-fashioned for our modern world.

Sunday becomes more and more a holiday, lacking any outside reference to its sacred associations. Little consideration is given to man's need for worship and rest and true recreation under God.

If a standard of living does produce the good life and if satisfying our personal desires does produce happiness, then all may be well, but Jesus said: "Seek ye first the Kingdom of God, and all these things will be added." He makes it clear that human life is so created that unless we do seek first the will of God, we will lose the very good things we seek.

We will do well to make all personal decisions on a deeper level than financial profit and personal satisfaction. God, not man, is the center of life and in Him we live and move and have our being.

OCTOBER 25   WHAT have I to dread, what have I to fear, leaning on the everlasting arms.

Elisha A. Hoffman, Hymn

WE WANT SECURITY, BUT WE LOOK FOR IT IN THE WRONG PLACES

Security is something everyone wants. Some say that this is the weakness of our day. They are wrong. We cannot live without having a sense of security. When you walk, your feet must be on solid ground. When you live, your life must rest on foundations that support you. Our problem is not that we want security but that we seek it in the wrong places.

The most popular place to seek security today is in money. Money does certain things but it does not bring an inner sense of security. If it did, America would be the most secure feeling nation in the world and the people who are financially comfortable would be relaxed and happy.

Security is an inner conviction. It is how you feel about things, regardless of whether they are good or bad. It is a confidence that the future will hold nothing that will finally defeat us. It is a thing of the spirit.

This sense of security comes in only two ways. It comes by believing right and by doing right.

1. It comes by believing the right things about God. You have to be a theologian, because you are a human being. Theology is the science of the knowledge of God. The security of your life depends on your knowing the truth about God and in trusting the truth you know. God has revealed Himself in a way that makes it possible to know Him. The Bible is open to you for this purpose. You can fail to know God by neglecting to acquaint yourself with His Revelation of Himself. You can refuse to believe the right things. However, you can not neglect and refuse God and ever know an inner sense of security.

2. We must do right. The wicked flee when no man pursues. "Conscience doth make cowards of us all." A great majority of our fears that rob us of peace stem from our failure to do the right thing as we know it. Economic, social and political pressures that play on all of us and make it hard for us to act as we know we should. The result is that we lose our inner sense of security.

It does not matter how much or how little money you have, or how much or how little education you have received in so far as your feeling of confidence is concerned. If you are one of those many people who feel terribly insecure, spend some time in discovering the truth about God. Begin trusting yourself to the truth you discover and then make a point of trying to do the right thing as God allows you to see it. You may be surprised at the results.

THE ANSWER LIES IN THE CHURCH

The word "member" is familiar to all of us. We are always looking for some way to bridge the chasm of our aloneness by being members with other people in various organizations.

In the heart of each there is a secret place where we are alone and the door to which is scarcely ever opened to admit anyone else. We long to have company in this secret place. We try so hard to break down the door that is kept so tightly closed. We join groups and often play out little games of make-believe. When it is over, we are still alone with ourselves in our secret place.

We cannot do without one another, yet so often our closest ties fail to unlock the door of our aloneness. The early Christians won the attentions of their pagan neighbors because they appeared to have found a solution to this problem. People said to one another, "Behold how these Christians love one another."

The Christians were members of one another. They used as an illustration of their close fellowship, the relation of the parts of the human body to each other. For a long time they were so close together that they had all things in common. They found the door into their aloneness broken down and, in the fellowship of the Church, they belonged to one another.

Perhaps we can find an answer to our aloneness in the way they found their answer. In the faith they shared, they came to understand that God loved them enough to give His Son to die for them. Such a God could be trusted. Trusting His love, they invited Him into their secret place. The door they could not unlock and that no human love could break down, God entered easily.

They were no longer alone and they found that then they could

426

love others because God first loved them. They invited each other into the secret places of their lives. This is the contagious fellowship that changed the world: they belonged to God and were members one of another.

If you are alone in spite of all you do, invite God into the secret place of your loneliness. Oneness in Christ will then become real. You will belong to others as they belong to you. This miracle takes place nowhere but in the fellowship of the church.

Only as the church, your church, offers such a fellowship, will its faith be contagious. When the world can say, "Behold, how the Christians love one another," the world will be won to the faith we profess. Jesus said, "By this shall all men know that ye are my disciples, that ye love one another."

OCTOBER 27   HOW firm a foundation, ye saints of the Lord, Is laid for your faith in His excellent Word!

Hymn, Author Unknown

THE FOUNDATIONS MUST BE RELIGIOUS

Everyone is running in all directions trying to do something about the many problems that afflict us and our society. Crime is increasing, the schools complain that young people are tearing up the libraries, mental health is breaking down, and taxes are too high. Everybody wants somebody else to do something about it all.

I am sure our problems will continue to grow until we put them back in an eternal frame. You cannot leave God out without having personal and social breakdown. It is a false idea to advance solutions that ignore religion as their basic foundation.

Religion is the insistence that behind all our material world, there is a world of the spirit where God reigns. Religion is the insistence that this spiritual world determines the course of the material world that we can weigh and measure. Jesus was giving sound, practical scientific advice when He said, "Seek ye first the Kingdom of God and His righteousness and all these things shall be added unto you." No moral or mental or social or physical order can long endure without a solid religious foundation.

The basic structure of moral order is set forth in the Ten Commandments found in Exodus 20. No amount of sophistication, cleverness or so-called maturity can shake these foundations. We either build on them or our life and our society will be nothing but an increasing number of unsolvable problems.

The first four commandments have to do with God. We must begin with our relationship with God or we might as well forget our good intentions and our good efforts. Jesus said the commandments are summed up in the first two: "Thou shalt love the Lord thy God with all thy heart, thy soul, thy mind and thy strength. And thou shalt love thy neighbor as thyself."

People are getting alarmed over our moral breakdown. Until the alarm sends us back to re-examine our relationship to God, our efforts will only aggravate the confusion. God gave us the Ten Commandments to show us the way. They are the spiritual supports for successful living in this world. To ignore them is to ignore reality. No one can keep them perfectly. God knows this and He has provided a way of forgiveness and revival to all who, in repentance, rise from failure to try again.

We can commit ourselves to the Ten Commandments to guide our lives. In so doing, we shall find cohesion of faith, singleness of purpose and fruitfulness in service. We must commit ourselves thusly or watch our present decline conclude in a final moral catastrophe.

OCTOBER 28   THROUGH the rise and fall of nations one sure faith yet standeth fast: God abides, His word unchanging, God alone, the First and Last. Amen.

George W. Briggs, Hymn

ONLY THE CHURCH STOOD FIRM

No one who knows the church would argue that it is free from serious faults. It is often limited in its vision, in its self-centeredness, in the hypocrisy of those of us who are its members. Yet with all its weaknesses, it may be the only foundation upon which our lives can rest and upon which any good civilization can be built. It is easy to brush it aside and to criticize it but those who do so must suggest something better. The church holds Christ forth to men and the power of this witness has given to us many of those things we prize most.

The church has been the source of our faith in the dignity of the individual. The humblest individual is seen as one whom God made, as one whom God so loved that the Word became flesh for his salvation. Such a man cannot be a cog in a machine or a tool to be used by another. Because the church sets truth and justice in an eternal framework as the will of God, it has been an unbreakable barrier to tyranny. The church calls men to act in love one toward another because God's love for us requires it of us.

We like to think of ourselves as good and kind people, as those who try to do the right thing and treat everyone as we want to be treated. Without roots in faith, it is not likely this kind of thing can be maintained. Indifference to the church may contribute to the loss of the very privileges you cherish.

After the Nazi movement gained control of Germany, Mr. Einstein, the famous scientist wrote: "Being a lover of freedom, when the revolution came to Germany, I looked to the universities to defend it, knowing that they had always boasted of their devotion to the cause of truth; but no, the universities immediately were silenced.

Then I looked to the great editors of the newspapers whose flaming editorials in days gone by had proclaimed their love of freedom; but they, like the universities, were silenced in a few short weeks....

"Only the church stood squarely across the path of Hitler's campaign for suppressing truth. I never had any special interest in the church before, but now I feel a great affection and admiration because the church alone has had the courage and persistence to stand for intellectual truth and moral freedom. I am forced thus to confess that what I once despised, I now praise unreservedly."

OCTOBER 29   **THE LORD is good, a stronghold in the day of trouble...and darkness shall pursue his enemies.**

Nahum l: 7, 8

EVIL IN THE WORLD WILL BE CAST OUT

Jesus told a story of a man who planted a field with good seeds. While he slept an enemy came and sowed weeds in the field. The weeds were of a kind that looked like the grain which came from the good seed. When it was discovered that the field was a mixture of grain and weeds the workmen wanted to go in and pull the weeds up. The owner decided against it. He said the good and the bad could more easily be separated at harvest time. He preferred to wait, because it was hard to tell the difference. Also, much of the grain would be destroyed in trying to root out the weeds.

This is an illustration of our world. It is an encouraging one. So much emphasis is put on the bad things in our lives until we tend to grow too discouraged about the good. Certain facts need to be remembered:

There is evil all through our world, but there is also good all through it. We need to be reminded that the world belongs to God and to the good. Evil is an intruder that must disguise itself. You never hear anyone take pride in being evil. The evils of gambling, of alcohol, of immorality are cloaked in nice words and nice surroundings. When you and I do wrong we either try to hide it or explain it in terms of something good.

The good grows and multiplies. A mother who leads her child in the ways of faith and goodness can count on her efforts to bear fruit. There are exceptions which bring grief, but they are exceptions. A man or woman who is faithful to God and to the things that are good and true will find their faithfulness bears fruit. The world is full of such people. They are up and down your street. They are in politics trying to give good government. They are in business trying to make business honest and useful. They are in education trying to plant good seed in our youth. They are in social life trying to stand for decent living. These are the people who bear their burdens with high courage, who bear one another's burdens with affection and who keep our homes, our communities and our nation from becoming a jungle.

Evil comes to harvest. Evil is always self-destructive. Leave it alone and it shows itself for what it is. Gambling brings scandal, immorality brings disaster and cruelty destroys itself. However strong evil seems, it always is on the way to defeat. God is on the side of the good.

Life moves toward a final accounting when the victory of the good will be manifested in God's last judgment and then evil will reach its end and be cast out forever.

OCTOBER 30 **BUILD a little fence of trust around today,
Fill the space with loving deeds and therein
stay; Look not through the sheltering bars
upon tomorrow, God will help thee bear
what comes of joy, or sorrow.**

Butts

LIVE FOR TODAY

We are always making plans for tomorrow. This is true of individuals and families. Business does it. Science calls its future planning "research." Education and government are busy planning for tomorrow and the future. Not only do we plan for tomorrow, but also many of us live in the future because we fear today. We try to escape into thoughts of what is ahead of us because we cannot bear to face what is present today.

Some live in the future because of our fear of the future. Others do not live today because they do not enjoy it, but they plan to have a good time tomorrow.

It is quite true that anyone who fails to provide for the future is foolish. I want to suggest, however, that anyone who fails to live today is equally foolish. Today is the only time we really have. Today is full of the things out of which life is made. If we fail to use them today, tomorrow will fail to bring us what we seek.

Jesus said once: "Be not anxious for the morrow for the morrow shall take thought for the things of itself." He was saying: "Live today."

1. If you are afraid of today and are trying to hide out in tomorrow, try facing your today. Look your fears straight in the eyes. Use what resources you have to handle your present situation. You will find your fears tend to disappear as you face them. Today will offer you good things which will surprise you.

2. If you are failing to live today because you are panicked by your

fear of tomorrow, try committing tomorrow to God. Determine to live each minute of today to the best of your ability.

3. If you are failing to live today because you aren't having much fun today but plan to enjoy tomorrow, look deeply into your purpose in life and into your conduct. If you are not enjoying today, you probably won't enjoy tomorrow. Spend part of today finding out why you are wanting to dodge it.

This is written as a protest against all the preparing and planning that goes on as a substitute for living. A young person is not only preparing for life, he is living in the only way he will ever live - one day at a time. This is an appeal for us to stop and ask: "Am I really living today? Am I enjoying the gift of today offered to me in my family, my work, my friends, and the glory of nature? Am I finding meaning in my relationship to God?"

Too many of us are not living at all, in spite of our outward appearance. We are missing a wonderful world by not living the only day we have - today.

OCTOBER 31   A GENTLE answer turns away wrath, but a harsh word stirs up anger.

Proverbs 15:1 (NIV)

SOME SUGGESTIONS ON 'GETTING EVEN'

How do you get even with someone who has done you wrong? "Getting even" is a motive in more things we do than we like to admit. All of us have a broad streak of selfishness in us. This means that we sooner or later do someone wrong and are done wrong.

There are countless ways in which this happens. Everybody likes to talk about people. We like to talk in a way that makes us feel important. It leads us to say things about others that injure their self-esteem. When this happens they want to get even.

433

People feel wronged by being unjustly excluded from some group or another. They are often wronged in the fierce competition of business or politics. Worse still there are those who give themselves in affection and are betrayed by the unfaithfulness of the one to whom that affection is given. The urge to get even often seems irresistible. How do you get even in such a way that both you and the one who wronged you are helped rather than hurt?

The Bible gives the only answer. It is not an easy answer. However, it is not an easy problem. It is not a question of finding an easy answer. It is a matter of finding one that will work. Jesus said we could ask God for anything we need, but He put a condition that is part of the answer.

Any hope of "getting even" begins by forgiving in your heart the one who has injured you. "And whenever you stand praying, you must forgive anything that you are holding against anyone else, and your Heavenly Father will forgive your sins." You forgive, not because the person deserves it, but because God forgives you who also do not deserve it. God cannot forgive you unless you forgive the one or ones who have injured you. If Christ could forgive those who crucified Him, you can forgive those who injure you.

The second step is to give up any idea of "getting even" and leave it up to God. Paul makes this point in writing to the Romans. "Don't pay back a bad turn by a bad turn, to anyone.... Never take vengeance into your own hands, my dear friends: stand back and let God punish if he will. For it is written: Vengeance belongeth unto me: I will recompense.

"The third step is also given by Paul. Find some way to be helpful to the one who has injured you when the opportunity comes to you. And these are God's words: "If thine enemy hunger, feed him; If he thirst, give him to drink; For in so doing thou shalt heap coals of fire upon his head."

If you are hurt and bitter, you will be amazed at what can happen to you and to those who have injured you if you will take these steps.

NOVEMBER

NOVEMBER 1   **BEFORE I was afflicted, I went astray: but now I have kept thy word.**

Psalm 119:67 (KJ)

RELIGION KEEPS US FROM GETTING LOST

It is easy to get lost in the crowd. Today it is almost impossible not to. The processes of our life are reducing us to numbers. If the trend continues, we may soon give each newborn baby a number instead of a name. This will take care of all cradle-to-grave arrangements of a benevolent government.

It will handle all the necessary banking. It will serve to identify you in your job. It will take care of your proper billing in all the clubs you belong to. Your charge accounts will be by number. About all that will be left will be the endearing pet names given to you by those that love you.

Big government, big business, big social organizations have little time to deal with people by name. Efficiency demands machines and cards and numbers. More and more we are the victims of people who know what is good for us. By number, they are going to do it to us whether we want it or not. The thin line that separates benevolence from tyranny is rapidly disappearing.

The only thing that stands in the way of the loss of the individual in the crowd is religious faith, the conviction in the soul that God has entered into a direct relationship with us one by one. He calls us by name.

Those who want to dominate people in government, in school, in welfare and in business are afraid of true religion. When a man walks with God, it is hard to make him conform to the demands of a human master.

435

Nazi Germany sought to displace the church. Russia sought to eliminate it from any place of influence. There are those in our land who would silence the church when it seeks to call to judgment certain aspects of our life, or to encourage individuals to stand out from the crowd.

NOVEMBER 2   **HE WILL give eternal life to those who patiently do the will of God...there will be glory and honor and peace from God for all who obey him...**

Romans 2:7-10 (TLB)

FOUR THINGS TO EXPECT FROM REAL RELIGIOUS FAITH

It is a rather common thing for us to try to use our Christian faith as an escape hatch from trouble. Another use that we seek to make of our faith is to achieve those things, which, in our own judgments, are good for us. We have been taught by some that the Christian faith can help you win friends and influence people; or it can be a key whereby you can find greater economic success; or it can be used as a tool so you will be healthier and better equipped in body and mind to tackle this world; or it can be used as a tool to defeat our enemies.

Then something happens. The troubles that we were using our religion to fend off hit us. We use religion as a tool to make us healthy, wealthy and wise - but then we find that we are neither healthy, wealthy nor wise.

We need to come to terms as to what God promises us by our faith.

1. The first is, He promises that whatever happens to you, you can take. "For there hath no trial taken you but such as is common to man." God is faithful and will not allow you to be tempted or tried above that you are able, but He will, in the temptation or trial, make a way of escape, "that ye may be able to bear it." And

436

you can. The witness of people everywhere is to the fact that those in whom Christ lives somehow make it - in spite of whatever happens to them.

2. He promises that in peace He will be with us, "what'er betide." "My peace," He said, "I give unto you. Not as the world giveth give I unto you. Let not your heart be troubled, neither let it be afraid."

3. He promises us that He loves us. The greatest burden in life is to be unloved. "For I am persuaded out of the experiences of life," Paul says that "neither death, nor life, nor angels, nor principalities, nor powers, nor things present, nor things to come, nor height, nor depth, nor any other creature, shall be able to separate us from the love of God, which is Christ Jesus, our Lord."

4. He promises at least one more thing. That is Heaven. These lives of ours have no meaning just in terms of this world. If all of your striving is for this world, it is a poor show. God promises rest at the end. Perhaps no more gracious words, certainly no more meaningful words, were spoken by Christ when He said, "In my Father's house are many mansions. I go to prepare a place for you and I will come again to receive you unto Myself that where I am, there you may be also."

These are the promises of faith.

NOVEMBER 3   **COMMIT to the Lord whatever you do, and your plans will succeed. The Lord works out everything for his own ends.**

Proverbs 16:3,4 (NIV)

SOME FIND THE SECRET OF HAPPY LIVING

Every now and then you run across someone who seems to have

found the secret of the happy life. I know such a person. It has been interesting to try to figure out the secret. She has no money except what her husband earns. They probably have only a very few hundred dollars in reserve. Her friends range from the very poor to the very rich. She appears equally at home with both and is accepted as an equal by both.

If she belongs to a club of any kind, I am not aware of it. Her home and yard are well kept, but neither absorb her attention in any major way. Her children are cared for, but she makes no major production of it; however, she fulfills her obligations to her children, husband and friends in a way that is the envy of those who know her. Surprisingly, she always seems to be relaxed and cheerful and she meets emergencies with a steady hand. She plays the piano a bit and reads a great deal.

This woman has found the secret of inner confidence: she has found love. She apparently never doubts the love that surrounds her. She and her husband have moved together through the years with unquestioning loyalty to one another.

She never doubts her love for her children or theirs for her. The family has certain rules that are necessary and they are enforced, but the children know that the parents keep rules, too. They have learned that only as the rules are kept by each can the home function.

She never doubts her affection for her friends and theirs for her. She makes little, if any, effort to spread herself out too thin in her contacts. She makes no effort to be accepted where she is not naturally accepted.

At the center of her life, she does not doubt the love of God. This is her secret. She deeply believes that her relationship with God is secure because of her faith in Christ. Her Bible is a daily companion and her church is her central loyalty outside the home.

She has known joy and sorrow, gain and loss. Apparently she has found God sufficient for all. She trusts God with her family and her daily life. She believes in a deep, quiet way that God works out all things for those who love and are loved by Him.

The influence of this person is great. I hope this story will help you break the grip of life's anxious, fearful rush.

Dr. Vernon Broyles Book ***"In The Cool of The Evening"***
Reflections related to "In God We Trust: The Future of Faith in America"

OUR father's God to Thee, Author of liberty, To thee we sing...

Samuel F. Smith, Hymn

OUR HERITAGE HAS CHRISTIAN ROOTS

The American heritage sinks its roots deep into the Christian faith. This is as true of its education and politics as of its religion. Our modern effort to divorce the Christian religion from education and the state is a strange denial of the foundation upon which our national values are built.

It may help to take excerpts from early documents.

"Our liberty to walk in the faith of the Gospel was the cause of us transporting ourselves...over the Atlantic Ocean into this vast wilderness." This was Governor John Endicott's statement to Charles II of England concerning the colonizing of Massachusetts.

The Mayflower Compact begins: "We whose names are underwritten having undertaken for the Glory of God and advancement of the Christian faith and honor of our king and country, a voyage to plant the first colony."

In 1636 the Massachusetts Colony Council said: "It seemeth to us to be a divine ordinance (and moral) that none shall be appointed and chosen by the people of God, magistrates over them, but men fearing God, chosen out of their brethren, saints."

The articles of the first Virginia settlement did "specially ordain, charge and require with all diligence, care and respect that the Christian faith be preached, planted and used and to make yourselves all of one mind for the good of your country and your own to serve and fear God, the giver of goodness."

Education came out of the church in the formative years of our country. Yale, Harvard, Princeton, Columbia University and nearly all colleges begun before 1850 were founded to further the welfare of man on the basis of the Christian faith. There was little secondary education outside the Christian church.

This is presented to you to bear witness to the true foundations of the American Way. The results of the American heritage of faith have been the best history records. However, you cannot destroy the foundation and expect our structure to long stand.

We must keep God at the center of our way of life to prevent the values we cherish to be destroyed.

NOVEMBER 5 **AND I will give you a new heart - I will give you new and right desires – and put a new Spirit within you. I will take out your stony hearts of sin and give you new hearts of love. And I will put my Spirit within you so that you will obey my laws and do whatever I command.**

Ezekiel 36: 26,27 (TLB)

THOSE WITH A CHIP ON THEIR SHOULDER NEED HELP

It is hard to live with a person who has a chip on the shoulder. What we sometimes forget is that it is a good deal harder to live with a chip on your own shoulder; such a person is always unhappy and knows it.

One day, by a well in Samaria, Jesus met a woman with a chip on her shoulder. (John's Gospel, Chapter 4). She lived by her resentments and resented her position as a woman and as a Samaritan. She resented herself most of all because she had made a moral shipwreck of her life. She lived on the defensive.

She had reason to feel resentment because in her day, women were definitely second-class citizens and were treated as such. Moreover, the Samaritans were a people of mixed race and were generally regarded as inferior. Personally, the woman's life was a mess, making her hostile to everyone and everything. Then she met Jesus. He led her to a new relationship to God and she was changed. She lost her resentments and became a happy, useful person.

This is what Jesus did to lead the unhappy, resentful woman out of her misery and bitterness:

1. He accepted her as she was. He did not look down on her because she was a woman or because of her race or because she was a sinner. He led her to see that however badly she felt about herself and however inferior she felt, God accepted her just the way she was. We must all remember that when we feel excluded and unwanted, God receives us just the way we are.

2. Jesus asked for her help. He needed water to drink. She resented him as a man and because of his race and because she was afraid He would lecture her on her conduct. She was disarmed by a request for help. In a very real sense, God needs our help and everyone we meet needs our help. God invites us to help where we can. Pick out the person you resent and look for something you can do to help. It will do much to dissolve your resentments.

3. Then Jesus went to the real source of her resentments - the woman herself. She was a moral failure and needed most of all the forgiveness of God. She needed to be able to accept herself. Jesus led her to see that she could accept the forgiveness of God revealed in Himself. She was able to worship Him in the depths of her own spirit and she went away, cured of her resentments.

Today, we are still plagued by resentments between men and women and between races. To solve these problems, we must begin with God's answer to personal moral failure, which is the forgiveness of sin. His forgiveness allows us to accept ourselves because we have been accepted by God.

EVERY good and perfect gift is from above, coming down from the Father of the heavenly lights ...

James 1:17 (NIV)

EVIL IS IN OUR WORLD, BUT GOOD HAS MORE POWER

You don't read much about it in the press, and our crisis-crying news commentators seldom mention it, but all over our world there are those who are busy, bringing shafts of divine light through this world's darkness. In the midst of hate, there is love. For despair, there is hope; for disease there is healing; for cruelty, there is kindness; for treachery, there is fidelity; for broken lives, there is redemption and for sorrow, there is comfort. God's Kingdom marches on and its steel framework of love still supports our world.

When you tend to grow discouraged by the passing parade of man's evil and selfishness, it helps to remember this is only part of the story - and the minor part, at that. I was reminded of this by a letter written by a priest in 1513 A.D. and reproduced in 1963 in a Honolulu church bulletin;

"Contessina, forgive an old man's babble. But I am your friend and my love for you goes deep. There is nothing I can give you which you have not got; but there is much, very much, that, while I cannot give it, you can take. No heaven can come to us unless our hearts find rest in it today. Take heaven. No peace lies in the future which is not hidden in this present little instant. Take peace!

"The gloom of the world is but a shadow. Behind it, yet within our reach is joy. There is radiance and glory in the darkness, could we but see; and to see we have only to look. Contessina, I beseech you to look.

"Life is so generous a giver, but we, judging its gifts by their covering, cast them away as ugly or heavy or hard. Remove the covering, and you will find beneath it a living splendor, woven of love, by wisdom, with power.

"Welcome it, grasp it, and you touch the angel's hand that brings it to you. Everything we call a trial, a sorrow, or a duty, believe me, that angel's hand is there: the gift is there, and the wonder of an overshadowing presence. Our joys, too; be not content with them as joys. They, too, conceal diviner gifts.

"Life is so full of meaning and purpose, so full of beauty (beneath its covering) that you will find that earth but cloaks your heaven. Courage, then to claim it, that is all! But courage you have; and the knowledge that we are pilgrims together, wending through unknown country, home.

NOVEMBER 7   **IT IS very helpful to make a habit, morning by morning, to give the troubles of the day just beginning to our dear Lord, accepting his will in all things, especially in all the little personal trials and vexations.**

H. L. Lear

HONESTY WOULD IMPROVE PRAYER

Maybe we would pray better if we prayed more honestly. We who are supposed to be Christian are sometimes more dishonest in prayer than non-Christians. We know how we are supposed to be because we know Christ. We know how we are supposed to feel about things and people, but often we don't. Rather than admit we don't, we pretend that we do.

Our minds wander in prayer because our prayers are about things our minds are not really interested in. We confess that we are unworthy sinners, but our mind tells us we are not so bad after all. We offer ourselves to God's service when what we want is a messenger boy to run an errand for us. We pray to God as Ruler of the Universe, but we have several suggestions as to how He might improve His administration.

We pray to be shown His will, but our mind is not interested in anything that will disturb our comfort or our program of activities. We pray for love and peace and good will among men, but with the exception of our national enemies and our neighbors who won't act as we know they should.

We pray for God to do something about the pain and sorrow in our world, but to find someone else to use in the job. We timidly thank God for the Cross of Christ, but we want none of it for ourselves. We are not sure what taking the cross would mean, but we make sure not to find out lest it be uncomfortable.

We want to pray for peace, but it makes the mind wander to think about all the billions spent for bullets. We pray for help in our emergencies, but something in us is honest enough to disturb our prayers by asking what use we will make of the answer.

We pray to be useful in serving others, but our minds remind us to be sure to serve in such a way as to get credit and perhaps, profit. You can't afford to be humble enough to get lost in the crowd.

Sometimes it seems that the only prayer left to us is that of the publican: "God be merciful to me a sinner." We read that the publican went away accepted of God. It is the secret of God's Gospel that He came to seek and to save the lost.

It will help in prayer if we come just as we are, just as we know we are. There isn't much pride in such coming, but there is acceptance by God and there is His forgiveness. There is reality in praying.

THE POSITIVE APPROACH IS MORE HELPFUL

Things are getting along well to be as bad as they are presented. For some reason - one not easy to figure out - everyone who presents facts to the public tries to push the panic button. We may be getting to the place where we are hardened to all the fear psychology that is being dished out in such heavy doses. Out of necessity, one is almost forced to discount many of the daily threats. Otherwise, we could not live normally at all.

We do live in a world that is in revolution; however, it is not helped by constant repetition of its awful possibilities. Racial problems are far from solved, but more effort is being made to solve them than at any other time in history. It is not encouraging to those who work at it patiently and intelligently to be constantly criticized and threatened because of the unhappy situations that remain. There are too many people who find it necessary to blow up all out of proportion every passing difficulty and make them all seem to be a threatening crisis.

We are constantly bombarded with campaigns to raise money for various health agencies, yet it is seldom pointed out that no nation has ever spent as much on health services with such good results.

The woods are full of experts on international relations who keep us well posted on the smallest friction. Bad crises arise, but most of the incidents pass without serious results. In the meantime, the gains in international understanding seldom get much attention.

We hear a lot about controversies in our communities, yet we tend to forget that most things are getting along fairly well. We hear about the failures of our young people, and especially about our school dropouts. It is a problem, but more than ever before, young people everywhere seem to be doing better than before.

These are a few examples of the negative approach that is caused, in part, by the fact that we are so well fed and so prosperous that we feel guilty. We feel it is necessary to beat ourselves over the head with our failures as self-punishment.

We do need to work on correcting our failures and to try to help all who need help - but we also need to remember that there is much that is right with life. We need fewer manufactured crises and less emphasis upon crime and tragedy.

We need more reminders of the great host of people in every walk of life who do their part in life with courage and fidelity. We need more emphasis on the successes in our human and political relationships. If we will dwell on the positive, then our problems and our real crises will be met with a good deal more hope.

NOVEMBER 9   NO man is poor who has had a Godly mother.

Abraham Lincoln

FAITH IN CHILDHOOD ABIDES THROUGH LIFE

Recently a letter came from a friend whose aged mother had died. He wrote: "My mother leaves me with a fine heritage. I shall do my best not to disappoint her." A few days ago, a governor of a midwestern state was being interviewed on radio. He was asked what influences were most powerful in his life. He replied that the influence of his parents had come first in his development. In both instances, the parents reared their children in homes where God was honored and where the church was faithfully attended by parents and children.

I would pay tribute to all parents who have had the divine wisdom to anchor the lives of their children in the eternal. The older you get, the more grateful you become for a heritage of faith that supports you in the difficult task of living. When troubles come, when storms threaten to overwhelm, when temptation seems almost unbearable, it is almost a miracle how strength and courage will well up from the memory of parents who walked with God. I wonder how many people there are who live with an inner security who do not rest their faith on that of a faithful parent.

I would encourage all parents who sacrifice today to lead their children in the things of God. It is not easy today to teach children the faith or to get them to Sunday school and to various groups where they are given religious training. It is not easy, but it leads the children to faith in God for which they were born. There comes a day when the children rise up and call their parents blessed.

It is important to do what you can to see that your child is trained in the things of this world. Skills must be learned. Social graces are desirable. Material things are necessary, but "life is more than food and the body more than clothes." We are made to be children of God. It is more important, therefore, to train your child in the things of God. These are the things that abide and that are eternal.

This is why strong men and women unashamedly pay tribute to parents who led them to faith regardless of whatever else they could or could not give. This is why countless young couples today work so hard to surround their children with the influences of the church and of God.

If you are not doing it, what are you putting in its place to insure that your child may have a heritage for which he will be grateful when the storms come?

THIS is my Father's world,
And to my listening ears
All nature sings, and round me rings
The music of the spheres.

Mattie Babcock, Hymn

GOD, MASTER OF HISTORY

Among the many changes that affect and afflict our day is the fact that almost no one can afford to be ignorant of history, not only as it takes place around us, but as it has occurred in the past. Our very commitment to life depends upon what we think about history. The Christian religion is an historical religion. It has been hammered out of the experiences of men and women as they have been a part of history in the making. It has been hammered out of the blood and tears and sacrifice of men and women who have lived as citizens of their communities down the ages. It makes a difference what you think of history.

There are choices to make about how we think about history. The first choice is that history is simply the record of man on his own: that the events and circumstances of life grow out of man's own inner necessity and that everything that happens can be explained in terms of what happens to man. It suggests that man is the center of life and that everything flows out of him and revolves about him. Most of history today is written in that context.

Combined with this view are the political principles: the great struggle of the weak against the strong. Those who would explain the affairs of our day in this light, pride themselves on their knowledge of power politics.

Another set of principles gathers around the term "sociological." The great push of people toward status changes history, we are told, and in this push of people upward, you have the explanation of revolts, rebellions and of the progress of history. No one can live very long, however, without becoming conscious that there hovers over us something that we cannot control. Our lives turn most unexpectedly when we have been thinking they would go in an entirely different direction.

While we hear a lot about history in the terms just described, there is a second view. That second view is the Christian interpretation of history. The Christian interpretation of the events of time says that at the heart of everything, there is a Sovereign God. The Bible tells us that, from the beginning, no man and no nation can live in rebellion against God.

God is in charge. We are saved only by the Cross of Jesus Christ. Pilate said to Jesus, I have power to crucify Thee. I have power to let Thee go." Pilate had in his hand all of the power of the most powerful Empire of that day. Jesus looked him squarely in the face and said simply, "Thou couldst have no power at all over Me except it were given thee from above."

In this day, when everything seems shaken loose from its moorings, perhaps we need the same message that God sent to Judah by Isaiah: "Go and say unto the cities of Judah, 'Behold your God!'" And so God would say to us today and throughout all history: "Behold, your God!"

NOVEMBER 11   **FOR home, where our affection clings, we thank thee Lord.**

Sarah B. Rhodes, Hymn

THE SECURITY OF HOME

There is a passage from II Samuel which recounts an incident in the life of David when he was surrounded by his enemies. He did not know whether he would come out alive or not. In that time of stress, pain and agony, he instinctively cried out for a drink of water from the well of Bethlehem, which was by the gate. David did instinctively that which every man does under pressure; he cried out for "home!" This little incident is a parable of what goes on in life every day, all about us. When we are afraid, when the unusual threatens, when danger looms, when crisis develops, our hearts instinctively want to go home.

I was in the hospital the other night for an hour or two with a family whose little boy, something short of four years old, had fallen off a wall and bumped his head rather severely and was showing some signs of possible concussion. They wanted to watch him there in the hospital. Every time anyone came toward him, he said, "I want to go home!" Every time they would wake him up, which they did to be sure that he could be waked up, he would say again, "I want to go home!" I have an idea that if the adults in that hospital could have shared his lack of inhibitions they would have joined this little four year old in his vocal statement, 'I want to go home!"

The only way you can stand erect in this world is if you have somewhere to lean, cushioned by affection. There is no other way to meet the pressures of our day. Happy and fortunate is the person who, when the clouds are leaden and the ceiling is zero; when the days become short and the nights are long, can go "home" and find at the end of the lane, assurance, security, peace and love. That was what Paul was talking about when he wrote to Timothy. He was calling Timothy to a life of great stress, calling him to life that would cut him off from normal associations, calling him to a life that could very easily lead to martyrdom. He said, "You know Timothy, I just want to be sure that you remember the marvelous heritage that you have in your home where God was honored. I just want to be sure that you remember that it was through the channels of this Godly home that you have received the things upon which life is built."

We live in a day when people are looking for security, a day of great pressure for young people, children and even small children, hustled about to this and that, giving them "advantages" from the French class to the dancing class, the music, Indian Guides - whatever. We hear about the insecurities of poverty. We hear a good deal about the "home" and how, unless the home can provide peace and security, they cannot be provided. How we worship the cold products of the human mind, yet these are not going to make good homes.

I believe that you will find that whenever it is possible to go home, either down the streets of your town or down memory lane, and find security and peace and rest and a solid foundation upon which you can stand to fight, I believe you will find that it is a home where God has been honored, or is honored. I do not believe that all of the sociological information that has ever been complied can make a good home, <u>without God</u>! You can learn things that can help you, provided that God is in the center, but you will never find a home that wells up like springs of living water, that is not founded upon the worship of God. That is what Paul was saying to Timothy. He reminded him of the wonderful heritage that he had in the home. Courage had taken the place of fear. Love and wisdom were firm foundations.

Love. We just cannot function without love. It is the only thing, really, that is absolutely necessary. To have a place that you can go, a place where you can go and shut out the carping world and know you are loved just for yourself and in spite of yourself, that is divine love! This is not human. You will never build a home that ministers to the hearts of men, unless you build it on the very love of God.

Wisdom. Just the sense to live. This is a gift. An old Presbyterian elder told me once, in a little country church where I first preached regularly, "I have been here seventy-six years and if you want me to give you a little advice, come to me and I think I can give it to you. But, Mr. Broyles, if you lack common sense, may God have mercy on your soul!" I have never forgotten it. Wisdom. You just do not learn it from books. You catch it from those who live close to God.

These are the gifts of God, received through homes founded in God. There many problems today, problems that matter. You cannot solve them by information. You cannot solve them by reading books. You will solve them only as, somehow, a Spirit comes into life.

NOVEMBER 12   ACKNOWLEDGE and take to heart this
day that the Lord is God in heaven
above and on the earth below. There is
no other. Keep his decrees and
commands...so that it may go with you
and your children after you and that you
may live long...

Deuteronomy 4:39,40 (NIV)

THERE ARE SOME THINGS THAT THE SPACE AGE HASN'T CHANGED

Everyone is talking about meeting the challenge of the space age. The vastness of space is supposed to force us to change all our thinking and acting. I want to submit that things have not changed much in the realm of religion and morals. God has not changed as men have roamed around space. He has not changed since we reached the moon. He is the same yesterday, today and forever.

The revelation we have of Him in the Bible will cover any discoveries men may make. He was in the beginning. He is the Creator, the First Cause of all that exists. He loves this world and gave Himself to the world in Jesus Christ because of this love. Round about the world, and all the space there is are the everlasting arms wooing it all toward Himself.

Man has not changed with all the modern discoveries. Change the names and the uniforms and the titles and one period of history reads about like any other. The wheat and the tares grow together.

There are the same struggles between the good and the evil in the hearts of modern space scientists that existed in Adam and Eve. Cape Canaveral has its churches and its dives as did ancient Babylon or Rome or Jerusalem. The heartaches in any modern city are the same as were those in ancient days. Guilt is present in the same way as it existed in David or Judas. Kindness and cruelty, greed and generosity, hatred and love can ride in space ships just as they rode in ancient chariots.

452

The ground rules by which men are made to live have not been changed. The Ten Commandments still mark the paths in which men must walk in this world, placing God first. Idolatry still leads to death. The name of God demands honor, as does one day in seven. Parental request is still divinely ordered. A respect for human life, fidelity in marriage, honesty, truthfulness and proper regard for what belongs to another, all hold true today.

It remains true that the only way we can live together in this world is to love God with our heart, soul, mind and body and our neighbor as ourselves. Also unchanged is frail man's need for forgiveness because he falls short of God's requirements.

As modern as tomorrow's latest scientific triumph is the ancient cry of the Gospel, "We beseech you in Christ's stead, be ye reconciled to God." Here God, and man, meet in peace. Only in this peace can modern man be saved from himself.

NOVEMBER 13 **...THEN HE stood up and rebuked the wind and the waves, and the storm subsided and all was calm.**

Matthew 9:26 (LB)

ON STILLING STORMS

In the book of Mark, we are told that Jesus cast out demons. The man possessed was called "Legion." We are also told that Christ spoke to a storm at sea and all became calm.

Jesus, by the word of His power, brought peace. He brought peace to the physical storm, and he brought peace to the torn and tortured mind of this man. These are what are known as miracles. We are not accustomed today to talk about or to think about miracles. It is not that secretly we do not hope for them.

Often we pray earnestly for them. But they fit in so little with our modern scientific approach that we simply evade any real confronting of our minds with them. We like to think that science has unlocked the door that gives us the meaning to the physical universe. We really believe we do not know the answer but that somebody does. We have an idea that human minds will read the secrets of the universe, unravel its laws, learn how to use them and solve all physical problems.

To understand miracles at all you must understand and move from the Grand Miracle, that miracle that really stretches the mind of man. The fact that God, the God who hung the stars in the skies and who created the universe, made it all and that God became incarnate in one single individual person. Sit down with that miracle. There is no human approach to this miracle, the very heart of the Christian Gospel. God was in Christ, reconciling the world to Himself. If God is in Christ, reconciling the world to Himself, then it is more remarkable if miracles do not happen than if they do. As He moves about, it is remarkable if strange and wonderful things do not come from it.

The storm at sea. No one can explain the evil in our world, but it is there. Somehow it is tied with the aberrations of nature that destroy. The storm at sea was raging. The sciences of meteorology would have vast descriptions of it. They could tell you about the currents. Finally they could tell you why the storm blew itself out. But at this particular moment, in the center of the storm, God, in Christ, spoke and the winds ceased and the waves quieted. He said, "Peace, be still!" and peace came. God was doing at that point what God is always doing. There has never been a storm that blew itself out that did not blow itself out because God said, "Peace, be still!" The weather that we have has been a bit unseasonable recently, yet somewhere in it, God is moving. God, in the stilling of this storm, did what God is doing always.

The man was driven by the storms of his inner life onto the rocks of disaster. I do not know what caused it and nobody does. He said his name was Legion. It may be that he had some terrifying experiences at the hand of the Roman Legions who were the rulers of the land. Nobody knows. But this wild man, unable to find help anywhere, suddenly, by the voice of Christ, is brought back to sanity, and we read that they found him clothed and in his right mind. We read further, "They were afraid!" Here God is doing nothing unusual. God, in Christ, did not create something here that was contrary to

454

nature. God, here, simply did suddenly, in His incarnation in Christ, what He is doing always. There are never any laws broken in miracles. They are just hurried a bit. In miracles, God works suddenly as He is always working normally.

If there are storms beating your own life, there is always God urging, "Come unto Me!" It is still true that with God all things are possible. The witness of Paul is still valid when he said; "I can do all things through Christ, who gives me strength." In the mighty works of Christ we have the assurance that God is with us, to work not only through His ordinary ways, but also time and again, to work what we call miracles. These are tremendous days in which to be alive, and our resources lie in a tremendous Gospel where anything can happen at any time in the building of His Kingdom.

NOVEMBER 14   **FOLLOWING after the Holy Spirit leads to life and peace, but following after the old nature leads to death...**

Romans 8:6 (LB)

DOES IT MATTER?

In midst of the religious confusion of our day, this question is one that Christians need to face.

As one reads the Bible in the face of things that are happening to people and in society one cannot escape the feeling that some things are "pushed under the rug" in much of what is said privately and publicly. Recently a poll claimed to show that a large percentage of people expressed a desire to go to heaven. No one asked how they expected to get there. Christ said "No man cometh to the Father except by me." You hear very little of this even in many of the churches. Does it matter?

The poll indicated a lack of faith in the Ten Commandments and, indirectly, in the teachings of Christ as the cornerstones of man's proper behavior. The Bible makes it clear that they represent reality by which all people must live. Does it matter?

The Bible makes it clear that one day in seven is to be set aside as a day to honor God, to rest and to do good deeds. Today it has become a "play day." Does it matter?

The Bible makes it clear that marriage was created to be a permanent relationship with few valid reasons for breaking the tie. The Bible sets forth the proper relation between husband and wife. In our day, marriage has come to be regarded by many as a convenience to be broken if it "does not work out." Does it matter?

The Bible teaches clearly that man is born into this world a sinner, unable to create lasting good unless changed by the grace of God in Jesus Christ. Today, society generally proceeds on the idea that man is intrinsically good and needs only good advice, money and education. Does it matter?

The Bible makes it clear that God in Christ rules all things in the affairs of individuals and of society and that relation to God determines the welfare of everyone in this world and in the world to come. Does it matter?

This is a personal question for each Christian. Think about it.

NOVEMBER 15   **LAY not up for yourselves treasures upon earth, where moth and rust doth corrupt, and where thieves break through and steal: But lay up for yourselves treasures in Heaven...**

Matthew 6:19,20 (KJ)

THE PRIMARY STRUGGLE IN EVERY SOUL

There is a fierce battle going on in the heart of the average individual you meet even as it goes on in your own. It is the struggle to find the right choice between your desire for the so-called rewards of the world and what you believe to be right.

Moses is the classic Old Testament example of what each of us faces. He was a prince in Egypt. He was popular and powerful. As a baby he had been adopted from slave parents by a princess. At the height of his power and privilege, he was faced with the inner challenge to serve his oppressed people. He would lose all he had been taught to regard as good. Personal power, privilege and security were in direct conflict with God's voice in conscience. What would you do?

In the hearts of men this question is answered and the answer determines what happens to the individual and to society.

What do you do? What do you do when your desire to get ahead and to make money comes into conflict with your deeper obligation to your family?

What do you do when the demands of the job and the ambition for power and position and privilege conflict with the obligations you have to Christ and to the church?

What do you do when you are faced with the choice of being popular with your group or of speaking out for, or doing, what you know is right?

Do you decide to ignore the call of conscience and openly give yourself to the pursuit of worldly goods? Do you just decide that principle is not as important as position? Or do you rationalize your actions? It is easy to decide to ignore conscience for a while in order to get power and position. If you do ignore conscience, you will use your place of privilege to do the things you know you ought not to do. Will you have the courage to stand up for your principles in the middle of the power structure? This is dangerous, for power structures have cruel ways of dealing with those who challenge their ways.

The writer to the Hebrews tell us: "By faith Moses, when he was grown up, refused to be called the son of Pharaoh's daughter, choosing rather to share ill treatment with the people of God than to enjoy the fleeting pleasures of sin."

Here is the decisive battle that every man must fight. No amount of worldly gain can compensate for a defeated conscience. Only by faith in God who speaks to us in conscience, who guides us by His providence, who forgives us by His grace, can we ever successfully fight this battle. Your soul, your home, your world depend on the answer you give to the question: What do you do when conscience and the demands of the world come into conflict?

NOVEMBER 16   FOR where your treasure is, there will your heart be also.

Matthew 6:21 (LB)

WEALTH OF GOODS, POVERTY OF SOUL

The wise men of human history have noted the deadly danger of material prosperity and have commented on it. No one has been more pointed in his comments than Jesus Christ. He said it would be easier for a camel to go through the eye of a needle than for a rich man to enter the kingdom of heaven. Today it is evident that people generally seem more interested in getting rich than in entering the kingdom of heaven. At best, they confuse the two.

However, there is enough evidence that material progress makes it difficult to grow spiritually to make it desirable to think seriously about our present worship of prosperity.

Jesus told a story of a certain rich man who prospered beyond his dreams. All the man could think about was the expansion of his holdings to take care of his increased wealth. In the process, the man lost his soul. Jesus noted that this is always the result when a man is not rich toward God.

The story illustrated the point that a man's life does not consist in the abundance of the things that he possesses. Deep within us we respond to this warning. When material things and our love for them rob us of inner peace, they cost too much. When they destroy the close relationships we have with our family and with our friends, we have lost the key to real life. When they destroy the moral standards that bind society together, material things have become our enemy.

458

When they crowd God out of our lives, we have lost our souls.

Our growing problems give evidence that we are in grave danger, despite our outward prosperity. Greed is making international relationships a jungle. The rising tide of mental illness should not be with us if possessions made people happy. Too many of our pretty homes are frames without pictures. Too many of our large businesses have been convicted of price-fixing. Sports are plagued by the breakdown in ethics. The streets of our fair cities are not safe after dark. Alcoholism is a growing menace. Until individuals and societies turn to God, problems can only grow. God is not mocked, and what we sow, we reap.

However far-fetched it may seem to those who believe you can build a life or a community by human wisdom, the hope for true life rests on the responses of hearts to the call of Christ: "Repent and believe the gospel.

NOVEMBER 17 **I PRESS toward the mark for the prize of the high calling of God in Christ Jesus.**

Philippians 3:14 (KJ)

THE PATH OF FAITH IS THE WAY TO VICTORY

These are days when we ought to stop and thank God for the Christian faith. It is good news in this time when good news is rare. It is a message of redemption, of healing and of hope. Reading, hearing and seeing the daily news, one can easily conclude that evil, destruction, hatred, division, sickness, dishonesty, immorality and death are the major forces of our day.

Writers deal in pessimism in plays, poems and books. Much of what appears in print can be found in this Scripture: "having no God and without hope in the world."

But this is not the main story. The main story is that our kind of world is greatly beloved by God. He was in Christ as He died on the cross, reconciling this world to Himself. He made sure that in the death of Christ, evil cannot win.

The fact of salvation is stronger than lostness; healing is more powerful than disease; love overcomes hate; honor shines more brightly than dishonesty; construction is more active than destruction and unity constantly presses against disunity.

You don't hear much about them, but wherever you are, there are those quietly seeking to be instruments of God's salvation and healing. There are individuals living with moral integrity and with unselfish devotion to whatever task is theirs. There are parents seeking to train children by their words and their lives in the way that is pleasing to God and useful in their generation. There are teachers dedicated to helping youth to know what is good. There are faithful physicians holding open the door, that God's healing can be known in sickness and disease. There are men and women in business who, in honesty and service, hold our economic structure together. There are those in public life honestly trying to make government work for the good of all. There are those of the church working to keep the doors of men's souls open toward God, allowing His grace to always be present to help in time of need.

To each of you who labor for the common good, God in Christ bids you to take hope. You are walking in the way of victory, a victory guaranteed by the resurrection of Christ from the dead. In a day when the voices of pessimism have the floor, we can be grateful for the Christian faith.

NOVEMBER 18   HEAR my prayer, O Lord, because you are faithful to your promises.

Psalm 143:1 (NIV)

STEPS TO INNER CONFIDENCE

There is a story that we read from the book of John in the New Testament that has to do with the healing of a sick boy – it is actually the story of how man found rest and peace and victory in life. It is the story of how a man through faith - found the answer to the problems of living.

What so many people thoroughly fail to understand is that the Christian faith is designated not only to furnish a home in heaven, but is designated to enable a person to meet the evils and problems of this life with victory and with a basic sense of confidence and peace underneath whatever outward storm there may be. There is a good deal more said in the New Testament about the deliverance of the Christian from the present evils and difficulties than there is about the providing for the Christian an eternal home.

Often we who are Christians bear our own burdens, fight our own sin and suffer defeat at the hands of that which is outside of us. One of the chief reasons why we are not more fruitful in our witness as Christians is that we are not actually different in our living. The Christian, basically, is supposed to be a person who lives with confidence and with joy in the midst of whatever life brings. If you will read the New Testament you will find that it is not concerned with problems, that it is not always solving dilemmas, but it is witnessing to a victory in the midst of that which ordinarily would defeat.

Now the man of faith in the story of the sick boy came out of strange soil. He was not a very likely prospect and if you had been looking for those of faith, you would probably have skipped him. He was a nobleman, an official in the court of Herod Antipas. It was a court that was known for its immorality, for its cruelty and for its carelessness in those things that mattered. In that soil, this man grew.

Then crisis came. One day there came into his home that which he could not repel. There stalked into the innermost part of his heart an anxiety he could not dispel. He had a boy, maybe an only son, and now this one was sick unto death. With all of the anxiety of the human heart he sought to handle the situation. He wanted to find an answer and there was no answer. His very extremity brought him to decide something about Christ.

This man then made two decisions and in those two decisions he found his God, and he found his salvation. He found the answer to life. He found out how to live with an inner confidence that nothing could shatter. He found how to face disaster and win.

The first decision that he made was to surrender himself to the Lord. He came and Jesus immediately tested him to see why he came. Jesus first said to the man, "Except ye see signs and wonders, you are not going to be interested in me. Unless I perform a miracle for you, you are not going to be interested." Jesus was saying this to this man because He wondered why he was there. Did he just want Him to help him in this specific instance? Did all he want from Jesus was to make his son well? Then he could go back to his own environment and live his life again as he wanted to do. That was not what the man had in mind at all, but that is what you and I have in mind a great many times. There is a difference between coming to God to get what you want and coming to God just to surrender to God and to say, "I have tried my best to run my life. I have tried my best to control it, but I know now I cannot handle it. It is beyond me and I want to come now and just turn myself completely over to You."

This man made his second decision. He decided to trust God, to trust Christ, to do what He said He would do. Jesus said to this man, "Go on home." Go about your way. Your son lives. We are always wanting proof before we believe. There is no such thing in the realm of the Spirit. God said to this man, "Go on home." And "the man believed the word that Jesus spoke unto him." He took God at his word.

Actually the crucial point of such faith lies in the words, "All things work together for good to them that love God and to them that are called according to His purpose." To believe as you stand before some unbearable burden, that God will let it touch you as only He sees fit, to believe that insofar as you are concerned, this is your pathway toward the good and to walk in it with no more proof than because God says so, is the way to peace. There is no other way.

NOVEMBER 19   ...ASK, using my name, and you will receive, and your cup of joy will overflow.

John 16:24 (LB)

PRAYERS AT MIDNIGHT

An unidentified phone caller asked: "What do you do when the circumstances of your life threaten to destroy you? What do you do when your best efforts do not help? What do you do when midnight descends on your life and there seems no possibility of dawn? What do you when you battle life and all of a sudden something threatens to overwhelm life?"

It is the glory of the Christian faith that it meets us at midnight more perfectly than at any other time. Jesus, our Lord, met his midnight at Gethsemane. Apparently, here was the end of the way for Him. He was perfectly human as well as perfectly divine. We do not accomplish what He accomplished by meeting our midnight, but we must meet it as He met His. It is the glory of our faith that He met it even as we must meet it. I would commend to you the story of Gethsemane.

It is a strange thing what friends can do at midnight. It is almost beyond belief what God does through our friends when we need them. Jesus took three disciples to Gethsemane and said, "Just sit here and keep awake. Just stand by me." Whatever you do, do not ever underestimate what it means as you hold some friend's hand in the midst of crisis. It is the kind of thing that enables a person who faces midnight to make it.

A second thing that we ought to remember is this: Jesus left these three and went a little further in the garden to be alone. In the deep crises of our lives, when it seems that all the stars have been blanked out and all hope has been squelched, at heart, we are alone. At the moment of our most desperate need, a human being is alone. We need to realize that this is something that is common to man. The experience of Jesus makes this clear.

The third thing is that Jesus was in agony. We keep up a front with even those we love best. We do not let ourselves go, because we have some idea that is not manly or womanly. But there in the darkness, by ourselves, we can pour out the agony of our souls. The Son of Man knows exactly how you feel "For in that He suffered, being tried, He is able to succor them that suffer."

In the fourth place, in the aloneness of life, Jesus talked to God! How many souls reach out in need into the vastness of his own loneliness, searching for God! And strangely enough, they usually find Him!

Jesus prayed, just as you and I pray. He prayed two things: He prayed, "God, if there is any way on this earth for me to escape this thing, let me do it!" We have all been there and prayed with all the agony of our heart to be allowed to escape. It is helpful to know that the Lord Himself did that. It was also at this point than an angel came and strengthened Him, but the angel did not take away the tension.

Finally, Jesus came to His second prayer - a prayer of victory: "Thy will be done!" This prayer was a positive committal, not a supine submission. It was the act of taking evil and holding it in His hand and hurling it back, finding that it was His chief weapon in the battle against evil.

The answer to the question, "What do you do when there is nothing you can do?" is prayer: prayer that is honest, prayer that leads to commitment, prayer that finds an answer at midnight.

NOVEMBER 20   **"...DON'T be afraid. From now on you'll be fishing for the souls of men."**

Luke 5:10 (LB)

HOW DO YOU "INVITE"?

You cannot do anything better for people than to invite them to come to church with you.

When you bring a person, you do not bring them to convince them of anything...you do not bring them to really hear a preacher preach a brilliant sermon...you do not bring them to hear great music; you bring them that the Spirit of God may play upon them and answer their needs and bring conviction of sin, forgiveness and reconciliation.

And something happens. It brings them strength for the day, every day, all the days of their life. Where else can you take them and say, "There is something here for you that will undergird your life as long as you live and it will never let you down. It will give you something to comfort a broken heart and something which will give you a sense of optimism and purpose?"

Inviting someone to come to church with you is rather simple for a thing so profound. You simply ask them to come to church.

Where are they? In your neighborhood...in your office...in your club. You don't have to push yourself, just be aware of the opportunities that arise daily in your everyday life.

Pray about it. You'll know when the time comes.

NOVEMBER 21   **IN everything give thanks: for this is the will of God in Christ Jesus concerning you.**

I Thessalonians 5:18 (KJ)

TWO LITTLE WORDS BRING HAPPINESS

Years ago a clerk in a store did me favor. I wrote him a note of thanks. He told me thanks. He told me it was the first thing of its kind to happen to him in 35 years. This may mean that one of the finest things in the life is also one of the rarest, namely, expressed gratitude.

Our concern for ourselves is so intense until we fail to understand how important it is to be conscious of our debt to others and to express our gratitude.

This Thanksgiving season is a good time to take stock of ourselves. Face the fact that you are dependent on God and on your fellowman for all you are and have. How long has it been since you have taken time to say: "Thank You"?

Here is a suggested checklist for Thanksgiving.

1. Follow the advice of the Psalmist: "O Give Thanks unto the Lord for He is good: His mercy endureth forever." He has given Himself to us in Jesus Christ that we may be the children of God. He has created a world that supplies our needs.

2. There are the members of your family who have made your life rich. It may have been a long time since you have broken down and told your husband or wife how grateful you are for all that your life together has meant. Take time this Thanksgiving to express your gratitude. It will bring joy to you both. Parents can make young hearts sing by letting children know of the happiness they bring. If your mothers and fathers are living, stop a moment and let them know how grateful you are for them. You will be surprised how often it will swell the heart with emotion until it squeezes tears from the eyes, just to hear a child say: "Thank You."

3. Friends are a precious possession. In this season you can do much to strengthen the ties by going to the trouble to say "thank you" to your friends for what they mean to you.

4. You have many outside contacts in your business or school or social life. You are in debt for favors done. Make it a point in this season to let them know you appreciate them and their kindness.

If you take time to be grateful, you will find whole new areas of happy living open to you because you have brought joy to others by the simple, but sometimes difficult, act of saying: "Thank You."

AND all the nations shall be gathered before me...

Matthew 25:32 (KJ)

AUTHORITY

We are a confused people living in a confused world. The author of Judges in the Old Testament ends with these words: "In those days there was no king in Israel: every man did that which was right in his own eyes." This pretty well sums up our day also. The underlying problem is the question of an authority which people everywhere can and will accept as the standard judge of their actions.

We Christians have an answer which we are sometimes very timid to make known. We believe that man was created in the image of God to live in His created world in proper relation to Him and in obedience to His word. All people everywhere are so made. Deviation from this brings eventual disaster in this world and in the next. Christians believe that the ills of this world are basically caused by rebellion against this way in which we were created to live.

We believe God in His love has provided a way whereby rebels against God's way can be restored to the proper relation to him; namely, by repentance and by faith in the death of Christ for the sins of rebellion and its consequences.

We believe God has revealed Himself and His purpose and actions in the Bible and in His earthly incarnation in Jesus Christ. In Christ we believe God Himself is present, the God who created, sustains, rules, judges and takes care of His own.

We Christians believe that these convictions about Christ come as God's gift of His grace through our faith. They come as we expose ourselves to the Bible, studying it faithfully with an open mind and heart. This faith is undergirded by fellowship with other Christians in groups and in worship in church.

We believe that in this search are found the answers to all the problems we read about. The Bible and Christ have very definite things to say about all of them: heaven, hell, death, guilt, fear, getting along with others, the relationship of men and women, marriage, sexual relations, ethical conduct, daily work, children, Sunday, church attendance and health of mind and body.

Answers to all these problems, which essentially are personal, await the witness of the Christian community. It begins with deciding whether you and I believe the Christian faith. It depends on our deciding to live by what the Bible and by what Christ teaches about our problems...asking the simple and life changing question: "What would Christ have me do?" When we Christians begin again to take seriously the Gospel to which we subscribe, God will move again to change our confused people and our confused world.

NOVEMBER 23   "...SONS, your sins are forgiven!"

Mark 2:5 (LB)

THE PEACE OF CHRIST

Puzzlement, anxiety and fear are the order of the day. There is a search for peace of heart and mind. This peace is available in the Christian faith. The New Testament repeatedly tells of this faith. "The Lord is at hand. In nothing be anxious. In everything by prayer and supplication, with thanksgiving, let your requests be known unto God and the peace of God will keep your hearts and minds through Christ Jesus." (Philippians 4:4-7). Jesus Christ said: "My peace I leave with you, my peace I give unto you. Not as the world gives, give I unto you. Let not your heart be troubled nor afraid." (John 14:26,27). Peace is available as we come to surrender our anxieties and fears to Christ in the confidence that He will take care of us and of our concerns.

This is not easy. It is not something we can just decide to do and it is done. Faith that gives release is a gift from God. You cannot achieve it; you can only receive it. "By grace are you saved by faith and that not of yourself, it is the gift of God." (Ephesians 2:8)

At one place in the Scripture God says: "Try me." Give God a chance. This will mean spending time - some real time - reading the New Testament. Take some of the time you spend watching television which only feeds your fears. Read the New Testament just as you read any other book. Then re-read it. Read it with an open mind with one main prayer: that if God has something to say to you, He will say it by the touch of His Spirit on your mind and heart.

Then go to church regularly with others who are seeking and finding. Do this with the same prayer used in reading the Bible. The Bible and the church are the chief peace instruments of the Holy Spirit.

Through the New Testament and the church, you will find information about God's promises and what He requires of you. Most of all, you will find a marked release from anxiety and fear as you are led to cast your care upon Him in Whose hands are the affairs of all people and of all nations.

NOVEMBER 24   I, THE Messiah, have the authority on earth to forgive sins...

Mark 2:11 (LB)

MAKING AN ADVENTURE OF OUR LIVES

These are days that threaten to overwhelm us. It reminds one of being grabbed by an undertow at the beach, finding yourself tumbling over and over, panicked by the fear of being carried out to sea. The events are too complicated and our wisdom too little.

There is a way to get control of life, to be saved, to use an old term. There are no quick fixes. It involves Christ's will instead of our own desires in the detailed thoughts and acts of our daily lives. It

469

means asking ourselves earnestly the question "What would Christ have me do?" instead of 'What do I desire to do?' This is not easy nor does it come naturally; however, honestly tried, it will change our lives. It will make an adventure out of living. We will be saved.

All this begins when we - to use another old term - come "under conviction." This means that we admit deep within us that we are lost, tumbling in the surf of life. It involves the growing feeling that there may be the help of salvation in Christ, the door to a right relation with God.

When we are properly troubled in our mind and in our conscience, we will then take seriously the disciplines and the instructions of the faith: the Bible, the worship of the church and the help of Christian friends. We must be led by the strange movement of God's Spirit, leading us to accept the death of Christ as the door to forgiveness of our sins. Only then will we begin to experience what it means to be guided by Christ rather than by our own desires.

With this, the adventure of life begins if we will seek to work out His resolution. It will be hard, sometimes rocky; sometimes a cross, but we will no longer be "tumbling in the surf." We will know the presence and power of the Lord.

NOVEMBER 25   **COUNT your blessing, name them one by one; Count your many blessings, see what God has done.**

Johnson Oatman, Jr., Hymn

TIME TO COUNT YOUR BLESSINGS

We are approaching the Thanksgiving season. The Psalmist wrote a long time ago: "It is a good thing to give thanks unto the Lord." It still is a good thing to do. We are in danger if we omit gratitude in our busy lives. We are living in the midst of plenty. In spite of this, we give the majority of our attentions to what we want, to what is wrong and to what we do not have.

If you would receive a blessing in the Thanksgiving season, take a little time out to be grateful for the good things in your life. In the words of an old hymn, "what the Lord has done" will surprise you.

If you are well in body and mind, you are blessed of God and man. Be grateful for all those who serve in medicine -they are God's channels of our health. You will be doubly grateful for them if you have experienced illness.

Remember your family that provides the strong framework of affection without which life is barren. There is a host of people where you work, plus public servants who guard your safety, deliver your mail, put out your fires and make government possible. Give thanks for these

Give thanks for country. Remember the things that are right about it. We are the most fortunate of people. Under God, this nation has found freedom. You and I are free to pursue our lives without fear of government terror. We freely elect our officials and, as a whole, we have good government. Our system of checks and balances works well. Freedom of the press allows the public to know what goes on and this serves us well.

Remember the church as you make your list. Through the church, the instinctive longing of the human heart for God is met. By the church we are reminded that God is the giver of every good gift. By its voice we are invited to bring to God our sins to be forgiven, our mistakes to be overcome and our weakness to be made strong.

Having made our list, let us say: "Thank you, God for everything."

O OUR God we thank you and praise your glorious name.

I Chronicles 29:13 (LB)

TAKE STOCK OF YOUR BLESSINGS AND EXPRESS YOUR GRATITUDE

The search for reality in prayer concerns us all. The God to whom we pray has not left us in the dark as to how we may find response to our praying. We must come to God believing that He exists and that He is the rewarder of those who seek Him. We must come in an attitude of repentance and with a willingness to obey Him as He allows us to see His will.

There is a further bit of light along the way as we are told to come with a thankful heart. "Give thanks unto the Lord" is a constant theme of the Bible. Paul wrote the Philippian Christians: "Have no anxiety but in everything make your requests known to God in prayer and petition with thanksgiving."

Gratitude is in short supply both in our dealings with people and with God. Stop and think for a few minutes about yourself. Make a mental list of the things people have done for you in the past 24 hours. There are those who have loved you. This love has expressed itself in the comfort of your whole life. There are those who have served your needs in every area of your life: in business and in recreation. The list is endless. In the last 24 hours what evidence have you given that you are grateful?

How about your gratitude to God? All our blessings are gifts of His hand. Surely you don't think you deserve them because you are such an excellent person.

Then there is a world you live in, ready made to support your life. You and I provide no wonders of nature. Its seasons and its fruits are so provided that we can live in this universe. There is mental and physical health which enables you to be active and useful. There is the movement of God's spirit in your soul leading you in right paths, forgiving your sins and lending purpose to the labors of your hands.

The list could be endless. What evidence is there in your life that you are grateful to God?

Once Jesus healed ten lepers. Only one returned to give thanks. We are all too much haunted by Jesus' question: "But where are the nine?"

You will find that prayer offers rich returns in the answers God gives to you if you will begin by counting your blessings in gratitude before Him. A part of the answer will come as God leads you to give more evidence of gratitude to those who do so much for you. By thanking others, you will be thanking God in word and in deed.

NOVEMBER 27   CHART and compass come from thee, Jesus, Savior, pilot me.

Edward Hopper, Hymn

IN OUR TROUBLED WORLD THERE IS A BEACON TO GUIDE US

Before we move too far away from Thanksgiving, I want to write about it one more time. We are an ungrateful people. We have much in common with the prodigal son about whom Jesus told. Luke 15 records the story. The boy was an ungrateful wretch who got all he could from his father and went away to live as he pleased. He went through five stages: 1) rebellion; 2) prosperity; 3) indication of want; 4) life in a pig sty; 5) return home.

As a nation, we appear to be following the prodigal. There is rebellion against God. Not many take Him seriously. We enjoy and live by the bounties of nature, yet we have no sense of a personal God generously providing for His own. We smile indulgently when anyone suggests that our personal relation to God is the most important question of our lives. We do not really believe that sin, which separates us from God, is responsible for our ills. We try to find purpose and meaning for our lives everywhere but in doing God's will day by day.

We have been prosperous. No nation has ever been more so. We are presently nearing the third stage of the prodigal's career. We see signs of being in want. Despite our pride in our military strength, we do not know what to do with a small nation like Cuba. We are in want morally as the merchants of sex and alcohol dominate our lives. We are in want spiritually, having no great loyalty to hold our scattered affairs together.

Maybe we will come to ourselves and be saved before we experience life in the pig sty - maybe not. In any case, there are some things for which we can be grateful in a day like this.

We can be grateful that God is still there. Although we may rebel, God is faithful to us. He remains good even though we are bad. He is still pure in the face of immoral living. He is still on the throne. The faithfulness of the prodigal's father makes us sure of a happy ending for the story. Our God gives assurance, even in our troubled world, that evil will not finally win.

We can be grateful that God works in the hearts of men, even as in the heart of the prodigal. We can be grateful that when a man comes home to God, there is always forgiveness and new life. God is always moving to save His people and the world.

This is the message of the story of the prodigal. It is the heart of the Christian Gospel. In our bewildered day, we can be grateful for it.

NOVEMBER 28 "...LOVE your neighbor as much as you love yourself."

Matthew 23:29 (LB)

ON GETTING ALONG

Think how much better the world would be if everyone got along with everyone else. Families would thrive, most lawsuits would disappear, crime would lessen, tension between the races would ease, and wars would cease. The energies and money spent in not getting along would go into constructive channels. It is really impressive how much trouble and expense we go to get along with one another.

There is a secret to getting along with people. You must first learn to get along with God. Think seriously about this statement. It is not just a "religious statement." It is either true or false. If it is true, as I believe it to be, then it is basic in all efforts of people who try to get along together. If it is true, then we are created to prosper in life only in relation to God and all our secular efforts will fall short of any real success.

In Christ's Great Commandment lies the secret of getting along: the first of all commandments is, "Hear O Israel: the Lord our God is one Lord: and thou shall love the Lord thy God with all thy soul, and with all thy mind and with all thy strength. And the second is like, namely this, thou shalt love thy neighbor as thyself."

Getting along with God depends on starting at the cross where Christ died for our sins. Although completely unworthy, we enter into a proper relation with Him by the forgiveness of our sins. Then we are able to love our neighbor and to seek his and her welfare, not because that person is worthy of it, but in gratitude for what God has done for us in Christ. We love because He has first loved us.

In history, whenever the Christian faith has been influential in meeting the problems of life, it has been when the world has seen a company of people who love God and one another. We worry about the problems of our day, all of which are people problems. As a church we will have a part in changing things, to the extent that we demonstrate care for one another and for all people.

NOVEMBER 29   ALL things come to Thee, and of Thine own have we given thee.

I Chronicles 29:14 (KJ)

OUR TRUE INTEREST IS FOUND WHERE WE PUT OUR MONEY

Some people don't like it when the church talks about money, yet nearly half the Gospel touches on the subject of money. Most of us would rather not hear about money in the church because it forces us to face some facts that we would rather ignore. You can claim faith and develop a good religious vocabulary and feel rather smug, but you cannot evade the question of the money you know you should give to your church.

If the church talked more about money, we might not be so in love with material things. Most of us need to face God's demands in this regard.

Giving money in a sacrificial way is not natural. I believe you will find little evidence of generous giving outside the places where the Christian influences have been dominant.

Paul wrote a letter to the Christians at Corinth in which he called attention to the need to give money. He told them it was part of giving ourselves. Jesus said that our heart's interest follows our money. Where we put our money, we put ourselves. One reason we are so interested in material things is that we put most of our money into them. If you want to get more from your religious life, you will have to put more money into it. A sure way to religious revival in your own heart and in your church is through sacrificial giving.

It is by our giving that we prove the sincerity of our love. This is true in our relations with one another. It is easy to profess love. Some do it for their own purposes and fail to give of themselves or of their money. In such cases, love is not sincere. This same thing is true of the love we profess to God and His Church.

We need to give in gratitude to God for His gifts to us. Everything we are and have is a gift of God. More especially, His gift of Christ who came from glory to redeem us is His gift which makes it possible for us to love with peace and hope.

We cannot forgive our own sins, or carry our own guilt or bear our own burdens. We cannot provide our own eternal future. These needs God meets for us in the supreme gift of His Son. Gratitude prompts our giving of ourselves to Him. Our money is a basic part of ourselves.

If God seems far away and you seem to seek Him in vain, check your checkbook with your conscience. You may find your answer.

**NOVEMBER 30   A FORWARD heart shall depart from me:
I will not know a wicked person.**

Psalm 101:4 (KJ)

CHRISTIAN REASONS FOR PERSONAL MORALITY

I would like for you to imagine that the great majority of people suddenly became victims of a fever epidemic and their fever rose and stuck at 102 degrees. Nothing could be found to lower that fever or to break it. After a while, people got tired of being sick because they had a fever of 102. After all, nearly everyone had this same temperature. There was no particular pain, so imagine that people got together and decided they would merely change the normal degree of body temperature from 98.6 to 102 degrees. They then declared that everyone was normal and well and went about their way. Physicians told everybody that 102 degrees of fever was still dangerous, but people paid no attention. People died, but they still had the notion that the physicians were simply trying to keep them sick, so they continued to ignore them.

This is a parable of what is happening to us morally. There is a fever of personal immorality sweeping across our world and it affects almost everyone, therefore, we treat immorality as normal. We are judged to be rather narrow-minded if we seek to protect ourselves against immoral influences. Consequently, we have developed this fantastic idea of a freedom of the press that allows all manner of filth to be poured into a community. What is the reason? It is because people no longer care. We could stop it if enough of us cared. The courts have let the system break down, but this is because of popular pressure from the people. Law is nothing but the reflection of what the people want.

We have changed our standards. We have changed the level of the fever chart and we think, thereby, to have changed something. We have not changed anything any more than we can when we decide that 102 degrees is a normal temperature. Nevertheless, we have suddenly decided there are no ground rules. Let everybody do as he pleases. This has infected our children and it will infect our children's children if the present attitudes continue. Nothing is going to be done about it until somehow something happens to the fever.

This is not the first generation where the fever has been raised. It was there back in Paul's day. Paul faced a society where personal immorality was not only socially accepted, but was religiously promoted. The largest temple in Corinth was the Temple of Aphrodite and we are told there were some three hundred prostitutes who were the "priestesses" of that temple. That is the kind of thing that he had to combat.

Paul gave the Corinthians specific advice. The first was: "...all things are lawful for me, but all things are not expedient." Then Paul said: "I will not be brought under the control of anything such as this."

Then Paul says, everything has a purpose, but, in the matter of the human body, it is something from God. In the fourth place, Paul said that God raised up Christ and so will He raise us up. He says that although our bodies will be changed they will be the same body, as a particular flower grows from a particular seed. Immorality stains the very seed of Eternity. We just cannot afford to do that.

Finally, Paul reminds us that our bodies are members of Christ and that they are the Temple of the Holy Ghost. God, through His Holy Spirit, moves into human beings.

These six facets of our relationship to Christ demand personal purity. In this day when the fever of immorality rises all about us, it is time for the Christian community to make clear where it stands and why it stands there.

DECEMBER

DECEMBER 1
THE LORD your God is with you, he is mighty to save. He will take great delight in you, He will quiet you with his love, He will rejoice over you with singing.

Zephaniah 3:17 (NIV)

GETTING READY FOR CHRISTMAS

Thanksgiving is over and it is full speed ahead toward Christmas. "Full speed" is a good description for the rush of getting ready for the season. There is probably no cure for the headlong pace, but there should be some way to slow up.

There ought to be a few things that will leave us in better shape religiously, morally, financially and physically when the season is over. All too often we stagger to the end of the holidays with our conscience, credit and our stomachs over-extended.

Christmas can be such a wonderful time. It offers us a reminder of God's presence in our midst. It carries to the heart the fact of God's coming to earth. It is a simple story that all can understand - the story of shepherds and angels and the birth of a baby in the stable of an inn. The story gives assurance that God is with us in every experience.

Christmas draws the heart of people together in affection. It makes us a bit ashamed of the tensions that keep us apart, whether in our families or in our neighborhood or in our world.

As we prepare for the season, the hurt of the rush and extravagance can be eased if we make sure not to miss the treasure that lies at the heart of it.

1. Put worship into your preparations. Find time during the days to read the Christmas story in Matthew or Luke. You can read it over and over and find it new every time. Read it until you and your family are familiar with it. Take advantage of opportunities to worship with your family in church as the weeks go by. The beauty of holiness can become very real as you worship together.

2. Be sure your love is expressed to those who depend on you for love. The gift can be very simple if it carries an expression of real affection. Sometimes expensive gifts are used to cover a lack of love. If within the circle of your family or friends there is tension, go the second mile to do what you can to ease it.

3. Find someone outside the circle of your obligations who needs an expression of real affection. All the needy folks are not poor or destitute. Someone you know is lonely or hurt or sick or saddened and has no one who really cares.

4. Make a real effort to keep the expenses of the season within your ability to pay.

5. Determine to keep the pleasures of the season within the levels that your conscience before Christ can command.

These suggestions can help you have a happy Christmas and can help you make it happy for others.

Isaac Watts, Hymn

WHAT YOU BELIEVE DOES MATTER

Who believes in miracles? The man who believes or disbelieves in miracles believes or disbelieves because of his theology, not because of his science. We are victims of a day when it is popularly said: "It does not matter what you believe. What matters is what you do." The moral standards of our day are being sapped because we no longer believe.

All the knowledge in the world is not going to help you until you believe the right things about God. And when you believe certain things about God, then miracles fit in.

At the heart of the Christian gospel is the grand miracle. This miracle - if believed - furnishes the foundation for all others. The grand miracle is that God became man - the God, who in the beginning was the first fact, out of which every other fact flows.

This is the miracle that staggers the minds of men. It should stagger our minds, because it is utterly beyond the comprehension of a man to conceive how the God of the universe could funnel Himself down into one person. That is what our Christian gospel says. It says it directly. It says it without any effort to make it appear rational or reasonable. It just says it because it is true.

This fact becomes the great central fact of history. Everything else takes its meaning and purpose from this central miracle. All science, all literature, all art and all learning must get their beginning and meaning and ending and purpose from this one central event. Outside the framework of the incarnation (God becomes man), any effort to study this world or to study man finally reduces itself to either foolishness or deviltry.

481

In this Christmas season, God presses on us the miracles of His grace. Because of the miracles of the incarnation, heaven has touched earth with rest. Sins are forgiven, the individual finds his true value, and all human effort has meaning and purpose.

Here you and I discover the deep miracles that God cares for us and in His love He would have us love one another. Miracles always follow love.

DECEMBER 3   **GET rid of all bitterness, rage and anger ...forgiving each other, just as in Christ, God forgave you.**

Ephesians 4:31,32 (NIV)

WALLS THAT WE BUILD AROUND OURSELVES

We are familiar with today's statistics that try to tell the story of what is happening to people in our urban society. Rising rates of crime, delinquency, alcoholism, cruelty, mental illness, all tell a sad story. They tell the story of people walled off from one another, people lost in their bewildered souls. They tell the story of people lost to love and striking out in their lostness to hurt as they have been hurt.

Much is being done in response to these needs and all that effort to help is commendable. The discouraging thing about so many of our efforts is that they fail because they never break through the walls that lost people build around themselves.

Our efforts often fail because those of us who try to help are lost ourselves. We substitute programs for real concern. We put our faith in the things we do and we fail to understand that why we do them is the secret of our success or failure.

All of this leads up to an appeal for an understanding of the

482

personal message: "God loves you." The message is so urgent that God came in human form to break down that wall you have built around yourself. In the mystery of His death, He took our sins upon Himself that we might be forgiven by the God who loves us.

It is only those who have been captured by the love of God who can convey this love to others, so that they may also be rescued from their lostness. It is the love of God that breaks through the walls which people build around themselves.

It is dangerous to deal with people in terms of techniques and methods alone, regardless of their correctness or efficiency. People quickly sense what is in the heart of those who serve them in their need. Loveless service breeds resentment. Love can be kept alive only by keeping the heart open toward God in faith and in commitment. We love because He first loved us.

By love, walls go down and lost people are saved. This is at the heart of what Christmas is all about.

DECEMBER 4 ...I CONSIDER everything a loss compared to the surpassing greatness of knowing Christ Jesus my Lord...

Philemon 3:8 (NIV)

WHOSE 'IMAGE'? GOD'S OR MAN'S?

Christmas speaks to our most pressing question: What is man? In our day of man's greatest advances, the individual finds himself disregarded. Automation brings the fear that a man is only a temporary asset waiting for a cheaper mechanical replacement. Art represents man as an ill-defined blob. Literature and the theater present man as a pawn of his greed and his passions. Psychology presents man as a poorly balanced set of drives and impulses. Science speaks of man as a pointless mass of cells.

When our self-image becomes blurred, our lives become pointless. We learn the truth of Christ's words: "A man's life consists not in the abundance of things which he possesses."

The message of Christmas comes to us in our confusion. Christ said: "I came to seek and to save the lost." Most of us have the feeling that we have lost the way that leads to abundant life.

Christ let men see that they were children of God, made in His image. He opened the way by which each one can live in this relationship. He challenged all who would debase man.

If you let this message of Christmas drop out of your life, your life loses its meaning and society will become a jungle where only the strongest survive. Only as your life and mine have eternal meaning can they have meaning for anyone. The Christmas message came through a peasant couple, lodged in a stable, visited by humble shepherds and surrounded by angels so that the lowliest people may understand that they are of infinite value to God.

Christmas is the divine warning that if man's so called progress fails to treat him as the loved of God, it can lead only to destruction.

DECEMBER 5   **GOD always fills in all hearts all the room which is left Him there.**
F. W. Faber

...LET every heart prepare Him room, and heav'n and nature sing...
Isaac Watts, Hymn

THE VOICE THAT PREPARED THE WAY

On Christmas we remember the birth of Jesus Christ. God invaded our planet. God in Christ comes to deal directly with people personally and Christmas finds its true meaning when Christ is born into our hearts. At Christmas we hear the "voice of one crying in the wilderness, prepare ye the way of the Lord, make his path straight."

The voice of John the Baptist can prepare our hearts for the entrance of Christ. That voice was so important that people came from everywhere to hear him. It was so penetrating that his hearers finally killed him to get rid of his voice, but the voice has never been stilled. He spoke to the consciences of men and this prepared the way for the Christ. He still answers our question: What shall I do?

He pointed to men whose lives were obsessed with making money and warned them to take no more than was rightfully theirs. He answered those in authority, and he spoke to their consciences about doing violence to those in their power, about accusing men falsely or trying to increase their incomes by dishonest means.

If you would prepare your heart for the entrance of Christ, John would say: Don't be selfish, don't be greedy and don't be cruel. If you take seriously what the voice says in your own conscience you will begin to be ready for a Savior.

As Christ came when John had made ready a people prepared for Him, so He still comes. He meets us in our efforts to overcome selfishness and greed and cruelty, efforts that quickly convince us that it is impossible to succeed by our own efforts.

The tidings of the great joy are the good news: "Unto you a Savior is born." It is a personal word of hope to all who have found how impossible it is to be what we ought to be and to do what we ought to do.

We are prepared by the voice that convinces us of our need. We are saved by the Christ who meets that need with forgiveness and with grace.

...LOVE one another. As I have loved you so you must love one another.

John 13:34 (NIV)

AT CHRISTMAS, SHOW AFFECTION

The fact that so many people dread to see Christmas coming is a sign of great sickness among us. It means there is something wrong with our way of doing things. If we cannot enjoy Christmas it is likely we can't enjoy anything.

Christmas ought to be the high point in our year. Do you remember when you felt sad because next Christmas was a whole year away? Now many are grateful that there are 12 months before we have to go through another one.

Christmas has become a burden and has lost its thrill for many because simple and plain affection has been crowded out of its heart. The fires of affection are the only things that can warm the hearts of human beings. Nothing is really worthwhile without love and love grows not without evidences of affection.

It is at Christmas that the fires of affection are kindled. We look to Christmas to set glowing again fires that have burned low. When this fails to happen, we come to dread Christmas because we fail to give or receive that which we need and long for most.

The Christmas memories that mean most to us are those that cluster around simple evidences of affection. There are memories of worship when God's love seemed very near as we bowed before the story of the Christ child. In the glow of candles and the music of the carols and the words of Scripture, we felt the affection of God.

There are memories of home at Christmas. There was the baking of the fruitcakes early that they might be ready for Christmas; the making of gifts that loving hands might witness to loving hearts. There were plans to have all the family together. There were the decorations and the tree and the stockings to be hung.

As affection took over the leading role, there was a relaxing of the routine of living. There was the singing of the carols and the reading of Luke's Christmas story. God's love for us and our love for God and for one another got all mixed up. The result was a wonderful Christmas.

The pace of life has changed, but people are the same and the need of the affection of God and of one another is the same. Christmas can be more nearly the Christmas of happy memories if we will try harder to make it so. It will mean putting the things of affection in the center of all you do; the things of God's love for you and of your love for others.

By so doing you can make the fires of affection burn more brightly in yourself and in others. You will also build memories for children which will warm their hearts all their lives and which will keep their lives guided by the Star of Bethlehem.

DECEMBER 7   **NOW this is the way to have eternal life: that they may know you, the only true God, and Jesus Christ, whom you have sent**

                                       John 17:3 (NIV)

REMEMBER WHO CHRIST WAS AS YOU OBSERVE CHRISTMAS

One wonders if we are not forgetting what the meaning of Christmas really is. Everywhere people are getting ready for the season that is supposed to be the season when we celebrate Christ's birthday. It is hard to believe we are making any real effort to put Him in the center of it all.

We celebrate people's birthdays because of who they are and what they mean to us. Maybe it will help if we remind ourselves who Christ is and what He means to us.

Jesus Christ was born in Bethlehem, grew up in Nazareth and lived and taught in Palestine. He was executed in Jerusalem, but was raised from the dead by the power of God. He reigns in glory and will return one day to judge the world.

In Revelation, John describes Him for us in a clear fashion. He is the faithful witness of God, showing us by His life what God is like. He is the first person born who brought hope to all who face death. He is the Prince of Peace. He is our confidence that in all the confusion of world politics, there runs the golden thread of God's purpose and power to work His will.

This Christ has loved us and continues to love us. The power at the heart of the universe is love. He has washed us from our sins in His own blood. Because He died, we find peace with God in the forgiveness of our sins. In addition, He has made us to be kings and priests unto the Father.

This is the Christ whose birthday is the occasion for Christmas. Certainly those of us who call ourselves Christians will want to make our celebration of the season one that will honor Him. We try to do this for our friends and family. We would not do less for Him who came to redeem our world. Christ has done so much for our world that even those who do not accept Him as Savior will want to pause to do Him honor.

In this season, spend some time remembering who He is and what He has done for you and for your family and for your world. Make sure your observance of the season is such that it will make Him glad. It may force some changes in your plans, but it will be worth it to you and your loved ones and to your world.

488

DECEMBER 8   O COME let us adore Him, Christ the Lord.

Latin Hymn

EARLY PREPARATION ENHANCES THE SEASON

Folks are getting ready for Christmas. You can feel it in the air. You can see it everywhere you go. The keeping of Christmas has come to be a burden to many people. It lays heavy demands on people who work in stores, and for that matter, on lots of people who buy in stores.

No one is going to change the present way of celebrating Christmas by writing or talking about it. Sooner or later, circumstances will do that. In the meantime, Christmas can mean more to us if we will prepare early for it, not only by buying and selling early, but also by reminding ourselves what it means.

If a man from Mars were to land in town and spend the day mingling with the crowds, he would have a hard time figuring out what it is all about. He might decide we are observing the birthday of Santa Claus by giving one another presents. He would learn that it is a "holiday season," at least for those in our schools. If he got acquainted with any group he would find that he was invited to stay over for a round of parties. Here and there, our man from Mars would run across unusual concern for the less fortunate. He would be hard pressed to discover the real meaning of it all.

It can help us all to remind ourselves of what Christmas really means. It is the season when we remember that God has landed on this planet. It becomes a little more real to us at Christmas that "God so loved the world that He gave His only begotten Son that whosoever believeth on Him should not perish but should have everlasting life." We don't talk about it much, but deep within us we need saving and we need everlasting life and Christmas speaks of this need.

God's love breaks through to us at Christmas. Our love for one another has a chance to express itself. In spite of all the pressures of Christmas, it is a gracious season because the eternal things of love touch our lives. We are more nearly human beings as we prepare tenderly for little children and as we see other people as those for whom we care.

We can have a good Christmas if we will prepare our hearts as well as our homes by keeping them open to God's coming. At Christmas, we sense that eternity has to do with time; that Heaven has a word for earth. He comes to share our joys, to forgive our sins, to comfort our sorrows.

It is a time when tired men and a tired world hear the gracious words, "For unto you a Savior is born which is Christ the Lord."

DECEMBER 9   THE WORD became flesh and lived for a while among us.

John 1:14 (NIV)

CHRISTMAS IS PACKED WITH GOOD NEWS

Everyone seems to be getting ready for Christmas. Let me suggest that we spend more time in turning our hearts to hear angels' voices. The eternal world has a message for us, a message of "glad tidings of great joy which shall be to all the people."

We can do with some glad tidings. So many people seem buried in problems, theirs and those of the world. There is lots of news and most of it is bad. It is easy to view all we see with alarm. If there is to be any good news, it must come from Heaven since the world is not able to supply it. The miracle of Christmas is that personal word has come from Heaven. God has spoken and His word is good news. This good news is for the fearful and confused, the burdened and sad, the lonely and troubled. It is for a world gripped by evil.

It is good news that God has come into our world. Mary was

promised a Son whose name should be "Emmanuel" which means "God with us." God is personally involved in all the confusion of our world and in every trouble of every person. God is neither an absent deity nor an impersonal "first cause." He is the God and Father of our Lord, Jesus Christ. He has not forgotten us. It is good news to know that in the midst of our disordered world, in the midst of all our personal difficulties, God is with us.

The name of Mary's son was to be Jesus "for He shall save his people from their sins." Deep within us, most of us know our troubles are caused by our sins. We are guilty and know it. When we try to save ourselves or to make a better world, it always ends in defeat. Evil is stronger than we are. Our sins hold us in a grip we cannot break. It is good news indeed that in Christ, God has come to forgive our sins and to make us new creatures in which the power of sin is broken.

It is good news to have the assurance of the Christmas message. He who came from Glory made it plain that Heaven is our home. We are made for Heaven and our spirits respond to angels' voices. We find joy even in our troubles in the assurance that He has prepared a place for us and will receive us unto Himself.

As you move toward Christmas, listen for angels' voices. Whatever your circumstances, they will bring you "glad tidings of great joy."

DECEMBER 10   IN THEE there is gladness...

Johann Linderman, Hymn

CHRISTMAS CUSTOMS LINK THE CENTURIES

Here are bits of information about some of our Christmas customs. There are at least two traditions as to how Christ's birthday came to b be celebrated on December 25. One is that in 125 A.D. Bishop Theophilus of Caesaria decreed that it was a proper date. Another tradition is that in the middle of the fourth century the Bishop of Jerusalem wrote the Bishop of Rome asking him to determine the date. He wrote back that investigation showed it to be December 25.

The first Christmas carol is the song of the angels. In the early centuries of the church's life, hymns were sung which had to do with Christ's birth. In the western world, the earliest recorded carol was written by King Canute in 1017 A.D. The carols were originally sung while dancing. The first book of carols appeared in 1517 A.D. Carols appear in all countries and the geography of each puts its stamp on the way in which the Christmas story is presented.

The manger scene is popular. It came into use under the influence of Francis of Assisi. He used it at Christmas in 1223 A.D. He lived in a cave above the town of Grecio, Italy. He placed a life-size image of the Christ child in a manager. A wealthy noblemen provided a donkey and an ox. Neighbors scattered straw on the floor. At night candles lighted the scene. Crowds were attracted and this simple act grew into a worldwide custom.

Santa Claus is thought to have grown out of the stories of St. Nicholas. Nicholas was Bishop of Myra in Lycia, Asia Minor, in the fourth century. Unexpected gifts came from unknown sources to people in need. It was thought those gifts were from Nicholas. The legend grew that he went around on December 6 on a white horse, leaving his gifts door to door. He left nice gifts for good children and switches for bad ones. St. Nicholas became the favorite of children in Holland and was brought to American by early Dutch settlers.

Martin Luther, the German reformer, is given credit for making popular the use of the Christmas tree in the early part of the 16th century. He brought an evergreen into his home as part of his Christmas celebration. He decorated it with candles to remind his household of the stars which shone in the sky over the stable where Christ was born.

Christmas cards are fairly recent in origin. The first cards offered for sale were printed in London in 1846. They were hand colored and were ordered and sold by Sir Henry Cole in his art shop.

So it is today that we join hands with all the centuries as we celebrate the "glad tidings which shall be to all people."

492

DECEMBER 11 ...come ye and let us walk in the light of the Lord.

Isaiah 2:5 (KJ)

BEST OF ALL GIFTS: A HAPPY MARRIAGE

If you are happily married, you are fortunate indeed because you have life's most precious gift. Cherish it. If you are unhappily married, this Christmas is a good time to remedy the situation. So many couples get divorces and others just put up with bad situations. This is a tragedy and where there are children, the tragedy is complete.

No one can deal with life as a minister does without knowing that there seems to be no solution for some situations. However, the number of these is small. Most couples don't find happiness together because they don't want to do the things necessary for it. Having promised love and fidelity "till death do us part," they just run out on their word. Men and women forget that once they are married, they are obligated to find happiness in and with one another. Where there are children, a couple has an added obligation.

If your home is failing to provide the wonderful blessing that marriage can bring, I would suggest that you give one another the greatest Christmas present in the world - love.

1. You will have to make up your minds to do it. Most of the reasons for divorce are excuses. Most of the marital unhappiness is caused by things that can be remedied if you want to.

2. Some evening after the house is quiet, go upstairs and together kneel down by the side of the bed and confess your sins to God. Confess yours, not your partner's. Ask God to forgive your trespasses as you forgive the one who has trespassed against you. Be honest with yourself before God. Be willing to make the first move toward understanding.

3. Accept God's forgiveness.

4. Ask God to help you love one another. "Beloved, if God so loved us we ought to love one another."

5. After your prayer, if you have anything to say to one another, say it. If not, don't.

6. Repeat this each evening.

7. On Sunday, go to church together. Pray, sing, listen. Go and be willing for God to work in your lives. Don't force anything. Just go with an open heart and mind. Go each Sunday. Find a church that meets your need. Join it.

These steps won't solve all your problems, but they will connect your lives with God, the source of love. Without this, you can solve all your problems and still be no closer together. This Christmas, receive God's love in His Son and share this love with one another. No child will thrill to the Christmas season as you will in the glow of love given and received.

DECEMBER 12   TELL me the story of Jesus, write on my heart every word; Tell me the story most precious sweetest that ever was heard.

Fanny J. Crosby, Hymn

THE STORY OF CHRISTMAS HAD GREAT AUTHORS

People all around the world will read, hear, repeat and love the Christmas story. Matthew tells of the angel's announcement to Joseph and of the visit of the wise men. Luke records the wonderful events surrounding the birth of John the Baptist, the visit of the angel Gabriel to Mary, her visit to Elizabeth and her song of praise.

Luke is the author who wrote down the tender story of the birth of Jesus. He preserved for us the song of the angels and allows us to go

494

with the shepherds to the crib of Jesus. Matthew also wrote an inspired account of our Lord's birth.

Before Matthew became a follower of Jesus he was a publican. This was a term of reproach. Publicans were usually Jewish collectors of Roman taxes. They ordinarily demanded more than was thought to be just and were despised. They were usually cut off from their own people and Jesus was severely criticized for including such a man among His disciples. It has always been hard for people to understand that folk like Matthew were the ones Jesus came to claim as His own.

Luke was a physician. He was a Greek, born - according to ancient historians Eusebius and Josephus - in Antioch of Syria. He is mentioned only three times in the New Testament. In Colossians 4:14 he is called "the beloved physician." Paul writes Timothy from prison in Rome (II Timothy 4:11): "Only Luke is with me." In Philemon 24 he is called "fellow laborer" with Paul. He went with Paul into Europe and probably was in Philippi for some seven years serving with the church there. After Paul's arrest in Jerusalem, he remained with Paul until his death in Rome some years later. Before being taken to Rome, Paul was in prison two years in Caesarea. Luke probably spent much of this time in securing information for his Gospel. Luke's care of Paul as a physician did much to make possible Paul's great work.

These two men gave to us some of the most loved words of the human language. We are indebted to this publican and this physician whom God so richly used.

DECEMBER 13   LORD, make me an instrument of Your peace.

St. Francis of Assisi

LET'S REMEMBER ITS DEEPEST MEANING

We are coming into the celebration of Christmas. It is one of those seasons when the Spirit of God touches the spirit of man. That which is divine in man comes nearest the surface. The commercialism and the dissipation have not buried the real nature of the season.

We celebrate the birth of Jesus Christ who is our Lord and Savoir. In the coming of Christ, God entered this world of ours in human form. Divine Love became Incarnate. It is a thing of great mystery. It is something that defies the human mind to describe, much less to explain. The human heart can only bow in reverence and in gratitude.

This is made more evident if we remind ourselves of the background of the coming of Christ into the world. It was something planned in the mind of God before the foundation of the world. The One who came had been with God and was God when creation began. John's Gospel begins by drawing back the very curtains of eternity and by introducing us to the glory that Christ had before the world came into being.

John makes bold to declare that "all things were made by him." He was the active agent of creation. His hand formed the space and the planets we now set out to explore. The orderliness of God is written into nature by His hand. He formed us and set within man the divine light to guide him all the days of his life.

The world's tragedy flows from the fact that He came into the world that was made by Him and the world knew Him not. He came into His own and they did not receive Him. Our hope lies in the fact that to those who do receive Him He gives the power to become the sons of God. By Him we are restored to the relationship to God for which we were made. This is the Word of God which was made flesh and dwelt among men. He lives today. In reverence, may we behold His glory in this Christmas season.

It is only as we behold his glory that we can be lifted out of our fears. Only as we behold his glory can we be freed from the shackles of this world. Only so can we feel the surge of the world of the Spirit as it flows about our world. Here is our assurance that God is very near to our troubled hearts and to our disturbed world. God was in Christ, reconciling the world to Himself. He set us a light, which no darkness can put out.

In all our Christmas celebrations, let us remember with reverence and with gratitude that its deepest meaning is Emmanuel – "God

With Us."

DECEMBER 14   COMMIT thy works unto the Lord.

Proverbs 16:3 (KJ)

CHRISTMAS PREPARATIONS CAN BE A CHORE OR A JOY

Some of us never enjoy today because we are so busy getting ready for tomorrow. This is what happens to so many people at Christmas. Getting ready for the holy day is such a burden that Christmas Day is an anticlimax. The season has become so filled with obligations until there is neither time nor energy to enjoy its true meaning and its precious privileges. We know Christmas represents the birth of Christ, but we never stop to think that its real meaning is Christ is also born anew in us.

It brings us the privilege of renewing our ties of affection with those we love, but if we wear ourselves out with preparations and parties, we fail to enjoy the renewal of love as we should. Christmas can be a gracious occasion and preparation for it can be a joy. All the commercialization and all the dissipation that go with Christmas can't ruin your celebration of the season unless you let it.

You can make Christmas what you want it to be. The whole point is the mastery of your time.

1. In the first place, you will have to be honest enough about it to give your time to the things that really matter. If you prefer to fill the time with a round of parties, don't complain if the joy of family life suffers. You and I can't have it both ways.

2. These joys come as you find time to think about the Christmas story. Read and reread the accounts in Matthew and Luke and John's first 14 verses. Be sure and go to church faithfully during these days.

3. As you send your Christmas cards take time enough to think about each one as you prepare it for mailing. Send your love with each card. It will help you and it will help each one who receives your card.

4. As you buy and wrap your gifts, let your affections select each gift and guide each wrapping. As you deal with each gift, remember with gratitude and love the person or persons who will receive it.

In your Christmas season, take time to lead the children of your circle into a real understanding of God's love given to us in Christ's birth. Take time to create for your children the traditions that will live in their memories. In so doing, your own heart will be touched.

Center your Christmas season in the church and in the home and in those whose circumstances make Christmas a difficult time. I know that these suggestions are easier to make than to carry out. They do, however, point in a direction that can make the season a happy one. We need so badly the steadying hand of God on our lives. Christmas is our assurance that God is present to help. The decision is ours.

DECEMBER 15   LOOK now! for glad and golden hours come swiftly on the wing....

Edmund H. Sears, Hymn

THERE ARE ABUNDANT REASONS TO BE GRATEFUL
FOR CHRISTMAS

I am grateful for Christmas. It gives a welcome break from the tensions of the day - from our preoccupation with business conflicts and conferences and from the endless process of trying to entertain ourselves. I am grateful for Christmas because it speaks to the divine in all of us. We are created in God's image and however far we have strayed from it, there is something that responds to the touch of God in our lives.

We are still sensitive to the rustle of angel's wings. Our hearts are all out of tune with the infinite, but the songs of angels still find a response in our tangled heartstrings. Many times it seems that all that matters to us is what we can physically enjoy or what we can figure out with our minds, but at Christmas we realize that these things are a long way from the truth.

I am grateful for Christmas because it gives the world of the spirit a chance to be heard, and in the hearing, our hearts are warmed. For a brief time at least, it makes sense deep within as we talk of God's coming to the earth in human form. We sense the reality of Heaven about us as angel visitors touch human lives and as the skies are broken through by voices from God's own world.

Our hearts respond with awe and reverence as we stand with Zacharias beside the altar of incense and hear the words of the angel: "I am Gabriel that stands in the presence of God." We hear with wonder that 'the angel Gabriel was sent from God into a city of Galilee named Nazareth, to a woman espoused to a man named Joseph.' We instinctively join in the chorus of the heavenly host: "Glory to God in the highest, and on earth peace, good will toward men."

I am grateful for Christmas because the self-giving of God makes selfish lives look shoddy in the heavenly light. For a moment, we believe as little children and love as we ought to love. The unquestioning faith and hope and love of little children become the most real things on earth. The clutch of a small hand and the joy in a small face becomes our greatest thrill. The light of love and the pressure of the hand of affection become our greatest possessions. We rejoice in God's promise to our world of His forgiveness for our sin, of His victory over evil, of His peace in all our conflicts.

At Christmas we know the glory of God in the face of Jesus Christ. Because we do, our earthly lives never quite escape the heavenly light that plays on them.

Thanks be to God.

DECEMBER 16   GOOD henceforth from heav'n to men, begin and never cease....

Nahum Tate, Hymn

A LIGHT IS SHINING FOR THE TROUBLED

I am sure that God will rejoice with all who are happy when this Christmas day arrives. Where there is good health, an unbroken family circle, the glee of little children, abundant food and shelter, then surely the heart of God is glad. But happy people are not the ones to whom Christ chiefly came with his glad tidings of great joy.

We often think of those who are free from trouble as the ones who are having a good Christmas. We feel that Christmas is ruined if there is misfortune during the season, but the truth of it is that it is on those who walk in darkness that the light hath shined upon. Jesus came to preach the good news to the poor, to heal the brokenhearted, to bring deliverance to the captives and to set the bruised at liberty. It was to the sick and the sorrowing, to the outcast and the lonely, that he came bringing new life and great joy. He came to seek and to save the lost.

If today you walk through the valley of the shadow of death, Christmas is especially for you if you will let Christ be born anew in your heart. He comes with His assurance of eternal life for your lost loved ones and with His promise to you, "My peace I give unto you."

If today you have a feeling of "aloneness" in the midst of the Christmas gaiety, Christmas is especially for you with the promise of the Christ, "Lo, I am with you always."

If on this Christmas day you are burdened with a deep sense of guilt for deep wrongs you have done yourself or someone else, Christmas is for you more than anyone else. If you will let Christ, into your heart, He will come with pardon and release and send you out with His gracious words, "Go in peace, thy sins are forgiven."

If your burden seems too heavy and you are weary in body and in mind from the load you carry Christ seeks to come into your life with the promise, "I will give you rest."

If you are discouraged over the turmoil and strife, the tensions and the conflicts of your heart, your nation and your world, Christ would remind you that it is exactly for the purpose of saving such a world that He came at Christmas. It was the promise of a better world that lay in the angel's song: "Glory to God in the Highest and on earth peace, good will toward men."

He would invite you to share His crusade for the Kingdom of God by taking your cross and following Him. He would invite you to join those who have found that "this is the victory that overcometh the world, even our faith."

DECEMBER 17   WAIT on God 'til you know you have met Him; prayer will then become so different.

Murray

IN PRAYER WE CAN ASK FOR ANYTHING

As we come to pray along the pathways marked out by God, He bids us come as those who are grateful and who approach Him in reverence and in sorrow for our sins. He reveals it to us. If we come in this way, we can ask for whatever is in our hearts. There are many who seem to believe that it is a low form of prayer to ask for what we need. The New Testament does not support this view. People came to Jesus with all sorts of requests and He never turned them aside as untrustworthy.

We are invited to come as little children. We are told that our prayers are to include everything. It is at the point of our need that we pray best. The best answer may turn out to be a closer walk with God but that does not make our request for help any less acceptable to God.

We do bad things and need forgiveness; we get sick and need healing; we get hungry and need food. We become lonely and need friends, afraid and need assurance. We love our family and friends. When they are in trouble our hearts cry out for a divine hand to help. We face the evils in our world and in our own hearts and we need a Redeemer.

For all these needs we pray. It is through the glory of our faith that God invites us to come boldly into the throne of grace to find help in our time of need. Nothing is too small or too great.

Strangely enough, we are invited by God to keep on asking. Deep within us we want to continue praying until we get an answer. Some people say that we should not beg God for what we want. He knows our need before we ask. He does, but for some reason we are urged to urge our needs upon Him.

Jesus told two stories that carry this message. One was of a man who had midnight guests for whom he had no food. He went next door and awakened his neighbor who refused to come down. The man hammered on the door until the neighbor came down and gave him what he needed.

The other story was of a judge who finally gave a woman justice because she worried him until he did. Jesus noted that if folks who don't care for you will respond to steady urging, you can expect far more from God who loves you.

If we pray in the right spirit and with persistence let our requests be known, God will hear and answer. He will say "Yes" or "No" or "Wait." Most of all, He will give the assurance of His presence which is the most satisfying answer we can receive.

DECEMBER 18   CARRY each other's burdens, and in this Way you will fulfill the law of Christ.

Galatians 6: 2 (NIV)

LIFE TAKES ON A SPECIAL MEANING AT CHRISTMAS

It is now full speed ahead toward Christmas. The things you see and hear most will have to do with shopping for gifts and with social occasions. Too much money and too much energy will be spent in these things. Many will come out of the season glad it is over and exhausted in body and in pocketbook. The receipts will be added up, and it will probably be called the best Christmas ever. You and I will share to some extent in all of this.

However, I am glad Christmas is coming. In the Christmas season, the things we live by find expression as at no other time. This old world hears the account of God's love for His people. Believers and unbelievers are stirred by the story of God entering our world as a baby for the purpose of saving sinners. It is a time when the depths of our affection find a way to surface. The thrill of a young couple who watch their first child, now old enough for his or her first Christmas; the renewing of love; the homes which have stood the test of the years; the coming home of boys and girls who have been away to school; the renewing of ties with family and friends and the chance to express the affection you feel for those who work with you - these are things we live by which come to the surface at Christmas.

At an even deeper level, the Christmas message of God's love answers the longing of the heart for those who are far away and can't come home and for those whom we have loved and whom God has received unto Himself. In the love of God given in Christ, we still have a fellowship with absent ones.

In the days ahead, think on these things. Take time for the things we live by and you will find that it will be for you and for yours a time of great joy because unto us a Savior is born.

DECEMBER 19   HOW beautiful a day can be when
               kindness touches it.

                                    Elliston

WAYS TO CELEBRATE CHRIST'S BIRTHDAY

There is a multitude of people who would answer correctly the question: "Whose birthday do we celebrate at Christmas?" But if a visitor from Mars were to walk our streets and visit our homes during the season, he would be hard pressed to answer the question based on his observations.

I asked some small children what they did to celebrate a person's birthday. One child immediately answered: "You try to make him happy." When the birthday of a family member comes around, we try to set aside the day - or part of the day - to make that one remember it as a happy day. We do some things the person wants to do. We give gifts that we think he would like to have and we treat him as he would like to be treated. We make a special effort to show our love and gratitude.

It will make Christmas a much happier occasion if we will remember that it is Christ's birthday. Surely no one would deprive any child of the thrill of Christmas with its toys and its fun, but the thrill can be made greater if children are led to understand what is behind it all. Surely it is part of Christmas to gather family and friends and to enjoy all that such gatherings can bring. These gatherings would be different if more of us really remembered whose birthday it is we celebrate and, in the end, the pleasure would be greater.

At Christmas we celebrate the central fact of human history: the coming of God into our world in human form; the Word made flesh. It is the Lord's birthday; therefore, is it not a time when we should try to make Him happy?

504

1. We will make Christ and ourselves happy as we show our love for Him by our worship. This is a season for the expression of our gratitude for God's gift of Himself in Christ.

2. Then we will want to do something for Christ. He said, "Inasmuch as ye have done it unto one of the least of these, my brethren, ye have done it unto me." We will make His heart glad if we make someone happy by our kindness who might otherwise be neglected. This will help us change the greeting of Christmas from "What did you get?" to "What did you give?"

On Christ's birthday, give Him your heart's devotion and some real evidence of your concern for those who need you. You will be happier at Christmas if you do.

DECEMBER 20 **LOVE is patient, love is kind. It does not envy, it does not boast, it is not proud. Love never fails.**

I Corinthians 13:4,8 (NIV)

WAYS TO EXPRESS CHRISTMAS LOVE

The steady theme of the Christmas story and of the Christmas season is love. It is the story of God's love for each of us and of the love He would have us show to one another. We can love only as we are loved. We love because He has first loved us. The story of Christmas holds us in its spell because it tells us over and over that God so loved the world that He gave His Son to save us.

The real happiness of the season comes as we pass on to others the love we have received from God. Love is very personal. You receive it from a person and you give it person to person. No one will seriously doubt that our happiness depends on receiving and giving love. The true joy of Christmas will come to those who make it a time of true affection.

1. It is a time to make sure that any tensions in the family circle are dissolved by love. Unless we receive and give love at home, it will not be given anywhere. It is sadly true that many family groups are divided by barriers that make them sources of misery rather than of happiness. Make sure you do what you can to dissolve the barriers in your family by the expression of your love.

2. Our friends need the reassurance of our friendship. In the rush of daily living, we just don't get around to keeping these ties strong. The pressures of "getting ready for Christmas" can make it impossible to strengthen these ties unless we are careful. You will find joy in the season as you renew the expressions of affection with friends in these days.

3. One of the most gracious messages of the Christmas season is: "Love your enemies." There are so many of us seeking our own things instead of the things of others. We are divided among ourselves in many ways. This is a time to increase our joy by doing what we can to remove barriers of unfriendliness. It will be a better Christmas if you will be sure there is an honest effort on your part to show good will to any person or group from whom you are separated by feelings of enmity.

4. There is a source of real happiness in making happier someone who is deprived of the normal blessings of life. Within reach of each of us there are those for whom we can make life brighter by a personal gesture of concern. It may be a shut-in or a sick person or one who is depressed by poverty. In any case, it will be someone who needs you.

DECEMBER 21   WHAT do we live for, if it is not to make life less difficult for each other.

Eliot

A FEW WORDS OF APPROVAL BUILD OUR SELF-CONFIDENCE

The tap dancing "commencement" was over. The children were coming out of the theater with their mothers. There was one little girl whose appearance did not lead one to suspect that she was the star of the show. There was apparently some kind of physical difficulty which this little one suffered. In a clear voice, she questioned her mother: "Did I do good, Mommy?"

With a bright smile the mother answered instantly: "You were wonderful, darling." A look of contentment settled over the little face and she was one step nearer victory in her small battle for self-confidence and self-respect.

Where little children and men and women do their best, whether with two talents or ten, their success hangs on the encouragement of affection. Love never compares with perfection. Love is not blocked by failure. Love sees the striving of the heart and the intent of the act. Love surrounds our best efforts, regardless of results, with "You were wonderful, darling."

Jesus told a story of two men who were given responsibility and who did their best, "Well done," He said. He found a woman who wanted to begin again after years of sin and He said, "Neither do I condemn thee." She went away in God's peace.

Whatever authority exists, no one denies the right of correction, but where authority exists, love must also be present to encourage others if our frail human lives are to have strength to go on.

Barnabas was known as the "Son of Encouragement." Humanly speaking, he saved Paul and John Mark for the preaching of the

Gospel by his encouragement of them at critical moments in their lives.

In this Christmas season, take note of people who really are trying. You will come into contact with courageous souls laboring under handicaps. Often the results of their efforts are not perfect, but you will find that the people themselves are wonderful. Tell them so.

Critics there are in abundance. Most of us are conscious of our shortcomings and failures. The critic doesn't help much. How it does lift the spirit to have someone see through the poor result to the sincere effort behind it! A word of approval drives depression away. It keeps us hoping. It makes life worth living.

Remember that for everyone there is the necessity of encouragement. Surely the art of encouragement is one of the finest fruits of the Christian faith. Surely there are no sweeter words, when you have really tried, than "You were wonderful, darling."

This is at least a part of what Jesus meant when He said, "Thou shalt love thy neighbor as thyself."

DECEMBER 22   FOR THE joy of human love, Brother, sister, parent, child....

Folliott S. Pierpont, Hymn

AT CHRISTMASTIME, WE THINK OF HOME

"Going home for Christmas" is close to the heart of what the season really means. It is a time when we want to gather the scatteredness of our lives and the loneliness of our hearts before the warm glow of the family fireside. It is a sure instinct of the human heart that joins our desire to be home for Christmas with our celebration of Jesus' birth; God's love, given fully in Christ, is the source of our love one for another. "We love because He first loved us." This love finds its sweetest expression in the family circle. So, at Christmas, we want to be at home where love dwells.

It is the time when the family gathers and the ties of affection are renewed. How much to be pitied are those families where the celebration of Christmas fails to destroy the barriers which break the flow of love among members of the family.

There are those family circles that have been broken by death. Christmas comes with bittersweet memories, yet the very memories make the season a kind of reunion. The absent one seems nearer. The familiar things prepared by the one no longer present are used again and the hurt of it brings its own healing. In the fellowship of faith, the family circle seems less broken at Christmas.

There are those who have no home of their own. Perhaps for these, memory crowds more closely. Every reminder of home brings to mind days when Christmas meant a home that no longer exists. At Christmas, the lonely need the message of God's love, the message given in Christ. So the special need is met by the special season. The open door out of the confines of loneliness is that of sharing the happiness of others and of bringing a bit of joy to someone who also needs a helping hand. The giving of self brings the reward of Him who gave Himself.

Most of all, the message of Christmas is to those lost to love by their own choice. To them, it is God's invitation to come home and to dwell again in the family of God and in the love of others. If some evil has cut you off from God and man or if you have cut yourself off by the pursuit of money and pleasure or if cynicism has frozen your soul, then God invites you to join those going home for Christmas. You will find the forgiving welcome of God and the love of those among whom you dwell.

May I take this opportunity to wish any who reads this an experience of real joy in these days. May the days ahead find the door fully opened into a happier and more useful life.

DECEMBER 23   WE hear the Christmas angels, the great glad tidings tell; O come to us, abide with us, Our Lord Emmanuel.

Philip Brooks, Hymn

WHEN THE ANGELS BROUGHT WORD TO THE SHEPHERDS: 'EMMANUEL'

The Christmas story has many facets that appeal to us. It speaks to the heart, and for a time we understand that those things that speak to the heart are more important than those that fret our minds. At the center of the Christmas message is the astounding fact that our welfare and the solution of our problems do not depend on us after all. It is discouraging to push as hard as we can and then find our problems do not depend on us after all. It is discouraging to push as hard as we can and then find our problems bigger than ever.

Into our discouragement comes the message of Christmas summed up in one word: "Emmanuel" which is being interpreted, "God with us."

The angel Gabriel is sent from God to an old couple to announce to them that a son will be born to them. In due course, Zacaharias and Elizabeth are the parents of John who, in the power of God, is to make ready a people prepared for the Lord.

Then the angel is sent again, this time to a virgin whose name was Mary, to announce to her God's choice of her to be the mother of the Lord by the power of the Holy spirit of God.

One of the loveliest parts of the story is the account of the time Mary and Elizabeth spent together before their children were born. Here heaven and earth meet together as they share their experiences of God's direct presence with them.

Mary comes home to be the espoused wife of Joseph. It is the angel of the Lord that opens the heart and mind of this troubled husband to the wondrous events in which he is to play so noble a part.

The time was fulfilled that Jesus was to be born and the glory of God broke out on a lonely Judean hillside where shepherds kept watch over their flocks by night.

The angel of the Lord appeared with glad tidings that a Savior was born. The angel's announcement was accompanied by the angelic chorus of heaven uniting the glory of God in the highest and man's highest good: peace on earth and good will among men.

And the story is not ended, for the hand of God moved wise men from the east to find Him that had been born "King of the Jews." A star guided them to their goal and the presence of God led them home again by a secret way lest they endanger the Child's life at the hands of Herod.

Since those days, men have known in their hearts that God is with us. This star of hope and faith and love has never gone out.

DECEMBER 24 THE GREAT man is he that does not lose his child's heart.

Mencious

IF YOU HAVE THE FAITH OF A CHILD, FEAR AND ANXIETY WILL EASE

In those rare moments when we are honest with ourselves we are conscious of the threat to our existence which we feel every moment we live. Every step we take is in the shadow of death. We walk a narrow catwalk over a yawning chasm into which we are in danger of falling at every step into the emptiness of living. The telephone rings at three o'clock in the morning and every sense awakens to the question: "Is this it?" The ambulance siren sounds in our street and we are tense until we are sure our child is safe.

511

Our insecurity, shared by every living person, is worse today because the things we have been taught to depend on have failed us. Prosperity has only increased our anxiety, education is bringing more tensions, science has produced the ability to destroy ourselves, and our idealism is bogged down in another blood bath of war.

Paul's ancient question: "Who shall deliver us from the body of this death?" is becoming relevant again.

Behind most of our anthill busyness today is a frantic effort to run away from facing the ache in our hearts.

The Christian message offers you an answer. At Christmas God offers you an invitation to enter the kingdom of God. The invitation is particularly attractive at Christmas and the kingdom of God is best entered into as little children. Jesus said, "Except you change your whole outlook and become as little children, you cannot enter the kingdom of God."

You enter the kingdom of God by believing as a little child in certain things which are at the heart of the Christmas story.

You are invited to believe simply and as a little child that God loves you and cares for you by name. God sent His Son to die for you so that you can become His child by the forgiveness of your sins. As His child He will care for you in all your needs.

The Christmas story invites you to put aside all your sophistication and to believe as a little child in the supernatural. Heaven has come to earth, God has become man. Nature and nations, individuals and groups of men are moved by God's hand to work His purpose of saving men by making His Son Savior and Lord. That supernatural power still works to rule our world in spite of its evil, to work His will and to care for His own.

If you will enter God's kingdom of love as a little child, you will find that the deep anxiety and fear of your heart will be eased. You will be held on the narrow catwalk of life by the everlasting arms. And you will discover that Christmas can be wonderful again.

THE SPACE RACE WAS WON BY GOD TWO MILLENNIA AGO

"The Space Race: Heaven put a man on earth - BC+AD." These are the words on a sign on the porch of Atlanta's North Avenue Church. They are from the mind and hand of Mr. W. Austin Williams, then one of its officers. These words express in quite modern way the Christmas message. God won the space race a long time ago. When Jesus Christ was put on the earth from Heaven, this world was turned into a new direction. Our calendars witness to this fact. Christmas is our annual reminder.

He came to this earth to save its people from their sins. He towers over history and modern events as the only answer to our complex problems that is adequate, trustworthy and eternal. It is not surprising that He is considered irrelevant by many who bear His name but call in question His power to save. This has always been true. But remember unbelief has never changed facts. The fact of Christ as Lord is still a fact whether one believes or not.

This is what Christmas really is saying. It is saying it to scientific reason which puts a man in space but which trembles before man's destructive use of its contributions. It says this to physical power that has fear and destruction as its results. It says it to selfish nationalism that breeds cruelty and hardness of heart. It says it to unworthy desires that seem to feel they can be called right if enough people share them.

The message of Christmas – "Unto us a Savior is born which is Christ the Lord" - is to all people. It comes with particular relevancy today in our country where men fly in space with no public gratitude to God, where man's justice no longer is anchored in God's justice, where men seek to practice brotherhood with no reference to a heavenly Father, where morality is judged by a majority vote.

513

It is relevant because the God of Christmas comes to save those who without Him face judgment. At its heart the Christmas message is the call to repent and to believe the Gospel.

The intuitive, instructive response to the stories and music of Christmas indicates more clearly than any argument the movement of God in our lives. The playing with words by clever men falls into the background. We feel at Christmas that the God who made it all, and us, loves us and cares for us. We feel we are responsible to Him for how we act and how we treat others.

At Christmas, in the Godman He put on earth, we feel close to God and are grateful. This is Christmas joy.

DECEMBER 26   I HAVE put my hope in your Word. I know O Lord that your laws are righteous.

Psalm 119:74,75

LET'S LOOK AGAIN AT THE GREAT MESSAGE

Christmas is over. For many, it has been a time of relaxation from the ordinary walk of life. Gleams of glory have sifted through countless hearts. A child's delight, a loved one's return home, a stray bit of Christmas music. These and other things have brought a lift to the spirit.

Now we are adjusting the pack to our shoulders and are preparing to take up again life's steady march. Before we get too far along the road from Christmas, it may help to remind ourselves of the message it sought to leave at the door of our heart.

It is the story of how the God of the universe, the God of space and time, the God who made and rules it all has come into this tiny planet of ours to dwell in one single, solitary individual. It is as through someone said to you, "Do you know that last Sunday, God was born in a garage back of a fourth-rate hotel. He was born of a

514

country woman who had come to town with her husband who had to straighten out some business with the Bureau of Internal Revenue."

In some such way He was born. Nothing could be more human. Then he grew up as a boy in a normal home. As a young man he worked in a carpenter's shop working as men work for a living. He went out to live and teach among people. He had no home, no earthly goals. He knew poverty as the poor know it. Finally He died as men die, but in a manner few are called to suffer. He died the shameful death of the criminal's cross. So in Christ God was reconciling the world to Himself. Surely only God would dare to be so human.

Because He came in this way, life is different for a vast host of people. Because He was born as a baby, there is a conviction that whenever babies are born; God is there in a mystic, wonderful way. Because he was a boy in a home, those who seek God's help in making their home a good one are encouraged. God understands the problems of parents and children, having grown up as a boy in a home.

God understands what it means to work with the hands to earn a living. God was in Christ working in a carpenter shop. Work has always had divine meaning for those who know the Divine Carpenter.

Because he died as men die and was raised from the dead, death has been robbed of its sting. The cry of the lonely heart for assurance in the valley of the shadow finds the answer because Christ was born.

As we move away from Christmas, it will make life different if we carry its message in our hearts.

CANDLES LIGHTED AT CHRISTMAS...HOW LONG WILL THEY BURN?

A story is told by Leonard Eyster of a Christmas candlelight service. Near its conclusion, every worshipper was given a candle that was then lighted from a taper in the hands of the minister. He suggested that each person try to reach home without the flame being blown out. It was dusk when the congregation left the church and soon the evening was bright with hundreds of flickering lights. In most cases, the wind blew out the tiny flames before the people had gotten to their cars.

This story can all too easily be a parable of Christmas. Most who read this have sensed its application. Our world is in a bad fix. There is darkness all around us. Never in this era has there been such a wide difference of opinion as to what is good and right. It is hard enough to do right when you know it, but when you can no longer agree on what is right, you are confused. And so are we all.

At Christmas we found ourselves warmed by divine love as we lighted our candle. We went out of our way to show affection in the family circle. We renewed contacts and recommitted ourselves to the circle of family love. It is over now and the mad rush of living is on again. How long will your newly lighted candle of love burn before the winds of selfishness or impatience or indifference or neglect blow it out?

Our candle carried with it the resolve to live more nearly as a Christian in all our business and social contacts. In its light we saw more clearly how God would have us live. We can do our part toward making our world better by being sure the winds of temptation do not soon blow out our candle.

516

The very fact that our candle was lighted by the light of God's love in Christ led us to resolve to stay close to Him. Our failure to be faithful in worship will surely blow out our candles.

He who fails to keep his own candle burning cannot complain of the darkness. Whatever light our world receives will come through simple folks who let their light so shine that men see their good works and glorify the Father who is in Heaven.

Our best resolution for the New Year is to determine to keep our candle burning.

DECEMBER 28   **WHATEVER is true, ... whatever is right, whatever is pure, whatever is lovely... think about such things ... put it into practice. And the God of peace will be with you.**

Philemon 4: 8,9 (NIV)

YEARS CHANGE, BUT SOME THINGS DON'T

These are days of overwhelming change. We find it hard to count on anything anymore. The material world is very attractive to us, but it offers a poor foundation for the future.

There is always the threat of disease to our physical bodies. You can't count on health. Even the mind is not immune to the attack of illnesses that we cannot control.

For an increasing number, jobs are insecure. Automation and foreign competition will increase and will cost some their means of making a living. Mergers throw men out of work - from presidents down to office boys. Inflation and rising costs close business houses. War and its destruction are always a possibility.

The more we think about it, the more possibility for changes we can see; however, there are some things that can be counted on. There are rules of the game of life that are the same whatever happens. Some of these things are presented in a list written out by a friend of mine. I am passing them to you just as they were given. The informality of these things may be more helpful than my editing of them.

1. There will be no free lunches next year. (Don't expect to get something for nothing. No matter what happens, SOMEBODY PAYS.)

2. Very little will be as we wish it. (We must develop the ability to make life flexible enough to accept the disappointment that will come when it isn't as we wish it.)

3. There will be reason for SOME happiness and quietude next year. (Even if every day is dark, no one can look back to another year and not remember something good that happened – "I was sorry that I had no shoes 'till I saw a man who had no feet.")

4. You're not getting a bit younger. (Is there something you have wanted to do, but haven't done it yet? Better get to it.)

5. God will be in charge of the Universe next year.

6. In the coming year, the 10 Commandments will still be in force. (We don't know what laws congress will make, nor what the legislature will do, nor what will happen in the city council, but the 10 Commandments are part of the plan of God!)

7. Love will still be the greatest thing in the world. (The love of God, manifest in Christ, not the sympathetic kind of love seen in movies, etc. We do the most good when we love people in the spirit of God with Christian charity and generosity.)

DECEMBER 29   BUT SEEK first his kingdom and his righteousness and all these things will be given to you as well.

Matthew 6:33 (NIV)

TAKING INVENTORY AT YEAR'S END

Christmas is over and we are busy wrapping up the old year. Business houses will "take stock" to see how they stand. It can be helpful if each of us will do the same thing. As an old year ends, we cannot escape thinking about it. For some it has been a good year, for others a bad year and - for most - a year marked by both bad and good. Most people hope, at least secretly, that the new year will be better. We are not quite sure what it is that makes our days good or bad.

1. Most people act as though they think the year will be better if they have more money. The chances are, however, that if they have been unhappy this year over money, more of it won't help much. What you have done with the money you have had is more important than the amount. Check your checkbook. If it reveals a pursuit of material things for your own comfort and pleasure as your major concern, chances are that more money won't make the year better.

2. It can be helpful for our future if we will check our conduct. It is very easy to blame the bad things that happen to us on others. This is very popular today. If we do wrong things, we are told that the fault really lies with our parents or with society. Until you and I are willing to assume responsibility for our own bad behavior, it is not likely that our future will be any better. We need to take stock of ourselves and try to honestly see whether our own choices and our own actions have caused some of our failures.

3. It is a good time to take stock of what we believe. You have the right to believe anything you want to believe. But you cannot

believe the wrong things and expect life to be good. God has revealed the truth about Himself and about us as people and about the world we live in. This Truth is clearly seen in Jesus Christ. This has been what Christmas is all about. You and I will find inner peace and outer harmony one with another only as we are reconciled to God by believing the Truth as revealed in Christ. We are creatures of His world. Surely it is not unreasonable to believe that we can find life good only as we live by God's revelation of Himself.

If we will check our checkbook, our conduct and our faith, we will find cause for repentance. Repentance is the first step toward faith, and faith is the door into the Kingdom of God. Jesus promises you that if you seek first the Kingdom, all things will be added.

DECEMBER 30   **SET your hearts on things above, where Christ is seated at the right hand of God. Set your mind on things above, not on earthly things.**

Colossians 3: 1,2 (NIV)

HERE IS A SAMPLE OF NEW YEAR'S RESOLUTIONS

Have you made any resolutions for the New Year? It used to be a popular thing to do. The end of the year was considered a good time to take stock of yourself and to try to do better where you could. Lots of New Year's parties took time out for resolution writing.

There used to be more confidence that we could improve ourselves and our way of living. Why this confidence is less today than it was some years ago, I am not sure. Perhaps the constant bad news about which we feel so futile is part of it. Maybe so many are victims of our bigness in all areas of life and they feel that there is so little any one person can do.

Whatever the cause, it is time we moved toward a confidence that we can change ourselves. The trouble lies not in things outside. If we are defeated by life it is because we have accepted defeat within ourselves. The past does not make our future. Our future is made by that to which we give ourselves, our goal, and our purpose. Where you are headed has more to do with your success or failure than where you have been.

Against this background, New Year's resolutions can be helpful. I suggest a few, not that you will adopt these, but that you will be encouraged to make some of your own.

1. To seek God's will for your life and try to follow it.

2. To worship God regularly and personally in the home and in your church. In worship, life finds direction and strength.

3. To try each day to encourage those with whom you come into contact. So many people are feeling blue when you meet them. An encouraging word helps them and you.

4. To lend a helping hand wherever you can. When we get too busy to help our neighbor, we are too busy.

5. To be more faithful in doing the things you are responsible for. We often fail to complete those things we agree to do.

6. To be true to those who depend on you.

7. To bear without complaint those things that must be borne.

8. To begin each day with a prayer for God's help and to end each one with a prayer for forgiveness.

Some such resolutions as these made with the prayer that God will help you can well make the coming year a new one indeed.

DECEMBER 31   A THOUSAND ages in Thy sight are like an evening gone.

Isaac Watts, Hymn

ONE LAST LOOK BACK, WITH THANKS

Another year is gone. Today is actually only another day and yesterday is no more than another leaf torn off the calendar. Yet in tearing the leaf off the calendar, it is different somehow. The year soon changes and we can't help thinking about the past, present and the future. There are plenty of people around to remind us of how bad the past has been and of the dangers and threats confronting the present and future.

I suggest that we pause on New Year's Day and give thanks for the good things of last year. Even in difficult years we have much to be grateful for. There have been friends and loved ones. There have been material comforts. There have been our jobs and the security of our country. There has been the privilege of faith, undisturbed by threats of violence and there we have seen special evidences of God's goodness. Spend time being grateful.

Perhaps the thing we can be most grateful for is God's forgiveness. He has not dealt with us according to our sins nor rewarded us according to our transgressions. We have found this divine forgiveness reflected in the hearts of those who love us.

For most of those reading this, the present is surrounded with evidence of God's love and care. Where the eyes of faith are open to behold His presence, He walks with those most particularly whose faith leads through dark places.

It will be helpful if you will pause to count the blessings you have today. There is so much complaining today and so much quarreling about things in general, but the truth of the matter is, most of us never had it better. It can help your New Year if you will begin it in gratitude for what you have today.

522

Dr. Broyles' first wife Bena Virden Broyles died prematurely after losing a long bout with cancer. On the Sunday following her death, Dr. Broyles preached the following sermon. It became his most requested and most beloved sermon and remained so during his long ministry.

All who have known sorrow will find these words to be immensely comforting and uplifting. This message, forged in the crucible of Dr. Broyles' own suffering during a personal walk through "the valley of the shadow" and the "dark night of the soul," rings with truth and victory.

COMFORT IN SORROW

There are ties that bind humanity together that are stronger than barriers that divide them. One of these things that binds all mankind is sorrow. I have sat in a Palestinian cave with an ignorant Arab peasant and mourned with him the death of a loved one. I have walked the ways of death in many parts of this country.

Somehow the ache is always the same and where men mourn that which they have lost, having loved it, they come very close together. This morning I would pass on certain things that have been helpful to those who walk "in the valley of the shadow." They are not perfectly connected but either singly or together they have been of service in bringing comfort to the hearts of men.

The first thing is this: When sorrow comes, it is no alien intruder. Sorrow is at home in the heart of God. We had a theological professor when I was in the seminary and one of his pet emphases was the impassiveness of God. That means, simply, that God is not capable of emotion. For him, God was so perfect that he could not feel what we know as emotion. That may be a position that you arrive at by theological deduction, but you cannot arrive at it by reading the Bible. I never could quite understand how this great saint held that position so tenaciously. I still do nor understand it, because there is suffering at the very heart of God. He loved the world so much that He gave His only begotten Son. He spared not his own Son but delivered Him up for us all. God was in Christ reconciling the world unto Himself. God was in Christ standing at the open grave crying for His friend out of grief. God was in Christ reconciling Himself the world unto Himself as He agonized in Gethsemane, saying "My soul is sorrowful unto death." Finally, hanging there on the cross, crying out as almost every heart sooner or later will cry out, or has cried out, "My God, why hast Thou forsaken me?" There is no trial given to us but such as it is common to man and grief and sorrow are a part of life as it is made and as it must be lived. Sorrow is not an intruder any more than joy is an intruder. It is a part of the threads out of which life is woven and we can accept it on that basis. So many people move through sorrow, feeling that they have been suddenly taken with something that is not in keeping with life. Sorrow is a part of life and more than most. It is one of those ties that bind all of mankind together.

The second thing about sorrow is that you and I choose it for ourselves. We choose it because the coin of love has two sides – a side of joy and a side of sorrow. The day you commit yourself to love somebody, the day you accept the love of someone, that day you choose to walk in the valley of the shadow of sorrow because joy is just one side of the coin of love and if you love, one day you are going to lose that which you love. Inevitably, you must lose. If, when you find someone to marry, God said to you, "Now, you may have twenty-five years of happiness, but at the end of that time there will come separation" – you would have chosen to marry, and felt yourself fortunate in the choosing Sorrow is just the expression of love when love has lost the object of its affection. We choose it as a part of our lives. You can escape it – you can escape sorrow – but if you escape it you must refuse love. And if you refuse love you cease to be a human being in the true sense of the word, because one thing a human being needs is love. We must have it and so we reach out and grasp it and in grasping it we choose sorrow.

The third thing about sorrow is that it is one of our most priceless possessions. The average person who grieves would not give it up if you could bring some remedy for it because it is in the "Garden of Sorrow" that we remember those we love. We remember them in sadness and yet with a sadness that opens the very Gate of Heaven and with a sadness that interprets the meaning of love. We would not give it up if we could.

Those things being said, there are now certain things to be said about comfort, "the comfort wherewith we are comforted that we may comfort others with the same comfort." You cannot say that if you will do three things the comfort of God will come. Comfort is a gift of God and He gives it on His own terms. Comfort is a part of the Grace of God; it is a part of the Mercy of God with which He has blessed human beings. But there is a certain path with certain landmarks along it that if you will follow, one day there will begin to walk by your side, the Presence of God. There are certain things we can do that God's comfort can find us.

The first of them is surrender. Surrender is the golden key to comfort. For that matter, surrender us the golden key to life. But surrender is that fist step when you admit to yourself that you have lost that which you have loved. You try to hold on to it – you try to pretend that it is not so – you reach out to grasp that which you have loved and lost – and pretend it is not gone. The first step along the way to healing comfort is just to admit your loss committing to Him, who is able to keep it into Him against that day. This surrender of the loved one to God is with the consciousness and conviction that God will do far more that we can ask or think. Then the surrender of yourself; just laying yourself in the arms of God. There is not a thing you can do for yourself other than that. You may batter at the very gates of Heaven and nothing happens until you surrender. Now this matter of surrendering is not easy. It is very like taking a rubber ball and throwing it up and asking it to stick to the wall. You keep throwing it and it keeps bouncing back. But it is not exactly like a rubber ball, for one day it will stick. But, for a while it will be very difficult. We are human beings and we never perfectly exercise our faith. Do not let it worry you if you surrender and then, all of a sudden, you have sorrow on your shoulders and in your heart again. Just surrender it and keep surrendering. You will find that even in the imperfection of your surrender, there begins to move His Presence.

The second thing is that, in the valley of the shadow, we must believe that all things work together for good to them that love God, to them that are called according to His purpose. Believe it against all evidence to the contrary. Believe it because God says so. Because God guarantees it by His own Son's death on the Cross and the Resurrection of that Son , which is the guarantee. While I was in the seminary, this incident happened. I have told it before, but it is the most dramatic illustration of a man's faith in Romans

525

8:28 that I have ever known. One of our professors, teaching the New Testament, was leading us through Romans and, the strange thing was, we were in the eighth chapter. After dinner one evening, he and his wife went out for a ride and a very fast train hit their car and killed his wife and severely injured him. When he came back to consciousness and to rationality the first thing he did was send word to his class to remember that Romans 8:28 still holds good. It does not answer all the questions – I know that as well as anyone of you knows it, but it does give to life meaning and significance. Where we cannot find the way, it means everything to believe that God does know the way. That is the second thing – to believe that God works all things for good.

Then the third thing that helps is to face frankly your questions. God knows your doubts. Everybody has doubts. Nobody can be absolutely sure. It would be knowledge then. Faith is a jumping out in the dark and finding you do not fall, but have about you everlasting arms. There come questions. The question that is most always in the heart is, "Why did this happen to me?" "Why did this happen to this loved one of mine?" It may sound a little blunt and brash, but the best answer insofar as I know is a simple question: "Why should it not happen to you?" It happened to the Son of God Himself. It happens sooner or later to everybody else in the world. Why should it not happen to you and to me? What privileged position do we have that, out of all the world, we should be allowed to escape it? It will help you, I think, if you put yourself back down in the caravan of common man and just accept life as it is. Find your place in the sufferings of men. You have company there, the company of all mankind.

Another good thing that helps is the marvelous way that God tells His love through the ministry of friends and loved ones. There is a lot wrong with life. There are a lot of people who are mighty wonderful. At times, even in the bad ones, there comes out the expression of marvelous concern. God works through those who are kind to those in sorrow. It is a perfectly marvelous thing the way God gets through as friends simply stand by. In the valley of the shadow you will do well to accept the very love of God as it is ministered through loved ones who care.

It does not help very much to live in the future – particularly where grief and sorrow have come, because as you project the future, all you can think of is the darkness. It matters not how far you look into the future, all you can see is the darkness. Therefore, we are invited by God to live a day at a time. Every day brings its own compensations – an unexpected kindness here, an unexpected opportunity there, an unexpected friend, an unexpected feeling of being lifted by a mysterious force. Every day God does something to light the darkness and if you try to project the future in the midst of your grief, you leave all that out. You just plod through darkness. But if you live a day at a time in faith that God will open the way, you will find that everyday brings some new marvel of His Grace, some new marvel that you never could predict, never could think of as coming of age. Therefore it is a false picture that you project. However bad your situation, if you try to project into the future, you cannot do it truly and you will only badger and bruise yourself. Just a day at a time, letting God take the future.

Then, this is not exactly in my field, but to a certain extent it is. There are those times when drugs are necessary and whenever a physician feels they are necessary I think they ought to be given, of course. But there is today, every time some unusual emotion strikes, a perfect rush to get into the hands of the person, tranquilizers or barbiturates. I want to say to you that these things are robbing men and women of some of their highest experiences. God meant us to live. He did not mean for us to run. Grief is something that is common to man and is often man's greatest opportunity to live as children of the King. They do the same thing in joy today. They take a bride or someone who is facing a happy experience and administer these tranquilizers which depress and confuse. Men and women are turning from that which God has offered as one of their greatest opportunities – to achieve the heights of human living. You will do well to leave drugs alone, unless they are necessary.

Also it is always important to do the thing that needs doing today. So many people sit back and say, "Well I just cannot face it – I cannot do it." There are times when they cannot, but most of the time they can. It is important just to do the things that are necessary that day. They will be different in different cases, but to evade the day's responsibility weakens you for tomorrow. It is always a helpful thing to get going in the ordinary pattern of daily living as soon as possible.

Now, these things are practical suggestions. Some of them go down to the roots of faith. They are way stations along the road to comfort. No one can tell you just where this feeling of the Presence will come. If you will walk down this road, you will suddenly find that walking by your side is one like unto the Son of God. You remember Mary – Mary and Martha had lost their brother. Mary was grief stricken. She felt that God had let her down. "If Thou hadst been here," she said, "this would not have happened." And all of a sudden, in her grief, she heard a voice say, "The Master has come and calleth for thee." Somewhere along the way, you will hear Him can you by name. So often you will walk down a long road through the valley of the shadow with a family, a road that is marked with lingering pain or lingering illness. At the end of that road you hear them say this: "God was with us." This is man's victory not in the fine spinning of answers to arguments, but in the Christian witness that in the valley of the shadow of death we shall fear no evil for God is with us. You can duplicate that time and time and time again. It comes to every person through surrendering and believing and walking. There will come along the way the Presence to comfort. It will be your witness and has already been that to many of you, that "God is with me." This is the victory that overcometh the world, even our faith.

Thou hast companied with us, Eternal God. Our past is the witness to They faithfulness. Leave us not, neither forsake us. Grant that we shall not forsake Thee but going forth from this place shall live more generously, more kindly, more lovingly; shall be more perfectly the representatives of that which we profess. We offer ourselves in Christ's name.

AMEN

DR. BROYLES' LAST SERMON
February 9, 1992

HOPE

(Note: This sermon was not included in the first printing.)

Two passages. The first from the 12th Chapter of II Corinthians beginning with the 7th verse.

Paul is writing:

"Lest I should be exalted above measure through the abundance of revelations (or the blessings), there was given me a thorn in the flesh, a messenger of Satan to buffet me, lest I should be exalted above measure. For this I besought the Lord three times, that it might depart from me.

And he said unto me, My grace is all you need: for my strength is made perfect in weakness. Most gladly therefore will I rather glory in my infirmities, that the power of Christ may rest upon me. For when I am weak then am I strong."

And, the last verse of the 8th Chapter of Romans, well, first the 28th and then the last verses: "For we know that all things work together for good to them that love God, to them that are called according to His purpose.

Who shall separate us from the love of Christ? Shall tribulation, or distress, or persecution, or famine, or nakedness, or peril, or sword? Nay in all these things we are more than conquerors through Him that loved us. For I am persuaded, that neither death, nor life, nor angels, nor principalities, nor powers, nor things present, nor things to come, nor height, nor depth, nor any other creation, shall be able to separate us from the love of God, which is in Christ Jesus or Lord."

There is a good deal today that makes life seem just a series of dead ends. Every step we take forward there seems to be reason to take two backward. There seems to be no solution that really works. And, you can read all about it wherever you read today.

I want to talk about something I have done before – but – just the simple matter of "keeping on keeping on" or better said "putting one foot in front of the other." Because in one way or another, sooner or later, life brings us the experiences where there seems to be no way out and it becomes almost impossible to put one foot in front of the other.

Now we have a great deal to encourage us in it. We take for granted so much today. We are such smart people. We are able to do so many things. And somehow we take for granted that we have by these processes learned to live. And, I will submit that we know less about the art of living today than I think has ever been true in my life. And by that I mean just confidence in life that it's going to be all right. But there is a lot to encourage us. We take so much for granted.

There is a lot in the physical world. I watched the sun come up this morning. My little study faces back east. And, out of the darkness, I saw the sun rise. You know, I didn't have a thing to do about it, not a thing. You didn't either. No human being ever had. But, those who study it knew exactly what second it was going to appear And they've known it for a hundred years, that today it would rise. And all of life, yours, and all the planet, everything depends on the fact that it come up this morning. And, it's rather remarkable because you and I depend on it.

And the seasons, they come. And, we don't have anything to do with it. And yet, they are our life. And, you plant a seed in the ground – just a dead looking seed. And buried in that seed is a spark of life. And so after the seed planting is the harvest... And, we take it for granted. Our food for granted. And, rarely stop to think, these things encourage you because they are supporting casts.

And, it is true in our physical body. We are able to do things. I don't know that anybody on earth knows why the heart keeps beating. Now, they can give you descriptions of the process. But, why the processes nobody knows. It just keeps on, keeps on, keeps on keeping on. And you can't produce it and so forth and so on.

An eye surgeon told me not long ago, he said "Vernon, anyone that studies the structure of the human eye and does not believe in a creator is beyond my understanding." Do you ever think why the eye sees? I don't know. Sometime I read somewhere that people that believe in evolution without God believe that there was a pressure on a point and it developed into an eye. That's idiocy. Why didn't it go...You could have grown them all over your head. I mean...these things...

Then in the body there is healing. No doctor, no physician ever healed anybody. They do remarkable things in removing the obstacles to healing. But you can count on that every time you cut...it heals. And, nobody knows why. Oh, they can describe it. But, these things that support us are mysteries that we live with daily.

And then we have in the relm of the spirit...When you say "I," whatever it is you mean, you are talking about your person, your personality, your spirit, your soul this thing that's entirely separate from the body yet absolutely related to it. Yes, it's a gift.

We have the instinct of God. Whenever you hear someone saying "I don't believe in God or that really doesn't matter." These are just...they are aberrations. They are marginal people.

The history of the world is basically the history of man's search for God. Wherever you go in history, looking back, there's the sun worship, and all kinds of worship, there are the trees that become sacred, the little areas that become sacred, the houses of worship of whatever kind. You travel all over this country, all over Europe, and all over Asia. You see those things built which represent man's search for God. And, sometime just drive around Atlanta and see all the churches and stop and take note of what that means. That means there are people who have been trying to find a relation to God. And so on, God is part of our standard equipment. You can't evade it. Even the man who practices profanity is making his negative witness of rebellion.

And then, finally get to what I'm talking about: HOPE. One the strangest things in the human heart is hope.

There is a very famous painting – and it's this woman playing an

531

instrument in the shape of a "U", which she holds in her hand. And, it has several strings. But all the strings are broken except one. And, she is playing that one string. The title of this picture is Hope. I'm sure you have seen it. I tried to find a copy of it, but I couldn't.

Hope. Did you ever think how remarkable that is? You watch television and you see these streams of refugees leaving their homes with a bag over their shoulder with their belongings or pushing a cart going somewhere and hoping it will be better. And, the very fact they are going rather than just sitting down and pawing the ground in despair is a miracle.

And, there isn't a person here that hasn't walked this way or stood by those who have given up the expectation of better things but nevertheless kept putting one foot in front of the other. And, it's an instinctive thing. We don't give up. It's one of those gifts God gave us to enable us to do it.

But, there's a lot set itself against hope. It's kind of hard to keep hoping in a world like ours. And then, the cards are just against us, if all you have to depend upon is whatever this world has to offer.

In the first place, I don't care how able you are and how much you have the things of your life in order. Age is going to get you. Then mental and physical life is going to weaken and you aren't going to be able to do it anymore. And, that's a game you can't beat. You can get your face lifted and your hair dyed but you're still going to make the same schedule with nature's deterioration.

And then, circumstances...In this day and time there are millions of people who thought they were comfortable but lost their jobs. They're sitting in desperation. And, what they thought they could depend upon is gone. There are those who have lost health and strength, who stand by as others suffer disease. And, it's hard to hope.

And sooner or later, if all you have to serve as a foundation for hope are the things of this world, you are going to lose. And you are either going to become a cynic or a critic or have your life tinged with despair or maybe something worse.

And so, God gave us a further gift. And, this is an area that we don't pay much attention to in this day and it's one of the reasons we are having a time hoping. That is, that God, as he has given us the instinct for God, gives us at least a receptive instinct to eternal life and to heaven – the consciousness that we are not in this world to make good in this world. We are in this world marching towards the Father's house.

And to the Christian and to the Christian alone in our world there comes the only foundation which will support hope in the midst of disaster. And, that is through Christ Himself. There is only one foundation which is laid and that is Jesus Christ, the Lord. If we are going to continue to hope just as human beings we are going to have to do something about our fear. This doesn't play a part in the thinking of our day much. But, the loss of hope comes more often from conscience in the light of the kind of people we are. We are just not good enough, we think. And so, Christ came and the cross of Christ is the only highway to peace. It is the place where we just give our sins to Him and believe that in God's sight, regardless of the fact that we are still not very good, He looks at us and sees in Christ's name that we are perfect.

And secondly, the resurrection. The fact that He lives. The fact that He lives in us. And, that day He said "You shall know that I'm in my Father, you are in Me, and I'm in you." That He lives within us to take care of us.

And God does take care in the details of life of His people and those who have trusted Him witness to it. And, He takes care of us when at the end of it all we enter the mansions of glory. And, you'll never really get the secret of the Christian faith until that becomes the welcome gate. Because there He promises the answer to all things.

Now I know this can sound very naïve and I know it's called by the critic "pie in the sky." But, I tell you right now we'd be better to have "pie in the sky" than hell somewhere else. ...I just recommend it.

Nevertheless, it has been the witness to the centuries and the stories of the faith that come down to us in inspiration are people who found that God did take care of them. "My grace is all you need. My strength is made perfect in weakness." And, it has been true in life where there are those who have accepted His cross of forgiveness and have been willing to lay their hands in His hands just to take care of them. And, I can walk the streets of Atlanta and I can point out homes from where I've seen where in the midst of tears there's been thanksgiving, where in the midst of weakness there's been strength. It's a fact. And, no critic or cynic can deny it.

Paul said, "I am persuaded that neither death nor life nor angels or principalities nor powers nor any other creation, nothing can separate us from the love of Christ." And, Paul wrote words like this under sentence of death in a Roman prison. He wrote it despite of the fact he had been beaten five times by the Romans, three times by the Jews and three times by the Romans had been stoned, shipwrecked three times, chased by his own countrymen, chased by the Gentiles, sick. Nothing can separate us from the love of Christ.

And you know there is a little story...A man appeared in heaven. And, He and St. Peter were talking about his life. And, it was sort of laid out where you could see the footsteps. And, all along there were two paths of steps, his and the Lord's, the man's and the Lord's. And, every now and then there were long stretches where there was only one path. And, man said, "Lord, what was...what about that long stretch? And the Lord said, "John, that's when I carried you."

***

Let us stand.

God, thank you for faith. It fades out on us so easily. Grant us the confidence that Thou are our Lord and that Thou dost take care of us. And now hear us as we pray the prayer that you taught us saying: Our Father, Who art in heaven, hallowed be Thy name. Thy kingdom come. Thy will be done on earth as it is in heaven. Give us this day our daily bread. And, forgive us our trespasses as we forgive those who trespass against us. Lead us not into temptation. But, deliver us from evil. For Thine is the kingdom and the power and the glory for ever.

And may the grace, mercy, and peace of our Lord, Jesus Christ, be with us in peace for ever.

AMEN